PERSONNEL AND ORGANIZATIONAL PSYCHOLOGY

The Irwin Series in Management and The
Behavioral Sciences

L. L. Cummings and E. Kirby Warren—Consulting Editors
John F. Mee—Advisory Editor

PERSONNEL
AND
ORGANIZATIONAL
PSYCHOLOGY

LAURENCE SIEGEL, Ph.D.
Chairman, Department of Psychology
Professor of Psychology
Louisiana State University

IRVING M. LANE, Ph.D.
Associate Professor of Psychology
Louisiana State University

1982 RICHARD D. IRWIN, INC.
Homewood, Illinois 60430

Georgetown, Ontario
Irwin-Dorsey Limited
L7G 4B3

ISBN 0-256-02721-8

Library of Congress Catalog Card No. 81–81551

Printed in the United States of America

1 2 3 4 5 6 7 8 9 0 MP 9 8 7 6 5 4 3 2

preface

From start to finish, this is a new book rather than a revision of our *Psychology in Industrial Organizations*, 3d ed., 1974.

Since the publication of the first edition in 1962, much has happened in the field, and to the one of us who did the original writing. As we thought about the task facing us, we came to a selfish realization: It would be easier for us if we began over.

We call this book *Personnel and Organizational Psychology* both to distinguish it from the earlier one and to reflect (equally) the antecedants and present concerns of industrial/organizational psychology.

Our discussion moves freely between theory and application as we attempt to emphasize how each reinforces the other. One of our messages is that professional applications are derived from, and contribute to, furthering the science of human behavior.

We have sought to keep our readers' backgrounds in perspective while delivering this message. The book is written for an undergraduate course. From our own experience, we know that although a few such students are psychology majors, most are not. Many have taken only one or two earlier psychology courses. For a fair number, including adult students returning to studies after some hiatus, this is either a first exposure to a psychology offering, or the first in many years. (And we recognize, finally, that even the institutional context for the course which might use this book varies. It is offered by departments in schools of business administration as well as in psychology departments.)

We have tried to be sensitive to the diverse backgrounds and interests brought to this book by its readers. Many choices about content coverage had to be made. Some topics (such as consumer behavior and job evaluation) are left untreated in our attempt to present a comprehensive, but not encyclopedic, overview of I/O psychology. Within those topics selected for discussion, we chose to sacrifice some breadth in favor of increased depth of coverage.

Certain judgments about what constitutes a balanced treatment are matters of personal preference in which considerable variation can be tolerated. Others are more important in their effect upon a book's teachability, fairness, and accuracy in representing its subject matter, and—for the student—readability. We endeavored to make judgments about the latter

vii

sufficiently well so that instructors and students alike would accept—even though they might not agree with—the former.

Not surprisingly, the book's primary organizing concept is *performance*. Its structure flows in two directions. First, the discussion moves from issues in defining and measuring performance, to performance prediction, to facilitation. Second, it moves from considering task performance by individuals to considering the behavior of individuals in an organizational context. Hence, the book's two major divisions: Personnel Psychology, and Organizational Psychology.

In spite of our best efforts, certain chapters in both sections are more difficult to read than others. None, however, require students to approach them with specialized backgrounds. We prefer to think that those particular chapters treat topics which, by their nature, require the reader to be intellectually active. These are the chapters which either consider issues typically unfamiliar to undergraduate students or consider familiar issues but in new (to the reader) ways. Chapters 7, Validity and Prediction, and 15, Leadership, are cases in point.

We see our field as vigorous, stimulating in its approach to questions and issues, and socially valuable. Those perceptions were reaffirmed in the process of preparing the manuscript. We hope we succeeded in communicating them.

There are some persons whose contributions to the manuscript must be acknowledged. The task of a critical field reader is sufficiently thankless that one wonders how our colleagues are ever talked into it. We had three readers who had substantial impact in shaping the book from its preliminary manuscript: D. L. Dossett, H. Takooshian, and M. S. Taylor. Their careful, objective readings led each of them to make invaluable suggestions. We agreed with, and therefore implemented, many of them. We may yet regret that we did not implement all of them.

Finally, several typists again did the impossible by helping us make deadlines. We particularly and gratefully acknowledge Linda Corona, A. Elaine Moore, and Dawn Scallan. And we here publicly promise that they will not again be asked to handle a manuscript while also readying an academic department to move across campus.

Laurence Siegel
Irving M. Lane

contents

decision making. Strategies. Difficulties. Two nontraditional approaches. Toward a theoretical integration.

section one

INTRODUCTION

1

chapter 1

What's in a Name?

Welcome to our book. We wrote it because we wish to share our enthusiasm for psychology in general and for our particular specialty, industrial/organizational (I/O) psychology.

It is easy to be enthusiastic about psychology. It provides the excitement of gaining new knowledge about behavior with the gratification of being able, through applying that knowledge, to improve human conditions. Additionally, it offers a way of thinking about the world, of formulating questions, gathering and evaluating information, drawing conclusions, and using these conclusions to ask still further questions. Finally, of all of the fields of knowledge concerned with advancing our understanding of behavior, psychology is unique in being both a science and a profession.

The professional psychologists who deliver psychological services do so with a scientific perspective: professional practice is applied research. Solving a real problem in the real world (like excessive absenteeism, "burnout" among air traffic controllers, training the hard-core unemployed, and so on) requires that the issues be defined, alternative solutions be evaluated, and the optimal solution implemented. The answers at each step come from research.

As an applied science, I/O psychology rests on a body of basic research and theory about behavior in general and behavior in organizational contexts in particular. The relationships between the basic and applied aspects of the science are reciprocal. Basic theory is tested both in laboratories and out in the field, but it originates in both places. Thus, I/O psychology both draws from and contributes to the broader base of knowledge about behavior—even in nonorganizational settings. This book is about a uniquely challenging and pertinent field, where science and its applications are merged to address the human issues appropriate to the one third of our adult lives that most of us devote to work.

Welcome.

BACKGROUND

You probably have noticed that we have several times referred to the field as *industrial/organizational* psychology. Why that, instead of simply *industrial* psychology, or *business* psychology or *organizational* psychology? In fact, the I/O designation is a fairly recent name change (dating to 1973) for a division of the American Psychological Association that formerly had been designated the Division of Industrial Psychology. The newer designation is meant to imply that the field has somehow been broadened. A historical overview helps to clarify the significance of this change.

Early history

We cannot carry our history too far back, since psychology as a separate discipline originated only about 100 years ago. The specialty of *economic psychology* within the broader field can be dated by the publication in 1913 of Hugo Munsterberg's *Psychology and Industrial Efficiency*.

Within the general context of psychology, Musterberg's book appeared shortly after Alfred Binet, a French psychologist, had formulated the notion of IQ, evolved techniques for its measurement, and demonstrated the usefulness of his intelligence test for screening children who were experiencing difficulties in school. That test, and test-building technology generally, were rapidly imported into the United States, elaborated, and applied to nonscholastic as well as school settings.

World War I provided an additional impetus for the development of one of two major threads in the fabric of I/O psychology—psychological testing. The army needed to screen inductees rapidly for optimal assignments. Within the space of just the few war years, psychologists became heavily involved not only in test construction and administration, but also in such areas as training and evaluating officers' performance. The emphasis was on finding the right persons for jobs (in terms of prerequisite skills and abilities) and, when necessary, training them to do the work required. The testing thread was elaborated to include several other activities related to personnel psychology.

A second approach to improving work performance was also being developed shortly before America's entry into World War I. In contrast to the emphasis on selection and placement which sought to match people to jobs, this second approach emphasized altering jobs and the way people do them. This approach, known as *industrial engineering* pretty much developed outside of psychology—at least initially. Henry Ford had introduced mass production. The weak link in manufacturing operations was the worker who could not keep up with the machine. Improved efficiency became synonymous with redefining criteria for a fair day's work to include increased worker speed (Taylor, 1911) and simplifying the motions entailed in job tasks (Gilbreth, 1911).

Although not part of these particular efforts, psychologists had a very sound tradition of experimental research, particularly on sensation and perception. The growing interest in fitting jobs to workers led some of the early experimental psychologists to study the impact of adverse work environments (noise, heat) upon job performance, fatigue, and boredom.

Inadvertently, this created a third major thread in I/O psychology's history. Studies conducted in the Hawthorne plant of the Western Electric Company beginning in 1927 were in the experimental psychology tradition. The initial intent was to investigate the effect of different illumination levels upon job performance.

We discuss this important series of studies at length in Chapter 13. For now we merely mention that what had started out as a one-year study of a relatively simple issue became progressively more involved as the investigation progressed. The entire series continued for 12 years. The initial study revealed unexpected productivity gains in spite of dramatic decreases in illumination—even to the point where visibility was considerably reduced! This effect, whereby subjects' performances initially improve in spite of what appear to be adverse conditions, is generally designated the *Hawthorne effect*.

It was clear to the Hawthorne investigators that appearances were deceptive. Something about the conditions surrounding their study had to be sufficiently favorable to offset the expected negative consequences of illumination decreases. Thereafter, their efforts were directed toward understanding this phenomenon. They discovered the importance, previously unsuspected, of employee attitudes, informal interpersonal relationships, perceptions about supervision, and organizational structure. By the time the studies were ended in 1939 (Roethlisberger & Dickson), the human relations movement was firmly entrenched as the third major thread in I/O psychology's history.

You can gain some additional feeling for these three major threads— personnel psychology, industrial engineering, and human relations—by thinking about them from the perspective of the times. Psychology applied to work was profoundly affected by the economic and social consequences of the Depression. Scarce jobs and overabundent labor imply opportunities to pick and choose from among the applicants. And the general atmosphere of shattered economic self-confidence also caused workers to question two former assumptions: (1) doing a good day's work insures job security and (2) management has the right to establish ground rules (hours, pay, production quotas) for work.

Management also began to question some of its assumptions as it became aware of the interdependence of its needs and those of labor. Companies provided the jobs generating the income with which labor could purchase goods and services allowing the company, in turn, to make a profit. Efforts to improve human relations at work were seen by management as positive steps toward healing some of the powerful schisms that had developed between the economic haves and have nots, and therefore in the company's self-interest.

World War II to 1950

Military manpower needs in World War II once again required an enormous personnel effort to which psychologists responded—now with considerable expertise. The techniques of personnel psychology leapt rapidly ahead.

The human relations movement also gathered steam in the producing sector because of the urgent national need to involve virtually all nonmilitary personnel in the war effort. Long shifts, short vacations, and nontraditional employment (for example, women engaged in heavy manufacturing) were the rule. Employers and employees were clearly involved in a mutual effort, and were united against shared external threats. Both were concerned with maintaining productivity through high morale and good supervision, and welcomed contributions from the human relations movement.

A fourth thread now began to emerge. Rather complicated equipment (aircraft, tanks, and so on) was being manufactured by inexperienced workers. And this complex equipment was to be operated finally by recruits after relatively little training. One solution was to modify the manufacturing machinery and the product design to meet the limitations of human operators. The field of engineering psychology was inaugurated, building largely upon the techniques and knowledge of experimental psychologists.

Psychologists with diverse interests ranging from statistics and test construction, to attitude assessment and change, to designing equipment and optimal working environments were drawn together as industrial psychologists by sharing an overriding common interest in work behavior.

The postwar years were ones in which psychology was rapidly assimilated into society. Industrial psychologists had established the value of their potential contributions—and industry was ready. The viability of this specialty within psychology was evidenced in 1950 with the publication of the *Handbook of Applied Psychology* (Fryer & Henry) which devoted approximately 50 percent of its two-volume coverage to work-related applications.

Later years

Dunnette compares the coverage of this earlier *Handbook* with the one he edited in 1976, *Handbook of Industrial and Organizational Psychology*, to clarify changes in the field during the intervening quarter century. He points out that the 1950 *Handbook* was directed almost entirely to practice; research was accorded little attention; theories of individual and organizational behavior were ignored. In contrast, the more recent *Handbook* gives heavy emphasis to research methodology, theories of behavior, and the interactions between organizations and persons. Here, research practice and theory are seen as interdependent, each derived from and contributing to the other.

THE FIELD IN OVERVIEW

It is convenient to indicate something of the range of issues addressed in I/O psychology by presenting an overview of the chapters that follow.

Although a book is divided into chapters and topics, we all realize that people and issues are not neatly and similarly segmented and packaged. They, and the organizations they comprise, are dynamic and vibrant. With this in mind, let us preview what follows.

Our title, *Personnel and Organizational Psychology,* reflects equally the historical antecedents and present concerns of I/O psychology. Accordingly, the book has two main sections: one for Personnel Psychology (Chapters 4–11); the other for Organizational Psychology (Chapters 12–18).

Section one. Introduction

Chapter 1. What's in a Name?   I/O psychology is only one approach to understanding people in organizations. Psychology as a discipline articulates with such other disciplines as sociology, economics, and political science. However, since people are biological as well as social organisms, psychology (unlike the more usual social sciences) adopts a biosocial view of behavior.

And as we have already discussed, I/O psychology is uniquely a science/ profession. It seeks through research to develop broadly applicable theories of behavior which allow us to better understand it. Further, it seeks through research to apply information about behavior to practical issues like prediction and change. The ultimate practical test of theories of behavior is their demonstrable usefulness for predicting behavior before it occurs and/or providing mechanisms whereby behavior can be modified in desired directions.

Chapter 2. Research.   Before we can plunge into the more substantial content, we need to clarify some things about the ways in which psychologists do research. A statement like: "Women cannot effectively manage organizations" is meaningless if the conclusion is based on incomplete or faulty evidence. Thus, the second chapter acquaints you with the psychologist's approaches to learning about behavior in organizations.

Chapter 3. Correlation and psychometric theory.   Psychological research often explores relationships between variables. When they are demonstrated to exist, such relationships permit predictions of one variable from knowledge about the other. Thus, an applicant's scores on preemployment tests may be used as a basis for making a hiring decision. Likewise, evidence of a relationship between certain supervisory behavior and work-group effectiveness may lead to modifications of the organization's supervisory training program. The third chapter discusses correlation as one way of examining such relationships.

Data about peoples' actions are typically derived from some sort of behavioral measures (like psychological tests). These psychometric measures must meet certain requirements, also discussed in this chapter, if they are to provide useful and meaningful data.

Section two. Personnel psychology

The object of personnel psychology is to understand and implement the conditions of effective job performance by individual employees. This entails three primary considerations, each covered in one of the parts of Section II.

Part A. Defining and measuring performance.   To the extent that all of I/O psychology seeks to understand, predict, and encourage effective job performance, Chapters 4–6 are relevant to everything that follows. Before these more ambitious goals can be realized, the differences between effective and ineffective performance must be clarified. Further, if we ultimately wish to predict and encourage certain kinds of job performance rather than others, we need to be able to measure it.

This part begins with Job Analysis and Occupational Classification (Chapter 4) as an indispensible preliminary to virtually everything else the I/O psychologist does. A job analysis summarizes the duties required on a particular job, and describes the environment in which the work is done. Without such analyses it would be impossible, for example, to intelligently decide which tests might be appropriate for employee selection, or how a job might be redesigned for handicapped employees, or how an organization might be restructured to facilitate rather than impede employee performance.

Chapter 5 considers alternatives in formulating definitions of effective job performance. And Chapter 6 discusses procedures for transforming those definitions into useful measures. These appraisals of employee performance are critical both for maintaining personnel programs (through, for example, periodic performance reviews), and as research criteria for evaluating the impact of changes directed toward modifying performance.

Part B. Predicting performance: Personnel selection and placement.   Most employers have the opportunity to choose new employees from among a group of job applicants. Hence, they face a prediction problem: Which applicant, if hired, will prove to be the most satisfactory employee? Chapter 7, Validity and Prediction, discusses the technology of employment selection. Some of the vital questions raised by applying this technology are also confronted. For example, how do we determine whether or not a preemployment test or job interview leads to accurate decisions? Are tests equally fair to everyone, including women and minority applicants?

Whereas employee selection makes use of preemployment tests and other devices as performance predictors, these measures also have many other applications to I/O psychology. The range of available measures of personal characteristics is explored in Chapters 8 and 9.

Part C. Facilitating performance.   Part C begins by assuming that the new employee has been selected and placed. The concern now is to facilitate job performance and satisfaction. We discuss two approaches, both of which are taken in most organizations.

Training (Chapter 10) attempts to help the employee learn appropriate skills, attitudes, and knowledge required by the job. Thus, it is a planned effort to help the employee adapt to the job. Although presented in the context of new employees, training efforts permeate most organizations at all levels, including top management.

An alternative, discussed in Chapter 11, Human Factors, is to modify the job (or at least some elements of the job) so it is more compatible with employee skills.

Section three. Organizational psychology

The context of work is a social one for most employees. With the exception of a few solitary jobs, most workers either are required to interact with one another or do so because such interactions are important to them. Furthermore, an employee brings a social history to the job. That history includes such group affiliations as family and neighborhood, and personal values including attitudes toward work and authority.

Section Three is also divided into three parts.

Part A. Individual variables.   Social history interacts with aspects of the job and work environment and with individual employee characteristics jointly to influence frames of reference, attitudes, and one's general posture toward the world as well as one's place in it. These in turn influence motivation (Chapter 12) and feelings of satisfaction or dissatisfaction with the job (Chapter 13).

Motivation is a complex matter. A person's goals reflect the interaction of present circumstances and past history. Thus there are widely ranging individual differences between employees in their attitudes toward work and the satisfactions they derive from it. One of the tasks for I/O psychologists is to discover broad principles of motivation transcending individual differences in specific work-related drives.

Part B. Individuals in groups.   Beginning with Chapter 14 our emphasis shifts from our prior consideration of employees as individuals to the interpersonal context of work. The two topics comprising Part B are Group Behavior (Chapter 14) and Leadership (Chapter 15).

The employee is viewed here from an organizational perspective—that is, in context with co-workers, supervisors, subordinates, and managers. We consider the kinds of reciprocal effects people have on each other as they work together to accomplish organizational objectives. Some of the questions addressed in these chapters are: How do groups make decisions affecting work goals and the way in which these goals are to be attained? What factors influence the quality and acceptance of those decisions? What constitutes effective supervision and management? What do we know about the circumstances conducive to effective leadership?

Part C. Organizational dynamics.   Our last three chapters address the big picture. We begin by examining the total organization from several theoretical perspectives (Chapter 16). These theories attempt to systematize what is known about the various forces and counterforces impinging upon organizations.

Chapter 17 discusses organizational development as the application of organizational theory. Here we consider several approaches to evaluating the organization's present status and helping it grow in new directions.

We conclude with Chapter 18, Organizational Change, by presenting detailed case histories of attempts to modify two organizations: one a university, the other, a manufacturing company. Since one of these change efforts failed whereas the other was highly successful, these cases give us a chance to clarify some of the practical as well as theoretical issues in working with organizations.

I/O PSYCHOLOGY AS A SCIENCE AND PROFESSION

We have thus far described something of the scope of activities of I/O psychologists. The breadth of possible applications is further amplified by the description taken from the *Dictionary of Occupational Titles* and quoted under the subhead "Functional Job Analysis" in Chapter 4. We urge you to read that description now even though you will see it again when you read that chapter.

How are these skills developed?

Educational background

Since I/O is but one of several specialty fields of psychology, all sharing a common concern for understanding, predicting, and changing behavior, the training of all psychologists has much in common. The main distinguishing feature of I/O training is that it emphasizes behavior in work or other organizational settings.

Most qualified psychologists in this country are members of the American Psychological Association. Although the association does not endorse the professional qualifications of any of its members, it has developed a code of ethical practice to which all members (over 50,000) are required to adhere.

The association is comprised of 39 divisions representing the members' specialized fields of interest and activities. One of these (Division 14) is the Division of Industrial and Organizational Psychology. There are also divisions of Consulting Psychology, Psychologists in Public Service, Military Psychology, the Society of Engineering Psychologists and Consumer Psychology.

APA standards hold that the title *psychologist* should apply only to persons with doctoral training (and, as discussed below, appropriate state certification or licensure). The association's policy further specifies that persons newly working in the field with less than the doctorate (Ph.D.) in psychology should work only under the continuing supervision of a fully trained psychologist.

The Ph.D. is a research degree. To earn it in psychology, the student ordinarily studies for four to five years beyond the bachelor's degree and completes an original research contribution to the field (that is, writes a dissertation). Ph.D. students in I/O psychology typically are provided with supervised on-the-job experience as part of their training.

Employment

Statutory regulations enacted in most states control the practice of psychology, including I/O psychology.

The laws are enacted to protect the public by ensuring that the professional practitioner meets or exceeds certain minimum standards of education, experience, and knowledge. Most such laws require the Ph.D. and one or two years of supervised experience (plus satisfactory performance on the licensing or certification board's examination) before permitting independent practice as a psychologist. A few states provide lower levels of certification (often as psychological associate) for persons with training at the master's level.

I/O psychologists typically are employed in three kinds of settings: academic, industrial research, and consulting (including private practice). A survey of the work activities of 1,586 members of Division 14 in 1978 placed the percentages in these three categories at 35 percent, 36 percent and 18 percent, respectively (Madden, 1980). The activities of the remaining members included miscellaneous administrative, governmental, military assignments and so on.

Although these are primary work settings, there is a degree of overlap. Thus, many I/O psychologists on university faculties also consult on a part-time basis; and many employed by industry or as consultants hold part-time academic positions.

SO WHAT'S IN A NAME?

Dunnette's *Handbook* was published three years after the Division of Industrial Psychology of the American Psychological Association changed its name to the Division of Industrial and Organizational Psychology. The name change is meant to make explicit two aspects of this field:

1. It has moved from emphasizing "cookbook" practice as relatively separated from theory to a scientific/professional orientation wherein both theory and practice are interdependent and mutually reinforcing.
2. Its orientation, theories, and techniques are equally appropriate to nonindustrial organizations (like government, education, and so on) as they are to industry.

There is every reason to believe that the growth and expansion of activity by I/O psychologists will continue in the future. The attainment of most of society's significant goals requires the kinds of knowledge that psychologists have already generated and will generate to an even greater extent in the future. With the oceans and outer space relatively unexplored frontiers, adjustments to energy-related issues an international priority, and an improved quality of life for humankind a world ambition, there can be no shortage of meaningful problems for I/O psychology.

REFERENCES

Dunnette, M. D. (Ed.). *Handbook of industrial and organizational psychology.* Chicago: Rand McNally, 1976.

Fryer, D. H., & Henry, E. R. *Handbook of applied psychology* (Vols. 1 and 2). New York: Holt, Rinehart & Winston, 1950.

Gilbreth, F. B. *Brick laying system.* New York: Clark, 1911.

Madden, J. M. Distribution of Division 14 members by state, type of work, and type of degree. *The Industrial-Organizational Psychologist,* 1980, *17,* 25–27.

Munsterberg, H. *Psychology and industrial efficiency.* Boston: Houghton Mifflin, 1913.

Roethlisberger, F. W., & Dickson, W. J. *Management and the worker.* Cambridge, Mass.: Harvard University Press, 1939.

Taylor, F. W. *The principles of scientific management.* New York: Harper & Bros., 1911.

chapter 2

Research

I/O psychologists are researchers as well as practitioners. Their training includes the Ph.D., which is a research degree; they contribute to the science of behavior; and they attempt to deal with practical issues from a sound theoretical and investigative orientation.

There is a richness and variety to research methods in I/O psychology. As you read about the several approaches, keep in mind that they complement each other; each provides a unique vantage point from which to understand behavior in organizations.

BASIC CONCEPTS

One topic discussed later in the book is group problem solving. Suppose you were interested in determining whether the size of the group influences the number of solutions generated in a certain amount of time.

You might reason, in advance, that larger groups would have an advantage. The greater the number of persons, the greater the total number of ideas generated, and hence, the greater the number of solutions to the problem. Or you might reason conversely that too many cooks spoil the broth; as the group gets larger, it becomes increasingly difficult for anyone to convey ideas; many people might attempt to talk at once and relatively few would listen; and the resulting disruption would reduce the total number of solutions.

One way to find out what actually happens is to investigate the issue. You might decide to study problem solving in four different sized groups: 2, 8, 14, and 22 people. After reading some of the literature on group problem solving, you might realize that your findings could be influenced by the type of problem these groups are asked to solve. So you build this into your design by having the groups deal with two different types of problems: one with correct solutions (for example, mathematics problems); the other without a single correct or "best" solution (for example, devising names for a new sports car).

You have now begun to conceptualize a 4×2 design. You will have four different sized groups, each solving two different kinds of problems. Before discussing strategies for implementing this design, we need to clarify five basic concepts and some terminology.

The independent variable

The *independent variable* is the factor we are investigating because we believe it may affect the outcomes of the study. Two independent variables are involved in our illustrative study: (a) group size and (b) the type of problem the group is asked to solve. I/O psychologists are interested in a wide range of independent variables including work environments, leadership styles, equipment designs, and so on.

Any factor that is systematically controlled so that it is allowed to operate under certain circumstances and not others (or for certain experimental subjects and not for others) could be an independent variable. As we discuss later, one of the advantages of laboratory research is that the investigator is able to actually isolate and manipulate the independent variable for study. Group problem solving could, of course, be studied outside of the laboratory using real groups facing real problems. But the investigator would have to take the groups as they were, without being able to systematically vary the conditions considered critical to the experiment.

The dependent variable

The behavior studied and measured as a possible outcome is a *dependent variable*. The investigator conducts the research to determine whether that behavior depends upon manipulations of the independent variable. The dependent variables of greatest interest to I/O psychologists are (a) task performance and (b) personal satisfaction.

For our illustrative research problem we hypothesized that the number of solutions generated by the group would depend upon the group's size and the type of problem. Hence the number of problem solutions is the dependent variable. You can undoubtedly think of several other dependent variables that could have been investigated in this same study. For example, we might also have wanted to study the effects of the independent variables upon the group members' willingness to return to participate in a follow-up study, or upon their feelings about whether their group came up with "good" or "poor" solutions, and so on.

Extraneous variables

Extraneous variables are factors *other* than the independent variable that may inadvertently (against the investigator's wishes) influence the dependent variable. If these extraneous variables are allowed to operate, the investigator cannot know whether to attribute any changes in the dependent variables to *them* or to the particular independent variable(s) isolated for study.

What extraneous variables might contaminate the results of our problem-solving study? Two possibilities are the (*a*) intellectual level of the participants and (*b*) previous contacts among the participants. It is likely that brighter persons generate more solutions to problems. It is also possible that groups comprised of persons who know each other beforehand are more productive than groups made up of persons meeting for the first time in the laboratory.

As experimenters, we would likely draw incorrect conclusions if one of our groups differed from the others in these respects. Therefore, sound experimental design requires us to isolate the variables we wish to study and somehow to eliminate the possible effects of extraneous variables: that is, those we do not wish to study.

Control

The potential influences of extraneous variables are either eliminated or held constant across the experimental groups by control procedures. The most typically used control procedure in psychological experiments is random assignments of subjects to groups. The effectiveness of randomization as a control procedure rests partly on the number of subjects in the experiment. Given enough subjects it is likely that by randomly assigning them to the different sized groups and the two different problem conditions, we will effectively prevent any one group from being different from the others with respect to the extraneous variables.

This is another way in which laboratory studies are superior (from a research design standpoint) to studies of behavior outside of the laboratory in "real life." Such field studies offer the investigator fewer opportunities to control extraneous variables.

Inferences about causality

If our experiment has been carefully designed and the results are statistically significant (meaning that changes in the dependent variable probably were not chance variations), we are able to infer that these changes were caused by manipulations of the independent variable.

Did the independent variable manipulation actually cause the accompanying changes in the dependent variable? We really do not know. Although this might be the case, there is always the possibility that the results are attributable to some still uncontrolled extraneous variable, or to some as yet unknown third factor causing changes simultaneously to occur in both the independent and dependent variables. Although causality is always inferred rather than proven, we become increasingly confident of a particular cause-effect relationship when a series of well-designed studies repeatedly produces the same findings.

EXPERIMENTAL DESIGN

I/O research is conducted in two types of settings: the laboratory, and the field. In either setting, the investigator may elect (circumstances permitting) to implement an experimental or nonexperimental approach to data collection. In this section we consider experiments conducted in the laboratory and in the field. Certain nonexperimental types of research are considered subsequently.

Laboratory experimentation

For reasons which will soon become apparent, I/O psychologists have more often conducted their research in the field rather than the laboratory. However, the unique strengths of laboratory research have caused several investigators (for example, Weick, 1965) to express concern that it has not been more often used.

Research procedures. Let us return to our problem-solving study and describe its implementation as a laboratory experiment.

Once the independent and dependent variables have been selected and the design worked out to control extraneous variables, the investigator is ready to begin. In order to carry out the group problem-solving study you would need to: (1) prepare the "cover story"; (2) recruit subjects; (3) conduct the experiment; (4) analyze the data. We will consider all but the last of these steps at this time. (Data analysis is discussed later in the chapter.)

1. The cover story. What will you tell your subjects when they come to your laboratory? The cover story is the rationale given the subjects for their participation. The simplest cover story entails giving the subjects a brief overview of what you are investigating and why.

However, there are sometimes problems with this direct approach. Although the cover should be believable and understandable, you do not want your subjects to correctly guess your hypothesis (Fromkin & Streufert, 1976). Subjects sometimes try to help investigators "prove" that they believe to be the expected finding. Also, the particular behavior you are interested in studying may be destroyed by calling the subjects' attention to it. (Although this would not be a particular issue for the problem-solving study, you can see how this might occur if you were investigating, say, the incidence of hostle remarks in groups of various sizes.)

Sometimes the effective implementation of research requires a certain amount of deception in framing the cover story. This is most often the case when the behavior you wish to study would be suppressed or substantially altered if the subjects knew what you were about. It is unlikely, for example, that fully informed employees would provide the investigator the opportunity to collect accurate data on tool theft in the plant, or unauthorized coffee breaks. Deceptive cover stories are used only after careful consideration, and only as a last resort when it is clear another approach will fail. Even then, in order to be ethically tolerated, the potential benefits of the investigation must clearly merit its conduct, and the investigator must make provision for debriefing afterwards, including an explanation to the subjects of why the deception was necessary.

2. *Recruiting subjects.* The most obvious consideration in recruiting subjects is availability. For this reason many I/O laboratory studies are conducted with college students as subjects.

However, a concern for generalizability of the findings may dictate drawing subjects from other populations. Results obtained with college students may not generalize to say homemakers, factory workers, or industrial executives. The appropriateness of a particular subject population becomes a concern whenever the subjects' characteristics (age, education, and so on) are different from those of the population to which we wish to generalize.

3. *Conducting the experiment.* Once you have recruited the subjects you are ready to deliver the cover story and perform the required manipulations.

Although not necessary for our hypothetical problem-solving study, the investigator is sometimes required to make a manipulation check. The purpose of the manipulation check is to make sure that the independent variable was manipulated successfully. For example, in a later chapter we present some studies on equity in which some subjects are made to feel underpaid for their work and others are made to feel overpaid. Here the manipulation check is a necessary follow-up to data collection in order to insure that the independent variable (subjects' feelings about the way they were paid) was successfully manipulated.

Laboratory versus field experiments

We have emphasized that laboratory experimentation permits the investigator a high degree of control over the variables. However, two potential characteristics of laboratory settings—artificiality and demand characteristics—may invalidate their use for particular purposes. This is not meant to minimize the contributions possible through laboratory investigation. But, as I/O psychologists are well aware, the investigation of particular kinds of problems sometimes requires field rather than laboratory study.

Artificiality and generalizability. Compared with real organizations where work is performed, laboratories are artificial environments. Like the question we raised earlier about the generalizability of research findings obtained with experimental subjects to actual employees, we can question the generalizability of laboratory findings to employment settings. This question of generalizability has been referred to as the question of *external validity* (Campbell & Stanley, 1966).

How can the external validity of laboratory studies be enhanced? The clear answer is to arrange the laboratory to approximate the important characteristics of the work setting to which we wish to generalize. Some of the major potential differences between working and laboratory environments are: (1) size of the work group; (2) duration of prior interpersonal contact; (3) importance of task outcome; (4) clarity of performance feedback; and (5) task interdependence (Weick, 1965). Employees ordinarily work in either smaller or larger groups than are accomodated in the laboratory, and have known their co-workers for a longer time (and perhaps more intimately) than is characteristic of experimental subjects. Further, job tasks and laboratory tasks often are qualitatively different. Job performance is more likely to have genuine consequences for salary, promotion, and so on; therefore employees are more likely than laboratory subjects to receive performance feedback. And whereas the laboratory is a fine place to isolate task and subtask performance for study as dependent variables, the interdependence of these tasks while doing the actual job may thereby be sacrificed.

Such factors can often be taken into account when designing and implementing laboratory studies without sacrificing experimental control. If they cannot, the investigator may need to consider field research as the only viable option.

Demand characteristics. Research subjects will often do what they believe the investigator wishes them to do (Orne, 1959, 1962). These ''good'' subjects divine cues from the situation (recruiting, cover story, research procedure) and attempt to infer the investigator's hypothesis or purpose.

These cues are termed the *demand characteristics* of the experiment. Good laboratory design requires that they be eliminated. The combination of such demand characteristics and subjects who attempt to help the investigator can easily generate erroneous findings. Since demand characteristics are a potential source of error in laboratory experiments, the investigator often conducts postexperimental interviews with the subjects to determine whether these cues have successfully been eliminated from the design.

Field experimentation

The primary difference between laboratory and field experiments is that the latter are accomplished in the work environment. The feature distinguishing field experiments from other kinds of field research is the treatment accorded the independent variable. If this variable is systematically manipulated by the investigator, an experiment is being conducted, and all of the requirements of sound experimental design apply.

Several difficulties are inherent in conducting sound field experiments.

Perhaps most obvious, you may not be able to arrange circumstances in the field to permit your desired independent variable manipulations. Think about the difficulty of doing the problem-solving study in the field. You would have to structure groups of employees into work groups of the desired sizes and assign them particular types of problems to solve.

Second, extraneous variables can be much more difficult to control in actual work settings because the random assignment of employees to experimental conditions often is not feasible. Thus, the results may be contaminated by such factors as employee age, sex, work experience, and variations between departments in the work environment.

The effect of uncontrolled extraneous variables is to generate ambiguous findings. It is impossible to determine with confidence that observed changes in the dependent variable are a function solely of the independent variable manipulation (Ellsworth, 1977).

In addition to the more usual kinds of extraneous factors, field experiments are vulnerable to a unique extraneous variable. Sometimes the experiment itself becomes an event or "happening" in the organization. That is, the presence of researchers, and the resulting discussions about the project, can become a more powerful experimental force than the independent variable!

NONEXPERIMENTAL RESEARCH PROCEDURES

There are other ways to do research besides conducting an experiment. Indeed, some kinds of researchable questions of interest to I/O psychologists are not really amenable to an experimental research design. To cite just a few examples: Are managers more or less satisfied with their employment than the employees they manage? Is there a relationship between employee age and accident frequency? Are there any personality traits that seem to characterize effective leaders?

Four nonexperimental sources of research information are discussed in this section: systematic observation, unobtrusive measures, research interviews, and questionnaire analysis.

Systematic observation

Systematic observation of actual on-the-job behavior is one of the most basic research approaches. Trained observers often note things that questionnaire or interview respondents either overlook or take for granted.

This procedure is appropriate to those situations in which the investigator has no way to manipulate the independent variable, and therefore must study its effects in the natural environment. (Hence, it is sometimes referred to as *naturalistic* observation.) Astronomers have always made effective use of this method. An I/O psychologist might use it, for example, in studying the effects of alcoholism upon productivity; or of a change in work procedure on accident record; or of labor contract negotiations upon job attitudes.

Objectivity in observation.   Objectivity is a goal of all research. It is especially difficult to attain when the research data are derived through observation because the observer inadvertently acts as a kind of subjective filter. Bouchard (1976) suggests the following rules for making objective observations:

1. Bolster your observational data with data collected from other sources. These sources might be other independent observers, interviews with participants, and so on.
2. Separate fact from interpretation.
3. Be aware of your prejudices, defenses, biases, and stereotypes.
4. Observe your subjects in as many different contexts as possible.
5. Be sensitive to changes in your own emotions. Such changes are clues to diminished objectivity.
6. Avoid identifying symbolically or emotionally with the group you are observing unless it is a tactical necessity.

Some difficulties. Assuming that the natural environment provides the desired circumstances and the observer is objective, systematic observation can provide much information not otherwise available. But there are also potential problems.

One is causal ambiguity. Whereas the experimenter manipulates the independent variable, and is therefore in a relatively strong position to infer causal relationships (particularly when the same results are repeatedly obtained), the observer takes variations in the independent variable as they come. Thus even when behavioral observations are systematically made, it is sometimes very difficult to isolate the causal agents.

A second difficulty is that systematic observations provide a different type of data than those obtained from experiments. Experimental data are usually measurements of some kind. Observational data, on the other hand, often need to be categorized, classified, or coded before they can be summarized. There can be no universally accepted classification scheme for such data because the appropriate scheme varies with the particular circumstances and issue being investigated (Guest, 1960). Hence, it sometimes proves difficult to compare observational results derived from different studies.

Unobtrusive measures

Behavioral data of interest to researchers can sometimes be collected without the subjects' knowledge. As the term implies, unobtrusive measures provide data without requiring the investigator to be an obvious intruder in the natural environment.

Cook and Campbell (1976) discuss four unobtrusive sources of information: (*a*) records regularly maintained by most organizations (salary, promotions, turnover, and so on); (*b*) physical traces (for example, wastepaper discards analyzed at the end of the day as an index of false starts by a typist); (*c*) recording devices (for example, a counter attached to a door to record how often that particular office is visited); and (*d*) unobtrusive observation (identifying communication patterns, for example, by having a secretary present at a conference actually keep tabs on communication while the participants believe she is taking conference notes).

In spite of their rather clear advantages for gathering certain data not otherwise available, Cook and Campbell note that unobtrusive measures are subject to certain deficiencies. The associated ethical issues relating to invasion of privacy can sometimes be complex; the archival records may not be trustworthy; and the range of problems that can be investigated in this way is limited.

Research interviews

We devote a large part of Chapter 8 to preemployment interviewing. In addition to their use for employee selection, interviews are widely used to collect research data. Sometimes the easiest way to discover what people want or how they feel is to ask them!

Successful interviewing. For interviews to provide meaningful research data, the interviewer must obtain the respondents' goodwill and trust (Stebbins, 1972). The likelihood that this will occur is increased when status differentials between interviewer and interviewee are minimized (Bouchard, 1976). The interviewer must also be perceived as an honest inquirer (Hund, 1959), asking meaningful questions about worthwhile issues (Scott, 1963).

Bouchard (1976) notes the following as important prerequisites to conducting successful research interviews:

1. Identify yourself and the project. Respondents ought to know why they are being interviewed, how they were chosen, and how much of their time will be required.
2. Maximize privacy and confidentiality.
3. Know who you are talking to (the respondent's name—which should be correctly pronounced—position in the organization, and so on).
4. Maintain neutrality. The interviewer attempts to gain information, not take sides.
5. Listen carefully.

Potential difficulties. One major source of potential invalidity of data generated from interviews is distortion caused by the interviewer. Through subtle signs of approval or disapproval, or almost imperceptible changes in the tone of voice, the interviewer may lead the respondent toward or away from particular answers. The usual precaution here is to provide thorough interviewer training, including supervised practice.

Causal ambiguity is a problem also for interviewers. Interviews may reveal, for example, that managers hold more favorable attitudes toward the organization than do lower level employees. A possible explanation is that status influences the level of job satisfaction. Equally plausible is the possibility that persons who are more satisfied with the organization tend to remain with it long enough to be promoted to managerial positions.

Finally, we note in passing that interviewing can be an expensive way to gather research data. The interviewers must be trained; data are collected individually from each respondent; and when responses are narrative, they need to be categorized or coded before interpretations can be made.

Questionnaires

Data obtained from questionnaires are used in research on such diverse topics as employee motivation, organizational communication patterns, leadership, and group processes.

As with interviews, questionnaires find out how people feel or what they think by simply asking them. However, unlike the unstructured or free-response interview, where the respondent answers freely and in his/her own words, the questionnaire limits the range of response. Thus the wording of questionnaire items can be critical to its usefulness for generating meaningful data.

Phrasing questions. Questionnaire writing is more art than science; rules for writing items are based pretty much on experience.

One recommendation that makes very good sense is to involve persons from the target research sample in helping to construct the questionnaire (among other things, to insure appropriate wording) (Bouchard, 1976). It is also usually critical to pretest the questionnaire in order to insure that the items are unambiguous and understandable.

Among other recommendations (Bouchard, 1976; Erdos, 1970; Kornhauser & Sheatsley, 1959; Payne, 1951) are such things as: eliminate unnecessary, repetitious, embarrassing or ambiguous questions and questions that could be answered more simply from organizational records; capture the respondents' interest; and so on. Several suggestions also have been made to enhance the likelihood that completed questionnaires will be returned: for example, include a cover letter and stamped self-addressed envelope.

Potential difficulties. Although questionnaires are subject to some of the same potential difficulties as interviews are (causal ambiguity and cost) there is one issue that is unique to questionnaire data—possible sampling error.

The objective is to generalize from the responses of the questionnaire sample to the population of persons that the sample is supposed to represent. Thus, a low return rate is devastating to questionnaire-based research. When the return rate is low, as it often is, the investigator cannot be certain that nonrespondents would have replied similarly to the respondents. (For this reason, it is disturbing to read newspaper and magazine articles summarizing research or polls based upon a relatively slim questionnaire return.)

DATA PROCESSING AND INTERPRETATION

Irrespective of the research design or sources of information, research generates data. The data from our hypothetical problem-solving study would be the number of problems correctly solved in, say, 10-minute work sessions, under 8 different conditions, 4 variations in group size, and 2 variations in problem type. Other types of studies produce other types of data—productivity records, accident rates, test scores, and number of persons answering "Yes" to a questionnaire item, to name a few.

These data somehow must be organized if we are to make sense of them. You are already familiar with several arrangements for organizing and summarizing data. Questionnaire responses can be tabulated and converted to percentages; income levels can be graphed as a function of educational background; an instructor can indicate standing relative to the rest of the class by noting the placement of your examination score in the distribution of class scores; and so on.

Data distributions

Figure 2–1 gives us some data to work with. The table on the right side of that figure shows the number of correct problem solutions for 50 different

FIGURE 2–1
Number of correct solutions: Four-person problem solving groups

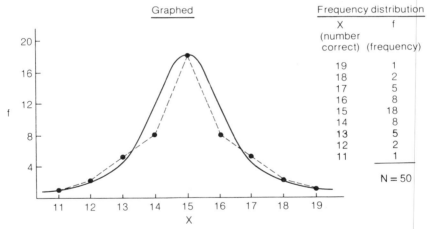

X (number correct)	f (frequency)
19	1
18	2
17	5
16	8
15	18
14	8
13	5
12	2
11	1
	N = 50

four-person problem-solving groups. The scores (number of correct solutions) are designated by a capital letter X; the frequency (f) column shows the number of groups attaining each score; the total number of observations (N) is, of course, 50.

The same data are graphed on the left side of Figure 2–1. The data points are plotted as dots (•) and connected by dashed lines. The overlaid solid curve is fitted to the data distribution in order to clarify its nature.

We have arranged these data to generate a normal frequency distribution. This type of distribution is often obtained (or assumed) for data processing and interpretation. The plotted distribution is symmetrical and has a single peak. (The formula for a normal curve has other properties which are beyond the scope of this discussion.)

It is quite possible to obtain data with nonnormal distributional characteristics. The obtained curve may be skewed (off-center toward one side or the other), multimodal (have more than one peak), or either atypically flat or tall.

Descriptive statistics

You already are familiar with certain kinds of descriptive statistics, although you may not have been aware that this is what they are called.

Descriptive statistics are numerical summaries of a mass of data. When we speak of the average test score or a range of scores, we are providing a kind of shorthand description of a set of data. The average says something about the group's typical score; the range provides information about the spread of scores from lowest to highest. Both sorts of information are required to fully describe a set of data. Thus, there are two types of descriptive statistics: central tendency, and variability.

Central tendency. Suppose we wished to calculate a single value best representing typical performance by the 50 groups represented in Figure 2–1.

One possibility, with which you are already familiar, is to calculate the mean (or arithmetic average). The formula for the mean ($\bar{X}$) is written

$$\bar{X} = \frac{\Sigma X}{N}$$

indicating that it is computed by adding (Σ) the separate scores (X) and dividing this sum by the number (N) of observations.

Although commonly used, the mean is neither the only, nor always the most useful, measure of central tendency. Two others are the median and mode.

The median is that score falling precisely at the midpoint of the distribution of observations. With data from 50 cases arranged in order from highest to lowest score (or vice versa), the median is the score falling between the 25th and 26th observation. The mode is simply the score that occurs most frequently.

Referring to the graph in Figure 2–1, it is obvious that the mode is 15. Looking at the data on the right side, the median score is also 15. (Half the observations fall above this score whereas the other half fall below it.) Finally, the mean of this same distribution is also 15. (Add the scores, remembering to add 18 twice, 17 five times, and so on, and divide the total by 50.)

It is no accident that the three measures of central tendency are identical for these data; we made them up to produce that result. The mean, median, and mode are always identical when the data distribution is normal. However, these measures diverge, as shown in Figure 2–2, when the distributions

FIGURE 2–2
Measures of central tendency in normal and in skewed distributions

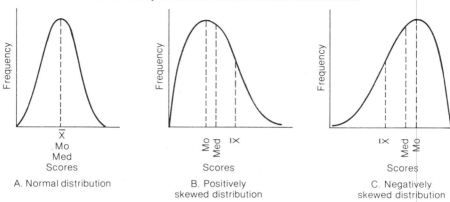

A. Normal distribution

B. Positively
skewed distribution

C. Negatively
skewed distribution

are skewed. Since the mean is more sensitive to the "tail" of a skewed distribution, it is therefore a less typical index of central tendency than is the median.

Variability

A measure of central tendency does not by itself provide an adequate description of a data distribution. It is quite possible for two distributions to have identical means even though their variabilities (spread of data away from the mean) are different. This is illustrated in Figure 2–3, in which we

FIGURE 2–3
Two normal distributions with identical means but different variabilities

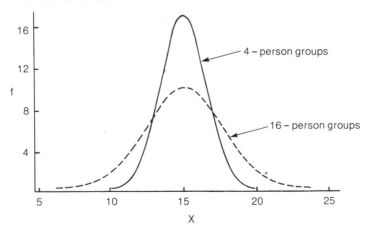

have taken the distribution from Figure 2–1 (results with 4-person groups) and superimposed another distribution (dotted line) showing hypothetical results from 16-person groups. Although the average number of solutions under both circumstances is identical, the larger group is shown as having greater variability, as evidenced by extreme scores in both directions.

We discuss only the most commonly used statistic of variability: standard deviation (s or the Greek letter *sigma, σ*).

If the data distribution is normal, approximately 68 percent (actually 68.26 percent) of the observations will fall between the scores delimited by one standard deviation on either side of the mean. This percentage is constant as a function of the formula for the normal curve regardless of the type of data plotted or of the distribution's mean.

The standard deviation of the data in Figure 2–1 is 1.57. (Although statistical computation is not treated in this discussion, one of the computational formulas for standard deviation is given below if you care to check our arithmetic.)[1] With a mean for that distribution of 15, and s of 1.57, the middle 68 percent of the observations fall between 13.43 (1 standard deviation below the mean) and 16.57 (1 standard deviation above the mean). The remaining 32 percent of the observations is equally divided, with 16 percent below $-1s$ and the other 16 percent above $+1s$.

Just as the percentage of observations between the limits of $\pm 1s$ is constant for normal distributions, so too are the percentages between the limits defined by two and three standard deviations on either side of the mean. The scores between $-2s$ and $+2s$ include 95.44 percent of the cases, while virtually all of the observations are included between $\pm 3s$.

The foregoing statements about standard deviation are summarized schematically for our illustrative data in Figure 2–4.

Looking back to Figure 2–3, would you infer that the distribution for 16-person groups generates a larger or smaller standard deviation than the 1.57 value obtained for 8-person groups? (Hopefully, you answered "larger." Since the data are spread further away from the mean, it takes a wider range of scores to accomodate a fixed percentage of observations.)

Information about standard deviation is useful in several ways.

One, discussed more fully in Chapter 9, relates to interpreting scores on psychological tests. Different tests generate different distributions of scores (that is, distributions with different means and standard deviations). In order to compare the scores meaningfully, it is necessary first to transform them to some common measurement scale. One such scale is provided by transforming raw test scores to scores expressed in standard deviation units. Since standard deviation always has the same meaning in normal distributions, one can directly compare such standard scores. A test like the Graduate Record Examination, or GRE, for example, yields scores converted to a scale where

[1]

$$s = \frac{\sqrt{N \Sigma X^2 - (\Sigma X)^2}}{N}$$

FIGURE 2–4
A distribution of data: Mean = 15, standard deviation = 1.57

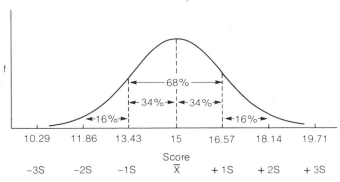

the mean is set to 500 and standard deviation is set to 100. A GRE score of 600 is a full standard deviation above the mean; one at 450 is one-half standard deviation below the mean; and so on.

Another application, more directly relevant to our concerns at this time, is making inferences and drawing conclusions from obtained data.

Statistical inference

Research data are accumulated from limited samples of subjects. This fact raises two related issues for the investigator. First, how much confidence can be placed in the obtained findings? Are they genuine reflections of the influence of the independent variable, or are they a fluke? Second, assuming that the investigator wishes to contribute to the scientific base of I/O psychology, a particular finding is meaningful only if it is generalizable beyond the particular research sample to other similar persons and situations. Thus, we didn't propose our group problem-solving experiment to draw conclusions relevant only to the particular subjects involved in that study; we hope to use the results to say something about group size and problem solving generally.

Both issues entail making inferences from research data. The starting point for the appropriate statistical analysis is the *null hypothesis:* that is, the assumption that whatever the study's findings, they can be attributed to chance.

Chance.   This is not merely perverse logic on the investigator's part. If an independent variable has no influence at all, the dependent variables will remain unaffected by it. However, this does not mean that the dependent variable score will be identical in a before-and-after comparison. The dependent variable measures are themselves imperfect. Productivity, for example, fluctuates with time of the day, whether or not the employee has a headache, and so on. The same can be said of any measure: each has some inherent *measurement error*. Measurement errors cause fluctuations in the dependent variable quite apart from any effects that might have been produced by the independent variable.

The null hypothesis assumes that the obtained results are entirely attributable to such chance fluctuations, and challenges the investigator (through statistical inference) to refute this assumption.

How does standard deviation—which signifies variability—relate to statistical inference?

In considering any distribution of data, some of the variability merely reflects chance fluctuations due to measurement error; the remainder is real in that it reflects true variations between people's performance. One task for statistical inference, then, is to sort out these elements of variability. To put it another way, if the independent variable exerts no effect upon performance, all of the observed variability in performance must be due to chance. What if the independent variable "works?" In that case it would produce a change in performance beyond the limits reasonably to be expected if chance alone were operating.

It is not our purpose to describe how statistical tests are made. We wish instead to clarify some of the underlying logic. Therefore, let us pursue the logic of one particular statistical test, the t-test.

The *t-test* is applied to test the obtained difference between two means. Thus we might use it, for example, to test the difference between the mean number of correct problem solutions in our four-person and two-person groups. We have already given 15 as the mean for the four-person groups; let us say the mean for two-person groups working on the same kind of problem is 12 correct solutions. It looks like four-person groups generate more correct solutions. The statistical question is one of chance variation. Could the difference between these means have originated solely by chance? If so, group size exerted no effect.

Since persons were randomly assigned to the groups at the beginning of the study, we can assume that extraneous factors were controlled. If this were true, then problem-solving effectiveness should be the same in the two groups, unless group size itself influences performance. The t-test approaches this by comparing the obtained difference between means to the magnitude of mean differences that could be explained solely on the basis of chance fluctuations. If the obtained mean difference is in the range expected by chance, the null hypothesis must be accepted: The independent variable exerted no systematic effect.

Statistical significance. What if we obtain a larger mean difference? Whatever its magnitude, there is some possibility (however remote) that chance alone caused it. Gamblers play the long shot because, although the odds of a payoff are slim, it just might happen. The casino plays the probabilities. It can afford to pay off on the occasional long shot precisely because it is such an infrequent occurrence.

Research data are interpreted with a similar gambler's perspective. We can never be absolutely and positively certain that our three-problem-mean difference between the problem-solving groups did not result from chance alone. But there is a point at which the likelihood that chance alone caused the difference is so remote that we are willing to "bet" on the independent variable as the determinant. At that point we say that we have a *statistically significant* difference.

Convention dictates that the probability that chance alone could have caused the obtained results must be 5 in 100 or less before we can claim to have a statistically significant difference. At this level of confidence, the investigator would report a p (probability) value of less than .05. If the likelihood were less than 1 in 100, the p-value would be reported as less than .01. Still lower p-values (.001, .0001) often are obtained, and give cause for still greater confidence in conclusions about the impact of independent variables.

Nevertheless, we note that all statistically significant findings are not necessarily also *practically* significant. Even relatively small differences between means may be statistically significant if the research groups are large. Whereas such differences may have important implications for theory, the practical question is always one of feasibility: that is, is the obtained difference important enough to justify the cost of its implementation? Can the company afford, for example, to restructure its organization to accomodate larger problem-solving groups? Or, as another example, is the anticipated reduction in employee turnover sufficient to offset the additional expense of improved employee selection procedures?

Postscript.   We do not wish to leave you at the end of this brief discussion of statistics for data analysis and interpretation believing either that the t-test is the only basis for making statistical inferences, or that inferential statistics are the only ones applied to I/O research data. We have occasion later in the book to cite results based upon other tests of statistical significance. And we devote most of the next chapter to correlation, which is a statistic for evaluating the relationship between two or more variables.

The immediately preceding discussion of statistical inference may seem somewhat intimidating if you have not had some prior formal background in statistics. If so, be reassured! You will not be inundated with statistics, even though you will read about conclusions and interpretations from research. The important point is that the conclusions cited subsequently followed careful and systematic data collection. Furthermore, those data were analyzed using appropriate statistics in order to conclude that the obtained results were unlikely to be merely chance occurrences.

SUMMARY

We began this chapter by considering three kinds of research variables: independent, dependent, and extraneous. An independent variable is the particular factor being investigated as a potential determinant of the research outcomes. It is the variable the effects of which are being studied. The dependent variables are the measurable behavioral outcomes. Thus, the investigator conducts the research to determine whether that behavior (the dependent variable) depends upon manipulations of the independent variable. Extraneous variables are factors other than the independent variable that may inadvertently (against the investigator's wishes) influence the dependent variable.

The researcher wishes to eliminate the effects of possible extraneous variables by attempting to control their influence. This is easier accomplished in laboratory studies, where subjects can be randomly assigned to treatment conditions, than in field studies. However, this advantage of laboratory experiments may be offset by two other considerations: artificiality, and demand characteristics. To the extent that the laboratory is an artificial setting, the results cannot confidently be generalized to employment settings. Likewise, if the laboratory design cues the subjects about the investigator's hypothesis or purposes, they may attempt to "help" by responding in terms of the experiment's demand characteristics.

Sound research does not always imply an experiment. We discussed four nonexperimental sources of research data: systematic observations, unobtrusive measures, interviews, and questionnaires. Each has its own advantages and disadvantages as noted in the chapter.

Irrespective of the research design or sources of information, research produces data which must be organized and interpreted.

Descriptive statistics facilitate data organization. Measures of central tendency provide a single numerical value as typical of the distribution of data. The three measures of central tendency considered here are the mean, median, and mode. The mean (or arithmetic average) is perhaps the most widely used measure of central tendency, except when the distribution of data is markedly skewed. Since the mean is particularly sensitive to the influence of atypical values in nonnormal distributions, the median is a more representative measure of central tendency in such cases.

Measures of variability describe the spread of data away from the central tendency. We considered only one such measure: the standard deviation. Standard deviation has a uniform meaning in normal distributions, irrespective of the raw score units. Approximately 68 percent of the data are contained within the score range defined by 1 standard deviation on either side of the mean.

Investigators attempt to generalize from findings obtained in the research sample to some appropriate population of persons. This raises a question basic to data interpretation: What is the likelihood that the obtained findings resulted from chance factors rather than from the independent variable? This question is answered by applying inferential statistics: that is, statistical tests allowing the investigator to make inferences about the generalizability of research findings.

Inferential statistics test the null hypothesis and establish confidence limits for its rejection. This hypothesis states that the findings can be attributed to chance (rather than to the independent variable). Thus, the more confidently it can be rejected, the greater the significance of the obtained finding. Convention dictates that the null hypothesis must be rejected with a probability level of .05 or less before statistical significance can be claimed. In other words, the likelihood that findings of the magnitude obtained in the study could have resulted solely by chance must be no greater than 5 in 100 before the investigator can reject chance as the explanation.

A final consideration for the I/O researcher is practical significance, as distinct from statistical significance. Even when findings are statistically significant there is always the question of feasibility—is the projected outcome sufficiently important to justify the cost of implementation?

REFERENCES

Blouchard, T. J.   Field research methods: interviewing, participant observation, systematic observation, unobtrusive measures. In M. D. Dunnette (Ed.), *Handbook of industrial and organizational psychology*. Chicago: Rand McNally, 1976, 363–414.

Campbell, D. T., & Stanley, J. C.   *Experimental and quasi-experimental designs for research*. Chicago: Rand McNally, 1966.

Cook, T. D., & Campbell, D. T.   The design and conduct of quasi-experiments and true experiments in field settings. In M. D. Dunnette (Ed.), *Handbook of industrial and organizational psychology*. Chicago: Rand McNally, 1976, 223–326.

Erdos, P. L.   *Professional mail surveys*. New York: McGraw-Hill, 1970.

Ellsworth, P.   From abstract ideas to concrete instances: Some guidelines for choosing natural research settings. *American Psychologist*, 1977, *32*, 605–615.

Fromken, H. L., & Streufert, S.   Laboratory experimentation. In M. D. Dunnette (Ed.), *Handbook of industrial and organizational psychology*. Chicago: Rand McNally, 1976, 415–466.

Guest, R. M.   Categories of events in field observations. In R. N. Adams & J. J. Priess (Eds.), *Human organization research*. Homewood, Ill.: Dorsey, 1960.

Hund, J. M.   Changing role in the interview situation. *Public Opinion Quarterly*, 1959, *23*, 236–246.

Kornhauser, A., & Sheatsley, P.   Questionnaire construction and interview procedure. In C. Sellitz, M. Jahoda, M. Deutsch, & S. Cook (Eds.), *Research methods in social relations*. New York: Holt, Rinehart & Winston, 1959.

Orne, M. T.   The nature of hypnosis: Artifact and essence. *Journal of abnormal and social psychology*, 1959, *58*, 277–299.

Orne, M. T.   On the social psychology of the psychology experiment: With particular reference to demand characteristics and their implications. *American Psychologist*, 1962, *17*, 776–783.

Payne, S. L.   *The art of asking questions*. Princeton, N.J.: Princeton University Press, 1951.

Scott, W. R.   Field work in a formal organization: Some dilemmas in the role of observer. *Human organization*, 1963, *22*, 162–168.

Stebbins, R. A.   The unstructured research interview as incipient interpersonal relationship. *Sociology and Social Research*, 1972, *56*, 164–179.

Weick, K. E.   Laboratory experiments with organizations. In J. G. March (Ed.), *Handbook of organizations*. Chicago: Rand McNally, 1965.

chapter 3

Correlation and Psychometric Theory

Research undertaken by I/O psychologists is often designed to explore relationships between variables. For example, we might wish to investigate whether employee age is associated with accident frequency, or whether annual income at age 50 is associated with educational background.

Correlation (r) is the statistic used to establish the existence of relationships between any two or more variables. Correlational values can range from +1.00 (signifying a perfect positive relationship) through 0.00 (signifying a total absence of relationship) to −1.00 (a perfect negative relationship). Given information in the form of a correlation coefficient, it is possible to predict one of the correlated variables from scores on the other.

Thus, in addition to studies like those mentioned above, correlation is central to exploring possible relationships between preemployment variables (applicant test scores, age, sex, and so on) and postemployment measures of actual job success. Here the investigator begins by hypothesizing the existence of a relationship between applicants' characteristics and their subsequent effectiveness as employees, and checks to determine if the hypothesized relationship is confirmed (Guion, 1976). If the hypothesis is confirmed, it provides a basis for establishing a preemployment selection program. Thereafter, employees can be selected from the applicant pool on the basis of predictions of their likely eventual success as employees. When used for this purpose, the correlation coefficient is termed a *predictive validity coefficient*.

TWO-VARIABLE CORRELATION

The simplest type of correlation involves just two variables. In selection research, this means one predictor and one criterion. If these measures correlate, the scores earned on them are covariant: that is, changes in one of the scores are accompanied by systematic (and therefore predictable) changes in the other.

Correlation as overlapping variance

One way to conceptualize covariation is as overlapping variance. You will recall from Chapter 2 that scores comprising any distribution spread away from the measure of central tendency. You will recall further that we can compare distributions having different means and standard deviations by transforming the raw scores for each distribution to standard scores. This z-score conversion (to standard deviation units) has the effect of setting the means of each distribution at 0.00 and the standard deviations at 1.00.

Assuming we have effected z-score transformations of a set of predictor scores and a set of criterion scores, we can visualize the covariation signifying the existence of a correlation between them as shown in Figure 3–1. The

FIGURE 3–1
Correlation as overlapping variance

correlation itself is an index of the amount of variance shared by the predictor and the criterion.

Regression

Computational procedures for calculating correlation are beyond the scope of this discussion. Instead, we will emphasize the meaning and uses of correlation, particularly as this statistic relates to employment selection programs.

A convenient format for visualizing covariation is the *scattergram;* that is, a crossplot of the scores on the two correlated variables. Such a scattergram is shown in Figure 3–2. Since the arithmetic test was administered to job applicants it is designated the *predictor.* The measure of job proficiency, available subsequent to employment, is the variable we wish to predict and is therefore termed the *criterion.* Again, because the distributions of scores for these two measures have different variances, each one has been transformed to z-score equivalents.

Visual inspection of this scattergram confirms that the two measures covary. Each dot represents one person's scores on both measures. The higher

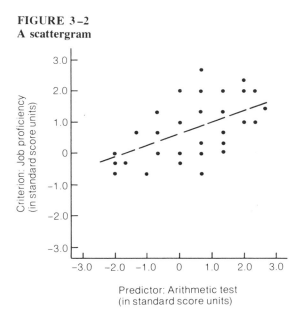

FIGURE 3–2
A scattergram

Criterion: Job proficiency
(in standard score units)

Predictor: Arithmetic test
(in standard score units)

job proficiency (criterion) scores are generally associated with the higher arithmetic test (predictor) scores, although there are exceptions. When computed, the correlation coefficient tells us about the strength and direction of this covariation.

The nature of the relationship between the variables can be mathematically expressed by the line which best describes all of the data points. This line of best fit is the *regression line* (shown as the broken line in Figure 3–2). When all data are represented as z-scores, as in this figure, the mathematical slope of the regression line is the correlation.

How do we know that the line which has been fitted to the scattergram is the one best fitting all of the data points? The solution whereby data are fitted to a mathematical function (like a line) is the *least squares solution*. This solution regards as "best" the particular function which represents the data in a way that reduces the deviations (differences between individual data points and the mathematical function fitted to them) to a minimum. Since such deviations can be positive or negative, the deviations are squared to produce this solution.

The least squares concept is illustrated schematically in Figure 3–3.

You may be wondering whether paired data of the sort contained in a scattergram are always best represented by a regression *line*. The answer is no. The relationship between two measures may be curvilinear rather than linear. This would have occurred with our earlier arithmetic test-job proficiency illustration, for example, if the most proficient employees were those

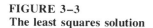

FIGURE 3–3
The least squares solution

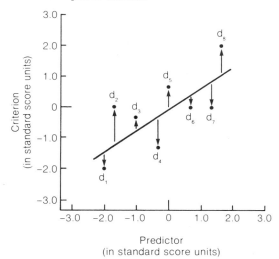

Predictor
(in standard score units)

The regression line provides the best fit by minimizing the sums of the squared deviations. It is the line producing the lowest value for the sum of $d_1^2 + d_2^2 + d_3^2 \ldots$

who had scored in the midrange of the arithmetic test. Conceivably one can have too much as well as too little knowledge to perform some tasks efficiently.

When a curvilinear relationship exists, the appropriate function of best fit is, of course, some kind of curve rather than a straight line. We will not consider procedures for making predictions from curvilinear functions. However, it is important to note that correlation assumes that the relationship between variables is *linear*.

Point prediction. Once the regression line is established, it permits point prediction: that is, prediction of the score on one variable (the criterion) from the score attained on the other variable (the predictor).

Point prediction is illustrated in Figure 3–4. The array of data points comprising the scattergram is shown as an ellipse. In this hypothetical situation, an applicant for a position as bank teller scores − 1.3 standard deviation units on the arithmetic test previously established as a valid predictor of job proficiency. On this basis, our best prediction of the applicant's likely level of proficiency, were he or she to be hired and placed on the job, is − 1.0. This applicant's preemployment test score was below average; the predicted proficiency level is also below average.

The accuracy of this prediction is partly a function of the magnitude of the

FIGURE 3–4
Point prediction from the regression line

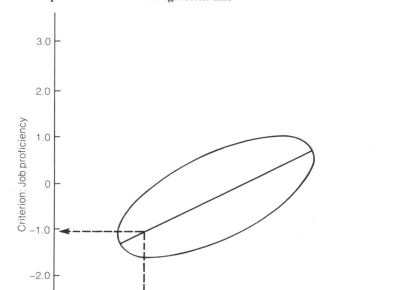

correlation upon which it is based. Given a perfect *r* (1.00), point predictions are error free. Given a 0.00 *r*, predictions have only chance accuracy. The correlation shown in Figure 3–4 is somewhere between these extremes.

Strength and direction.   In addition to indicating the magnitude (strength) of covariation, correlation signifies its direction. A *positive* correlation indicates direct covariation between two sets of scores: Higher scores on one variable are associated with higher scores on the other. A *negative* correlation signifies inverse covariation: Higher scores on one variable are associated with lower scores on the other. Thus, were we to find that age and accident frequency were negatively correlated, it would mean that older employees as a group had fewer industrial accidents than younger employees as a group.

Representative scattergrams for various magnitudes of positive and negative correlations are shown schematically in Figure 3–5. Note that as the average deviation from the regression line increases (represented by a wider elipse) the magnitude of *r* is diminished. Ultimately, when *r* is 0.00, it is impossible to fit any regression line.

FIGURE 3–5
Illustrative scattergrams

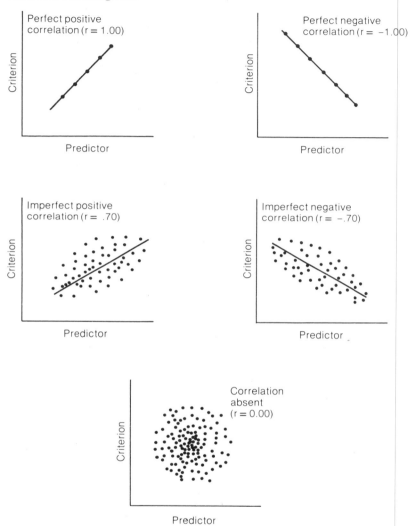

Interpreting correlations

Correlations are not percentage values in spite of their appearance. A correlation of +.60 is *not* 60 percent of anything. It is not 60 percent of a correlation of 1.00; and it does *not* signify 60 percent covariance.

Coefficient of determination.   When prediction is at issue, the value of r^2 (coefficient of determination) tells us the percent of criterion variance predictable from the predictor. Thus, given a validity coefficient of .60, the test predicts 36 percent of the criterion score variance.

Obviously, the higher the correlation, the higher its predictive efficiency. However, remember that the magnitude of this improvement in predictive efficiency is a function of *r-squared* rather than of *r* itself. Thus, for predictive purposes, a correlation of .85 is about twice as powerful as a correlation of .60 and about three times as powerful as a correlation of .49.

You may intuitively, but incorrectly, feel that negative correlations are somehow less useful for making predictions than positive correlations. Brief reflection upon the paragraph above concerning the coefficient of determination will confirm that positive and negative correlations of identical magnitude generate equally efficient predictions. Comparing coefficients of, say, +.60 and −.60, both signify the same covariance (36 percent). If these coefficients represented predictor-criterion correlations, both predictors would generate equally accurate criterion estimates.

The significance of the sign is solely directional. When the coefficient is *positive,* higher predictor scores are associated with *higher* criterion scores. Given a *negative* validity coefficient, higher predictor scores are associated with *lower* criterion scores. The latter is a relatively uncommon, but not unheard of, occurrence. For example, we might anticipate such an inverse relationship between tellers' errors while handling routine financial transactions (a criterion) and arithmetic test scores (a predictor).

Statistical significance. You already know that higher correlations are "better," but how high must a correlation be in order for it to be useful?

This apparently simple question does not allow an easy answer. The answer depends upon the correlation's intended use, and on the existing state of affairs. If, as we discuss in Chapter 7, the purpose is to predict subsequent job performance, the answer is conditioned by such things as the efficiency of selection without using this predictor, the ratio of job applicants to available positions, and the stringency of the definition of satisfactory job performance.

However for many other applications of *r*, we wish merely to know whether the obtained correlation can be taken as evidence of the existence of a relationship. Here, the investigator asks whether the correlation is statistically significant, that is, whether it is really higher than a value that might have resulted just by chance when the "true" *r* is really 0.00. Convention requires a probability level of 5 percent or better. In other words, for an obtained correlation to be regarded as significantly different from a value of 0.00, the probability of its occurrence as a chance variation from a "true" value of 0.00 must be 5 percent or less. Table 3–1 shows the value of *r* required for statistical significance at both the 5 and 1 percent levels for selected *N*s (number of pairs of observations).

Note that the size of *r* required for statistical significance decreases as the number of pairs of observations from which *r* is calculated increases. Thus, when the correlation is calculated from 1,000 pairs of observations, a value of .06 is statistically significant at the 5 percent level of confidence.

TABLE 3–1
Values of r required for significance at the 5
percent and 1 percent levels

N	5 percent level	1 percent level
10	0.63	0.77
25	0.40	0.51
50	0.28	0.36
75	0.23	0.30
100	0.20	0.26
500	0.09	0.12
1,000	0.06	0.08

Source: After L. D. Edmison, in J. E. Wert, C. O. Neidt, &
J. S. Ahmann, *Statistical Methods in Educational and Psychological Research* (New York: Appleton-Century-Crofts,
1954), p. 424.

A word of caution about statistical significance is appropriate here. Statistical significance alone does not signify *practical utility*. Although a relatively
low correlation may be significantly different from a correlation of 0.00, this
fact does not establish its usefulness for making predictions. As shown in
Table 3–1 even very low r's can attain statistical significance if they are based
upon a large number of paired observations.

MULTIPLE CORRELATION

We have thus far limited our discussion to two-variable correlation. The
usual predictive study attempts to maximize the efficiency with which a
criterion (or criteria) is (are) predicted from combined scores on several
preemployment measures, each weighted optimally. The statistical technique appropriate to correlation involving more than two variables is multiple correlation (R).

Assume we are considering using two preemployment tests jointly to predict a criterion. We would not ordinarily be considering the possible use of
both predictors unless we had established that each, alone, was valid. The
question resolved by multiple correlation is: Will joint use of these two
predictors materially improve the validity obtained when either predictor is
used alone?

Compare the three sets of covariance diagrams drawn in Figure 3–6.
These three examples show the predictor-criterion co-variances when the
two predictor tests are: (1) totally independent; (2) partially independent; and
(3) totally dependent, and therefore share identical variances.

The essential differences between the three conditions in Figure 3–6 is in
the magnitude of the coefficients of determination (r_{12}^2). In Case A, the predictors are uncorrelated $(r_{12}^2 = 0.00)$; hence each accounts for a unique portion of the criterion variance. At the other extreme (Case C) $r_{12}^2 = 1.00$;
therefore both predictors account for the identical criterion variance.

FIGURE 3–6
Multiple covariation

Case A: $r_{12}^2 = 0.00$

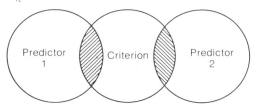

Case B: $r_{12}^2 =$ some value between 0.00 and 1.00

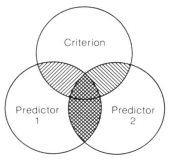

Case C: $r_{12}^2 = 1.00$

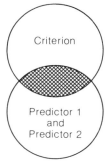

Just as r^2 indicates the amount of criterion variance accounted for by a single predictor, R^2 indicates this value for multiple predictors. When, as in Case A, the predictors are uncorrelated, R^2 is equal to the sum of the two separately calculated coefficients of determination ($R^2 = r_{1c}^2 + r_{2c}^2$). We will illustrate by substituting some correlation values. If each predictor had a validity coefficient of .40, and if r_{12} is 0.00, R^2 is .32. The calculated value is that for the coefficient of *multiple determination*. Since the value for R is found by taking the square root of $.32, R = .57$. Hence, the multiple correlation substantially improves predictive efficiency over that obtained using either test separately.

Case B complicates this situation because the predictors are themselves correlated. This means that some of the criterion variance is predicted as efficiently using either test alone as it is by using the combination of predictive tests. Other things being equal, improvements in predictive efficiency through multiple prediction are inversely related to the size of the correlation between the predictors. As you can see in Case B, the total amount of predictor-criterion covariance is less than it is for Case A.

Case C is the extreme, and hypothetical one, in which the predictors are perfectly correlated with each other. Since this is so, they both overlap with identical criterion variance. No improvement at all over the predictive efficiency of either predictor 1 or predictor 2 used alone is possible. Although hypothetical, this situation can be illustrated by considering a test scored for number of correct answers as "predictor 1" and the same test scored for number of wrong answers as "predictor 2." Whatever the separate validity of either predictor, this coefficient cannot be improved by combining the two into a multiple predictor.

The general rule for multiple prediction is that such prediction is enhanced by jointly using measures each of which correlates substantially with the criterion but only negligeably with the other predictor(s).[1]

PSYCHOMETRIC THEORY

As we have seen, one of the major reasons for taking measurements is to facilitate prediction. A score obtained at a particular moment in time (for example, on a typing test administered to a job applicant) may permit predictions of the score on that variable at some later time (projected typing test score after, say, three-months' employment), or of the score on some other variable correlated with the predictor (for example, supervisory evaluation of secretarial effectiveness six months after employment). It follows that measurement inaccuracies will detract from the accuracy of predictions based upon those measures.

It has been convenient, thus far in the chapter, to speak of correlating psychological variables or measurements (like test scores) without regard for the accuracy of those measures. However, all measures, including psychometric ones, are subject to potential sources of inaccuracy. The measuring instrument itself may be insufficiently refined to allow the required discriminations. Thus, we would not use an ordinary desk ruler to measure the kinds of close tolerances required for machining a space-shuttle

---

[1] The use of a test as a suppressor variable is an exception to this generalization. However, the implementation of suppressor variables is regarded as uncommon and therefore omitted from this treatment.

component. Alternatively, the measuring instrument may have some inherent defect (for example, an electronic short circuit) causing it to give inconsistent, and therefore untrustworthy, readings even under successively identical circumstances.

This generalization holds equally well for measures of psychological and physical characteristics. Thus, it is important to recognize that a person's earned score on any psychometric measure is only an estimate of his/her hypothetical "true" score. The more closely the earned score approximates the true one, the greater its potential value as a basis from which to make predictions.

The nature of psychometric error

The deviation between the obtained and true scores may occur in either direction. That is, the obtained score may either overestimate or underestimate the true situation. If we designate the hypothetical true score as T and the actual earned test score as X, the relationship between these scores can be expressed:

$$X = T + B + E.$$

This formulation (Brogden & Taylor, 1950) incorporates two major sources of psychometric error. One of these is bias (B); the other is really a cluster of several factors grouped together as error (E) factors. To the extent that bias and error can be removed from a psychometric measure, the obtained score is a more accurate estimate of the true one.

The potential sources of bias are discussed later (in Chapter 5). For now, we will be concerned only with the error component of the formula.

A definition of reliability. A reliable instrument is one yielding consistent or stable scores.

The requirement that a measuring instrument be reliable is no less important for psychometric devices than it is for instruments used in making physical measurements. An unreliable voltmeter, for example, is defective because it yields erratic voltage readings which are either above or below the true voltage. Its unreliability results from some defect (like a loose wire) in the instrument itself. Similarly, an unreliable psychometric instrument yields inconsistent or erratic scores over time when the true score has actually remained unchanged. In terms of the expression,

$$X = T + B + E$$

a perfectly reliable instrument yields scores with a zero-error component. To the extent that error components operate, the instrument is unreliable.

How does this relate to the earlier discussion of correlation? It may already have occurred to you that one way to estimate the size of the error component in test scores is to correlate two independently made estimates of the true score. If the correlation is relatively high, the test must be measuring reliably; that is, with little error. Conversely, a low correlation signifies a high error component, a high bias component, or both.

Reliability and validity.   What is the distinction between the two major concepts involving correlation introduced in this chapter, validity, and reliability? In practice, validity entails correlations between scores on a test (or other measure) with some independently measured criterion—behavior on the job, score on some other test, and so on. Reliability refers to the correlation between two separately made estimates of the true score yielded by an instrument.

For both reliability and validity, the higher the correlation, the more worthwhile the potential use of the test score for making predictions of future behavior. Nevertheless, it is entirely possible for a test to be highly reliable and yet be invalid. However consistent the readings taken from a psychometric test (its reliability), its validity is limited to predictions associated with the particular characteristic it measures. Although we may have a very reliable test of physical dexterity, for example, the resultant scores would be valueless for predicting a faculty member's "instructional effectiveness."

Finally, both concepts—reliability and validity—are similarly important to both psychometric predictors and criteria. There is little point to attempting to predict an invalid criterion. And it is impossible to predict an unreliable one.

Source of the error component.   Suppose we were using a work-output measure as a criterion of employee efficiency in a manufacturing operation. The criterion score is the number of work units produced per hour. The reliability of this criterion would be evidenced by the extent to which hourly productivity is a stable reflection of employee efficiency. The three major sources of unreliability in this or and other measure are (*a*) chance factors, (*b*) transitory personal factors, and (*c*) sampling inadequacies.

Chance factors are unpredictable, and therefore cannot be eliminated before they occur. An unforeseen power outage, a mechanical breakdown, or a raw materials supply bottleneck all illustrate some of the ways in which chance might depress hourly productivity. If one or another (but not all) of these adverse conditions is a normal feature of the job environment, then the simultaneous occurrence of all three during a given work period would artificially cause the criterion score to be depressed for that period. Conversely, the atypical absence of all three during another work period would cause the criterion score for that period to be artifically inflated.

Since, by definition, chance factors operate sporadically and irregularly, they are an inevitable source of unreliability whenever any measurements are made.

Transitory personal factors also influence the relative agreement or disparity between obtained and true scores. A person's productivity fluctuates because of temporary conditions such as fatigue, boredom, inattentiveness following preoccupation with something outside of the job, a hangover or cold, and so on. Although such factors usually have adverse effects, this is not always the case. The obtained score may be temporarily inflated by such transitory and sporadically occurring conditions as an impending performance review or a temporarily heightened feeling of well-being emanating from circumstances outside the job.

The third potential contributor to measurement error is *task sampling*. All psychometrics allow only a limited sample of observations. The 50 or 60 particular items or questions contained in a test are only a very small sample of the total universe of items that might have been written. The test score approximates the true score only to the extent that this sample of test items is truly representative of the universe of possible items.

Similarly a criterion measure, like hourly productivity, may vary with the time of the day or the day of the week. The true criterion score presumably reflects output over all time periods. However our particular criterion score can only be based upon observations taken during a finite sample of work periods. Included among these observations may be some in which performance is atypically weak or strong.

ESTIMATING RELIABILITY

Assuming the absence of bias, the correlation between obtained and true scores is inversely related to the magnitude of measurement errors. Should such errors be nonexistent, the obtained and true scores would, of course, be identical and the correlation between these scores would be 1.00. However, measurement errors do exist. They degrade the obtained scores, causing them to deviate from the hypothetically true values. The greater the measurement error, the greater the amount of score degradation, and hence the lower the correlation between obtained and true scores.

Thus, from a theoretical standpoint, the correlation between obtained and true scores is the index of reliability.

Obviously, this correlation cannot be calculated since the true score is unknowable. Therefore, the index of reliability must be estimated from the obtained scores alone. The correlation between two sets of scores earned by the same persons on the same psychometric test is taken as an estimate of the correlation between obtained and true scores on that test.

The several procedures for accomplishing this differ in two respects: (*a*) the meaning of *same psychometric test* (*b*) the time interval permitted to elapse between obtaining the two sets of scores. As we will see, the methodological approach to each of these matters has specific implications for the way in which the three major sources of measurement error (chance, transitory personal factors, and sampling inadequacies) are treated.

Depending upon the procedure, a source of error may be treated as a random or systematic source of variance. *Random sources of variance* affect the pair of obtained scores for each subject in different directions: that is, if they inflate one they are presumed to deflate the other. *Systematic sources of variance* influence the pair of obtained scores for each subject in the same direction: both are thereby inflated or deflated.

What is the effect of permitting a source of error to operate systematically upon the two sets of scores being correlated in a reliability study? By definition, the effects of error should be randomized: Overestimates and underestimates of the true score should cancel each other. When the procedure of the reliability study causes these error effects to operate systematically rather than randomly, the correlation between the two sets of scores is artifically inflated.

The specific procedures for estimating reliability are designated (*a*) test-retest, (*b*) equivalent forms, (*c*) split-halves. No procedure is superior on all counts. They differ in the type of errors they permit to contribute to systematic variance. Therefore, there is no one best procedure for estimating reliability; each is appropriate under particular circumstances.

Test-retest

An obvious way to obtain two sets of scores from a group of persons is to test them twice with the identical instrument. When done to estimate predictor reliability, the same test is administered each time. When done to estimate criterion reliability, the identical criterion measure is taken on two separate occasions. For either application, the correlation between the scores on the original measure and the retest is taken as the estimate of reliability.

The retest can follow the original measurement immediately or after a time interval. As discussed below, some time interval is desirable in order to permit certain sources of error to contribute to random rather than systematic variance. The danger with an overly long interval between the original test and the retest is that some of the persons may change with respect to the function being evaluated. Given an interval of, say, three months for a test-retest criterion reliability study, considerable improvement might be anticipated for those employees who were hired at about the time the study was initiated. A parallel improvement would probably not be demonstrated by the more experienced employees. The appropriate time interval is one that is sufficiently brief to prevent the contaminating effects of changes due to employee training, development, and experience, but sufficiently long to prevent measurement error from operating systematically. This must be determined separately for each test-retest reliability study.

How does the test-retest procedure (both with and without a time interval between the initial test and retest) treat each of the sources of unreliability? As shown in Figure 3–7, two of the sources of error—chance, and transitory personal factors—contribute to random variance when an appropriate interval is permitted to elapse between the test and the retest. Without such an interval, these sources of error are likely to contribute to systematic variance because, although the conditions themselves are transitory, we have taken

FIGURE 3–7
Treatment of measurement errors by alternative procedures for estimating reliability

| | Treatment of measurement errors by | | | | |
| | Test-retest procedure | | Equivalent-forms procedure | | Split-Halves procedure |
Source of measurement error	Without time interval	With time interval	Without time interval	With time interval	
Chance	Systematic variance	Random variance	Systematic variance	Random variance	Systematic variance
Transitory personal factors ...	Systematic variance	Random variance	Systematic variance	Random variance	Systematic variance
Task sampling.........	Systematic variance	Systematic variance	Random variance	Random variance	Systematic variance

both measures at essentially the same time. The third source of measurement error—unrepresentative task sampling—exerts a uniform (therefore systematic) effect upon the results of both the original test and the retest, irrespective of the time interval.

Equivalent forms

One way to treat sampling inadequacies as a source of random rather than systematic variance is to administer two equivalent forms of a test. Although the specific items comprising equivalent forms differ, their content coverage and statistical characteristics (item difficulty and item validity) are alike.

Assuming equivalency of the forms is accomplished, the correlation between scores on the two forms estimates reliability expressed as the stability of two independently taken measures of the same psychological function.

As with the test-retest method, equivalent forms can be administered sequentially with varying time intervals. Most of the considerations affecting the optimal time interval between test and retest apply also in the case of equivalent forms, except that the latter entirely eliminates one of the possible contaminants inherent in the test-retest procedure. Since the two scores for the equivalent-forms reliability estimate come from two entirely different sets of items, the second test score is entirely immune to the possibility that subjects may remember (and attempt to duplicate) their performance during the initial administration.

The equivalent-forms procedure is ordinarily more suitable for estimating the reliability of predictors than of criteria. It is difficult to structure two parallel but different forms of a criterion measure. However, studies of interrater agreement can be conceptualized as an application in the realm of criterion reliability. Two raters making independent judgments about employee performance are, from this standpoint, providing equivalent forms of the same measure.

As shown in Figure 3–7, equivalent forms with a suitable time interval between administrations provides what is potentially the most meaningful estimate of score stability. This procedure is the only one permitting all potential sources of unreliability to contribute to random rather than systematic variance.

One practical objection to the equivalent-forms procedure is that the expense of developing equivalent forms is not justified when they are constructed solely for a reliability study. However, there are some other reasons for developing two or more forms of a test. It is advantageous, for example, to have multiple test forms when one wishes to evaluate change following a formal training program or as a result of job experience. Furthermore, multiple forms of a test are extremely useful whenever a large group of persons is to be tested in a room that does not permit adequate spacing between seats in order to prevent copying.

Split-halves method

One practical objection to both the test-retest and the equivalent-forms procedures is that they require two separate testing sessions. The split-halves method makes it possible to estimate reliability from a single test administration or set of criterion observations. The most common procedure requires that the test be split into separately scored halves, usually the odd and even numbered items. The correlation between these scores (corrected as noted subsequently) is taken as the reliability estimate.

There are certain parallels between the split-halves method and the equivalent-forms method. Both procedures correlate the scores earned on two forms of an instrument. However, whereas these forms are deliberately structured for equivalence in the equivalent-forms procedure, the split-halves method correlates two forms that are, at best, crudely comparable. Furthermore, the split-halves method correlates the scores on two half-length forms. Thus, the resultant coefficient is an estimate of the reliability of a psychometric test only half as long as the one actually under consideration.

Since reliability is partly a function of test length, split-half estimates of reliability must be adjusted upwards by means of the Spearman-Brown prophecy formula. The generalized Spearman-Brown formula estimates the reliability of an instrument increased in length k times, and is stated

$$R_{tt} = \frac{kr_{11}}{1 + (k - 1)r_{11}}$$

where R_{tt} is the reliability of the lengthened psychometric test, and r_{11} is the obtained correlation. Following a split-halves correlation, the reliability estimate must be adjusted for double length. Thus, if the correlation between scores on the halves of a test (r_{11}) is .80, the estimate of reliability for the total test $(k = 2)$ is 1.6/1.8, or .89.

In appraising the split-halves method (see Figure 3–7) it must be remembered that there is no time interval between administration of the halves. From this perspective the reliability estimate (corrected for length) approximates those provided by the test-retest and equivalent-forms procedures without elapsed time between the first and second administrations. Rather than reflecting score stability over time, split-halves reliabilities estimate internal consistency: that is, stability from one portion (half) of the instrument to another.

A special problem arises when the split-halves method is used to estimate the reliability of speeded tests where the time limit prevents persons from answering all questions. Here the odd-even correlation tends to overestimate the test's reliability. This is so because the unanswered questions are distributed evenly between the two halves, thereby exerting a uniform (systematic) effect upon the person's rank position for each half. The usual solution is to administer each half of the test separately, with its own time limit.

The Kuder-Richardson formulas for estimating reliability are variations of the split-halves procedure. Here, instead of dividing the measure into two halves, each test item is treated as a separate subtest. Essentially, the Kuder-Richardson formulas determine the average intercorrelation between every pair of test items. This, of course, generates an average reliability estimate for a one-item test. This estimate is then adjusted upwards (using the generalized Spearman-Brown formula) for the actual number of test item pairs.

SUMMARY

This chapter considered the correlation statistic in the context of employment selection. Correlation indicates the strength and direction of the relationship between two or more variables. The variables at issue in employment selection are predictors and criteria.

The simplest type of correlation examines the relationship between two variables. To the extent these variables are related, they are covariant: that is, changes in one of the scores are accompanied by systematic (and therefore predictable) changes in the other. The magnitude of the relationship is expressed by the numerical value of the correlation coefficient, which can range from 0.00 (absence of relationship) to 1.00 (a perfect relationship). The direction of covariation is signified by the sign carried by the correlation coefficient: a + sign indicates a direct relationship; a − sign signifies an inverse relationship.

The value of the correlation is given by the slope of the regression line. This regression line is the line best fitting the crossplotted data points in a scattergram once the raw scores have been converted to z-score (standard score) equivalents. Thus, by fitting a line to the data, correlation assumes that the relationship between the variables is linear. (If this assumption fails, and the relationship proves to be curvilinear, statistics other than correlation must be applied to the data.)

In spite of their appearance, correlations are not interpreted as percentages. One kind of interpretation is possible through squaring the correlation. This coefficient of determination indicates the percent of criterion variance that is predictable. The higher the correlation, irrespective of its sign, the greater the predictive efficiency signified by it.

The discussion of the correlation statistic was followed by a consideration of certain aspects of psychometric theory. The chapter emphasized the concept of psychometric error and its implications for estimating reliability.

A reliable instrument is one yielding consistent or stable scores. From a theoretical perspective, the correlation between obtained and true scores is an index of reliability. Thus, unreliability results from measurement error, that is, the fact that the obtained scores differ from the true ones. The three major sources of unreliability are (a) chance factors, (b) transitory personal factors, and (c) sampling inadequacies.

Since there is no way to actually know the true score on any measure, test or criterion reliability must be estimated entirely from obtained scores. Three approaches to estimating reliability were considered: test-retest, equivalent-forms, and split-halves procedures. Each approach has its own implications for the way in which the major sources of measurement error are treated.

REFERENCES

Brogden, H. E., & Taylor, E. K.   The dollar criterion—applying the cost accounting concept to criterion construction. *Personnel Psychology,* 1950, *3,* 133–154.

Edmison, L. D., In J. E. Wert, C. O. Neidt, & J. S. Ahmann   *Statistical methods in educational and psychological research.* New York: Appleton-Century-Crofts, 1954.

Guion, R. M.   Recruiting, selection, and placement. In M. D. Dunnette (Ed.), *Handbook of industrial and organizational psychology.* Chicago: Rand Mc-Nally, 1976, 777–828.

section two

PERSONNEL PSYCHOLOGY

51

DEFINING AND MEASURING PERFORMANCE

part A

Employers seek to hire those applicants who have the best potential for performing the job effectively. Thus they attempt to predict the likely future performance of each applicant. Erroneous predictions are costly. In falsely rejecting an applicant who would, if hired, have proven to be a satisfactory employee, the organization suffers an irretrievable loss. Likewise, by hiring an applicant who subsequently proves to be ineffectual, the organization suffers direct adverse consequences.

Although critical to organizational health, correct hiring decisions alone do not insure it. The organization must thereafter arrange circumstances to help its employees realize their potential for effective performance.

New employees typically are given information about the particular employer's policies and procedures. Job skills may have to be taught and/or refined. Furthermore, organizations often take responsibility for maintaining continuous career development programs. Here, experienced employees are encouraged to elaborate their present skills and develop new ones preparatory to assignments of increased responsibility. In addition to supporting the job-related development of individual employees, organizations must arrange the total physical and social work environment to encourage maximally effective job performance and satisfaction.

53

Since effective job performance is one of the goals of all of these efforts, our discussion of personnel psychology begins with it. Part A considers ways of defining and measuring performance. Job analysis (Chapter 4) underlies this as well as virtually all other activities undertaken in I/O psychology. Among other things, the job analysis suggests one or more possible definitions of effective job performance.

All further psychological investigation requires that these suggested definitions be translated into specific and measurable performance criteria. Without sound criteria it is impossible to evaluate organizational efforts. Criteria may include such reflections of job effectiveness as productivity records, spoilage, supervisory ratings of effectiveness, safety record, and tenure. The issues in criterion development are explored in Chapter 5. That chapter also discusses considerations in one of the uses made of criteria: performance prediction. Chapter 6, Performance Appraisal, translates these issues into their implications for measuring employee performance.

chapter 4

Job Analysis and
Occupational Classification

A job analysis summarizes information about the duties entailed in performing a job and the surroundings (both physical and social) in which these duties are performed. Such a comprehensive description of a particular job is an indispensible preliminary to many of the activities undertaken by industrial/organizational psychologists. In addition, the study of jobs leading to their classification in terms of their common elements may serve as an end in itself. The resulting clarification of the structure of job families and occupations across employers and organizations provides the information base needed, for example, by vocational counselors and can contribute to shaping pertinent curricula in vocationally oriented training programs.

SOME USES OF JOB ANALYSIS

Figure 4-1 summarizes the major ways in which job analysis is used in industrial/organizational psychology. These applications preview much of the content of the remainder of this book.

Selection and placement

A selection program consists of one or more predictors of job success. These predictors, administered to job applicants, may include psychological tests, recommendations from previous employers, evidence that certain educational requirements have been completed, demonstrated proficiency in specific skills, and so on. One requirement for including a predictor in the selection program is that it *works:* that is, applicants'scores on these measures correlate with their subsequent job performance.

Thus, predictor validity is established by research. One of several approaches to this research (discussed in Chapter 7) entails administration of trial predictors to applicants, hiring them, obtaining a subsequent measure of on-the-job performance, and determining which trial predictors efficiently forecast actual job performance.

FIGURE 4–1
Some uses of job analysis

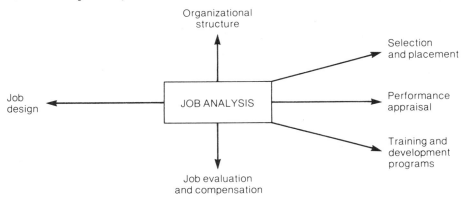

Predictive validity studies thus entail empirical tests of hypotheses about the influence of human characteristics, skills, and backgrounds upon their job behavior (Guion, 1976). The hypotheses have two elements: (1) human characteristics meriting exploration as possible predictors are specified; and (2) certain job behaviors are chosen to serve as criteria against which the potential selection devices will be validated.

As with all scientific hypotheses, those related to selection must have some logical or plausible justification. That justification originates in the job analysis, which gives direction to selection research by permitting informed judgments about likely predictor-criterion relationships meriting investigation.

Performance appraisal

The criteria mentioned above entail appraisals of actual job performance after the applicant is hired, placed, trained (if necessary), and has become acclimated to the job. They may include such things as productivity records, supervisory judgments about the employee's readiness for enlarged job responsibility, accuracy of work, and so on.

Besides serving as possible criteria for selection research, such appraisals of employee performance are the dependent variables for other types of research. Furthermore, they usually serve as partial bases for personnel actions (promotions, salary increases, terminations) affecting individual employees.

In order for performance appraisals to be useful for personnel actions, they must reflect how well the job is being done by each employee under consideration. Therefore, periodic reviews of individual employee effectiveness are limited to those behaviors clearly specified in advance of his/her job duties and responsibilities.

Training and development programs

Newly hired employees usually receive some kind of training during the initial period of their employment. More experienced employees often are identified to receive additional training and development to prepare them for assuming more responsible positions within the organization.

The nature of training and development programs varies extensively between organizations and even between jobs within an organization. Such programs may be highly formalized and include classroom-type instruction as well as proficiency testing. Others are relatively informal, requiring only that the trainee observe and work under the close supervision of the trainer.

The object of the training or development program may be to teach certain skills, to develop attitudes (perhaps with respect to safety practices or managerial style), or to provide other kinds of information of value to the trainee. The training objectives logically follow a thoroughgoing job analysis. It is necessary to know what a job entails before employees can be properly trained for satisfactory job performance.

Job evaluation and compensation

The purpose of job evaluation is to determine the relative worth of each job in an industrial organization. One of the primary applications of such an evaluation is the establishment of equitable salary ranges for various jobs within a company. By way of simple illustration, some jobs may expose employees to hazardous working conditions but may not require much in the way of formal education. Other jobs may require graduate training of some sort but do not expose employees to undue hazards. A job evaluation under such circumstances would lead to a weighting of the factors of working conditions and educational requirements in order to establish an equitable basis for paying employees on both kinds of jobs.

The determination of the worth of each job within an industrial organization requires a comparative study of the job duties and the working conditions. Thus, job evaluation must be preceded by an analysis of every job to be evaluated.

Job design

A job analysis may be performed as a preliminary to motion studies designed to develop more efficient methods of work. An analysis for such purposes may reveal, for example, that a particular job requires employees to do considerable walking or an excessive amount of heavy lifting. Rearrangement of the working environment or of materials may reduce the extent of such nonproductive physical activity, leading to a consequent reduction in fatigue and increased productivity.

Certain jobs, by their very nature, expose employees to personal danger. Unnecessary exposure to noxious fumes or radiation, for example, may be discovered by the job analyst and the working conditions revised in order to reduce or eliminate such conditions. Similarly, job analysis may reveal that certain features of machine operation are unduly hazardous, leading thereby to redesign of the equipment.

Organizational structure

Even small businesses and offices employing relatively few workers may utilize job analyses. A major source of bickering and discontent in such organizations results from the lack of clarification of duties of individual employees and delimitation of authority. An analysis leading to the definition of duties of each position may serve to eliminate this source of discontent.

The delimitation of personnel functions may likewise be helpful to larger industrial organizations by suggesting changes in current administrative patterns. Over the years the areas of responsibility assumed by a manager are likely to reflect his/her personal interests and strengths. This is particularly true of companies at the forefront of technological change. Such companies are continually creating new jobs not even conceptualized several months or years earlier. Once created, the job is usually subsumed under some existing administrative unit of the company. Hence a periodic reassessment of all jobs in a company with a view toward their most appropriate administrative allocations may suggest needed changes in present management patterns.

The foregoing description of applications of job analysis is not exhaustive. It is sufficient, however, to indicate the diversity of uses for information of the type provided by such analyses. The specific emphasis in any given job analysis will, of course, reflect the purpose for which the analysis has been performed. Job analyses written to provide clues to more efficient industrial operation will highlight different aspects of the job than will analyses prepared for the purpose of evaluating the relative worth of jobs within an industrial organization. However, aside from minor differences in emphasis as a function of intended application, all job analyses are basically alike in that they are designed to provide a detailed description of the analyzed jobs.

TYPES AND SOURCES OF INFORMATION

Although all job analyses entail descriptions of job duties, responsibilities, and the work context, their specific focus—and to some extent, the way in which information is obtained and summarized—is influenced by the intended use of the analysis.

A job analysis preliminary to selection will call particular attention to employee knowledges, skills, and abilities prerequisite to satisfactory task performance. An analysis preliminary to improving work methods or equipment design will emphasize potentially fatiguing motions (lifting and carrying) for which mechanical devices might be substituted. And as the initial step in establishing equitable wage ranges, the job analysis will emphasize the similarities and differences between the positions under consideration with respect to their value to the organization.

Considerations of intended purpose and constraints imposed by the job itself influence the analyst's decisions about the (*a*) type of information to be collected, (*b*) form for obtaining and presenting the information, (*c*) method of analysis, and (*d*) agent (person or device) used for collecting the information (McCormick, 1976). Some of the options in these respects are shown in Table 4–1.

Given the diversity of available and appropriate agents, methods, and data-collection formats, as well as variations in intended purposes for making job analyses, it is impossible to provide a *best* or *model* format for recording the required information. In various ways, all job analyses attempt to summarize and clarify the following:

1. The nature of the work performed: what the employee does, how it is done (including equipment used), and why it is done.
2. The skills and knowledge required for satisfactory job performance.
3. Personal characteristics (physical, mental, experiential, educational) prerequisite to selecting employees for the position.

FUNCTIONAL JOB ANALYSIS

One of the difficulties in preparing and interpreting job analyses follows from the constraints of language. Job analyses, once written, sometimes seem sterile or to lack the essence of the job described. Variations between analysts in language usage and implied connotations may even obviate comparisons between jobs analyzed by different analysts.

Hence, the United States Employment Service has instituted *functional job analysis* to reduce some of the language-related problems in describing jobs (Lewis, 1969). The two keys to functional job analysis are:

1. Its use of a standardized language to describe *what workers do* (as opposed to the effects or outcomes of their actions);
2. Its approach to assessing the *level* at which workers engage in these activities (Fine & Wiley, 1971).

This orientation to job analysis has been reflected in the most recent edition of the *Dictionary of Occupational Titles* (1977) which contains descriptions of approximately 20,000 occupations.

Worker activities

The descriptions in the *DOT* reflect the view that every job requires a worker to function, in varying degrees, relative to *data, people,* and *things.*

Data-oriented activities are intangible. They include manipulation of numbers, words, symbols, ideas, and so on.

TABLE 4–1
Types and sources of job analysis information

Type of information	Form in which information is obtained	Information collection	Agent

1. Work Activities
  a. What is accomplished (e.g., work processes, procedures, activities)? Accountable to whom? Responsible to whom?
  b. What has to be done to accomplish the work (e.g., decision making, physical demands, movements involved, fatigue)?
	1. Qualitative: narrative description of job tasks
	
	2. Quantitative: expression in terms of measurable units of job information (e.g., oxygen consumption, percent of time lifting, etc.)
	
	3. Mixed: combination of qualitative and quantitative format
		1. Observation of incumbents
		
		2. Individual interview with incumbents
		
		3. Group interview with incumbents
		
		4. Conference with experienced personnel (including supervisors)
		
		5. Questionnaire
			1. Individuals:
			  a. Job analyst
			  b. Supervisors
			  c. Incumbent
			
			2. Devices
			  a. Cameras
			  b. Physiological recording devices
			  c. "Force platforms" for recording movements in three dimensions, etc.

2. Machines, tools, equipment, and work aid used?

3. Job-related tangibles and intangibles: products made; services rendered?

4. Appraisal: work standards: error analysis?

5. Job context: physical working conditions; schedule; social context; incentives?

6. Personnel requirements: knowledge, skill, education, personal attributes?

6. Diary (e.g., daily log of activities)

7. Critical incidents characterizing excellent or inferior performance

8. Equipment design information (e.g., blueprints)

9. Recordings of job activities (film, videotape, etc.)

10. Personnel and equipment records

Source: After E. J. McCormick, "Job and Task Analysis," in Dunnette, ed., *Handbook of Industrial and Organizational Psychology*, pp. 652–654. Copyright © 1976 by Rand McNally College Publishing Company. Adapted by permission of Houghton Mifflin Company.

People-oriented activities include all instances of interaction with other human beings (selling, supervising, and so on). In addition, activities in which an animal is dealt with on an individual basis are subsumed under this heading.

Things-oriented activities include all manipulations of inanimate objects.

Functional level

Within each of the above areas, employees function at some level of complexity. Functional job analysis standardizes the language of activity levels as shown in Figure 4–2. This figure is arranged so that each successive

FIGURE 4–2
Summary of activities and functions used in the *Dictionary of Occupational Titles*

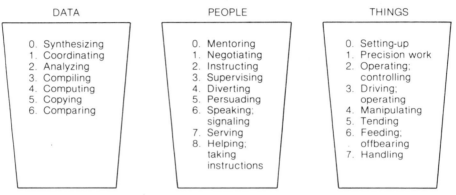

DATA	PEOPLE	THINGS
0. Synthesizing	0. Mentoring	0. Setting-up
1. Coordinating	1. Negotiating	1. Precision work
2. Analyzing	2. Instructing	2. Operating; controlling
3. Compiling	3. Supervising	3. Driving; operating
4. Computing	4. Diverting	4. Manipulating
5. Copying	5. Persuading	5. Tending
6. Comparing	6. Speaking; signaling	6. Feeding; offbearing
	7. Serving	7. Handling
	8. Helping; taking instructions	

Source: *Dictionary of Occupational Titles,* 4th ed. (Washington, D.C.: U.S. Government Printing Office, 1977), p. xviii.

function usually or typically involves all those that follow it. Thus, the code designation *O* is assigned to the most inclusive behavior in each area.

An illustration

Using the scheme shown in Figure 4–2, the *DOT* codes the industrial/organizational psychologist's relationship to data, people, and things respectively as *1-0-7*.

With respect to data, the code 1 signifies *Coordinating* defined as "Determining time, place, and sequence of operations or actions to be taken on the basis of analysis of data."

With respect to people, the code 0 (*Mentoring*) signifies, "Dealing with individuals . . . in order to advise, counsel, and/or guide them."

The code 7 for things indicates that the I/O psychologist is only minimally involved with manipulations of inanimate objects.

The full description of the industrial/organizational psychologist's job is as follows:

045.107-030   PSYCHOLOGIST, INDUSTRIAL-ORGANIZATIONAL

(profess. & kin.)

Develops and applies psychological techniques to personnel administration, management, and marketing problems: Observes details of work and interviews workers and supervisors to establish physical, mental, educational, and other job requirements. Develops interview techniques, rating scales, and psychological tests to assess skills, abilities, aptitudes, and interests as aids in selection, placement, and promotion. Organizes training programs, applying principles of learning and individual differences, and evaluates and measures effectiveness of training methods by statistical analysis of production rate, reduction of accidents, absenteeism, and turnover. Counsels workers to improve job and personal adjustments. Conducts research studies of organizational structure, communication systems, group interactions, and motivational systems, and recommends changes to improve efficiency and effectiveness of individuals, organizational units, and organization. Investigates problems related to physical environment of work, such as illumination, noise, temperature, and ventilation, and recommends changes to increase efficiency and decrease accident rate. Conducts surveys and research studies to ascertain nature of effective supervision and leadership and to analyze factors affecting morale and motivation. Studies consumer reaction to new products and package designs, using surveys and tests, and measures effectiveness of advertising media to aid in sale of goods and services. May advise management on personnel policies and labor-management relations. May adapt machinery, equipment, workspace, and environment to human use. May specialize in development and application of such techniques as job analysis and classification, personnel interviewing, ratings, and vocational tests for use in selection, placement, promotion, and training of workers, and be designated PSYCHOLOGIST, PERSONNEL (profess. & kin.). May apply psychological principles and techniques to selection, training, classification, and assignment of military personnel, and be designated PSYCHOLOGIST, MILITARY PERSONNEL (profess. & kin.). May conduct surveys and tests to study consumer reaction to new products and package design, and to measure effectiveness of advertising media to aid manufacturers in sale of goods and services, and be designated MARKET-RESEARCH ANALYST (profess. & kin.) II.

PERSONNEL SPECIFICATIONS

Personnel specifications delineate the employee characteristics prerequisite to satisfactory job performance. The development of these specifications is often the primary reason for undertaking job analyses. This is particularly true of job analyses preliminary to initiating selection, placement, and training programs.

Although all approaches to extrapolating personnel specifications from job analyses require some degree of judgment, it is convenient to classify them into three categories: (1) judgment only, (2) measurement, and (3) synthetic estimates.

Judgment only

Based upon a review of the job analysis, perhaps supplemented by his/her own direct observations and interviews with incumbents, the analyst or employment manager may formulate judgments about the employee prerequisites to satisfactory performance. This widely used approach to personnel specification is a rather crude one. The specifications thereby delimited are typically rather ambiguous and undifferentiated with respect to each one's relative importance.

A more systematic approach begins with a comprehensive list of job skills, abilities, and traits that might be important for *any* job. Every item in the list is carefully defined and accompanied by a rating scale on which the analyst estimates the degree of importance of each characteristic for the job in question. The pattern of ratings for a given job constitutes its *profile*, and a comparison of profiles for various jobs indicates the relative importance of the various worker characteristics across jobs.

This more systematic approach to securing judgments about personnel specifications imposes a degree of uniformity upon the process by compelling the analyst's attention to a wide array of potential prerequisites, each of which is defined with some clarity. However the approach is somewhat limited by possible omissions from the list of potential prerequisites to be considered. There is always the possibility that certain crucial prerequisites might have been overlooked in formulating the set of rating scales.

Granting the existence of a comprehensive pool of potential prerequisites to be considered by the analyst, there is evidence that judgments about the relative importance of certain kinds of prerequisites (for example, mental ability) are more accurate than judgments about others (for example, physical aptitudes). Furthermore, judgments of both types are more accurately made from first-hand observation of employees' actual job performance than from reviewing written descriptions of that performance (Trattner, Fine, & Kubis, 1955).

Measurement

Instead of requiring analysts to estimate personnel requirements subjectively, the measurement approach rests upon direct evidence that certain specific abilities and other psychological characteristics differentiate between the more and less satisfactory employees. This approach requires that psychologically relevant measures (test scores, educational history, and so on) be secured for a sample of employees, each of whom has been independently classified in terms of some criterion of job proficiency. The magnitude of the correlation between each psychological characteristic and the proficiency criterion determines which particular characteristics will henceforth be specified as prerequisites to employment.

This basic selection model is extensively discussed in the following chapters. For now it is sufficient to mention only that it assumes an adequate criterion by which to differentiate between more and less proficient employees.

In addition, small sample size may preclude computing the required correlations. Relatively small businesses with, say, two or three employees in a particular job cannot provide the employee sample necessary to empirically determine relationships between employee characteristics and job proficiency. This difficulty can sometimes be overcome by combining employee samples across employers. Thus, if we were interested in developing personnel specifications for hardware-store salesclerks, the measurement approach might be implemented by combining data obtained from 20 or 30 different stores, each employing several clerks. However in order to effect this combination we would have to assume that both the personnel prerequisites and the performance criteria are not store-specific.

Finally, there remains the matter of deciding which tests to include in the battery: that is, which characteristics to measure as potential correlates of job proficiency. In attempting to strike a reasonable balance between the cost of the program, time available for test administration, and comprehensive coverage of the psychological characteristics measured, there is always the danger that measures of certain important characteristics will inadvertently be excluded from the battery. The concern here parallels the similar one raised in the discussion of the judgmental approach to personnel specification.

Synthetic estimates

Although the measurement approach to personnel specification is generally the most acceptable and defensible procedure for delineating potential characteristics for selecting new employees, the sample of incumbents may, as indicated earlier, be too small to permit implementation of the procedure. A newly created position which, by definition, presently has no incumbents, is an extreme instance of this limitation to measurement as the basis for deriving personnel specifications. In such cases, synthetic estimates of personnel specifications provide an empirically based alternative to subjectively based judgments about the likely prerequisites to satisfactory job performance.

The underlying logic of *synthetic validity* initially advanced some time ago (Lawshe, 1952) and elaborated subsequently by McCormick (1959) is as follows:

a. The relatively large number and variety of jobs can be characterized by a much smaller number of activities and components, each of which is required to a greater or lesser extent by virtually all jobs.

b. To the extent that a particular work activity (for example, supervising subordinates) is common to several jobs, those jobs ought to have the same personnel requirements.

c. Therefore, the personnel specifications for any job can be synthetically (rather than empirically) derived—assuming one knows the job's crucial components—by accumulating the prerequisites to performing each of the components.

McCormick (1976) illustrates this logic with the hypothetical example shown in Table 4–2. Each job activity or component (A, B, C, D, . . . , N)

TABLE 4–2

A hypothetical example of synthetic estimates of personnel specifications

Job activity	Psychological prerequisite performing the activity	Importance of job activity in three jobs			Personnel specifications for three jobs		
		X	Y	Z	X	Y	Z
A	a	5	1	0	5a	1a	—
B	b	1	0	5	1b	—	5b
C	c	0	4	1	—	4c	1c
D	d	3	0	2	3d	—	2d
.	.	.	.	.	.	.	.
.	.	.	.	.	.	.	.
.	.	.	.	.	.	.	.
N	n	0	3	1	—	3n	1n

Source: After E. J. McCormick, "Job and Task Analysis," in Dunnette, ed., *Handbook of Industrial and Organizational Psychology*, p. 689. Copyright © 1976 by Rand McNally College Publishing Company. Adapted by permission of Houghton Mifflin Company.

has its own personnel prerequisite (a, b, c, d, . . . , n). The relative importance of each activity is described for each of three jobs (X, Y, Z). The total personnel specification for each job is then inferred to be a summation of the specific prerequisites (each appropriately weighted to reflect the relative importance of the underlying attribute) pertinent to that particular job.

Much of the research involving the Position Analysis Questionnaire by McCormick and his colleagues, as described in the next section, is directed toward identifying "core" job activities and their parallel psychological prerequisites.

In one direct test of the synthetic approach to personnel specification (Marquardt & McCormick, 1974b) the authors compared synthetically-derived personnel specifications with those obtained for the same jobs using the measurement approach. At issue were 141 jobs for which the United States Employment Service had records of actual test scores earned by incumbents on nine aptitude tests (comprising the General Aptitude Test

Battery). Without reference to these scores, the investigators synthetically constructed the personnel prerequisites for each job using the logic of Table 4–2. (The specific procedure whereby this was accomplished entailed data from the Position Analysis Questionnaire, the discussion of which is deferred to the next section). The correlations between synthetically derived personnel prerequisites and the actual scores earned on the aptitude test battery by incumbents was impressive. The median correlation coefficient across the nine tests of the battery was .71.

OCCUPATIONAL CLASSIFICATIONS

The United States Employment Service functional job analysis scheme, with which you are already familiar, illustrates one approach to developing a classification for describing and comparing jobs. Occupational classifications call attention to essential similarities and differences between jobs.

One reason for identifying pervasive job tasks and clustering occupations on the basis of task similarities may have become evident to you during the preceding discussion of procedures for deriving personnel specifications. We mentioned then that a concern with both the judgmental and measurement approaches is that crucial prerequisites might be overlooked in designing a comprehensive list of job skills, abilities, and so on, which are either to be related (in the case of judgmental procedures) or tested (in measurement procedures). One of the benefits of developing occupational classifications is that they help insure the desired comprehensiveness of the original set of potential prerequisite skills and abilities.

Further, the rationale for making synthetic estimates of personnel prerequisites depends upon the prior determination of clearly delineated components of the universe of jobs. Unless these components are delineated it is impossible to determine which ones are embodied within the job for which the synthetic estimate is to be made.

There are essentially two bases upon which similar jobs may be clustered. Jobs can be grouped according to similar content (that is, duties and responsibilities), or on the basis of similar worker attributes or prerequisites to performance. We will discuss a representative effort of each type prior to discussing an approach using both.

A classification reflecting job content

We have already noted the job classification scheme used by USES in structuring the *DOT*. Particular reference was made to the *DOT* classification of jobs on the basis of their relative involvements with data, people, and things.

This system of classification goes still further in reflecting job content by subsuming the data-people-things classification under a superordinate occupational classification. The major occupational categories, each of which has subcategories, are as follows:

1. Professional, technical, and managerial occupations.
2. Clerical and sales.
3. Service occupations.
4. Agriculture, fishing, forestry, and related occupations.
5. Processing occupations (e.g., ore refining and foundry occupations).
6. Machine trades occupations.
7. Benchwork occupations (e.g., fabrication and assembly).
8. Structural work (e.g., welder).
9. Miscellaneous occupations.

This overriding classification into occupational groups and subgroups, together with the subordinate classification of each listed job in terms of its relative data-people-things focus, revolves around the duties and responsibilities entailed in performing each analyzed job. It is, of course, possible to make inferences about employee prerequisites to satisfactory performance from such a comprehensive analysis of employee functions. But a concern for prerequisites is not central to this particular classificatory scheme.

A classification reflecting worker prerequisites

Instead of classifying together jobs in which workers engage in similar activities, this approach catalogs jobs on the basis of similar worker requirements for satisfactory performance.

Ability is one such category of prerequisites. Certain occupations, like dentistry and drafting, require spatial visualization (the ability to visualize in three dimensions); others require facility in dealing with numbers; yet others require coordination, strength, dexterity, and so on. Prerequisite abilities are not, of course, mutually exclusive. Most occupations require combinations of abilities, and those with similar requirements can be classified together.

An attempt to develop a taxonomy of motor skills illustrates this approach to job classification. A comprehensive group of 37 rating scales (the *Task Assessment Scales*) was developed to assess the array of human motor abilities (Theologus & Fleishman, 1971). Included among these scales are measures of perceptual speed, reaction time, finger dexterity, arm-hand steadiness, and so on. Expert judges were asked to consider a list of motor activities and for each activity to indicate (*a*) which of the abilities measured by the Task Assessment Scales were involved in doing the task and (*b*) what level of ability was prerequisite to errorless performance of that task. The resulting analysis permitted classification of the motor activities into just eight categories reflecting the central underlying skills prerequisite to engaging in each category of activity: choice reaction time, reaction time, speed of limb movement, wrist-finger speed, finger dexterity, manual dexterity, arm-hand steadiness, and control precision. These eight skills provide a potential basis for cataloging virtually all jobs in terms of their prerequisite motor abilities. One can envision similar classificatory possibilities based upon other kinds of abilities as well.

Job dimensions: A dual classification

McCormick and his colleagues have undertaken a most comprehensive analysis of characteristics common to a wide variety of jobs viewed both from the perspective of worker *activities* (job content) and *prerequisites* (attributes) (McCormick, Jeanneret, & Mecham, 1969).

The *Position Analysis Questionnaire (PAQ)* is a checklist of 182 job elements describing activities in which workers may engage. Most of these 182 job elements were rated for 3,700 different jobs, and the ratings were factor analyzed. (Factor analysis is a statistical technique for examining the intercorrelations among the constituents of a set of data. Its purpose is to derive the minimum number of relatively independent clusters or subsets of data— that is, factors—contained within the original mass of data.) The factor analysis of the original 182 job elements contained within the PAQ reduced these to 30 job dimensions which, in turn, were subsumed under just six major activity categories [Marquardt & McCormick, 1974(a)]:

1. Worker activities involving *information input:* for example, reading dials, evaluating gauge readings, awareness of environmental changes.
2. Activities involving such *mental processes* as decision making and information processing.
3. Activities required to effect *output:* for example, operating controls, adjusting machines.
4. *Interpersonal activities* (communicating instructions, supervising others).
5. The *job context* in which work is performed (stresses, hazards, and so on).
6. *Miscellaneous* aspects of the work activities (work schedule, clothing worn, etc.).

The interesting thing about the above list, generated from an analysis of worker *activities,* is that it parallels a classification of worker *attributes* developed by an earlier study (Marquardt & McCormick, 1972). Here, the investigators asked a sample of colleagues in the American Psychological Association to consider a list of 68 personal attributes (including aptitudes, like arithmetic reasoning, and characteristics like ability to deal with people). The respondents were asked to estimate the relevance of each attribute to virtually all of the 182 worker behaviors specified in the PAQ. The resulting organization of worker attributes was essentially similar to the list of worker activities mentioned above.

Occupational classification and job analysis

This chapter began with a discussion of particular jobs and is ending with a discussion of classifications of jobs in general. We started by describing job analysis procedures: that is, procedures for obtaining information about the duties, responsibilities, and work surroundings associated with the work assigned to a particular employee (or to groups of employees engaged in identical assignments).

However, it should by now be evident that all of the applications of job analysis summarized in Figure 4–1 entail clustering jobs on the basis of their similarities. Such clustering may focus upon such things as common duties and responsibilities, physical and psychological requirements, educational and experiential prerequisites, and so on. A meaningful classification of jobs in terms of their similar prerequisites facilitates selection efforts by identifying potential predictors of performance on those jobs. Occupational classifications calling attention to similarities and differences in job demands and in the relative worth of the resultant activities to the employer undergird the development of sensible wage and salary structures. As a final illustration, occupational classifications are prerequisite to vocational counseling and guidance where the objective is to identify groups of jobs making relatively similar physical and psychological demands, and which are compatible with the counselee's abilities and inclinations.

Aside from the very practical need to make job analyses and the tangible implications of grouping jobs into job families, this research direction promises to add generally to our understanding of: (a) the way in which human attributes are patterned, and (b) the attributes required for successful job performance (Pearlman, 1980).

SUMMARY

A job analysis summarizes information about required job duties and the surroundings in which these duties are performed. Thus, it is an indispensible preliminary to much of the work of I/O psychologists. The specific type of information, the form in which it is obtained (narrative or quantitiative), and the way in which it is collected and summarized, is influenced by the intended use to be made of the analysis.

The chapter describes the particular approach to job analysis, termed *functional job analysis,* taken by the United States Employment Service in preparing the *Dictionary of Occupational Titles*. This approach uses a standardized language to characterize and code all jobs on two dimensions: (*a*) the duties entailed relative to manipulating data, people, and things and (*b*) the level of complexity with which each duty is performed.

One of the major outcomes of job analysis is personnel specification. Such specifications delineate the employee characteristics prerequisite to satisfactory job performance, and thus are critical to initiating personnel selection, placement, and training programs. The chapter discusses three approaches to extrapolating personnel specifications from job analyses: (1) expert judgment based upon the statement of job duties, (2) measurement of abilities and other psychological characteristics differentiating successful from unsuccessful incumbents, and (3) synthetic estimates. The judgment and measurement approaches to personnel specification derive the psychological prerequisites to performance from the job analysis itself. Synthetic estimates infer these specifications from a body of background research on occupations.

Synthetic estimates of personnel requirements for any particular job rest upon (*a*) identifying the critical performance components of that job and (*b*) knowing the abilities, skills, and so on prerequisite to performing those components. The latter information is derived by studying occupations with a view toward classifying them in terms of their common elements, that is, worker activities and psychological prerequisites. The research to develop such occupational taxonomies has largely entailed wide administration of the Position Analysis Questionnaire, and is still in progress. A master template relating particular job duties to particular associated psychological prerequisites has been provisionally constructed. Synthetic estimates of personnel requirements makes use of this template by matching it against the worker activities on the job in question. The prerequisites to satisfactory performance of the tasks comprising the particular job are presumed to be identical to those demonstrated by the taxonomy to be generally associated with those tasks.

REFERENCES

Dictionary of Occupational Titles   (4th ed.). U.S. Employment Service. Washington, D.C.: U.S. Government Printing Office, 1977, xviii.

Fine, S. A., & Wiley, W. W.   An Introduction to functional job analysis. *Methods for Manpower Analysis. Monograph #4.* Kalamazoo, Mich.: W. E. Upjohn Institute, 1971.

Guion, R. M.   Recruiting, selection, and job replacement. In M. D. Dunnette (Ed.) *Handbook of industrial and organizational psychology.* Chicago: Rand McNally, 1976, 777–828.

Lawshe, C. H.   Employee selection. *Personnel Psychology,* 1952, 5, 31–34.

Lewis, L.   Job analysis on the United States Training and Employment Service. In *Proceedings,* Division of Military Psychology Symposium: Collecting, analyzing, and reporting information describing jobs and occupations. Lackland AFB, Texas: Personnel Research Division, Air Force Human Resources Laboratory, September 1969, 33–41.

Marquardt, L. D. & McCormick, E. J.   Attribute ratings and profiles of job elements of the position analysis questionnaire (PAQ). Lafayette, Ind.: Purdue University, Occupational Research Center, Department of Psychological Sciences, *Report No. 1,* 1972.

Marquardt, L. D., & McCormick, E. J. The job dimensions underlying the job elements of the Position Analysis Questionnaire (PAQ), Form B. Lafayette, Ind.: Occupational Research Center, Department of Psychological Sciences, Purdue University, *Report No. 4,* June 1974. (a)

Marquardt, L. D., & McCormick, E. J. The utility of job dimensions based on Form B of the Positional Analysis Questionnaire (PAQ) in a job component validation model. Lafayette, Ind.: Purdue University, Occupational Research Center, Department of Psychological Sciences, *Report No. 5,* July 1974. (b)

McCormick, E. J. The development of processes for indirect or synthetic validity: III. Application of job analysis to indirect validity. A symposium. *Personnel Psychology,* 1959, *12,* 402–413.

McCormick, E. J. Job and task analysis. In M. D. Dunnette (Ed.), *Handbook of industrial and organizational psychology.* Chicago: Rand McNally, 651–696, 1976.

McCormick, E. J., Jeanneret, P. R., & Mecham, R. C. A study of job characteristics and job dimensions as based on the Position Analysis Questionnaire. Lafayette, Ind.: Purdue University, Occupational Research Center, Purdue University, *Report No. 6,* 1969.

Pearlman, K. Job families: A review and discussion of their implications for personnel selection. *Psychological Bulletin,* 1980, *87,* 1–28.

Theologus, G. C., & Fleishman, E. A. *Development of a taxonomy of human performance: Validation study of ability scales for classifying human tasks.* Technical Report No. 10, Washington, D.C.: American Institute for Research, 1971.

Trattner, N. H., Fine, S. A., & Kubis, J. F. A comparison of worker requirement ratings made by reading job descriptions and by direct observation. *Personnel Psychology,* 1955, *8,* 183–194.

chapter 5

Criterion Development

You are by now familiar with the fundamental reason for psychologists' concern with criteria. They are evaluative standards. Thus, criteria are the dependent variables of interest whenever behavioral research of any kind is undertaken.

From a research standpoint it is insufficient to accept performance improvement, either by individuals or an organization, as an article of faith. Such improvement must be verified by demonstrating appropriate changes in suitable criterion measures. Thus the concern for developing adequate criteria is central to the science of human behavior.

When employee performance is at issue, the criteria provide some indication of job success or effectiveness. Although this chapter emphasizes evaluations of employee job performance, the broad issues of criterion development are equally appropriate to developing standards for assessing change in such things as consumer attitude, employee job satisfaction, managerial effectiveness, and so on.

Irrespective of the intended use, the purpose of any criterion is to measure differences between persons or groups. Thus, the criterion must somehow be scored and that score must be interpretable. We might, for example, wish to interpret criterion score differences between persons within a group: Which employees currently in the training program are sufficiently proficient that they are ready for job placement? Or we might wish to compare mean criterion score differences between groups of persons receiving alternate treatments (for example, product purchases following TV and magazine advertising campaigns). Or the criterion measure may be taken on a single group in a preposttreatment design: Has there been an increase or decrease in accident frequency following the introduction of new plant equipment?

Since criteria are behavioral measures they must meet all of the requirements of any other psychometric device. They must, in addition, satisfy certain largely nonpsychometric requirements like practicality, acceptability to management, and plausibility.

PSYCHOMETRIC REQUIREMENTS OF CRITERIA

Criterion measures are, broadly speaking, subject to the same requirements as are psychological tests. This important notion may require you to enlarge your view of what constitutes a *test*. Any device, set of questions, observation, or judgment used to differentiate between and/or rank order persons with respect to their psychological characteristics or behavior is, in effect, a psychometric device.

The purpose for which the psychological measure is devised is irrelevant to the requirement that it be psychometrically sound. Thus, even though a criterion measure may serve as the standard against which the usefulness of some other test is judged, the fact remains that the criterion is itself also a psychometric device.

Neither the type of data nor the format by which these data are collected alter this fact. Application blanks and interviews used totally or partly as bases for differentiating between applicants are tests, and must therefore meet the usual psychometric requirements. The same is true of production records, supervisory judgments of proficiency, estimates of managerial potential, counts of absences, and all other approaches to differentiating between employees.

One essential characteristic of psychometric devices, reliability, was discussed in detail in Chapter 3 and therefore will not be further considered at this time. In that same context we alluded to two other requirements—validity, and freedom from bias—which are discussed below as they pertain to criterion development.

Criterion validity

Since the criterion is the standard by which predictors and interventions are evaluated, it follows that the criterion measures themselves must be appropriate and relevant to this purpose. It is meaningless to establish that a preemployment test correlates with some sort of behavior unless that behavior truly reflects actual job proficiency. Conversely, evidence of a low predictor-criterion correlation, when that criterion is contaminated or otherwise inadequate, might cause us, incorrectly, to discard a truly useful predictor.

There are really two issues involved in criterion validity: (*a*) validity of the goal or objective itself and (*b*) validity of the specific measure(s) of that goal or objective (Smith, 1976). Suppose we are seeking a criterion against which to validate a preemployment battery. What is it that we wish the battery to predict? Clearly, we want it to predict the applicant's likely level of effectiveness as an employee. But *effectiveness* is a construct. It is a quality that must be inferred or deduced from certain more tangible indicators such as sales performance, stable tenure as an employee, receptivity to training, and so on. The process of justifying such inferences is discussed in Chapter 7. For now it is sufficient merely to reemphasize the critical importance of a careful job analysis as a basis for making informed and rational judgments about the relevance of potential criteria.

Having decided upon our criterion objective(s), we still must settle on the specific indicator(s) to be used. For simplicity in this discussion, let us assume that we have reduced the broad objective of *job effectiveness* to the single more specific one of *sales performance*. The important issue here is that whatever we use as our measure of *sales* must, in fact, reflect effectiveness as a salesperson and must not be contaminated by irrelevant circumstances.

Two considerations in deciding how we are to take this criterion measure are *time* and *type* (Weitz, 1961). When, and for what period of time will we record sales? Will we initiate data collection immediately after the salesperson has been hired, or will we wait until after some initial period of training and acclimatization? Are we interested in selling effectiveness at the end of the first year or at the end of the tenth year? And what type of measure will most accurately indicate what we mean by sales effectiveness? Total sales volume? Sales volume less returns? Number of new accounts opened? Number of old accounts terminated? Dollar volume of sales? Profitability of sales to the organization?

Freedom from bias

You will recall that a person's earned score on any psychometric measure is only an estimate of his/her hypothetical true score. The earned score is a composite of this true one, errors of measurement (contributing to unreliability), and bias.

Bias associated with subjectivity.   Perhaps the most obvious source of criterion bias is that associated with making ratings or other subjective estimates of the quality of performance. Anytime judgment enters into score determination the characteristics, predilections, and idiosyncrasies of the evaluator become a part of the measuring instrument. The evaluator may be consciously or unwittingly biased in favor of or against a particular employee or employee group. Either way, the resulting judgment of performance misrepresents the true situation.

Other sources of bias.   Even objectively derived criterion measures (that is, those that do not depend upon someone's judgment to yield a score) may be biased because of contamination. A *contaminated* criterion is one on which the score is falsely elevated or depressed because of the systematic influence of irrelevant factors beyond the control of the evaluatee.

Criterion contaminants are both pervasive and often quite subtle. Suppose we are developing predictors of sales performance and take, as our criterion, seasonally adjusted sales volume. (The seasonal adjustment is required to remove one rather obvious source of criterion contamination.) Sales territory, nature of the product or service sold, and level of advertising support

FIGURE 5–1
Spuriously high predictive validity resulting from criterion contamination

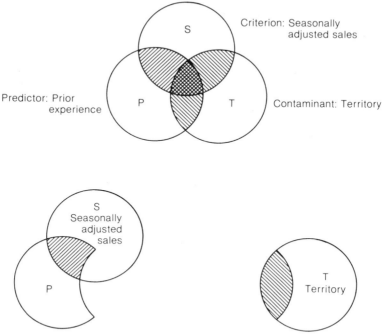

The predictive validity (correlation between P and S) is erroneously inflated by the correlation between Prior Experience and Territory because T also correlates with the criterion.

are clearly other possible contaminants. These are factors beyond the salesperson's control but which nevertheless have an impact upon his/her sales effectiveness. And to the extent that a potential predictor correlates with one or more of these contaminants, its value for predicting sales effectiveness will be overestimated.

One such situation is illustrated in Figure 5–1. Here, prior sales experience is shown to correlate with seasonally adjusted sales. However, the magnitude of this correlation is inflated because experience also correlates with sales territory which, in turn, contaminates the criterion. (This contamination might have resulted from a company policy of assigning potentially more lucrative territories to its more experienced salespersons.)

MULTIDIMENSIONALITY OF CRITERIA

The ultimate criterion is an abstraction. It is the complete and ultimate standard by which to judge the outcomes of a particular selection or other personnel program (Thorndike, 1949). Thus, it encompasses the essence of everything the satisfactory employee is expected to do. The ultimate objective in selecting bank tellers, for example, may be to identify those applicants who will count money easily, make change accurately, attend to possible irregularities in financial transactions (like a forged signature), know about the range of banking services available to customers, effectively sell new banking services to present customers, and so on.

Clearly, no single criterion measure can reflect all of these areas of performance. The ultimate criterion is comprised of several relatively independent (and therefore uncorrelated) measures. Yet the realities of selection and placement require a single decision: hire or reject; place as a teller or a savings counselor. The practical issue is self-evident: How can various criterion measures reflecting performance on different and often uncorrelated aspects of a job be used to facilitate making a unidimensional hiring decision?

The answer to this very practical question rests upon theoretical concerns about the appropriateness or inappropriateness of combining separate criteria into a single overall performance index. When several criteria are combined into a single index, we speak of a composite criterion. The alternative is to deal separately with each constituent criterion rather than combining them.

A classification of criteria

Smith (1976) has suggested the three-dimensional classification of criteria shown in Figure 5–2. (Although the axes of this figure really are continuous, each is artificially segmented for clarity.) Every criterion measure entails observations of behavior (a) following employment or administration of pre-employment predictors by some time interval, (b) varying in generality, and (c) representing some level of proximity to societal and organizational goals. The shaded cell in the lower right corner of the figure approximates what we earlier described as the ultimate criterion. The shaded cell in the upper left corner represents a measure of a very specific criterion behavior taken on essentially new employees.

Time.   When establishing a selection program, one has the option of predicting short- or long-term job performance. Similarly, when developing criteria as dependent variables for assessing the impact of some manipulation (for example, a safety campaign or a changed pay plan) the immediate or delayed effects can be studied. In either case, immediate and delayed criterion scores are often poorly correlated even when the specific criterion measure on both occasions is the same. Thus an efficient predictor of productivity after, say, three months on the job may not correlate well with productivity after 10 years. And the short-term beneficial effects of some environmental manipulation may be dissipated rather quickly with a consequent reversion to the original level of performance.

Thus criteria are dynamic (Ghiselli & Haire, 1960). Organizational demands may change over time. Also, relatively experienced (and generally

FIGURE 5–2
Classification of criteria

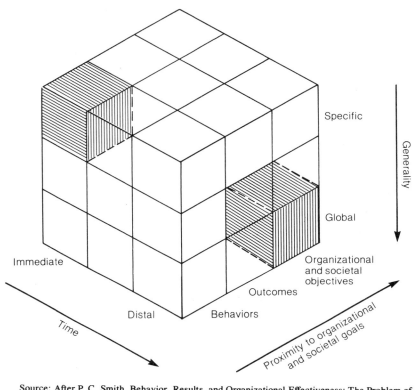

Source: After P. C. Smith, Behavior, Results, and Organizational Effectiveness: The Problem of Criteria, in Dunnette, ed., *Handbook of Industrial and Organizational Psychology*, p. 749. Copyright © 1976 by Rand McNally College Publishing Company. Adapted by permission of Houghton Mifflin Company.

older) employees may use different abilities than they did earlier to maintain their performance levels.

Two implications follow from the dynamic character of criteria:

1. Investigators cannot be sanguine about the long-term effectiveness of their preemployment predictors unless they have actually been validated against long-term criteria. In practice, the delay in validity studies between gathering the predictor scores and accumulating the criterion measures is usually brief—six months to one year. Longitudinal follow-ups, although rarely undertaken, are required (Guion, 1967).

2. Criteria developed as dependent variables by which to evaluate the impact of environmental or other manipulations must be time relevant. The effectiveness of a new management development program is more properly evaluated against measures of eventual managerial performance than against participants' scores on tests or simulations administered while they are engaged in the development program itself.

Generality.   Granted that criteria provide an index of employee effectiveness, the definition of effectiveness can range from very specific to very broad. Where effectiveness is narrowly defined by output rate, for example, the appropriate criterion measure is a very specific one: productivity. As the notion of effectiveness is broadened to encompass other aspects of employee behavior (like receptivity to supervision, commitment to organizational objectives, flexibility, progressive enlargement of skill and knowledge, and so on) the criterion must undergo parallel elaboration.

Proximity to organization and societal goals.   In practice, most criterion measures are taken from the outcomes segment of this continuum. They measure employee performance.

The measurable outcomes of individual effort originate from engagement by that person in a set of specific behaviors (lifting, walking, drilling, placing an order, talking, thinking, and so on). Further, each person's performance outcomes combine with those of all other persons within the organization to affect the attainment of broad organizational objectives, and across organizations to influence the realization of broad societal objectives. (See Figure 5–3.)

There is a major implication of this linkage between measurable outcomes by which we judge employee effectiveness and the variety of individual behaviors that contribute to reaching those outcomes. Different persons may be able to attain the same level of job performance through different and relatively idiosyncratic combinations of ability and behavior. A visually handicapped employee may, by substituting touch for sight, be quite capable of maintaining qualitatively and quantitatively superior output. Thus, a uniformly applied selection standard of visual acuity would be inappropriate in this instance.

The linkage on the other side of Figure 5–3—that between broad organizational and societal objectives and measurable work outcomes—calls attention to the importance of value judgments in structuring practical and useful measures of employee effectiveness. Those outcomes which an organization chooses to emphasize (and hence, the character of the work force it will recruit and the performance incentives it will offer) both mirror and influence organizational values. Whereas maintaining satisfactory contacts with present customers may be prized by organizations which are not seeking to expand, developing new accounts may be the reinforced outcome for salespersons in another organization which seeks an annual growth rate of, say, 10 percent. Likewise, an organization seeking to encourage its employees to use their leisure time creatively may be inclined to experiment with (and evaluate the effects of) flexible work schedules and enrichment opportunities offered at a nearby junior college.

Composite versus multiple criteria

All arguments against combining criteria into a single composite index rest upon the notion that criteria are multidimensional rather than unidimen-

FIGURE 5–3
Linkages between measurable outcomes, behavior, and organizational/societal objectives

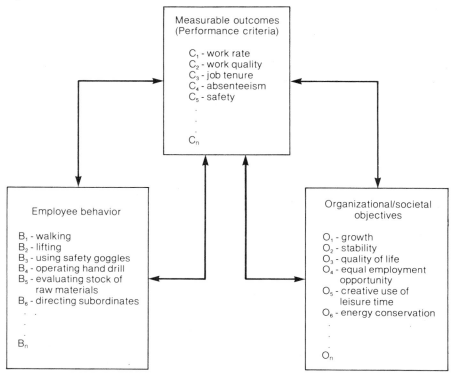

sional (Ghiselli, 1956; Guion, 1961; Dunnette, 1963; Wallace, 1965). It is theoretically irrational to combine into a single index several measures which are essentially unrelated to each other. In the case of a bank teller, combining measures of skill at accurately handling cash and effectiveness as a salesperson is conceptually akin to adding heights and grade-point averages to describe students.

In addition to the fact that criterion multidimensionality may conceptually preclude their combination into a single or overall composite, such a composite may misrepresent the very thing we wish our criterion to reflect: employee effectiveness. We have already noted that two different persons holding the same job may both be effective, but each in a different way (Ghiselli, 1956). Although the bank may wish to hire tellers who are both cash handlers and salespersons, clear superiority in *either* function could justify a decision to hire or promote. From an organizational standpoint, both functions need to be handled—but not necessarily by the same persons. Some tellers could be assigned as cash handling specialists; others as banking service specialists. This arrangement would imply that multiple criteria (and separate predictors of each) are necessary because we are really dealing with two different jobs: teller-cash transactions, and teller-salesperson. When viewed this way the development of a single composite criterion to be applied to all tellers makes no more sense to proponents of criterion combination than it does to proponents of multiple criteria. Different jobs call for the use of different criteria.

Thus, the theoretical controversy over multiple criteria versus a single overall criterion reduces to one major caveat: To the extent that two or more criteria for the same job are essentially uncorrelated with each other (even though each is a valid partial index of performance) they should be separately predicted. This view has an important implication. Criterion combination ought not be attempted unless the evidence indicates that (a) each criterion validly measures some aspect of job effectiveness and (b) the various separate criterion measures are sufficiently intercorrelated to support the contention that effectiveness for the job in question is a unitary concept. At least one author (Wallace, 1965) holds that the typical practice of combining criteria without such preliminary supportive evidence has limited the level of obtained predictive validity coefficients.

Combining criteria into a composite

Assuming that the stipulations above are satisfied (that is, the various criteria are demonstrated to sample different aspects of a single performance dimension) there remains the issue of weighting each measure as a constituent of the composite. There are three fundamental approaches to such weighting: judgmental, statistical, and economic. Unless there is clear justification for differential weighting in forming the composite, the subcriteria can be combined by a fourth approach: uniform weighting (Nagle, 1953).

Judgmental bases.   Management usually has certain notions, sometimes fuzzy, about the relative importance of various aspects of job performance. The assignment of judgmental weights to subcriteria attempts to make these notions explicit. The judgments can either be made independently by knowledgeable managers and the resulting values averaged to obtain consensual judgment (Toops, 1944), or weights can be extrapolated and made explicit by analyzing the personnel policies and actual personnel practices (Slovik & Lichtenstein, 1971).

Statistical bases.   This approach takes into consideration certain statistical properties of each subcriterion considered separately and/or the nature of the interrelationships between the several subcriteria. Thus, other things being equal, the subcriteria can be weighted proportionally to their reliabilities (because we might be more inclined to trust the most consistent measures). Alternatively, the weights can be set in such a way as to maximize individual differences in composite criterion scores (Edgerton & Kolbe, 1936), or to maximize the validity of the predictors (Hotelling, 1935).

The presumed advantage of statistical over judgmental weighting is that the former is based upon hard data rather than opinion. But statistically-based weighting neglects the very consideration that is central to judgmental procedures and intuitively provides the soundest rationale for differential weighting: the relevance of each subcriterion. However imprecise the judgmental weighting process, it does at least attempt to assign heavier weights to those criteria which are most pertinent to job effectiveness.

Economic bases. If one accepts that various subcriteria in profit-making organizations differ in importance to the extent that each reflects the employees' contributions to organizational profits, then the "dollar criterion" (Brogden & Taylor, 1950) is an appealing notion. Here, the assignment of weights reduces to a cost-accounting issue: How economically valuable is each element of job performance (reflected in each subcriterion) in terms of generating dollar profits and/or reducing costs?

While this approach is potentially useful in profit-making organizations, it is inapplicable to such nonprofit organizations as school systems. Furthermore, its use in profit-making organizations is severely limited by the infeasibility of effectively costing out such aspects of job performance as creating good will.

Uniform weighting. The foregoing discussion has not been particularly positive concerning any of the approaches to differential weighting. Each approach suffers deficiencies precluding its use as a generally preferred solution, although circumstances in a particular situation may suggest one procedure more than the others. Overall though, the arguments for differential weighting are not overwhelmingly persuasive.

An alternative when formulating composite criteria is uniform weighting: that is, to have each subcriterion contribute equally to the composite measure. The explicit assumption made—that the subcriteria are equally important to organizational objectives—is probably no more erroneous than are the assumptions made by the various differential weighting schemes. Indeed, unless there is clear evidence that certain subcriteria are more relevant than others, uniform weights probably yield the most defensible composite criterion.

APPROACHES TO EMPLOYEE SELECTION

The foregoing arguments generally favorable to the use of multiple criteria rather than a composite, overall criterion have been partly responsible for influencing current views of the employee selection process. The following sections contrast this more contemporary differential prediction approach with the earlier, traditional approach to selection.

The traditional approach

As shown in Figure 5–4, the traditional approach screens all candidates with the same predictor or predictor combination, and applies a uniform

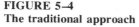

FIGURE 5–4
The traditional approach

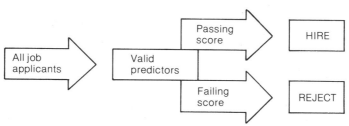

passing (or critical) score. This approach rests upon a prior search for the most powerful predictor-criterion correlation(s). Thus, it reflects the belief that (*a*) the same criterion (or criteria) should be predicted for all applicants, (*b*) valid predictors are equally useful for all applicants, and (*c*) a uniform critical score applied to all applicants enhances the probability of hiring the greatest number of potentially successful employees.

More recent experience has compelled a reconsideration of these beliefs and have led to changes in the traditional approach. In the 60 or so years that validity studies (involving test-criterion correlations) have been undertaken, there has been relatively little improvement in the demonstrated predictive efficiency of preemployment measures. A comprehensive review (Ghiselli, 1966) of many such studies confirms that correlation coefficients above .50 have rarely been obtained. The coefficient of determination (r^2) for a correlation of .50 is 25 percent. Although this is a substantial improvement over chance prediction, it still signifies that 75 percent of the criterion variance is unaccounted for by the predictor. Many predictor-criterion correlations obtained through traditional procedures are, of course, considerably below .50.

The search for explanations of this apparent ceiling on traditionally obtained validities has focused attention on both the criterion and predictor sides of the issue.

The traditional criterion.   In the final analysis, preemployment testing must eventuate in a decision to hire or reject the applicant. (The decision may not always appear to be this dichotomous. It is possible to hire provisionally, train, retest, and then to decide whether to employ permanently or reject the applicant.) Traditional programs translate this unidimensional employment decision into a single criterion for test validation. Generally, one or more predictors is validated against some overall index of employee efficiency.

However, as was previously noted, employee efficiency is not a unidimensional concept (Dunnette, 1963). Some "efficient" employees are high producers (defined by output quantity). Other equally effective employees may produce less but have fewer merchandise returns or production errors. Besides, there are other aspects to effectiveness. What about the employee who produces only moderately, but rarely loses any time because of absenteeism or accidents; or the employee who produces well but is relatively inflexible in adopting new work procedures or altered work schedules?

The decision to hire or reject an applicant should reflect a prediction of some synthesis of the diverse components of job success. But the point has been made that different persons may achieve equivalent total performance through different patterns of work behavior. This implies that improvements in validity may result from efforts to predict different criteria, all of which may influence effectiveness, for different applicants.

The traditional predictor. The traditional approach also oversimplifies the nature of the predictor. By searching for the single most powerful predictor (or predictor combination) it erroneously assumes that the same characteristics predispose effective job performance for all persons. This is like saying that academic ability is the sole determinant of your course grade. Although ability clearly is important, various students with different ability levels earn similar grades. Higher levels of motivation, time available for study, preparation through background courses, and so on, can moderate the impact of lower ability levels. Similarly, satisfactory job performance by one employee can be attributed to (and therefore predicted from) characteristics different from those encouraging satisfactory performance by another.

The differential prediction approach

It is clear that the traditional approach to employee selection is relatively insensitive to individual differences among applicants and among employees. In emphasizing a uniform criterion, it fails to take into account that there are often alternative (and equally acceptable) ways of accomplishing the same job tasks. In applying a uniform predictor to all applicants, it neglects the likelihood that a given outcome can be predected from various antecedants (Rundquist, 1969). Since there is no prediction model fitting all applicants, the assumption that one exists imposes a ceiling on traditionally obtained validity coefficients.

What is required, then, to remove this ceiling is an alternative assumption: that is, that job success for different applicants can be most efficiently predicted by different predictors. The ultimate (and, of course, unworkable) extension of this assumption would require selecting each employee on the basis of an individually-tailored predictor. A more moderate but workable extension assumes that applicants can be classified into subgroups, each of which has its own optimal selection program.

This assumption is represented in the selection research model shown in Figure 5–5. The model cails attention to the complex interactions between predictors, individual employees, work setting, and organizational consequences. The job behavior of subgroups of employees may be differentially predicted from various predictors, or from differentially established passing

FIGURE 5–5
A differential prediction approach to selection research

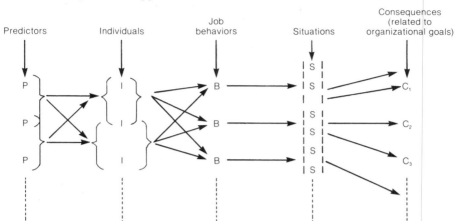

Source: After M. D. Dunnette, "A Note on the Criterion," *Journal of Applied Psychology* 47 pp. 317–323. Copyright 1963 by the American Psychological Association. Reprinted by permission.

scores on the same set of predictors. The model also makes the important point that job behavior itself is situational. The same or similar job behaviors may, depending upon specific organizational circumstances, have quite different organizational consequences (Dunnette, 1963).

Moderator variables. One of the implications of Figure 5–5 is that a predictor which works, for example, for men may not work equally well for women; one that predicts job efficiency for older applicants may predict either less or more efficiently for younger applicants; and so on.

Any such variable which systematically influences the relationship between two other variables (for example, the relationship between a predictor and a criterion) is termed a *moderator*. Virtually any basis upon which persons can be classed into subgroups is a potential moderator variable: race, age, sex, motivational level, educational history, and so on. Selection research increasingly has investigated the first three to determine whether, in given situations, they do in fact moderate the validity (predictor-criterion correlation) coefficient. The reason this research has focused particularly upon race, age, and sex as potential moderators is that these variables characterize classes of persons protected under the Civil Rights Act. We will say more about this matter in Chapter 7.

Selection and placement decisions. The approach shown in Figure 5–5 implies that a selection program should embody several decision points and offer several alternatives. This contrasts with the traditional approach embodying a single decision point (upon completion of preemployment testing) and a single decision alternative (hire or reject).

The flow of an applicant through this more contemporary selection pro-

FIGURE 5–6
The personnel decision process

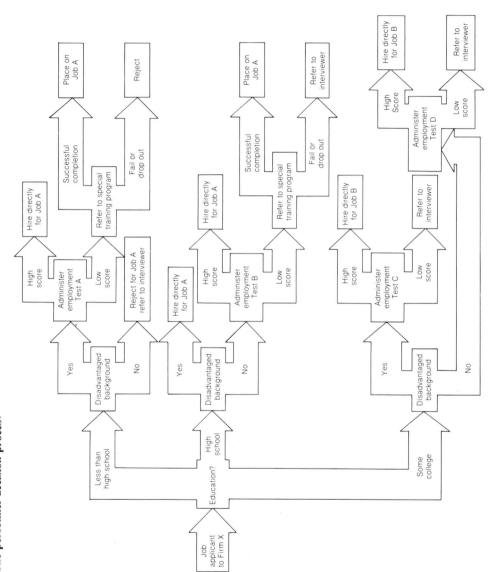

Source: After M. D. Dunnette, "Personnel Selection and Job Placement of the Disadvantaged: Problems, Issues, and Suggestions," *Integrating the Organization*, ed. H. L. Fromkin and J. J. Sherwood (New York: Free Press, 1974), p. 62.

cess is diagrammed in Figure 5–6. This flow chart illustrates how selection might proceed when educational level and socioeconomic background have been established by the research as useful moderator variables.

SUMMARY

Criteria are the dependent variables of interest whenever behavioral research of any kind is undertaken. Since criteria are behavioral measures they must satisfy the requirements of any psychometric device. Thus, they must be valid, free from bias, and reliable.

A three-dimensional classification of criteria for employee selection was presented. Any performance criterion incorporates time (short- versus long-term job performance), some level of specificity or generality, and a degree of proximity or distance from societal and organizational goals. This type of classification has two primary implications. First, any measurable outcome by which employee effectiveness is evaluated can be attained in different ways by different employees. Second, the decision about the relative importance to attach to the three major characteristics of criteria is a matter of judgment by the organization. Some, for example, will wish to emphasize long-term potential performance rather than short-run performance in making their hiring decisions, and so on.

The practical decision in employment selection ordinarily is a dichotomous one: hire or reject the applicant. This decision must somehow reflect a synthesis of predicted performance on all aspects of the job. Such a synthesis can be effected by predicting (a) a composite criterion combining all significant elements of job performance into a single overall index and (b) multiple criteria.

All arguments against combining criteria into a single overall composite index rest upon the notion that criteria are multidimensional rather than unidimensional. From a theoretical standpoint it does not make sense to combine several essentially unrelated performance measures into a single overall performance index. Thus, the use of multiple criteria is advocated except where there is clear evidence that the several criterion measures sample different aspects of the same performance dimension.

Given such evidence, the several measures can be combined into a single composite in which the components are assigned either uniform or differential weights. Unless there is clear and persuasive evidence that certain criteria are more relevant to the composite than others, uniform weights probably are the more defensible.

The arguments favorable to using multiple criteria rather than a composite, overall criterion are partly responsible for influencing current views of the employee selection process. The historically traditional approach sought to discover the best predictor, and to apply it uniformly to all job applicants. In contrast, more recent selection research has emphasized differential prediction. This emphasis recognizes that predictors may have different levels of efficiency for different subgroups of applicants.

The subgroup classifications ordinarily of greatest interest are race, age, and sex because of the implications of these variables for compliance with the Civil Rights Act of 1964. Any such variable with potential to influence the relationship between two other variables (for example, a predictor and a criterion) systematically is termed a *moderator*. To the extent that moderator variables actually exert their potential influence, the differential rather than the traditional approach to selection becomes imperative.

REFERENCES

Brogden, H. E., & Taylor, E. K.   The dollar criterion—applying the cost accounting concept to criterion construction. *Personnel Psychology,* 1950, *3*, 133–154.

Dunnette, M. D.   A note on the criterion. *Journal of Applied Psychology,* 1963, *47*, 251–254.

Dunnette, M. D.   Personnel selection and job placement of the disadvantaged: Problems, issues, and suggestions. In H. L. Fromkin & J. J. Sherwood (Eds.), *Integrating the organization,* New York: Free Press, 1974.

Edgerton, H. A., & Kolbe, L. E.   The method of minimum variation for the coordination of criteria. *Psychometrika,* 1936, *1*, 185–187.

Ghiselli, E. E.   Dimensional problems of criteria. *Journal of Applied Psychology,* 1956, *40*, 1–4.

Ghiselli, E. E.   *The validity of occupational aptitude tests.* New York: Wiley, 1966.

Ghiselli, E. E., & Haire, M.   The validation of selection tests in the light of the dynamic character of criteria. *Personnel Psychology,* 1960, *13*, 225–231.

Guion, R. M.   Criterion measurement and personnel judgments. *Personnel Psychology,* 1961, *14*, 141–149.

Guion, R. M.   Personnel Selection. *Annual Review of Psychology,* 1967, *18*, 191–216.

Hotelling, H.   The most predictable criterion. *Journal of Educational Psychology,* 1935, *26*, 139–142.

Nagle, B. F.   Criterion development. *Personnel Psychology,* 1953, *6*, 271–289.

Rundquist, E. A.   The prediction ceiling. *Personnel Psychology,* 1969, *22*, 109–116.

Slovik, P., & Lichtenstein, S.   Comparison of Bayesian and regression approaches to the study of information processing in judgment. *Organizational Behavior and Human Performance,* 1971, *6*, 649–744.

Smith, P. C.   Behavior, results, and organizational effectiveness: The problem of criteria. In M. D. Dunnette (Ed.), *Handbook of Industrial and Organizational Psychology.* Chicago: Rand McNally, 1976, 745–776.

Thorndike, R. L.   *Personnel Selection.* New York: Wiley, 1949.

Toops, H. A.   The criterion. *Educational and Psychological Measurement,* 1944, *4*, 271–297.

Wallace, S. R.   Criteria for what: *American Psychologist,* 1965, *20*, 411–417.

Weitz, J.   Criteria for criteria. *American Psychologist,* 1961, *16*, 228–231.

chapter **6**

Performance Appraisal

We turn now to some of the specifics of performance appraisal. These appraisals are the criteria against which predictors are validated, the dependent variables by which the relative merits of alternative treatments are judged, and the evidence by which personnel decisions are made.

It is useful to distinguish between objectively and subjectively derived appraisals or, as we do in this chapter, between performance *measures* and performance *evaluations*.

Objective performance measures are ones for which the raw data are matters of record; they are essentially judgment-free. Job tenure (length of employment), present salary, sales volume, hours lost because of accidents, are illustrations. Note that although the raw data are hard in the sense that they are objectively verifiable, their interpretation ultimately entails some kind of judgment. What rate of turnover is excessive? What sales volume is satisfactory? And so on.

The data for subjectively derived criteria are totally judgmental: they rest upon subjective evaluations of performance. Their use is necessitated when hard data pertaining to the desired criterion are unavailable. This is usually the case, for example, when we wish performance evaluations of employees in service-oriented rather than product-oriented jobs. Appraisals of managerial, supervisory, and professional/technical personnel typically rest upon subjective criteria. And evaluations of future potential (i.e., of "promotability") are subjective even though the rater's judgment may depend, in part, upon hard data.

PERFORMANCE MEASURES

The most apparent objective indicator of performance is some measure of productivity. Therefore, we begin by considering its usefulness as a criterion and proceed to such other tangibles as promotions and salary, tenure and turnover, and so on.

Productivity

Intuitively, some countable measure of work output would seem to provide an ideal performance criterion for jobs in which the employee does something tangible. In reality, however, productivity counts are rarely used as criteria except for rather routine jobs (Schultz & Siegel, 1961). The type of job that most lends itself to an objective productivity count is one in which (a) a large number of employees are performing the same task under the same circumstances and (b) the task is one that is sufficiently short-cycle and free of external constraints so that there is leeway for the manifestation of individual differences in productivity. It is rare for jobs to meet either, let alone both, of these specifications.

Even though sizable numbers of employees may be engaged in what superficially appears to be the same work, subtle differences in the task and job environment may invalidate direct comparisons of their output. Word output counts for technical manuscript typists and correspondence typists, for example, are not comparable. In order to effect a comparison, the output for each would somehow have to be converted to a uniform scale in which the measurement units express each one's level of productivity relative to some standard for persons engaged in that kind of typing. Any such conversion usually entails a preliminary time study and rests upon such a highly subjective determination of what is standard in each case, that the appearance of objectivity is illusory.

The second prerequisite to meaningful productivity counts—short-cycle work free from external constraints—is equally difficult to satisfy. Although there are still many repetitive jobs in manufacturing and assembling, their number is declining and the number of employees assigned to each is diminishing as plants are automated. Further such work, when it exists, is rarely free from constraints which, although beyond the employee's control, nevertheless influence the output rate. Limitations may be imposed by covert work-group standards, availability of raw materials, maximum machine speed, and so on.

Even when circumstances meet the prerequisites noted above, the resulting productivity counts may be subject to sampling error. An employee's productivity may fluctuate with the time of the day, the day of the week, the season (for example, whether immediately preceding or following a vacation) and so on. Since productivity criteria sample rather than continuously monitor output, the *representativeness* of the sample of observations is critical to approximating the true index of productivity.

The foregoing discussion emphasized two circumstances potentially militating against developing productivity criteria: (1) Even when employees produce some kind of tangible output, the output rate is often subject to contamination adversely affecting both the reliability and validity of the production index and obviating comparisons between employees. (2) Productivity counts are unavailable for or irrelevant to much of the work performed in our society. What type of output should be recorded, for example, for teachers, managers, supervisors, technical service representatives, and so on?

Either or both of these circumstances may influence the investigator to look toward some measure of effectiveness other than output.

Promotions and salary

Present job level and/or salary may sometimes provide an objective index of effectiveness—particularly for managerial and technical personnel. The rationale, of course, is that job level and salary are tangible reflections of the organization's assessment of individual merit. The validity of these criteria rests upon the tenability of this rationale. They are invalidated as indices of merit when promotions and salary increments reflect favoritism or other contaminants.

Assuming validity, present job level and salary must be interpreted in the light of the person's age (and experience). Thus for appraising executive performance one investigator suggests a correction reflecting the difference between actual salary increase and the magnitude of the increase predicted on the basis of job tenure (Hulin, 1962).

Tenure and turnover

Tenure refers to length of service; turnover is the obverse side of the tenure coin. Assuming the employee is performing satisfactorily, tenure is cost-effective to the organization. No organization likes to contemplate the prospect of training or developing employees only to have them accept placement with a competitor who thereby reaps the benefits of the training investment.

In addition to certain factors over which management has relatively little control, turnover reflects employee dissatisfaction with the job. Therefore, it is most effectively predicted from employee interest and background (Schuh, 1967). As we will discuss in Chapter 8, the standardized application blank is one source of information from which tenure predictions can sometimes be made.

Miscellaneous

Among the other job behaviors of concern to investigators and sometimes used as criteria for preemployment prediction are accidents, tardiness, and absenteeism.

It is usually incorrect to take these measures as indirect indications either of productivity or job satisfaction. All three are influenced by a host of situational factors, many of which are beyond management's control and some of which are beyond the employee's control. Therefore if they are to be used as criteria at all, their use must be justified on the basis of their own relevance rather than because of a presumed relationship with more fundamental indices of employee effectiveness.

ERROR AND BIAS IN PERFORMANCE EVALUATION

We have previously noted that measurements of performance are either infeasible for or inappropriate to many kinds of work. The alternative to measurement is subjective evaluation. The element of subjectivity in such appraisal is at once the peculiar strength and weakness of performance evaluation.

Its strength derives from the fact that it provides otherwise unobtainable criteria for test validation and personnel decisions. Even when performance measures are available, these must often by subjectively synthesized to formulate judgments of managerial potential or promotability.

Hence, subjectively based performance appraisals may entail evaluations of selected elements of job performance, overall job performance, or potential for subsequent development.

The fundamental weaknesses of performance evaluation follow also from its subjective character. Other things being equal, judgments are often less reliable and less valid than are objectively obtained measures. This is, in part, a function of the evaluative procedure itself—as we will see when we discuss methods of performance evaluation. It is attributable also to evaluator errors and biases—the issue to which we now turn.

There are two general approaches to reducing the adverse impact of evaluator error and bias: (a) training designed to help the evaluators avoid the potential pitfalls and (b) modification of the evaluative format to mitigate such errors and biases. These approaches are not antagonistic; both are characteristics of sound performance evaluation procedures. They are best understood from the perspective of the kinds of errors they are designed to counteract.

Distributional errors

Theoretically, there is some true distribution of the performance evaluations for any particular group of employees. Unless there is some persuasive reason to think otherwise, this distribution is likely to approximate normality. Assuming a normal distribution is the true one, Figure 6–1 illustrates three kinds of distributional error: leniency, severity, and central tendency.

Some evaluators are disposed to be either erroneously lenient or severe. Of the two, leniency is the more likely direction whenever the evaluator believes that management will take poor ratings assigned to subordinates as a reflection of ineffectual supervision. Should the evaluator be rating members of some other supervisor's work group, deliberate or unconsciously motivated competition would likewise contribute to severity.

FIGURE 6–1
Distributional errors

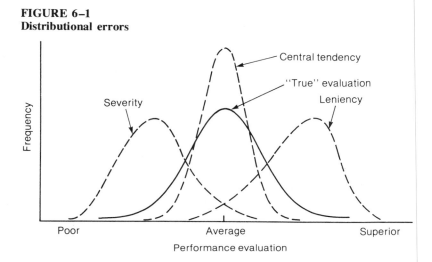

By themselves, leniency and severity errors do not signify deliberate or unwitting ulterior motives. Like teachers, some job performance evaluators have overly stringent standards and others have overly liberal ones.

Central tendency error is also shown in Figure 6–1. This is the disposition to assign average ratings to virtually all workers. This might reflect a systematic reluctance to rate anyone either as "very poor" or as "superior." It can result, also, when the evaluator has been asked to rate persons about whom he/she has insufficient information to make discriminating evaluations. (This occurs, for example, when a relatively new supervisor is required to make performance evaluations too soon after placement in the position or when premature evaluations are required of a relatively new subordinate.)

Probably the most widely used practice for counteracting distributional errors is the *forced distribution* of ratings. Forced distributions compel an assignment of ratings consistent with a normal distribution. If a five-category graphic scale is used, for example, we would anticipate that about 7 percent of the ratees would receive ratings at each of the extreme categories, 38 percent in the middle or average category, and 24 percent in each of the remaining categories.

Forcing supervisors to adhere to a normal distribution of ratings assignment overcomes any disposition they might have toward systematic bias. There is the danger, however, that forced distributions of ratings may actually produce some unfairly harsh appraisals when the department as a whole is better than average. Similarly, a forced distribution will produce a number of overly lenient ratings in departments with substantial numbers of relatively ineffectual employees.

The dilemma of forced distributions for ratings is quite analogous to curved grades. It is advisable to make a study of the legitimacy of requiring a normal distribution before deciding to force either merit ratings or course grades to such a distribution. How can we know whether or not it is legitimate to impose a normal distribution upon merit ratings? We would have to examine both the personnel selection program and the training program before answering this question. If employees were carefully selected through the application of rather rigorous standards and if they were carefully trained, it would be erroneous to require the supervisor's appraisals of their performance to conform to a normal distribution. The anticipated distribution under these circumstances should contain a relatively large proportion of favorable ratings. Conversely, if the selection and training programs were relatively weak, we should anticipate a skew in the opposite direction.

Halo effect

You are well aware of the lasting consequences of first impressions because of the halo effect. We tend to generalize from our present experiences to our subsequent ones, and to form pervasive impressions based upon only partial information. Thus, although a rating form may contain 10 or 15 separate scales, the supervisor may respond carefully only to the first two or three, marking the remaining ones on the basis of the initial impressions. Or the evaluations of all aspects of job performance may be tinged, for better or for worse, by the evaluator's perceptions about the one or two elements of job performance that the evaluator considers especially important.

Evaluator training concerning the pervasiveness and subtlety of potential halo effects—both positive and negative—probably is helpful in controlling its influence (Borman, 1975). In addition, two procedural mechanisms sometimes prove useful: horizontal ratings and reversal of the rating poles. Horizontal rating requires that all employees be rated on a single trait or characteristic at a time. Random reversals of the rating poles (placing the "favorable" pole sometimes on the left and sometimes on the right) compels the rater at least to examine each scale carefully enough to determine which end is favorable!

Egocentric effects

This type of error results particularly from an untrained evaluator's tendency to use his/her self-perception as the standard against which to evaluate ratees. The resulting errors may entail contrast or similarity bias.

Contrast error refers to an inclination to rate others differently from the way in which the evaluator perceives him/herself, almost as if to say, "Since I am the supervisor, none of my subordinates can possibly be as good as I." *Similarity* error, as you might expect, is the inclination to rate others congruent with the way in which we perceive ourselves.

Sequential effects

As we have already noted, subjective appraisals often entail evaluating each ratee on a series of scales, each devoted to a single aspect of performance. Whereas the intent is to obtain a set of independent judgments about these aspects of performance, the evaluator may strive to appear consistent by following a favorable rating on a particular scale with another that is somewhat higher than it should be. Alternatively, some evaluators tend toward balance; they follow particularly favorable ratings with ones that are somewhat lower than the ratee deserves.

Since this type of error depends upon the internal order in which the elements to be evaluated are considered, a solution is to develop multiple forms in which the order of the rating scales is randomized.

Evaluator bias

The foregoing types of subjective error are relatively simple to address in evaluator training. (This does not imply that the errors are easy to overcome. It implies only that the sources of error are not emotionally laden; hence their discussion during training is relatively unthreatening.)

Evaluator bias is quite a different matter. Bias is evidenced when the evaluation reflects the influence of factors that really are irrelevant to the dimensions under consideration. Potential sources of bias (often unintentional) in performance evaluations are such things as the employee's job level or classification, age, seniority, sex, race, and religion. Some such biasing factors undoubtedly produced the finding of a positive correlation between performance evaluations of West Point cadets after 14 weeks and the cadets' names and home addresses as predictors (Vielhuber & Gottheil, 1965)! Our early impressions about people often reveal more about our own stereotypes than they do about the characteristics or behavior of these persons.

Because of the distinct susceptibility of subjectively based evaluations to rater bias, it is generally desirable to interpret such evaluations relative to the employee's own reference group. Generally speaking, all of the considerations elaborated in our earlier discussion of bias in testing (Chapter 3) apply also to the issue of evaluator bias.

APPROACHES TO RATING

Given that performance often must be subjectively appraised, several procedures are available for making and collating the required judgments. All procedures seek to generate maximally reliable and valid evaluations. Furthermore, the evaluations must somehow be scored: that is, they must order persons along a continuum of "overall effectiveness" or along several continua each addressing some more limited aspect of criterion behavior.

Overall ratings are most appropriate to decisions about whether an employee ought to be discharged, promoted, given a merit increase, and so on. More circumscribed ratings are most useful for diagnostic purposes when alternative or remedial courses of action (for example, additional training or transfer to another section) are available.

Irrespective of whether we wish to obtain a single overall score or multiple subscores (or a combination of the two), it is useful to distinguish between (*a*) relative versus absolute procedures and (*b*) direct versus derived procedures.

Relative versus absolute

Relative procedures compare the persons being appraised with each other. Thus, the resulting scores are relative. One of the difficulties is that the person evaluated as "best" among a particular group may nonetheless be performing only marginally, or even unsatisfactorily. Alternatively, given a group of outstandingly effective employees, the one evaluated as "worst" may nonetheless be quite satisfactory.

Absolute procedures compare the persons rated to some external group or standard. This eliminates one problem of the relative procedures: the designation of one person as better or worse than another does not imply that either is necessarily effective or ineffective.

The potential validity of such externally-referenced rating procedures is largely a function of the appropriateness to the criterion of the items (characteristics or behavior) on which ratings are sought. If the scale is to measure effectiveness, then each item contributing to the score must concern some salient aspect of whatever is meant by effectiveness.

One source of rating scale items is, of course, the job analysis (see Chapter 4). Another is the *critical incidents approach* (Flanagan, 1954). Here the items to be rated are actual job behaviors (rather than traits or characteristics presumed to mediate job behavior). The key to the critical incidents approach, in addition to its focus upon behavior, is that the behavior to be evaluated has been shown to be critical to the quality of job performance. Typically, critical behaviors are suggested as possible rating scale items by supervisors who are asked to recall actual incidents in which employee actions enhanced or diminished the quality of job performance.

Direct versus derived ratings

This distinction (suggested by Landy & Farr, 1980) classifies procedures in terms of the requirements made of the rater. When making *direct* ratings, raters actually assign numbers representing their performance evaluations. *Derived* ratings are procedures in which the rater makes a series of discrete judgments about the ratee. These judgments then are combined to derive the performance rating.

The distinction between direct and derived ratings is a convenient basis for organizing the following discussion of specific rating procedures. We first discuss two direct procedures—ranking and graphic ratings—and behaviorally anchored rating scales as a relatively recent elaboration of the latter. The following section (on derived procedures) includes discussions of paired comparison ratings and checklists. Two more recent elaborations of checklists—forced choice procedures, and mixed standard ratings—are also considered in that context.

DIRECT RATING PROCEDURES

Ranking

The rater using this technique merely orders the ratees from best to worst, generally assigning a rank of 1 to the person judged to be highest or best, a rank of 2 to the second best, and so on. Often two or more raters are asked to provide independent sets of rankings, which are then averaged, in order to reduce the possible impact of subjective error and bias. The method is a simple one and may be applied either by assigning "man-as-a-whole" ratings or "trait" ratings. In the former case, the employee is assigned a rank on the basis of the supervisor's overall impression about his/her efficiency. Ratings of traits, on the other hand, may require the supervisor to rank employees on several specific characteristics like cooperativeness, initiative, or versatility. Such trait ratings are sometimes averaged to yield a composite index of the supervisor's opinions.

The ranking method is susceptible to two deficiencies that may have deleterious effects upon the validity of the resultant information: (1) the hair splitting necessitated by differentiating between adjacent ranks in the middle of the continuum and (2) the fallacious appearance of equal intervals along a scale of ranks. Thus, if 50 employees are to be ranked, the supervisor very likely will experience difficulty in differentiating between the one who should be ranked 23 and the one who should be ranked 24. Furthermore, it is unlikely that the magnitude of the difference between employees ranked 2 and 3 is of the same order as the difference between the employees ranked 26 and 27, even though only one rank separates each of these pairs.

Certain procedures for minimizing these deficiencies have been suggested. It often is desirable, for instance, to differentiate ranks only for persons in the upper and lower quarter of the total group, assigning a common middle rank to the remaining 50 percent of the group. This modification of the ranking procedure obviates the necessity for making impossibly fine discriminations between persons in the middle of the range. It should be apparent, however, that the ranking method is a crude one. Its usefulness is limited to situations in which relatively few employees are to be rated. Furthermore, it is applicable only when the rating is intended to order employees from best to worst without providing an indication of how much better or worse one employee is than another.

Graphic ratings

Graphic scales are one of the older and most generally familiar approaches to rating. Each scale consists of a trait label (such as *dependability*), a brief description of the trait, and a line with adjective guideposts extending from *most* to *least, highest* to *lowest, best* to *worst,* and so on. The line may represent a continuum or be divided into several discrete categories. In either case, the rater indicates a judgment by marking on the line or in the box.

Graphic ratings of several aspects of behavior are sometimes combined into a single overall criterion evaluation. The considerations in effecting this combination were discussed in the preceding chapter.

Although graphic scales are very widely used, largely because they are simple to comprehend, they are especially susceptible to distributional errors. Part of the reason for their susceptibility to these errors is ambiguity in the rating scale anchors. Phrases like *extremely dependable, about average,* and *extremely undependable,* mean different things to different raters.

Behaviorally anchored scales

Behaviorally anchored rating scales (BARS) seek to reduce this ambiguity by illustrating various positions on the rating scale with actual behavior (Smith & Kendall, 1963). A BARS developed to evaluate grocery checkers is shown in Figure 6–2. This was one of seven such scales developed for checkers. In addition to knowledge and judgment, considered by the illustration, the other scales considered such characteristics as organizational ability and human relations skill (Fogli, Hulen & Blood, 1971).

The primary objective of behaviorally anchored scales is to provide all evaluators with the same frame of reference for making their ratings, thereby improving interrater agreement. The interrater reliabilities of the seven scales for grocery checkers ranged from .97–.99. This is considerably higher than the level of agreement obtained with other types of graphic ratings.

A major disadvantage is the time (and hence, expense) required to develop behaviorally anchored scales. The scale for grocery checkers illustrates the typical sequence:

1. Critical instances of effective and ineffective behavior were isolated through interviews with staff personnel from a large grocery chain. The interviewees were asked to, "Remember incidents in your store that displayed vividly poor (or effective) performance. It might help you to describe the behavior you would expect from the worst (or best) checkers you have ever known."

2. The investigators reviewed the critical behaviors and extrapolated eight provisional functional dimensions (later reduced to seven) which appeared to them to encompass all of the cited behavior. Thereafter, a sample of staff personnel were asked independently to allocate each

FIGURE 6–2
A behaviorally anchored rating scale: Knowledge and judgment

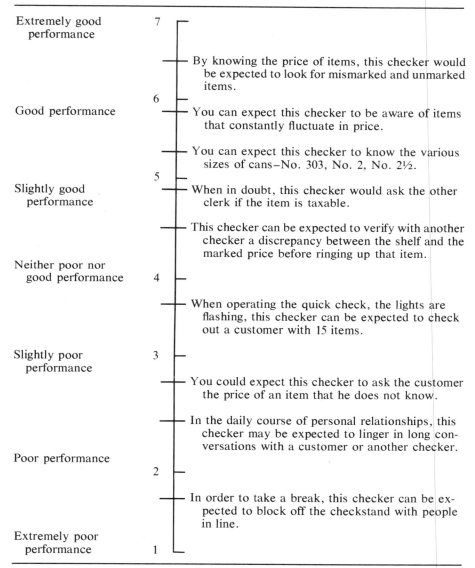

Extremely good performance — 7

By knowing the price of items, this checker would be expected to look for mismarked and unmarked items.

6

Good performance — You can expect this checker to be aware of items that constantly fluctuate in price.

You can expect this checker to know the various sizes of cans–No. 303, No. 2, No. 2½.

5

Slightly good performance — When in doubt, this checker would ask the other clerk if the item is taxable.

This checker can be expected to verify with another checker a discrepancy between the shelf and the marked price before ringing up that item.

Neither poor nor good performance — 4

When operating the quick check, the lights are flashing, this checker can be expected to check out a customer with 15 items.

Slightly poor performance — 3

You could expect this checker to ask the customer the price of an item that he does not know.

In the daily course of personal relationships, this checker may be expected to linger in long conversations with a customer or another checker.

Poor performance — 2

In order to take a break, this checker can be expected to block off the checkstand with people in line.

Extremely poor performance — 1

Source: L. Fogli, C. L. Hulin, and M. R. Blood, "Development of First Level Behavioral Job Criteria," *Journal of Applied Psychology,* 55: p. 6. Copyright 1978 by the American Psychological Association. Reprinted by permission.

behavior to one of these eight dimensions. This resulted in sets of critical incidents assigned by a majority of these judges to each dimension. *Knowledge and judgment* was one such dimension.

3. Another, considerably larger, sample of staff personnel was asked independently to rate the degree to which each incident indicated good/poor (scaled from 1 to 7) performance on the dimension to which it had been provisionally assigned. These ratings produced two types of information about each critical behavior:

   a. Ambiguity: Disagreement between the judges about the placement of an item on the point-rating continuum generated a distribution of judgments having a relatively large standard deviation. Since this meant that the judges did not agree about quality of the performance signified by the behavior described in the item, it was discarded from further consideration on the basis of ambiguity.

   b. Scale value: For unambiguous items, the mean rating (on the seven-point scale) was taken as that behavior's scale value on the dimension to which it has been assigned in Step 2.

4. The behavioral items surviving the analysis as described above were constituted into scales like the illustration in Figure 6–2. These scales were then used to evaluate particular checkers.

Reviewing studies comparing BARS with graphic scales, as part of their comprehensive review of performance rating generally, Landy and Farr (1980) conclude that the initial enthusiasm greeting the introduction of the procedure has not been supported empirically. The use of BARS tends to be restricted to organizations in which the number of employees to be evaluated warrants a significant financial investment in developing the evaluative procedure. Further, reported gains in the form, for example, of improved interrater reliability and diminished halo, probably result less from an inherent property of the BARS technique than from the manner in which it can be implemented (Bernardin, 1977). One of the advantages of the rather elaborate preliminaries to structuring behaviorally anchored rating scales is that these tend to *involve* the persons who will ultimately use the scale, and facilitate incorporation into the scales of terminology specifically appropriate to the job.

DERIVED RATING PROCEDURES

We next consider several procedures in which the rater makes a series of discrete judgments from which a composite rating is derived.

Paired comparisons

This method requires the rater to rank employees considered one pair at a time. In other words, every employee is compared with every other employee, and for each pair the rater judges which is the better.

FIGURE 6–3
Paired-comparisons evaluation of five employees

						Summary: Number of times ranked superior
Ratee	A	B	C	D	E	
A	—	A	A	D	A	A = 3
B		—	B	D	B	B = 2
C			—	D	C	C = 1
D				—	D	D = 4
E						E = 0

Each cell entry indicates the member of the particular pair ranked as superior. The summary column indicates the total number of times each employee was chosen as the superior member of the pair comparisons.

The grid in Figure 6–3 illustrates the procedure for a five-person group. For this illustration, the rater judged employee A to be superior to employees B, C, and E but less effective than employee D, and so on. As shown in the summary column, the "best" employee is D, chosen as the superior member in all possible comparisons. The "worst" employee is E.

The paired-comparisons method has two distinct advantages over the ranking method:

1. Instead of necessitating simultaneous consideration of all members of the group, the paired-comparisons method narrows the field for consideration by the rater to just two persons at a time. Thus, the kind of judgment required is greatly simplified.

2. The paired-comparisons procedure generates ratings which can be taken as reflections of the subjectively perceived distance between the evaluatees (Lawshe, Kephart, & McCormick, 1949). This kind of interpretation of paired-comparison ratings is shown in Figure 6–4 which summarizes data secured by one of the authors. The data for this figure were obtained from paired-comparisons ratings of 20 savings and loan branch managers independently made by four officers. The figure shows the average percentage of times each branch manager was chosen as the superior member of the pair. (Every manager was, of course, compared to each of the 19 others.)

A very important limitation of the paired-comparisons procedure is that its implementation can be quite time-consuming. The number of pairs of persons to be considered is given by the general formula $N(N-1)/2$ where N is the number of people being evaluated. Hence, the data for Figure 6–4 required each rater to make judgments for 190 different pairs of managers (that is, $(20 \times 19)/2$. Given a group of, say 50 persons, 1,225 comparisons would be required.

FIGURE 6–4
Paired-comparisons summary: 20-branch
managers

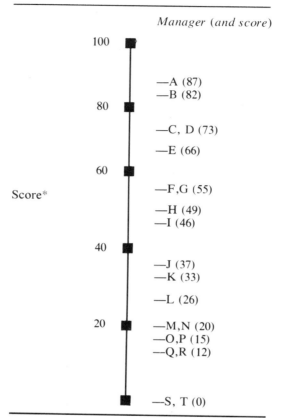

Manager (and score)

Score*

* The score is the average percentage of comparisons in which the particular manager was ranked as the more effective member of the pair.

Checklists

Whereas graphic scales require evaluators to record their judgments about the degree or extent to which each ratee demonstrates the behavior or evidences the characteristics in question, checklists require a simple dichotomous response. The rater records whether or not each listed adjective or descriptive statement applies to the employee. The format usually requires placing check-marks next to the applicable items.

When the checklist items are treated as uniformly important signs of effectiveness, the score is simply the total number of affirmative items checked. Alternatively, if the checklist contains both positive and negative items, the score is the algebraic sum of the +1 weights (for positive items) and -1 weights (for negative items). Since every item in the checklist carries the same numerical value as part of the composite, this is termed an *unweighted* checklist.

A *weighted* checklist is one in which each item is weighted to reflect its relative importance. Thus, the items comprising a weighted checklist must undergo prior scaling in order to determine the weight each should carry. (The scaling procedure is similar to that described above for developing a behaviorally anchored scale.)

Although the supervisor responds similarly to weighted and unweighted checklists, they are scored differently. The ratee's score on the weighted checklist is the composite weight—often the median scale value—of the particular items checked as descriptive of him/her. The intent is to permit more important characteristics to carry proportionately heavier weights in the overall evaluation.

A comprehensive weighting endeavor scaled 2,000 statements describing behavior for widely varied jobs (Uhrbrock, 1961). A small sample of these items and their weights is reproduced in Figure 6–5.

FIGURE 6–5
Some generally applicable worker descriptions and their scale values

	Item	Mean	Standard deviation
1.	Is dynamic leader who stimulates enthusiasm.	109.38	2.42
2.	Is an expert on his job.	107.50	4.33
3.	Shows top potential for advancement.	107.50	4.33
4.	Has exceptional skill in motivating others.	105.63	6.09
5.	Quality of work is exceptional.	105.63	6.09
6.	Has an unusual sense of responsibility.	103.75	5.99
7.	May be counted on in a crisis.	103.75	6.96
8.	Is excellent prospect for advancement to position of greater responsibility.	103.75	10.53

Source: R. S. Uhrbrock, "2,000 Scaled Items," *Personnel Psychology* 14 (1961):377.

Forced choice

One difficulty with the checklist, both weighted and unweighted, is transparency. The rater can tell whether he is giving a favorable or unfavorable evaluation. The forced-choice procedure (evolved from research conducted for the military services during World War II) was specifically developed to overcome this potential source of rating error.

In the forced-choice procedure the rater completes a checklist in which the items are grouped (usually in sets of four) as described below. The rater is forced to mark the one statement of the set that is most descriptive and the one that is least descriptive of the ratee. (Variations of this general procedure use sets of two, three, or five statements and instructions to mark only the most or the least descriptive.)

An illustrative tetrad for rating college teachers might be:

a. The instructor used clear and understandable examples and illustrations.
b. The instructor tried to increase the interest of the class in the subject matter.
c. The course material was presented in sufficient detail.
d. The instructor was readily available for consultation with the students.

Certain of the statements in a forced-choice tetrad look more favorable than others. In fact, each tetrad is composed of two pairs of statements with constituents that appear superficially to be equally desirable (or undesirable). However, only one statement of the pair *actually* differentiates between more and less satisfactory performance. In the above illustration, a and b comprise one pair of statements; c and d comprise the other. Although the members of each pair contribute similarly to students' interest in the classroom presentations, items a and c are more critical than their counterparts to the instructor's actual teaching effectiveness.

Prior research establishing two indexes for each statement is prerequisite to pairing the statements. One is an index of *desirability* (or preference) indicating how good or desirable the stated behavior appears superficially to be. The second is a scale value of *importance* of that behavior to the characteristic being rated. Paired statements have similar desirability values but dissimilar indexes of importance.

Since the rater is permitted to mark only the one statement of the pair that is most descriptive, the procedure forces a choice between alternatives that superficially look equally attractive or unattractive. Theoretically it is possible for a supervisor to respond by marking only items which look desirable and yet to assign the ratee an unfavorable evaluation.

Returning to the illustrative tetrad for college teachers, the preference and discrimination indexes established through prior study are given in Figure 6–6 along with the scores generated by various combinations of student responses.

Since the respondent must choose the one most descriptive and the one least descriptive statement, you can see that the instructor is assigned the best score (+2) when students select either (a) or (c) as most descriptive and (b) or (d) as least descriptive of his/her behavior. The converse of these choices generates the lowest score for the tetrad (0); and other choice combinations produce an intermediate score (+1).

Forced-choice checklists have been used for rating in many different occupations including law enforcement, engineering, teaching, and medicine. In addition to their application to performance evaluation, forced-choice procedures have been put to various other psychometric uses including interest, personality, leadership, and attitudinal assessment (Zavala, 1965).

FIGURE 6–6
Scoring a forced-choice tetrad

Instructions to rater: Select the one most descriptive and the one least descriptive statement,

Alternative	Preference value*	Discrimination value*	Scoring weight when chosen as	
			Most descriptive	Least descriptive
a	3.4	3.4	+1	0
b	3.3	2.9	0	+1
c	3.9	3.2	+1	0
d	3.8	2.7	0	+1

* Values estimated on a 4-point scale.

Most studies comparing forced-choice with more conventional rating procedures conclude that forced-choice ratings are more resistant to leniency bias. However, forced-choice rating is no panacea. Extensive preliminary research is required to establish the bases for pairing statements. A further major limitation is its inappropriateness to providing the person rated with diagnostic feedback. Although forced-choice rating may yield a useful criterion measure for making personnel decisions or validating predictors, it does not generate the kind of information that informs persons about their individual strengths and weaknesses.

Mixed standard scales

The mixed standard rating scale is another fairly recent variation of the checklist in an attempt to reduce rating bias and transparency (Blanz & Ghiselli, 1972). This scale consists of statements like those in a checklist. However, instead of merely checking the ones that apply, the rater is asked to indicate whether the person rated is better than, equal to, or worse than the behavior described.

There is also another important difference between mixed standard scales and the more usual checklists. Research preliminary to assembling statements into mixed-standard scales establishes two scale values for each item. The first is a value for the behavior dimension (for example, job knowledge, interpersonal skill, and so on) sampled by the statement. The second is a value for importance or pertinance to that dimension. (This latter value is similar to, but calculated differently from, the importance index developed for forced-choice and weighted checklist items.)

The scale is assembled by randomly arranging statements tapping several performance dimensions and representing various degrees of importance.

The scoring weight given to each response (*better than, equal to, worse than*) is a function of that item's importance to one of the dimensions underlying the scale. Mixed standard scales seek to reduced bias by concealing from the rater both the weights and dimensions attached to each item.

This intriguing approach is still too new for much evidence of its effectiveness to have been accumulated. Although it seems to reduce halo errors, the reliability of the resulting scores is lower than obtained with other procedures (Saal & Landy, 1977). Furthermore, as is true of forced-choice and BARS, the required preliminaries to scale construction are extensive.

WHO SHOULD RATE?

Although performance evaluations ordinarily are the province of the immediate supervisor, there has been considerable research on ratings made by peers, subordinates, and oneself. The primary reason for considering these alternatives to ratings by superiors is that supervisors' familiarity with the ratees' actual behavior (rather than with hearsay about that behavior) may be open to legitimate question. This is clearly the case, for example, with ratings of teacher effectiveness made by department heads who cannot possibly make sustained observations in the classroom.

First-hand familiarity with on-the-job behavior is a clear prerequisite to reliable and valid performance evaluation. Interrater reliabilities in assessing the performance of engineers, for example, were demonstrated to range from only .24 when the ratees were superficially known to the raters up to about .80 when the raters were well-acquainted with the ratees (Landy & Guion, 1970).

For several reasons, the most often explored industrial alternative to supervisory evaluation is peer or co-worker review rather than self-evaluation or evaluation by subordinates. Self-ratings are obviously open to positive bias when a person is, in effect, asked to help determine his/her own salary or future fate within the organization. Self-ratings are, however, sometimes solicited for the purpose of contrasting these with supervisory ratings as a constructive approach to performance feedback (Bassett & Meyer, 1968).

Peer ratings have been fruitfully applied to predicting trainee success in Officer Candidate School and combat effectiveness (Hollander, 1954). Nevertheless, and without implying that one is more accurate than the other, supervisors and peers may be observing or emphasizing somewhat different behavior in making their evaluations (Lawler, 1967). The extent to which supervisory and peer ratings differ is largely a function of differences in the raters' frames of reference: that is, notions about the elements of effectiveness (Borman, 1974). This, together with the likelihood, previously noted, that peers often have a sounder observational basis for making their evaluation probably accounts for differences between ratings obtained from peers and supervisors.

FIGURE 6–7
Supervisory versus peer ratings

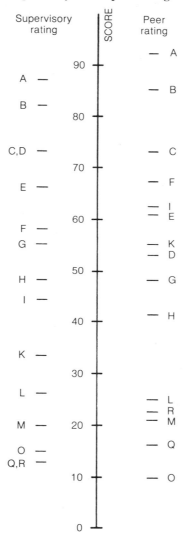

One potentially useful application of securing both supervisory and peer ratings is that the latter can provide additional perspective to supervisors charged with making certain critical personnel decisions. This was the case, for example, with the savings and loan branch manager assessment shown in Figure 6–4. The officers making the assessment were attempting to identify four incumbents for promotion: one to assistant director for operations, and three to district manager. Reasoning that these promotees would have to have the confidence both of top management (the officers) and of the persons who would subsequently become their immediate subordinates, paired-comparison evaluations were solicited from peers as well as the officers. The instructions for both sets of ratings were identical: "Assuming these persons were managing similar branches in similar locations, which would be the better branch manager?" The two sets of ratings, scored as described previously, are shown in Figure 6–7 on the preceding page.

These two sets of ratings are highly correlated (rank-difference correlation = .88) largely due to the fact that all raters were encouraged to evaluate only persons about whose performance they had first-hand knowledge. As you can guess from looking at Figure 6–7, three of the four contemplated promotions were settled easily. The two sets of ratings agreed that branch managers A, B, and C were the strongest candidates. A was promoted to assistant manager for operations; B and C were named district managers. The remaining opening posed something of a problem. As usually occurs with ratings, there was better agreement on the very strongest and weakest persons than on those at neither extreme. The compromise selection made by top management after considering these ratings was to promote E (rather than D) to the remaining district managership. In spite of management's high opinion, candidate D seemed to have too little peer support.

SUMMARY

Appraisals of employee performance may be made for several purposes. One of these, particularly emphasized in this chapter, relates to test validation. Some criterion measure of employee performance is required to validate preemployment predictors.

The chapter distinguishes between performance measures and performance evaluations. The former are objective; the data are matters of record and are essentially judgment-free. Thus, performance measures include evidence of productivity, job tenure, hours lost because of accidents, and so on.

Performance evaluations, on the other hand, are subjectively derived. They often take the form of supervisory ratings, and are necessitated when more objective data are not available.

Although some index of productivity would seem to be an ideal performance criterion for jobs in which employees do something tangible, they are appropriate only when (a) large numbers of employees perform essentially the same task under very similar circumstances and (b) the task is relatively short-cycle and free from external constraints. When these circumstances do not exist, the investigator seeking objective performance measures must turn to such indices as promotions and salary record, job tenure, absenteeism, and so on.

It is usually incorrect to take measures other than productivity as indirect reflections either of productivity or job satisfaction. They are often contaminated by situational factors beyond management and/or employee control.

Therefore, if they are to be used at all, their use must be justified on the basis of their own pertinence rather than because of some presumed relationship to the more fundamental indices of employee effectiveness.

The particular strength of subjective performance evaluations is that they can be made available in the absence of objective measures. However, their subjectivity implies their susceptibility to error and bias. The specific factors potentially invalidating subjective evaluations are distributional errors (leniency, severity, or central tendency), halo effect, egocentric effects (contrast or similarity errors), and sequential effects. Such errors can be controlled somewhat by (a) providing the evaluators with appropriate training and (b) arranging the evaluative format to conteract or minimize the likelihood of error and bias.

Given that the best available appraisal for a particular situation often is subjective, that evaluation may be either relative or absolute. Relative rating procedures compare persons with each other. Absolute ratings compare persons with some external group or standard.

Another distinction between procedures is that between direct and derived ratings. With direct ratings, raters record their evaluations as numerical values. The alternative is to derive the performance evaluation from a set of discretely made judgments.

The discussion of particular approaches to rating considered the relative advantages and disadvantages of ranking, graphic scales, behavioral anchored scales, paired comparisons, checklists, forced-choice procedures, and mixed standard scales.

The chapter concluded with a discussion of alternative raters, including peers and subordinates as well as supervisors.

REFERENCES

Bassett, G. A., & Meyer, H. H.   Performance appraisal based upon self review. *Personnel Psychology*, 1968, *21*, 421–430.

Bernardin, H. J.   Behavioral expectation scales versus summated scales: A fairer comparison. *Journal of Applied Psychology*, 1977, *62*, 422–427.

Blanz, F., & Ghiselli, E. E.   The mixed standard scale: A new rating system. *Personnel Psychology*, 1972, *25*, 185–199.

Borman, W. C.   The rating of individuals in organizations: An alternate approach. *Organizational Behavior and Human Performance*, 1974, *12*, 105–124.

Borman, W. C.   Effects of instructions to avoid halo error on reliability and validity of performance evaluation ratings. *Journal of Applied Psychology*, 1975, *60*, 556–560.

Flanagan, J. C.   The critical incident technique. *Psychological Bulletin*, 1954, *51*, 323–355.

Fogli, L., Hulin, C. L., & Blood, M. R.   Development of first-level behavioral job criteria. *Journal of Applied Psychology*, 1971, *55*, 3–8.

Hollander, E. P.   Military research and industrial applications. *Personnel Psychology*, 1954, *7*, 385–395.

Hulin, C. L.   The measurement of executive success. *Journal of Applied Psychology*, 1962, *46*, 303–306.

Landy, F. J., & Farr, J. L.   Performance rating. *Psychological Bulletin*, 1980, *87*, 72–107.

Landy, F. J., & Guion, R. M.   Development of scales for the measurement of work motivation. *Organizational Behavior and Human Performance*, 1970, *5*, 93–103.

Lawler, E. E.   The multi-trait multi-rater approach to measuring managerial job performance. *Journal of Applied Psychology*, 1967, *51*, 369–381.

Lawshe, C. H., Jr., Kephart, N. C., & McCormick, E. J.   The paired comparisons technique for rating performance of industrial employees. *Journal of Applied Psychology*, 1949, *33*, 69–77.

Saal, F. E., & Landy, F. J.   The mixed standard rating scale: An evaluation. *Organizational Behavior and Human Performance*, 1977, *18*, 19–35.

Schuh, A. J.   The predictability of employee tenure: A review of the literature. *Personnel Psychology*, 1967, *20*, 133–152.

Schultz, D. G., & Siegel, A. I.   Generalized Thurstone and Guttman scales for measuring technical skills in job performance. *Journal of Applied Psychology*, 1961, *45*, 137–142.

Smith, P. C., & Kendall, L. M.   Retranslation of expectations: An approach to the construction of unambiguous anchors for ratings scales. *Journal of Applied Psychology*, 1963, *47*, 149–155.

Uhrbrock, R. S.   2,000 scaled items. *Personnel Psychology*, 1961, *14*, 375–420.

Vielhuber, D. P., & Gottheil, E.   First impressions and subsequent ratings of performance. *Psychological Reports*, 1965, *17*, 916.

Zavala, A.   Development of the forced-choice rating scale technique. *Psychological Bulletin*, 1965, *63*, 117–124.

PREDICTING PERFORMANCE: PERSONNEL SELECTION AND PLACEMENT

Part B focuses on one major aspect of personnel psychology: personnel selection and placement. The elements and chronology of prediction in employment selection are summarized in Figure II–1 on the following page. Note that this sequence begins with the job analysis and then branches in two directions (the "criterion" side, shown on the right, and the "personal characteristics" side, shown on the left). Ultimately, these two directions are brought together to conduct validity studies.

Once the provisional predictors and criteria are identified or developed, the next step is an empirical one. The purpose of the validity study (Chapter 7) may be to investigate the utility of provisional predictors: Which ones efficiently predict the criteria? The results of such a study would delineate the nature of a preemployment selection program. As discussed in Chapter 7, validity is a broad concept extending beyond predictor-criterion relationships to establishing meaningful relationships between other types of variables.

Since the criterion side of this figure was discussed earlier, Chapters 8 and 9 are devoted to assessing personal characteristics like skill, knowledge, aptitude, work history, and so on. When these characteristics are assessed before the criterion measure becomes available (say, as a basis for selecting employees) the associated measures are designated *predictors*.

part B

FIGURE II–1
Employment selection: Investigating predictive validity

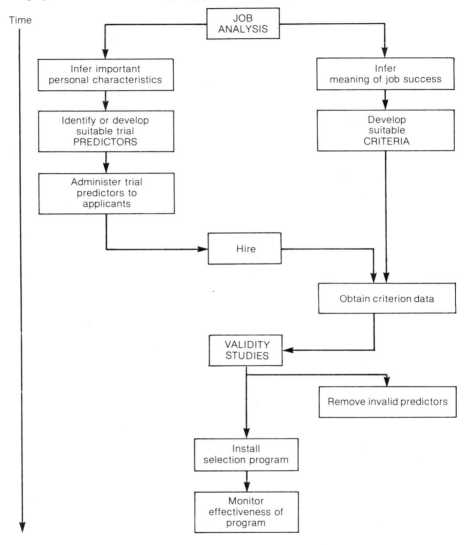

chapter 7

Validity and Prediction

In its broadest definition, validity signifies two concepts. A valid test or other measure (1) accurately reflects the characteristic it purports to measure and (2) permits reasonably accurate predictions or inferences about some other independently obtained measure. This chapter emphasizes the latter concept. However, the two notions are so inextricably related that both merit initial discussion.

TWO TYPES OF VALIDITY

The essential distinction between the two aspects of validity is one of focus. One aspect, designated *descriptive validity*, emphasizes a property of the measuring instrument itself. The other, *criterion-related validity*, emphasizes the utility of the instrument for providing information (or permitting predictions) about something extraneous to the test (APA et al., 1974; Messick, 1980).

Consider a tape measure. It yields readings or scores expressed in inches, feet, and so on. *Descriptive validity* is a property of the tape measure as an instrument. Its scores reflect length and height. The tape measure lacks validity for describing anything that cannot be expressed in these units.

The *criterion-related validity* question applied to the tape-measure asks about characteristics that are systematically associated with (and therefore can be predicted from) the readings or scores it yields. Can we, for example, predict with better than chance accuracy a person's height at maturity from length of trunk measured during infancy? Or, given a person's height can we infer his likely weight more accurately than we could without this information?

Descriptive validities

We do not have direct access to psychologically significant characteristics such as motivation, abilities, and job satisfaction. Indeed, we do not have direct access to what a person knows or can do. All available evidence about such characteristics is indirectly obtained from observing behavior. Persons act; and by systematically observing and measuring these actions we are enabled to *infer* something about the characteristics that make such actions possible.

A psychological test is merely a device for making such systematic observations and measurements. The accuracy of the resulting descriptions of the test-takers is at issue when we speak of descriptive validity.

It is important to recognize that a test, conceptualized as a set of questions which must be answered, is not the only available descriptive device. Any aspect of a person's behavior (including such things as safety record on the job, output or performance data, and absenteeism) is a potential basis for generating broad descriptions of that person as an "effective employee" or a "skillful manager." Thus we need to be concerned with descriptive validity as it relates both to tests of applicant suitability for employment and to criteria of employee effectiveness.

Content validity. The grade you are assigned in a course presumably reflects what you have learned as a result of having taken the course. However, the course examinations cannot possibly give you an opportunity to display everything you have learned. Instead, the examinations are comprised of questions which sample your knowledge. For the examination to have content validity, it must sample the desired knowledges *representatively.* The student who complains that the course examination neglected coverage of important content is questioning the examination's content validity.

As you can see, content validity is largely a matter of judgment. The person responsible for determining what skill, knowledge, or performance is to be measured must also determine whether the test questions provide a comprehensive and representative sample of the larger domain from which they are drawn.

The judgmental basis for establishing content validity may well be empirically grounded. For example, when there is evidence that productivity fluctuates with time of day, the criterion measure of productivity must take this into account by sampling output at various times. Content validity is of concern whenever we wish to generalize from observations of a sample of behavior to the universe or full domain of that behavior.

Construct validity. Often, the measured behavior is taken as a reflection of some more basic or underlying characteristic. We might, for example, wish to infer something about "motivation" from observations of job performance, or about "intelligence" from answers to a set of test questions.

Motivation, intelligence and similar traits are *constructs.* They are concepts which have been constructed lawfully to integrate several related observations. Although constructs cannot be seen or otherwise directly sensed, their existence is deduced from behavior. Thus, the issue of construct validity reduces to a question: Does this so-called intelligence test really measure intelligence? Does this presumed measure of employee effectiveness really reflect characteristics which are part of the construct "effectiveness"?

One way to establish the construct validity of a measure is to examine its relationships with other independently obtained measures of the same construct. In the case of a new intelligence test one could, for example, administer it along with another, more generally accepted, intelligence test. A strong positive correlation between these scores would signify that the two tests are measuring something in common. If we are willing to accept that the more established test measures intelligence, the existence of a positive correlation would then support the construct validity of the new test.

But what about the construct validity of the established test itself? Ultimately, demonstrations of construct validity must rest upon a second approach: that is, hypothesis testing. If intelligence is a reasonable construct, it ought to be associated with such things as learning speed, memory span, and so on. Taking the hypothesized relationship with learning speed, we can empirically ascertain whether persons scoring higher on our test actually learn more quickly. If they do not, either the hypothesis needs revision (and, by implication, something is wrong with the construct) or the new test is measuring something other than intelligence (that is, it lacks construct validity).

Thus, construct validity is less concerned with the usefulness of a psychological measure than it is with the intrinsic nature of that measure. Demonstrations of construct validity merely signify that the scores provide a measure of whatever we intend for them to measure. To establish that an intelligence test has construct validity and that an index of employee effectiveness has construct validity establishes nothing about the relationship between these two measures. That relationship, which is critical to employment selection, requires a demonstration of criterion-related validity.

Criterion-related validities

By now you are well aware that the creation and installation of a preemployment testing program is an empirical endeavor. As with all research, selection studies test hypotheses. The hypotheses tested by these studies concern presumed relationships between one or more predictors (data obtained from applicants) and one or more criteria (data obtained from employees). To the extent that the study supports the hypothesis that the predictors and criteria correlate, we have evidence for criterion-related validity.

We have previously noted that content or construct validity may be established for the predictor and the criterion without implying that there is a relationship (that is, criterion-related validity) between the two. The converse is likewise true. Criterion-related validity can be demonstrated in the absence of content or construct validity. One danger, should this occur, is that of bias. Even though the predictor "works" by allowing accurate forecasts of the criterion, it may work to the detriment of certain classes of job applicants. This issue is expanded later.

There is a second, somewhat subtle danger inherent in interpreting predictor-criterion correlations as evidence of criterion-related validity when descriptive validity has not also been established for both the predictor and the criterion. If, for example, the criterion measure does not really assess the characteristic we wish to predict (say, job effectiveness or some of its constituent elements) the predictor measure is invalid in spite of a correlation with that criterion. To illustrate, suppose the criterion is taken from supervisory ratings made some time after employment. Further, suppose that these ratings themselves lack construct validity. Instead of providing an index of job proficiency, they are heavily contaminated by the rater's assumption that more verbal employees are more "satisfactory." Finally, suppose that the rater's assumption is incorrect. Under these circumstances, a test of verbal fluency administered to applicants would probably correlate with the subsequently obtained supervisory ratings. But since those ratings are themselves invalid (they don't measure what they purport to measure) the correlation is not evidence of useful criterion-related validity.

Predictive validity. The object of establishing criterion-related validity is to develop a basis for making predictions about behavior at some future time. Preemployment selection tests are administered to applicants. We wish to infer, from the applicant's test score, whether he/she would, if hired, be a satisfactory employee.

Therefore, the predictive validation model is the appropriate one for employment testing (Guion, 1976). In general terms, this model requires a demonstration for each predictor that scores earned on it by applicants correlate with subsequently demonstrated proficiency by these same persons as employees. The time lapse between taking the potential predictor measure(s) and obtaining the criterion measure(s) is critical to establishing predictive validity.

Predictive-validity studies can only be undertaken in organizations which have a sufficient flow of applicants and a large enough number of job openings to generate data for meaningful predictor-criterion correlations. What about smaller organizations wishing to include testing in their selection programs? The limitation imposed by small organizational size may require reliance upon *synthetic validity.*

Rather than a study to yield an actual estimate of predictive validity, synthetic validity rests upon the assumption that the same predictors will work for all jobs which make identical human demands (and therefore can be presumed to have identical employee prerequisites). An oversimplification of the synthetic validity concept is to say that a test for which predictive validity has been established in a large organization will likewise be valid for the same job in a small one. The reason this is an oversimplification is that jobs which go by the same title are, to some extent, situation-specific. The duties, and hence the personnel requirements, differ somewhat from one setting to another.

Thus, for synthetic validity to be acceptable, the underlying evidence from which it is assumed must be more convincing than the assertion that the same battery predicted employee success over at company XYZ. One approach to generating the type of basic data required for synthetic validity, with which you are already familiar (from Chapter 4), is to analyze jobs into elements and to identify efficient predictors of those elements (McCormick, 1976). Should this approach succeed in identifying a taxonomy of job elements and of valid predictors for each, synthetic validity would thereby become a plausible substitute in small organizations for predictive validity. The choice of appropriate predictors in such instances would rest upon a careful analysis of the elements of the particular position followed by matching those elements to the comprehensive taxonomy.

Concurrent validity. Correlations between tests and criteria *without* an elapsed time interval are indices of concurrent validity. The usual procedure is to administer the tests being considered for inclusion in a selection battery to a sample of incumbent employees for whom criterion data are also immediately available. The resulting correlations are then often incorrectly taken as estimates of the likely predictive validity of those tests.

Although this procedure is expedient, it does not necessarily substitute for an actual predictive validity study. The expedience is undeniable. Concurrent validity yields an immediate estimate of test-criterion correlations. And management is not required, as with predictive validity, to hire a group of applicants while totally disregarding their scores on the tests undergoing validation.

There are several potentially important differences between concurrent and predictive validation circumstances. The time interval required by predictive validity has important ramifications; employees change between the time they are applicants (and take the tests) and are on the job long enough to provide suitable criterion measures. During this interval they may be specifically trained in work methods; they certainly gain experience; and many of the less satisfied or less proficient employees terminate their employment.

Another potentially important difference between applicants and employees is test-taking motivation. Applicants are presumed to try to do their best on preemployment tests; employees who are subjects for concurrent validation may not be similarly motivated.

It is clear that concurrent validity is not a substitute for predictive validity. Nevertheless, recent comparisons indicate that the practical importance of such conceptual differences between predictive and concurrent validity may have been exaggerated—at least for cognitive predictors (Jensen, 1980; Barrett et al., 1981). This issue bears further study. But caution is still indicated. When concurrent validity studies are undertaken as estimates of predictive validity, their results must be regarded as provisional, pending the outcome of a follow-up analysis of the actual predictive validity of the selection devices.

This is not to say that concurrent validity studies are undertaken solely as an expeditious approximation of predictive validity. Circumstances in which we wish to establish relationships between variables operating in employment itself specifically call for concurrent validity studies. A time lapse between acquiring data for the correlated measures is not called for, for example, when we wish to inquire into the existence of relationships between such things as employee age and work proficiency, employee experience and safety record, or job level and job satisfaction.

TWO ISSUES: SHRINKAGE AND RESTRICTION OF RANGE

Both of these issues are considerations whenever population generalizations are made from data obtained from only a sample of persons from that population. Although they are of broader concern, they are grouped together and discussed here because of their relevance to criterion-related validity.

Shrinkage

Both predictive and concurrent validity estimate the relationship between a predictor (or predictors) and a criterion (or criteria) as that relationship exists for a sample of applicants or incumbents. Once validity is established, the selection program becomes operational. Predictions of job proficiency are thereafter made from the regression line or, more typically, from the appropriate regression equation. Thus, the persons for whom the predictions are made are different from the ones providing the initial validity data.

The effect is to reduce the accuracy of predictions in the new group. The magnitude of such reduction is most marked when predictions involve multiple regression.

That predictive accuracy should be diminished is not surprising. As discussed in Chapter 3, the regression equation is fitted through a least squares solution. In multiple correlation, the predictor weights are empirically established from the data at hand. They best fit a particular set of data generated by a particular sample of persons comprising the validation group. Since no other sample of persons can generate the identical set of data, this regression equation subsequently applied to another group of persons (job applicants after the program has become operational) cannot possibly fit their data as well.

The term *shrinkage* refers to the decline in predictive efficiency from the original sample to the follow-up sample. The practical significance of shrinkage is twofold:

First, the original validity estimate must be obtained from as large a sample of persons as possible. To the extent that sample size is increased, the data thereby obtained come closer to approximating those data for the population.

Second, the original validity estimate must be rechecked using a follow-up sample to which the original regression equation has been applied. This revalidation with a new sample is termed *cross-validation*. Some authors (Campbell, 1976) recommend that a double cross-validation be undertaken. Here, the best estimate of a predictor's true validity is given by averaging the validities obtained by deriving two independent regression equations from two independent samples, and applying each equation to the sample from which it was *not* derived (see Figure 7–1).

FIGURE 7–1
The double cross-validation design

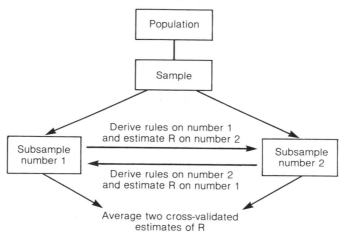

Source: J. P. Campbell, "Psychometric Theory," in Dunnette, ed., *Handbook of Industrial and Organizational Psychology*, p. 214. Copyright © 1976 by Rand McNally College Publishing Company. Used by permission of Houghton Mifflin Company.

There are statistical formulas for estimating shrinkage in R when the obtained multiple regression equation is applied to another sample. However useful such formulas may be for allowing an initial determination about whether the test battery deserves an operational trial, they do not substitute for actual cross-validation.

Restriction of range

Circumstances in test validation (as well as other kinds of research) may cause restriction in the range of available scores. As shown in Figure 7–2, restriction of the predictor or criterion range (or both) enlarges the relative spread of data away from the regression line, thereby lowering the correlation.

What kinds of situations involving validity might generate restriction? Since concurrent validation is undertaken with incumbents, it is reason-

FIGURE 7–2
Restriction of range reduces the correlation

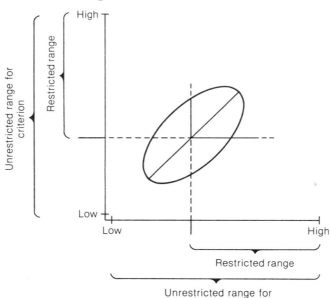

able to assume that the criterion is probably attenuated. Very unsatisfactory employees are probably not included in the sample; they have either terminated their employment voluntarily or have been fired. Additionally, suppose that the covariation you are seeking does, in fact, exist. The restriction in criterion range will then be paralleled by some restriction of the predictor range. The computed validity will thus underestimate the true covariation.

Predictive validity studies also are subject to restriction of range. Since time must elapse between acquiring the predictor and criterion scores, some of the unsatisfactory employees may not remain with the organization long enough to provide you with criterion data. Here the investigator has partial information; whereas the full range of predictor scores is available, the range of the criterion scores may quite possibly be curtailed.

A final illustration will suffice to clarify the problem of range restriction. Selection often involves multiple hurdles: Applicants must pass some initial screening requirement(s) (like demonstrating typing proficiency, or giving evidence of high school graduation) before the remaining selection instruments are administered. To the extent that the initial hurdle correlates with the remaining selection instruments, its use in eliminating candidates reduces the survivors' ranges of scores on the remaining tests. Further, to the extent that the initial hurdle is itself valid, its use also restricts the range of criterion performance which ultimately will be displayed by these survivors.

Various correction formulas can be applied to estimate the magnitude of the validity as if the full range of scores had been available (Thorndike, 1949; Gulliksen, 1950). However, in common with all correction formulas, these make certain assumptions which may deviate significantly from the realities of particular situations (Linn, 1968).

PREDICTION FOR SELECTION

Assuming we have established the existence of a correlation between predictor and criterion scores, two issues yet remain to be resolved: (1) We must determine whether the correlation signifies a sufficiently strong relationship to justify using the predictor for preemployment screening. (2) If a screening test is used, the minimum acceptable (passing) test score must be established.

As we will see, the resolution of these matters is conditioned by both statistical and nonstatistical considerations. The latter involve decisions about such things as: the definition of satisfactory job performance; the cost-benefit ratio of further improvements in the existing selection program; the possibility and/or desirability of recruiting more intensively in order to generate a larger and stronger applicant pool; whether it is preferable to select only applicants who have a very high probability of job success, or to provide employment opportunities to applicants for whom such success, although possible, is less probable. Certain of these decisions, like the last one cited, are overlain with value judgments.

Two kinds of selection errors

Whereas preemployment tests and the criteria against which they are validated are ordinarily continuous variables (with scores for each ranging from very low to very high), selection programs usually lead to a dichotomous determination: The applicant is hired or rejected. Given this outcome, the practical questions about validity usually reduce the predictor and criterion to discrete, often dichotomous, variables. Has the applicant passed or failed the test? Will he/she be a satisfactory or unsatisfactory employee?

The consequences of selection when the variables are dichotomized are shown in Figure 7–3. Satisfactory criterion performance is arbitrarily defined for this figure as job proficiency at level p or better. Since we wish to predict a minimum criterion score of p, the best point prediction results from test score t. All applicants scoring at or above t will be hired.

As usual, the correlational scattergram is schematically delineated by an elipse. The lettered segments of this elipse signify the following consequences of selection based upon prediction from the regression line:

A. *Accurate positives:* Applicants passing the test (and therefore hired) who subsequently prove to be satisfactory employees.

FIGURE 7–3
Prediction outcomes

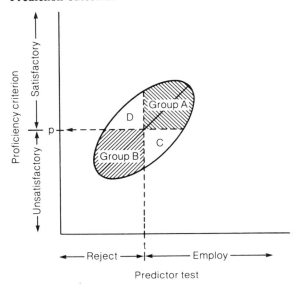

Predictor test

B. *Accurate negatives:* Applicants failing the test (and rejected) who would, if they had been hired, have proven to be unsatisfactory employees.
C. *False positives:* Applicants passing the test (and hired) who subsequently prove to be unsatisfactory employees.
D. *False negatives:* Applicants failing the test (and rejected) who would, if they had been hired, have proven to be satisfactory employees.

The predictions for Groups A and B are correct; those for Groups C and D are incorrect. Hence, the proportion of accurate predictions is

$$\frac{A + B}{A + B + C + D}$$

This proportion is fixed by the magnitude of the validity coefficient, the distributions of test and criterion scores, and the definition of satisfactory job proficiency.

Two emphases in selection

Given some proportion of accurate predictions, is this proportion sufficiently high to warrant using the test for selection? And if this predictor *is* used, *how* should it be used?

The answers to these questions require a judgment about the erroneous predictions. Is it worse for the selection program to generate false positives or false negatives? Or are both types of error equally deleterious to organizational and societal objectives?

The traditional emphasis in selection has been to structure the program to reduce the incidence of false positives; that is, to reduce the number of ultimately unsatisfactory employees who are passed by the preemployment screening test. This emphasis has a human cost: Reductions in the incidence of false positives are accompanied by increases in the incidence of false negatives. Not only do the potentially satisfactory employees thereby rejected suffer; the organization also suffers, since it is deprived of their services.

Whether the traditional emphasis is justified depends upon one's values and how one reckons costs. Intangible human cost and the values issue aside, the traditional approach may entail more extensive (and expensive) applicant recruiting efforts by the organization. The dollar cost has to be weighed against the organization's saving through reducing the incidence of false positives. And there are undesirable direct and indirect costs to society (with employing organizations each carrying a share of the burden) of willing and potentially satisfactory employees who are unemployed.

Clearly, this is a set of issues which will not be resolved in these pages. Indeed, a generalized resolution cannot be formulated.

What are the alternatives to the traditional emphasis upon reducing the proportion of false positives? One rather obvious one is to emphasize reductions in the incidence of false negatives. Since this would simultaneously increase the number of false positives, it is rarely seriously entertained. A second alternative, often preferable to the traditional one, is to optimize selection: that is, to structure the program so it maximizes the proportion of correct decisions consistent with minimizing the selection errors of both types.

The implementation of programs directed (a) solely towards reducing false positives and (b) towards optimizing the false positive-false negative balance are considered in the following sections.

Reducing false positives

You know from our earlier discussion that, other things being equal, higher validity coefficients lead to more accurate predictions. Assuming a constant validity coefficient, two other interactive elements influence the nature of selection programs focused on reducing the incidence of false positives: (a) the base rate and (b) the selection ratio. We will discuss each element briefly before considering the nature of their interaction.

Base rate. The base rate is the proportion of employees performing satisfactorily *before* the selection program is introduced. Suppose of the present group of employees selected without the predictor in question, only 30 percent is regarded as "satisfactory." There clearly is room for improvement of the selection process. And some improvement can be anticipated even by adding a predictor with only moderately high validity.

However, the situation is quite different when a high proportion (say 80 percent) of the present employees are regarded as satisfactory. With the existing selection program the chances are only 2 in 10 of making an incorrect hiring decision. To reduce this chance of an erroneous hiring decision even further requires insertion into the selection program of a predictor with very high validity.

Selection ratio.   The selection ratio is simply:

$$\frac{\text{Number of applicants hired}}{\text{Total number of applicants}}$$

An organization that must hire 80 of each 100 applicants in order to fill its vacancies cannot afford to be as choosy as one that hires only 20 of each 100 applicants. The latter organization is in the advantageous position of having a low selection ratio. Therefore, it can afford to be stringent in setting the passing score for any new test considered for inclusion in the selection program. When the selection ratio is high, the company is compelled by its need to fill vacant positions to hire most applicants—even those with relatively low predictor scores.

Setting the passing score.   The relationship between the base rate, the selection ratio, and the passing score established for a preemployment test is clarified in Figure 7–4.

FIGURE 7–4
Relationship between selection ratio and proportion of satisfactory employees

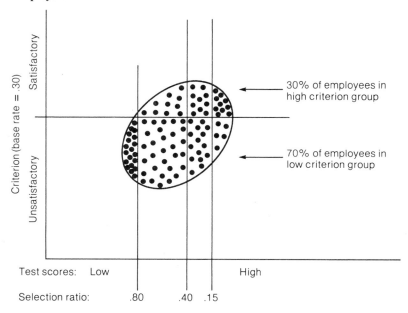

This figure shows a scatterplot of test scores against criterion performance for 100 employees in a company in which 30 percent of the employees are regarded as satisfactory. If we disregarded the new test and selected on the old basis, it is likely that we would continue to find that 30 percent of our newly hired employees would prove to be in the satisfactory criterion group.

Note what happens to the proportions of satisfactory and unsatisfactory employees as a function of establishing various passing scores on this test. A high selection ratio (say, .80) signifies proportionately few applicants relative to the number of vacant positions. As shown in Figure 7–4, of each 80 applicants thus selected, we will obtain 30 who will eventually be in the satisfactory criterion group and 50 who will eventually prove to be unsatisfactory. Given this selection ratio, the new test will improve the proportion of satisfactory employees from the present figure of 30 percent to 37.5 percent (30/80).

Predictive efficiency is improved further if the passing score can be set for a lower selection ratio. Suppose we had a sufficient number of applicants relative to vacancies to be able to select only 40 of each 100 applicants. As shown in Figure 7–4, this will have two effects. First, a number of applicants will be rejected who would have proven to be satisfactory employees. However, the number of such false negatives will be much lower than the number of potentially unsatisfactory employees simultaneously rejected (accurate negatives). Thus the second effect of this more stringent passing score will be to improve the program still further. In this case we would obtain 20 employees who will eventually be in the satisfactory criterion group and 20 who will eventually be in the unsatisfactory criterion group. The selective efficiency is here improved from its present level of 30 percent to 50 percent.

Finally, if the labor market permits, a still greater gain in predictive efficiency will come from setting the passing score even higher. Figure 7–4 shows what will happen if the selection ratio can be reduced to .15. For every 15 applicants selected, 10 will be satisfactory and only 5 will be unsatisfactory employees. Predictive efficiency under these circumstances has risen to 10/15 or 67 percent.

Group predictions.   We have seen, *given a particular validity coefficient,* that the efficiency of a particular passing score for reducing false positives is influenced by two factors: the base rate and the selection ratio.

The practical question when installing a new selection program might be phrased: "Given our selection ratio and a predictor with a specified validity (say, .55), how much improvement in criterion performance will be generated by this program?" (This question can, of course, be modified by substituting desired criterion performance as one of the givens and solving either for the needed selection ratio or for the prerequisite validity.

Naylor and Shine (1965) formulated tables which answer this question in terms of the *change in average criterion score* from the original situation (before the new predictor is used) to the anticipated situation after introducing the new predictor. Another approach has been provided by the Taylor-

Russell tables (1939) in which improvement is expressed in terms of anticipated increase over the base rate. Thus, to use the Taylor-Russell tables we need to know the original base rate (proportion of satisfactory employees) in addition to the selection ratio and the validity coefficient.

The full set of Taylor-Russell tables is reproduced in the Appendix. There is one such table for each base rate in increments of 10 percentage points.

To illustrate their use, let's assume we have a selection ratio of .60 (that is, we hire 6 of every 10 applicants), a base rate of 70 percent (7 out of 10 present employees perform satisfactorily) and a validity coefficient for the proposed new predictor of .55.

We need to consult the table for a base rate of .70, portions of which are reproduced as Table 7–1. Entering this table for the appropriate column (a

TABLE 7–1
Portions of the Taylor-Russell table where proportion of employees considered satisfactory is .70

r						Selection Ratio					
	0.05	0.10	0.20	0.30	0.40	0.50	0.60	0.70	0.80	0.90	0.95
0.00	0.70	0.70	0.70	0.70	0.70	0.70	0.70	0.70	0.70	0.70	0.70
0.05	0.73	0.73	0.72	0.72	0.72	0.71	0.71	0.71	0.71	0.70	0.70
0.10	0.77	0.76	0.75	0.74	0.73	0.73	0.72	0.72	0.71	0.71	0.70
0.15	0.80	0.79	0.77	0.76	0.75	0.74	0.73	0.73	0.72	0.71	0.71
0.45	0.94	0.93	0.90	0.87	0.85	0.83	0.81	0.78	0.76	0.73	0.72
0.50	0.96	0.94	0.91	0.89	0.88	0.86	0.83	0.81	0.78	0.74	0.72
0.55	0.97	0.96	0.93	0.91	0.90	0.87	0.85	0.82	0.79	0.75	0.73
0.60	0.98	0.97	0.95	0.92	0.92	0.89	0.86	0.83	0.80	0.75	0.73
0.90	1.00	1.00	1.00	1.00	0.99	0.98	0.95	0.91	0.85	0.78	0.74
0.95	1.00	1.00	1.00	1.00	1.00	0.99	0.98	0.94	0.86	0.78	0.74
1.00	1.00	1.00	1.00	1.00	1.00	1.00	1.00	1.00	0.88	0.78	0.74

Source: Taylor & Russell, "The Relationship of Validity Coefficients to the Practical Effectiveness of Tests in Selection: Discussion and Tables," *Journal of Applied Psychology*, 1939, *32*, pp. 595–600.

selection ratio of .60) and row (predictive validity of .55), we see that adding this test to present selection procedures would improve our predictive efficiency: 70 percent of the employees acquired through the old program were satisfactory; the new program increases this to 85 percent.

Examine the entries in Table 7–1 for other combinations of selection ratio and predictive validity. Note that an invalid test ($r = 0.00$) cannot improve the proportion of satisfactory employees irrespective of the selection ratio. Holding the selection ratio constant, the proportion of satisfactory employees increases as a function of increased validity.

Finally, note how the selection ratio itself interacts with the other determinants of predictive efficiency. Since predictive accuracy increases with increased validity, management can be more selective. For example, with a validity coefficient of .55, the proportion of satisfactory employees selected will be 97 percent with a selection ratio of .05, but only 73 percent with a selection ratio of .95.

Both the Naylor-Shine and the Taylor-Russell tables assume that the predictor-criterion correlation is linear (Smith, 1948). They cannot be used for curvilinear relationships. Also, both sets of tables make no predictions about the likelihood of success of an individual applicant; they permit estimates of selection efficiency for the group of applicants as a whole. (Other tables—Lawshe, Bolda, Brune, & Auclair, 1958—address the issue of predictor accuracy for individual applicants.)

"Optimizing" selection

The alternative to a selection program designed solely to reduce false positives is one designed to minimize decision errors of both kinds: that is, to bring the total number of false positives and false negatives to a minimum.

Locating the critical score. The critical score is that score on the test which minimizes all decision errors. Therefore it is the passing score set for the predictor when selection is to be optimized.

Look again at Figure 7–3, and visualize the distributions of predictor scores earned by satisfactory employees (groups A and D combined) and unsatisfactory employees (groups B and C combined). You should have visualized distributions like those shown in Figure 7–5. Since the predictor and criterion are correlated, the mean predictor score for the satisfactory employees must be above the mean for the unsatisfactory employees.

The critical score is given by the point of intersection of the two distributions (Cureton, 1957). Were this to be established as the passing score, the small shaded area of Figure 7–5 would represent false positives and the small

FIGURE 7–5
Critical score

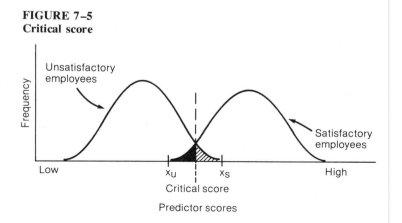

blackened area would represent false negatives. You may wish to visually manipulate the indicated critical score upward and downward: Movement in either direction will increase the *total* number of erroneous predictions, although such manipulation will reduce *either* the number of false positives or false negatives.

So far so good! The critical score minimizes both types of prediction error. And if the validity coefficient were increased, the difference between subgroup means would become greater, causing the critical score to generate still fewer prediction errors. But there are exceptions.

Predictive utility

Irrespective of the selection focus—whether on reducing false positives or on optimizing selection—its cost-effectiveness is an issue of theoretical and practical concern.

The theoretical formulations of this issue (for example, Cronbach & Gleser, 1965) deal with programs for optimizing selection. The key unknown with which these formulations grapple is specification of the program's utility or payoff. Intuitively, efficiency for managerial selection has greater utility to the organization (offsetting additional selection costs) than does efficiency in selecting employees for more routine assignments. But how can these relative utilities be specified? And what are the relative utilities of false negatives versus false positives, or of accurate negatives and positives (Darlington & Stauffer, 1966)?

These questions, though critical to making final decisions about selection program effectiveness, are usually ignored by organizations implementing that program (Campbell, 1976). We anticipate that further development of utility theory will ultimately lead to improved practice in this respect.

FAIRNESS IN SELECTION

In addition to being valid, selection programs must be fair to all applicants. Some of the technical ramifications of "fairness" are discussed later in this chapter. However, the intent is not technical at all. Title VII of the Civil Rights Act of 1964 makes it illegal to hire (or promote or set salaries) on the basis of tests which are biased in favor of a particular race, color, religion, or national origin and, by extension, of either sex. The administrative interpretation of this act appears in the *Uniform Guidelines on Employee Selection Principles* (EEOC, 1978). These *Guidelines* and subsequent decisions about their implementation properly broadens and clarifies the meaning of tests to include all personnel screening measures including interviews, application blanks, tests of physical strength or coordination, and so on.

A landmark legal decision on this matter was *Griggs* v. *Duke Power Company* (1971). In its decision the U.S. Supreme Court held that the interpretations of the enforcement agency (EEOC) were entitled to "great deference." Further, the Court held that the *employer* bears the burden of proving that employment selection measures are job related.

Unfair personnel practices are, by definition, those producing an adverse impact upon a group protected by Title VII without satisfactorily demonstrating business neccessity. The established legal sequence is essentially as follows (Gordon, 1978).

The courts tend to look first at whether the use of a selection procedure appears to be illegal by disproportionately disqualifying a protected minority group. If so, the selecting organization must provide the court with evidence of the validity of its selection program for differentiating between potentially satisfactory and unsatisfactory employees. Even if the employer provides satisfactory evidence of validity, "it remains open to the complaining party to show that other tests or selection devices, without a similarly undesirable social effect, would also serve the employer's legitimate interest in efficient and trustworthy workmanship." (*Albermarle Paper Co.* v. *Moody,* 1975, p. 1184.)

From the foregoing it is clear that fairness and validity are related but separate concepts. Consider a rather widely used preemployment requirement: high school graduation. The 1980 *Statistical Abstract of the United States* published by the U.S. Bureau of Census reports that as of 1979, 69.7 percent of all whites had completed high school as compared with 49.4 percent of blacks and 42 percent of persons of Spanish origin. Thus, proportionately fewer nonwhite applicants can be expected to satisfy the requirement of high school graduation.

Whether or not the requirement *actually* is unfair depends upon both the data concerning adverse impact and the data concerning validity. Census figures to the contrary, an organization may, through its intensive minority recruiting efforts, succeed in holding to this educational requirement without adverse impact upon protected minorities. Assuming adverse impact, the legality of the requirement hinges upon justification through demonstrated validity. Thus, the Equal Employment Opportunity Commission ruled that a union representing bricklayers working for a steel manufacturer violated Title VII by not admitting blacks into its apprenticeship training program. The union argument (that blacks were excluded because none had graduated from high school) failed because the union could provide no proof of a relationship between high school graduation and successful performance as a brick mason (EEOC Decision No. 72-0495, 1971).

Conversely, a court ruling in another case (*Head* v. *Timken Roller Bearing Co.,* 1971) found that the employer did not violate Title VII by requiring apprenticeship applicants to have graduated from high school—with a grade average of C—even though many fewer blacks than whites satisfied the requirement. The ruling in favor of the company took into account that the employer had established the job-relatedness of this requirement.

A concept of fairness

A test is not unnecessarily unfair or biased because different subgroups earn different mean scores on it. Women as a group, for example, score less well than men on tests of arm and hand strength. This alone does not signify that the tests are biased; they probably reflect a genuine difference between groups. Furthermore, knowing that there is variability in any set of test scores, you are aware that this difference between group means does not specify any *individual's* strength. In spite of the mean difference, some women will score higher on these tests than some men.

Judgments of possible bias in selection rest upon the use made of test scores. The score itself has no intrinsic value; its value depends upon the accuracy of predictions from it. Hence, for a test to be fair it must predict the criterion equally well for all persons to whom it is given.

This notion of fairness has been embodied in several related concepts advanced by different authors. Guion (1966, p. 26) speaks of discrimination when "persons with equal probabilities of success on the job have unequal probabilities of being hired for the job." Given two persons who would prove to be equally satisfactory employees if given the chance, a test causing one to be hired and the other to be rejected is, by this definition, unfair to the rejected applicant.

How could such a situation arise? To the extent that a test requires us to display knowledge acquired at some previous time (and this requirement is characteristic even of most so-called intelligence and aptitude tests) two persons' scores have the same intrinsic meaning only if both have had equal learning opportunities. Equal opportunities for learning implies more than merely going to the same (or essentially equivalent) schools. It implies, in addition, the same cultural emphasis upon learning, time not otherwise committed (for example, to supplementing family income), and informal opportunities for learning from books, magazines, adult models, and so on. Furthermore, it implies the same conviction that learning is itself profitable, and that society will not judge you on the basis of such irrelevancies as who you are, where you come from, your race, sex, or age.

It is therefore not surprising that a test score may have different intrinsic meanings for members of different racial or other subgroups. *When such differences in intrinsic meaning of the test score are paralled by comparable differences in criterion performance, the test is not biased.* Certainly no one will argue unfairness when the patient asks the prospective brain surgeon to provide some preoperative assurance that he/she knows how to do brain surgery!

However, when differences in the intrinsic meaning of the test are *not* paralleled by comparable differences in the criterion, and when that test is used to predict performance on that criterion, the selection program is biased. It unfairly rejects persons who might have done as well or better on the job than the persons selected.

Dunnette (1974) enlarged the concern for individuals to a concern for groups in stating "discrimination against a minority group occurs when, over the long run, a firm's personnel decisions yield higher proportions of reject errors for members of the minority group than for members of the majority group.'' To prevent such a situation from occuring, he suggested implementation of the selection model shown earlier in Figure 5–6.

Both Dunnette's statement about fairness and Guion's statement (presented earlier) have a straightforward implication: An employment test is unfair when it systematically overestimates or underestimates likely job success for members of any applicant subgroup. The usual connotation of unfairness is that the test underestimates for minority applicants and/or overestimates for nonminority applicants. Consequently, it leads to rejection of a disproportionate number of minority applicants who would, if they had been hired, have proven to be satisfactory employees.

Thus, a test is unfair if it generates different validities for minority and nonminority subgroups, and if appropriate correctives are not applied. Evidence that the test is fair consists of demonstrating either that no such differential validity exists or, if differential validity is established, in demonstrating that appropriate corrections have been applied to insure unbiased selection.

However, differential validity coefficients are not the only basis for potentially biased selection. As we will describe in the next section, there are circumstances in which the validity coefficients in two subgroups are essentially similar, and which nonetheless are potential sources of biased selection.

Whenever a corrective is applied, it implies that predictions must be made differently for applicants from each subgroup in order to insure fairness. It is to the broad issue of *differential prediction* (including, but not limited to, differential validity) that we now turn our attention.

CIRCUMSTANCES REQUIRING DIFFERENTIAL PREDICTION

A validity study that does not attend to the issue of possible bias ignores applicant subgroups when the predictor and criterion are correlated. Such a study combines all data into a single scatterplot generating a single regression line from which predictions are made in the same way for all applicants. Systematic prediction errors for one or another subgroup following this procedure would constitute evidence of bias (Cleary, 1968).

Possible bias in selection can take numerous forms, each of which has several variations (Bartlett & O'Leary, 1969; Barrett, 1978.) For our purposes, these are reduced to just five: two cases shown in Figure 7–6 where differential prediction is not called for, and three cases shown in Figure 7–7 requiring differential prediction.

Both figures are arranged similarly. Each case compares the validity coefficients separately obtained in two subgroups: Group A (solid regression line); Group B (dashed regression line). The validity coefficients are shown as ellipses defining the limits of their scattergrams. The slope of the regres-

FIGURE 7–6
Cases not requiring differential prediction

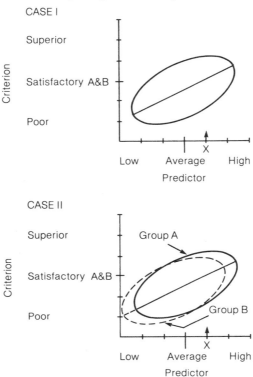

sion line corresponds to the validity coefficient. For all cases shown in both figures, the minimum level of criterion performance we wish to predict is designated "satisfactory."

Differential prediction not needed

Two general cases not calling for differential prediction are shown in Figure 7–6.

In Case I both groups have identical validity coefficients and score distributions. Since this is so, the correlation elipses overlap completely. The predictor operates with the same efficiency for Groups A and B. Therefore, predictor score X is equally appropriate as a preemployment requirement for both subgroups.

In Case II the validity coefficients are again identical. However, here Group A scores higher than Group B on both the predictor and the criterion. Assuming the criterion itself is not biased, a uniformly applied passing score

FIGURE 7–7
Cases requiring differential prediction

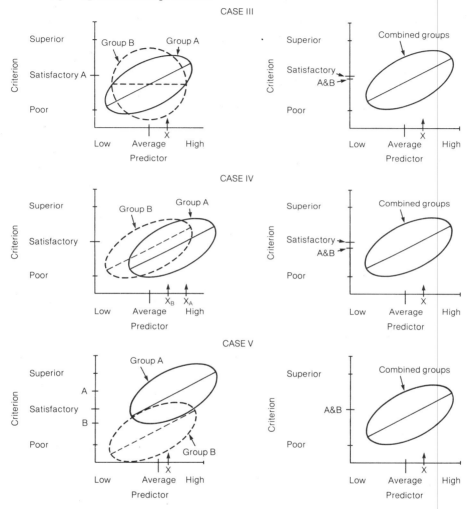

on the preemployment test is indicated, even though this will cause more Group A than Group B applicants to be hired.

Differential prediction is required

Three general cases are shown in Figure 7–7.

Case III shows a situation in which the predictor is valid for Group A, but invalid for Group B. This is an extreme illustration of differential validity, assuming that the difference between the two validity coefficients is statistically significant.

As you know, a correlation of 0.00 signifies only chance accuracy in prediction. Hence, use of this predictor for selecting employees from Group B would be unjustified. However, selection from Group A could still proceed on the basis of a minimum required test score of X.

As shown in Figure 7–7, the existence of differential validity is obscured when the data from the two subgroups are combined. For the combined group, a test score of X still predicts satisfactory criterion performance. But predictions from the combined regression line will systematically underpredict performance for persons in Group A, and overpredict performance for members of Group B.

Such systematic prediction error defines bias. The effect, in this case, is to cause unjustified rejections of Group B applicants. Likewise, it causes rejection of a number of Group A applicants who would, if given the opportunity, have proven to be satisfactory employees.

Another instance calling for differential prediction is shown as Case IV. Here differential validity is not evident; the correlations in the two groups are identical. However, note the difference in the regression line *intercepts:* that is, the point at which they cross the ordinate. This difference results because, while Group A outscores Group B on the predictor, both groups evidence the same criterion performance. Thus, the appropriate critical score for selecting applicants from Group A is X_A whereas the appropriate one for Group B applicants is X_B.

Again, this difference is masked without a moderated analysis. As shown for the combined data, a uniformly applied critical score of X would have unfairly favored applicants from Group A over those from Group B.

Case V is a variation of Case IV. The validity coefficients for the subgroups are again the same, but the intercepts differ because of differences in both the predictor and criterion score distributions. Were the data to be combined and a common regression line used for prediction, job performance would be underestimated for Group A and overestimated for Group B.

The standard recommendation for all three cases shown in Figure 7–7 is to predict separately for each subgroup (Kirkpatrick, Ewen, Barrett, & Katzell, 1968). By so doing, each applicant is evaluated with respect to the level of criterion performance predicted for his/her own group.

Differential validity

We have seen that the need for differential prediction to insure fairness may result from two sources: (*a*) differential validity, as in Figure 7–7, Case III, and (*b*) different intercepts, as in Cases IV and V, in spite of identical validities. Some further comments about differential validity are in order.

Evidence for its widespread existence is not overwhelming. What appears at first glance as differential validity is often shown, upon closer examination, to be a statistical or procedural artifact (Boehm, 1972; Humphreys, 1973). Reviewing 31 studies containing 297 instances of significant validity for at least one subgroup, Boehm (1977) found only 24 instances of differential validity (contained in 16 different studies). She does not regard this as persuasive evidence that differential validity is a frequent occurrence.

Others are either somewhat more (Katzell & Dyer, 1977) or less (Hunter & Schmidt, 1978) disposed to conclude that differential validity is a real occurrence. But most agree with Guion (1972) that it occurs rarely, if at all.

This is not to say that the possibility of differential validity can be ignored. Test validation procedures must still take into account that differential validity may be demonstrated. And in the relatively rare instance where its existence is verified, differential prediction is required.

SUMMARY

We differentiated between two complementary types of validity: (1) descriptive validity, which emphasizes validity as a property of the measuring instrument and (2) criterion-related validity, which emphasizes the instrument's usefulness for providing information (or permitting predictions) about something extraneous to the test.

Two varieties of descriptive validity are (a) content and (b) construct validity. Content validity is largely a matter of judgment that the measure in question reflects a representative sample of the behaviors it purports to assess. Construct validity implies empirical corroboration that the measure assesses the intended construct. Neither content nor construct validity by themselves establish the value of the measure as a basis for predicting criteria.

Thus, the second type of validity (criterion-related) is critical to selection research. This research tests the hypothesized relationship between the provisional predictor(s) and the criterion (or criteria). The model for testing criterion-related validity is the predictive validity model. Here, the provisional selection tests are administered to applicants who are hired without regard for their test scores. These scores are then correlated with a subsequently obtained criterion. This model has two important features from a research perspective: (1) the predictors are administered to job applicants. (2) A period of time is allowed to elapse before the criterion measure is made available.

Concurrent validation procedures are more expedient. Here, predictor-criterion correlations are established using a sample of persons (usually incumbents) for whom both measures are simultaneously available.

Two issues when generalizing from obtained correlations are particularly relevant to criterion-related validity: shrinkage, and the effects of restriction of range. Once the selection program becomes operational, the subsequently obtained predictor-criterion correlation will usually shrink below the value originally estimated. Although there are statistical formulas for estimating likely shrinkage, these estimates do not substitute for an actual follow-up (cross-validation) study. In addition to reflecting possible shrinkage, correlations obtained through cross-validation tend to be lower than the original estimates for another reason: restriction of score range. Once the test battery is used for selection, applicants who score low are rejected. In effect, this causes the bottom ends of the predictor and criterion distributions to be "lost." Therefore, obtained cross-validation coefficients are ordinarily statistically adjusted to compensate for range restriction.

Because validity coefficients are imperfect, employment selection programs are likewise imperfect. The prediction errors are of two types: false positives (hiring applicants who subsequently prove to be unsatisfactory employees), and false negatives (rejecting potentially satisfactory applicants). Traditionally, selection programs concentrated on reducing the incidence of false positives. This strategy simultaneously increases the proportion of false negatives, thereby raising several socially significant value judgments. An alternative is to design the selection program to minimize decision errors of both types.

In addition to being valid, all personnel assessment procedures (including preemployment tests) are required to be fair. Fairness and validity are related but separate concepts. For an employment test to be fair it must predict the criterion equally well for all persons to whom it is given. In other words, it must not exert a systematic adverse impact upon specific groups of applicants (women, blacks, and so on).

Differential validity (indicating that the test is more valid for one group than another) has clear implications for appropriate corrective action in order to insure fairness. Although the evidence accumulated over the past 20 years or so indicates that differential validity is a relatively rare finding, differential prediction (setting different passing scores) may nonetheless be appropriate. As emphasized in this chapter, fairness in selection requires that persons equally likely to succeed on the criterion must be provided equal employment opportunities.

REFERENCES

Albermarle Paper Company v. *Moody*, 45 L. Ed. 2nd 301 (1975).

American Psychological Association, American Educational Research Association, & National Council on Measurement in Education. *Standards for educational and psychological tests*. Washington, D.C.: American Psychological Association, 1974. Seventy-six pages.

Barrett, G., Phillips, J., & Alexander, R. Concurrent and predictive validity designs: A critical reanalysis. *Journal of Applied Psychology*, 1981, *66*, 1–6.

Barrett, R. S. *Statistical diagrams for zetetic for testers II*. Hastings on Hudson, New York: R. S. Barrett, 1978.

Bartlett, C. J., & O'Leary, B. S. A differential prediction model to moderate the effects of heterogeneous groups in personnel selection and classification. *Personnel psychology*, 1969, *22*, 1–17.

Boehm, V. R. Negro-white differences in validity of employment and training selection procedures: Summary of recent evidence. *Journal of Applied Psychology*, 1972, *56*, 33–39.

Boehm, V. R. Differential prediction: A methodological artifact? *Journal of Applied Psychology*, 1977, *62*, 146–154.

Campbell, J. P. Psychometric theory. In M. D. Dunnette (Ed.), *Handbook of industrial and organizational psychology*. Chicago: Rand McNally, 1976, 185–222.

Cleary, T. A. Test bias: Prediction of grades of Negro and white students in integrated colleges. *Journal of Educational Measurement*, 1968, *5*, 115–124.

Cronbach, L. J., & Gleser, G. C. *Psychological tests and personnel decisions*. Urbana, Ill.: University of Illinois Press, 1965.

Cureton, E. E. A recipe for a cookbook. *Psychological Bulletin*, 1957, *54*, 494–497.

Darlington, R. B., & Stauffer, G. F. Use and evaluation of discrete test information in decision making. *Journal of Applied Psychology*, 1966, *50*, 125–129.

Dunnette, M. D. Personnel selection and job placement of the disadvantaged: Problems, issues, and suggestions. In H. L. Fromkin & J. J. Sherwood (Eds.), *Integrating the Organization*. New York: Free Press, 1974.

EEOC Decision No. 72-0495, 4 FEP Cases 307 (1971).

Equal Employment Opportunity Coordinating Council. Uniform guidelines on employee selection procedures. *Federal Register*, 1978, 38290–38315.

Gordon, S. R. The impact of fair employment laws on training. *Training and Development Journal*, November 1978, 29–44.

Griggs v. *Duke Power Co.* 401 U.S. 424(1971), 3EPD P8137, 3FEP 175.

Guion, R. M. Employment tests and discriminatory hiring. *Industrial Relations*, 1966, *5*, 20–37.

Guion, R. M. Implications for governmental regulatory agencies. In L. A. Crooks (Ed.), *An investigation of sources of bias in the prediction of job performance*. Princeton, N.J.: Educational Testing Service, 1972.

Guion, R. M. Recruiting, selection, and placement. In M. D. Dunnette (Ed.), *Handbook of industrial and organizational psychology*. Chicago: Rand McNally, 1976, 777–828.

Gulliksen, H. *Theory of mental tests*. New York: Wiley, 1950.

Head v. *Timken Roller Bearing Co.*, 6 FEP Cases 803 (1972).

Humphreys, L. G. Statistical definitions of test validity for minority groups. *Journal of Applied Psychology*, 1973, *58*, 1–4.

Hunter, J. E., & Schmidt, F. L. Differential and single group vallidity of employment tests by race: A critical analysis of three recent studies. *Journal of Applied Psychology*, 1978, *63*, 1–11.

Jensen, A. R. *Bias in mental testing*. New York: Free Press, 1980.

Katzell, R. A., & Dyer, F. J. Differential validity revisited. *Journal of Applied Psychology*, 1977, *62*, 137–145.

Kirkpatrick, J. J., Ewen, R. B., Barrett, R. S., & Katzell, R. A. *Testing and Fair Employment.* New York: New York University Press, 1968.

Lawshe, C. H., Bolda, R. A. Brune, R. L., & Auclair, G. Expectancy Charts III: Their theoretical development. *Personnel Psychology,* 1958, *11,* 545–599.

Linn, R. L. Range restriction problems in the use of self-selection groups for test validation. *Psychological Bulletin,* 1968, *69,* 69–73.

McCormick, E. J. Job and task analysis. In M. D. Dunnette, (Ed.), *Handbook of industrial and organizational psychology.* Chicago: Rand McNally, 1976, 651–696.

Messick, S. Test validity and the ethics of assessment. *American Psychologist,* 1980, *35,* 1012–1027.

Naylor, J. C., & Shine, L. C. A table for determining the increase in mean criterion score obtained by using a selection device. *Journal of Industrial Psychology,* 1965, *3,* 33–42.

Smith, M. Cautions concerning the use of the Taylor-Russell tables in employee selection. *Journal of Applied Psychology,* 1948, *32,* 595–600.

Taylor, H. C., & Russell, J. T. The relationship of validity coefficients to the practical effectiveness of tests in selection: Discussion and tables. *Journal of Applied Psychology,* 1939, *23,* 567–578.

Thorndike, R. L. *Personnel Selection.* New York: Wiley, 1949.

chapter 8

Biodata and Preemployment Interviews

The two previous chapters considered criteria and their development. This chapter and the following one consider the other set of variables in validation research: *predictors*.

Predictors are of three types: personal history data, interviews, and psychological tests. Personal history and interview predictors are discussed here; tests as predictors are discussed in Chapter 9. We pointed out earlier that the psychometric prerequisites for acceptability are identical for all three. In order for a predictor, irrespective of its nature, to be useful, legally defensible, and psychologically sound, it must be reliable, valid, and unbiased.

PERSONAL HISTORY

To the extent that personal history and past experience influence subsequent behavior, that behavior ought to be predictable from factors like previous work experience, educational background, quality of performance on earlier jobs, and so on. This kind of information is elicited by an application blank and, in elaborated form, by a biographical information blank. (Although similar information may be obtained by a preemployment interview, this is not the interview's primary strength. Therefore, the preemployment interview is discussed separately.)

Application blanks

Letters of application and responses on more formal application blanks are typically used as preliminary hurdles in selection. Such information clearly is useful for screening applicants relative to certain minimum job prerequisites. If, for example, the job specification unequivocally indicates that satisfactory job performance requires a reasonable level of literacy, and the letter of application is written by someone who clearly has difficulties with the language, further investigation of the applicant's credentials is unwarranted.

A cautionary word is appropriate here. Employers sometimes make unsupportable inferences about minimum personal history prerequisites. Such inferences may unwittingly generate discriminatory hiring practices. Often some minimum level of formal education is specified because "it stands to reason that the employee has to be a high school graduate in order to do this work." Or, as another example, female applicants might routinely be rejected because "they lack the strength and endurance to do the job." The point, of course, is that *any* prerequisite, whether established from application blank responses or some other device, must stand the test of demonstrated job-relatedness.

The issue is that of *item-validity:* Each bit of information solicited on the application blank for use as a partial basis for making employment decisions must be correlated with the criterion. In rare instances a single application blank item may eliminate certain candidates from further consideration. (An applicant not licensed to drive cannot be hired as a chauffeur.) More typically, the application blank is comprised of several items, each with significant (but less than perfect) validity.

The weighted application blank. You may have correctly inferred from the preceding sentence that a scoring key can be developed for those application blank items used to screen potential employees. The item response contributing to the scoring key can carry unit weights ($+1, 0, -1$) or differential weights (for example, $+1, +2, +3$). Either way, the resulting score is a composite of responses to several personal history items.

The development of a weighted application blank parallels the steps for constructing many other kinds of psychometric instruments (England, 1971).

Item analysis establishing the relationship between each application blank item and the criterion, is the first step. Since tenure is a criterion often predicted from weighted blanks, we will use it to illustrate a procedure for establishing item validity and setting item weights.

Typically, the sample of current and previous employees for whom completed application blanks are available is divided into high and low criterion subgroups. Using tenure (length of employment) as the criterion, a long-tenure group might be defined by continuous employment for, say, two years or more. Persons terminated before two years would be assigned to the short-tenure subgroup.

The replies to the individual application-blank items then are tallied separately for the members of each criterion subgroup, and the data are analyzed to determine each item's validity. Consider an item like *age* either requested directly or indirectly (date of birth) on virtually every blank. Four hypothetical patterns of response to this item are shown in Table 8–1. In Organization A the long-tenured employees were older as applicants; the younger applicants tended to terminate employment sooner. Since age is positively correlated with tenure, the item should be weighted to favor older applicants.

TABLE 8–1
Analysis of an application blank item: Four hypothetical examples

Age reported on application blank	Organization A		Organization B		Organization C		Organization D	
	Short tenure	Long tenure	Short tenure	Long tenure	Short tenure	Long tenure	Short tenure	Long tenure
Under 20	50%	5%	5%	50%	40%	20%	33%	33%
20–40	30	30	30	30	20	60	33	33
Over 40	20	65	65	20	40	20	33	33
	100%	100%	100%	100%	100%	100%	100%	100%

The converse is true in Organization B. Here the item should be weighted negatively (that is, to favor younger applicants). The relationship in Organization C is curvilinear; the age range associated with long tenure (and therefore the range to be weighted most heavily) is 20–40. Finally, since age and tenure are uncorrelated in Organization D (that is, age is an invalid predictor) it would not enter into the scoring key at all.

Chi square is a frequently used statistical test for establishing item validity. This statistic compares the distributions of item responses made by persons in the criterion subgroups. When these distributions do not differ significantly (like the illustration for Organization D in Table 8–1) the item is discarded on the grounds of invalidity.

Once item validity is established, the response alternatives are weighted to reflect the character of the item-criterion relationship. One such weighting scheme is the extremely simple one based upon *horizontal percentages* within the high or desirable criterion subgroup. For the illustration in Table 8–1, this subgroup is comprised of the long tenure employees. The item response percentages by employees in that subgroup are used to establish relative weights. Thus, the weights in Organization A (Table 8–1) would be 1, 6, and 13 respectively for responses "under 20," "20–40," and "Over 40." (The percentages for the long tenure group were divided by 5 as the least common denominator.) The same responses would be assigned weights of 5, 3, and 2 in Organization B, and 1, 3, and 1 in Organization C. Since applicant age is unrelated to tenure in Organization D, the response alternatives would carry equal weight signifying that the item should be excluded from the scoring key.

The applicant's total score on the weighted blank is obtained by summing the weights of responses to all valid items.

Situational considerations. Before the weighted blank can be used as part of the selection battery, the instrument must be cross-validated as discussed in Chapter 7. Likewise, as also discussed in that chapter, the possibility of differential validity for individual items as well as total score must be investigated in order for the blank's use not to be discriminatory (Pace & Schoenfeldt, 1977). Evidence of the existence of differential item validity would suggest that item responses should carry different weights in the various moderator groups. The predictive efficiency and the response weights appropriate to the age question might, for example, differ for minority and nonminority employees or for employees in different jobs within the same organization.

Furthermore, additional periodic cross-validations of the item weights must be conducted after the weighted blank has been incorporated into the selection program. Subtle changes over time in the labor pool, the job market, the organization or the job itself may invalidate the original weights.

Because application-blank item validities are situation-specific, it is impossible to develop a weighted blank for use across organizations even when similar jobs are being considered. Although, as we will see, weighted blanks have demonstrable validity against several criteria and for a wide range of positions, the particular items comprising each blank (and the weights attached to those items) vary from one organization to another.

Biographical information blanks

The Biographical Information Blank (BIB) is an elaboration of the weighted application blank. Because of the situational character of weighted application blanks, their scientific (as opposed to practical) utility is rather limited. Research with weighted application blanks has not materially increased our understanding of the fundamental relationships between personal history and job performance (Guion, 1967).

The character of a weighted application blank also somewhat limits its practical utility. Typically, the blank yields a single critical score for a particular hiring or placement decision. To the extent that prior personal history does indeed predict future behavior, the identification and validation of different and discrete personal history patterns should prove more useful than validation of just a single pattern. Viewed thus, personal history data should enable us to go beyond simple dichotomous decisions (for example, hire or reject). More comprehensive theoretical formulations linking the individual's prior history to subsequent behavior might permit using biodata to make optimal assignments of applicants to position openings, of incumbents to alternative career development pathways, and so on (Schoenfeldt, 1974).

The key to effecting both objectives—improved scientific understanding and refined practice—is a biodata inventory yielding several scores, each for a different facet of personal history. The BIB is such an inventory.

The content coverage of a BIB is considerably broader than that of the usual application blank. The latter is pretty much restricted to data concerning previous employment, scholastic history, and the like. In contrast, BIB questions range more widely over factual background data in areas like health, hobbies, and family history, and often tap interests, attitudes, and values.

The two critical features of BIB items are : (a) they are autobiographical and (b) they typically are cast in a multiple-choice format. BIB items inquire both into the historical inputs to our behavior (through questions about parents, siblings, social and economic history, and so on) and the effects of these inputs upon such things as reading preferences, school grades, and job history. Some illustrative BIB items are shown in Table 8–2.

The information obtained from a BIB can be used in two ways: (a) to generate a single score predicting criterion performance for a particular job and (b) to generate multiple scores for each of several relatively homogeneous and independent biographical factors.

Predicting a specific criterion. What we have already said about the development of weighted application blanks applies to BIBs intended for situation-specific prediction. Each BIB item is analyzed to determine its

TABLE 8–2
Illustrative BIB items

1. *Yes-No*
   Have you found your life to date to be pleasant and satisfying?

2. *Continuum, single choice*
   What is your weight?
   (*a*) Under 135 pounds; (*b*) 136–155 pounds; (*c*) 156 to 175 pounds; (*d*) 176 to 195 pounds; (*e*) Over 195 pounds

3. *Noncontinuum, single choice*
   What was your marital status at college graduation?
   (*a*) Single; (*b*) Married, no children; (*c*) Married, one or more children; (*d*) Widowed; (*e*) Separated or divorced

4. *Noncontinuum, multiple choice*
   Check each of the following from which you have ever suffered.
   (*a*) Allergies; (*b*) Asthma; (*c*) High blood pressure; (*d*) Ulcers; (*e*) Headaches; (*f*) Gastrointestinal upsets; (*g*) Arthritis

5. *Continuum, plus "escape option"*
   What was your length of service in your most recent full time job?
   (*a*) Less than six months; (*b*) Between six months and one year; (*c*) One to two years; (*d*) Two to five years; (*e*) More than five years; (*f*) No previous full-time job

6. *Noncontinuum plus "escape option"*
   When are you most likely to have a headache?
   (*a*) When I strain my eyes; (*b*) When I don't eat on schedule; (*c*) When I am under tension; (*d*) January first; (*e*) Never have headaches

7. *Common stem, multiple continua*
   Over the past five years, *how much* have you enjoyed each of the following?
   (Use continuum 1 to 4 from the column on the right.)
   (*a*) Loafing or watching TV
   (*b*) Reading   1. Very much
   (*c*) Constructive hobbies   2. Some
   (*d*) Home improvement   3. Very little
   (*e*) Outdoor recreation   4. Not at all
   (*f*) Music, art, or dramatics, etc.

Source: W. A. Owens, "Biographical Data, in Dunnette, ed., *Handbook of Industrial and Organizational Psychology*, p. 613. Copyright © 1976 by Rand McNally College Publishing Company. Used by permission of Houghton Mifflin Company.

empirical relationship to criterion performance; valid items are retained and keyed; these items are then administered as a test, scored on the basis of the key developed during the item analysis, validated, cross-validated, and in general handled like any other psychometric device.

As we will discuss later, biodata inventories developed in this way have effectively contributed to selection programs for widely ranging jobs. However, they suffer many of the limitations of weighted application blanks.

Since they are situation-specific, the use of such a BIB is limited to making predictions (1) for applicants from a relatively circumscribed applicant pool and (2) of performance on the particular criterion measure(s) used in the validation studies.

Furthermore, since this BIB development procedure generates a single empirically derived scoring key (reflecting a particular set of item-criterion correlations), the resulting instrument is not particularly helpful to differential placement decisions.

Finally, the empirically keyed single score BIB is a totally practical instrument. Its development depends upon demonstrating relationships between particular elements of life history and subsequent behavior. However, it does not generate the type of data required to explicate the nature of the linkages between personal history and present or future behavior.

Biodata dimensions. The practical predictive utility of biodata supports the basic axiom that future behavior is predictable from past behavior. A corollary is that persons who have behaved similarly in the past and who have experienced similar life histories will behave similarly in the future (Owens, 1976). An understanding of the linkages between life history and subsequent behavior thus depends upon the delineation of the similarities and differences between different personal histories. For this reason, a body of research on personal history dimensions has been developing. Using factor analysis or related statistical procedures, it is possible to group BIB items into subsets (or clusters, or factors). All items in a subset share a common element.

The common element defining a BIB cluster may be the type of activity common to all items in that cluster. This was the case, for example, with items administered to high school seniors and organized into subsets concerned with social activities, religious activities, economic independence, and so on (Siegel, 1956). Alternatively, it has been suggested that our understanding of the personal backgrounds contributing to employee effectiveness can be enhanced by developing clusters of biographical items about such traits as level of maturity, rate of maturation, social adaptability, job interest, and energy level (Henry, 1965).

Once items are grouped into *homogeneous* (that is, with a common element) factors, the subset of items is scored as a biographical subtest. Thus, each dimension is separately scored. One value of this kind of analysis is that it permits additional understanding of the relationship between personal history and job success. Instead of merely contributing to improved prediction, dimensional analysis facilitates the discoveries of answers to *why*, in terms of personal history, some persons are more satisfactory employees than others. Further, by comparing biographical factor scores earned by employees in different positions, it becomes possible to hypothesize the relationship between differences in personal histories and success or failure in various kinds of positions.

All of the foregoing assumes that differential validity can be established for the biographical factors. This assumption is supported. Distinctive patterns of BIB factor scores have been associated with widely ranging criteria including measures of perception, creativity, learning and memory, interests, attitudes and values, and personality (Owens & Schoenfeldt, 1979).

Furthermore, biographical dimensions are relatively stable. Given a set of BIB items, those items group into similar clusters across age (Schmuckler, 1966) and sex groups (Owens, 1971; Schoenfeldt, 1979). Additionally, criterion-related validities of BIB items and scores typically are not moderated either by race or socioeconomic status (Cherry, 1969). Thus, biodata give promise of being *relatively* race- and culture-free predictors.

The italics are meant to emphasize that the assumption of fairness cannot, in practice, be taken for granted (Pace & Schoenfeldt, 1977). The investigator must remain alert to the possibility that biodata items involving such issues as formal education and socioeconomic background are potentially contaminated by race and sex. Recently one of the authors discovered that even such a relatively innocuous appearing background item like, "How were you referred for a job with us?" required different weights for minority and nonminority applicants. A positive weight for referral by one of the organization's present employees was justified for nonminority applicants. However, the item lacked validity for minority applicants—presumably because the organization employed relatively few minority group members who could make such a referral!

Veracity

One of the frequently cited strengths of biographical predictors is that replies are likely to be truthful because they are subject to verification (Owens & Henry, 1966). The possibility always exists, as far as an applicant is concerned, that the prospective employer will check upon the veracity of information recorded on the application form or BIB.

Nevertheless, one might wonder about the truthfulness of replies under selection conditions in which applicants might be expected to shade the truth by presenting themselves in the most favorable light. Self-reports of previous wages, length of prior employment, and previous job duties were found to correlate closely with the actual situation for persons applying for sales and office positions (Mosél & Cozan, 1952). Similarly, responses to 17 items (covering marital status and history, previous military service, employment history) by a sample of incumbent police officers yielded an average correlation of .94 with the responses by these same persons at the time they were job applicants (Cascio, 1975).

To the extent biodata items request factual information which *might* be objectively verified (even if it often is *not*), the likelihood is high that responses will be honest. However, as we mentioned earlier, BIB items can range rather widely over one's personal history, broadly conceived to include attitudes, preferences, and so on. Applicants may give themselves the benefit of the doubt in replying to such items.

Biodata validity

In his comprehensive review of validity studies of various predictors, Ghiselli (1966) found biographical data consistently to be the most successful predictor (1) of progress in job training and (2) of job proficiency. The average validity coefficients respectively were .44 and .41. Furthermore, two other literature reviews (Schuh, 1967; Asher, 1972) report considerable power for biodata predictors of turnover. We cannot know the incidence of *unsuccessful* attempts to predict turnover and other criteria from biodata since negative findings are often not reported in the literature (Schwab & Oliver, 1974). However, the number and variety of circumstances in which predictive validity has been established argues compellingly in favor of exploring the potential utility of biodata for employment selection and placement.

Personal-history data have been reported to predict job performance successfully in a wide range of positions including, among others, sales personnel (Scollay, 1957), seasonally employed production workers (Dunnette & Maetzold, 1955), office-clerical personnel (Fleishman & Berniger, 1960; Cascio, 1976), and research scientists (Smith, Albright, Glennon, & Owens, 1961), We will sample just two studies: one predicting turnover of clerical personnel; the other predicting performance by research scientists.

Turnover. Employee turnover (both voluntary and involuntary) is costly. Cascio (1976) reports a successful use of a weighted application blank to reduce turnover among clerical personnel from an initial level of 48 percent terminating within the first year to 28 percent. The items surviving both the item analysis and the subsequent cross-validation concerned: age, marital status, children's ages, education, tenure on previous job, previous salary, friend or relative employed by the company, location of residence, home ownership, and length of time the applicant was living at the present address. (This list is fairly typical of the types of items contributing to weighted application blank scores.)

Applying the scoring key developed from the original item-analysis group to the application blanks completed by members of a "hold-out" cross-validation group produced correlations of .58 for minority employees and .56 for nonminority employees. The differences in mean scores of short- and long-tenure employees *within* the minority and nonminority groups were statistically significant; the mean differences between minority and nonminority employees were *not* statistically significant. Hence, the weighted blank proved to be equally effective and fair for predicting tenure for both minority and nonminority applicants.

Performance by research scientists. A more elaborate BIB was validated against three criteria obtained for petroleum research scientists: (1) overall performance ratings, (2) creativity ratings, and (3) number of patent disclosures. Concurrent cross-validity coefficients were .61, .52, and .52 respectively (Smith et al., 1961). In a subsequent study designed to clarify patterns of life history experience and the significance of these patterns, the investigators (Morrison, Owens, Glennon, & Albright, 1962) factor analyzed all of the biodata items which correlated with one or more of the three criteria. The items were found to cluster into five factors: (1) favorable self-perception, (2) inquisitive professional orientation, (3) utilitarian drive, (4) tolerance for ambiguity, and (5) general adjustment (see Table 8–3).

TABLE 8–3

Biographical factors contributing to successful performance by petroleum research scientists*

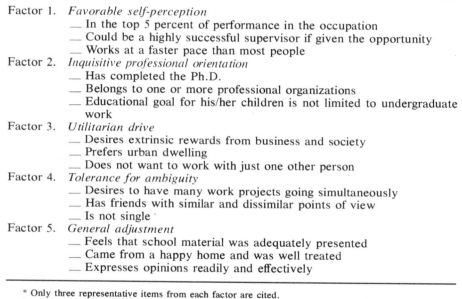

Factor 1. *Favorable self-perception*
__ In the top 5 percent of performance in the occupation
__ Could be a highly successful supervisor if given the opportunity
__ Works at a faster pace than most people

Factor 2. *Inquisitive professional orientation*
__ Has completed the Ph.D.
__ Belongs to one or more professional organizations
__ Educational goal for his/her children is not limited to undergraduate work

Factor 3. *Utilitarian drive*
__ Desires extrinsic rewards from business and society
__ Prefers urban dwelling
__ Does not want to work with just one other person

Factor 4. *Tolerance for ambiguity*
__ Desires to have many work projects going simultaneously
__ Has friends with similar and dissimilar points of view
__ Is not single

Factor 5. *General adjustment*
__ Feels that school material was adequately presented
__ Came from a happy home and was well treated
__ Expresses opinions readily and effectively

* Only three representative items from each factor are cited.
Source: R. F. Morrison, W. A. Owens, J. R. Glennon, and L. E. Albright, "Factored Life History Antecedents of Industrial Research Performance," *Journal of Applied Psychology* 46 (1962):pp. 281–284 and drawn from entire article.

One of the interesting findings from this study was that two rather distinct personal-history factor patterns were discovered for these scientists. Those who received high ratings on performance and creativity tended also to score high on the factors designated: favorable self-perception, utilitarian drive, and general adjustment. In contrast, scientists with many patent disclosures (the third criterion measure) tended to earn low scores on these factors, but high scores on the two remaining ones: inquisitive professional orientation, and tolerance of ambiguity.

From a theoretical standpoint this research goes beyond mere performance prediction by contributing to our understanding of the biographical antecedants of certain kinds of behavior. From a practical standpoint, it also reinforces a point discussed at length in Chapter 5: persons with different histories, skills, and so on may legitimately be expected to contribute to the attainment of different, but nonetheless equally important, organizational objectives. The challenge is both to delineate the objectives and to structure the organizational environment—beginning with selection—to facilitate the attainment of these objectives.

SELECTION INTERVIEW

Although interviews are conducted for many purposes including managerial assessment, attitude surveys, and employee counseling, our discussion here is limited to the preemployment or selection interview. Such an interview, together with a personal-history summary, is incorporated into virtually every selection program.

The interview typically serves several functions in the preemployment context. The one of primary concern to us now is that of assessing certain personal characteristics which are critical to job performance and either inaccessible to or only partly accessible to other evaluative procedures. Among the interview's other functions, largely ignored in this discussion, are providing information to the applicant about the job, the employer, and the terms of employment and clarification and elaboration of the applicant's responses on the application form.

The unique feature of the interview as a selection device is its interpersonal character. Its pertinence to employment decisions rests upon evidence that such things as personal characteristics, physical appearance, career motivation, and social behavior are critical job requirements. Its potential value rests upon evidence that such characteristics are better evaluated by an interview than by other means. Evidence that the interview is pertinent to selection would come from the job analysis. Assuming its appropriateness, its value in selection rests upon the usual considerations of validity and reliability.

Methodological issues

Two methodological issues bearing upon the way in which validity studies of the selection interview are interpreted have been highlighted in a review article by Ulrich and Trumbo (1965). One concerns a possible source of contamination of the interview inputs; the other concerns the nature of predictions made from interview data. Since these issues are inextricably bound to the question of validity, we will examine them briefly before considering the validity evidence itself.

The interview elicits face-to-face interaction which is the source of direct first-hand data available to the interviewer. But the interviewer typically also has available several secondary sources of information—letters of reference, the application form, test scores—which are subjectively combined with the direct observational data to formulate a selection decision. If our purpose is to validate the interview itself we need to separate the relative effects of these two input sources. Otherwise we cannot establish whether or not the predictive accuracy of the decision results from the available secondary information or from the interview as a uniquely valid predictor (Bellows & Estep, 1954).

Unfortunately, much of the research purporting to validate the interview has failed to make this distinction. Such research tests the validity of the *interviewer's* predictions from composite information to which the interview as a procedure has made an unknown contribution. Indeed, it is conceivable that certain reported validity coefficients might have been increased by eliminating the interview and relying solely upon the other available sources of information!

The second issue concerns the nature of the prediction process itself. Typically, the interviewer integrates whatever data are available to formulate an overall subjective impression and a prediction of the applicant's likely success as an employee. The factors contributing to the prediction and the relative importance of each component are not made explicit, and may change from time to time. Predictions following such a subjective synthesis of imputs have been described as *clinical* (Meehl, 1954). It is likely that interview validity is improved by using *actuarial* rather than clinical prediction: that is, by treating the interview as a psychometric device and entering the results from it into a regression equation.

Interview validity

In spite of the almost universal use of employment interviews, evidence concerning their validity is relatively sparse and largely negative (Mayfield, 1964).

Concurrent validity. Studies of this type typically correlate trait ratings made by interviewers with some other, independently made measure of these same traits. Positive correlations are usually reported for evaluations of intelligence and mental ability (Wagner, 1949).

This evidence alone is not persuasive concerning the usefulness of the selection interview for two reasons. First, intelligence and mental ability are by no means uniform prerequisites to satisfactory job performance. When these traits are irrelevant to performance, the fact that they can be evaluated during an interview is likewise irrelevant. Even worse, precisely because they *can* be evaluated, the interviewer may erroneously assume their relevance and weight them heavily in the selection decision. Second, even when mental ability *is* positively correlated with job performances, it almost invariably will be evaluated more reliably by ability tests than by interviews.

Predictive validity. Many estimates of predictive validity are contaminated by the interviewer's access to other, noninterview, information about the candidate. As noted earlier, this makes it impossible to estimate the validity of the interview as a procedure as distinct from the interviewer's clinical synthesis of information obtained from various sources.

One attempt to effect this separation established the invalidity of the interview as a procedure (Kelly & Fiske, 1951). The objective was to predict academic performance in graduate psychology programs. Several predictors were validated sequentially. The first predictor in the sequence was application credentials, yielding a validity coefficient of .26. When supplemented by a one-hour interview as a second predictor, the validity of the composite (credentials and interview) was .27. An improvement in validity, to .36, was obtained by predicting performance from the combination of application credentials and objective test scores. The further addition of a two-hour interview to this more valid composite predictor reduced the validity coefficient to .32!

How might we explain such negative findings? One possibility is that the type of behavior elicited from applicants during an interview is essentially unrelated to their subsequent criterion performance. The interview elicits interpersonal behavior. Therefore, we should expect predictive validity only against criteria entailing interpersonal interaction as an important ingredient.

Another possibility is that while the interview itself is potentially valid, the interviewer is at fault in not correctly interpreting the elicited behavior. Both explanations have merit.

Those selection interviews which are narrowly focused upon eliciting evidence of the quality of interpersonal relations and/or motivation to work show greatest evidence of validity. The interview's greatest promise is for assessing the applicant's potential fit into the social context of the job. His/her potential fit in other respects is better forecast by other predictors (Ulrich & Trumbo, 1965).

Interview reliability

As suggested earlier, the interviewer's attempt to clinically synthesize the data provided during the interview may reveal more about that particular interviewer's biases and preferences than about the interviewee. To the extent that interviewers' interpretations are idiosyncratic, we would expect interview-generated ratings to be unreliable. And this expectation is confirmed. The level of interinterviewer agreement, generally speaking, is considerably below that of reliability coefficients regarded as acceptable for making individual predictions.

The less structured the interview, and the more latitude afforded the interviewer, the lower the reliability. This suggests several things that might be done to improve the reliability (and hence the potential validity) of the interview: (a) limit the interview's scope to eliciting information about two areas—interpersonal behavior, and job motivation, (b) standardize the interview protocol to facilitate comparisons between the interviewees' behavior under essentially similar circumstances, (c) restrict the use made of interview ratings to predictions about specific aspects of job performance rather than a global prediction of anticipated overall performance, and (*d*) train the interviewers to be objective (unbiased) evaluators (Schmitt, 1976).

Interview dynamics

Much interviewing research focuses on factors influencing the interviewee's behavior and the interviewer's perceptions of and reactions to that behavior. Analytic studies of the interview as a dynamic process with continual give-and-take between the participants have suggested ways in which the validity and reliability of the selection interview can be improved. Such studies have also suggested certain limitations to the interview as a selection tool.

The dynamic character of the interview is schematically shown in Figure 8–1. The interview is seen as a continuous interaction entailing mutually dependent sets of cues and behaviors. The applicant and the interviewer each hold self-concepts, needs, attitudes, and so on, leading them to behave in certain ways. Each participant's behavior impinges upon that of the other by providing positive or negative feedback, and creating a climate of mutual

FIGURE 8–1
Interview dynamics

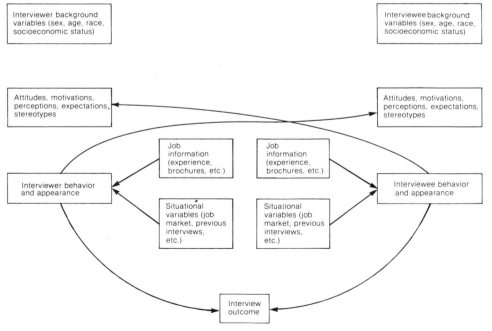

Source: N. Schmitt, "Social and Situational Determinants of Interview Decisions: Implications for the Employment Interview," *Personnel Psychology* 29 (1976): p. 93.

behavior modification. This is perhaps most clear for the applicant who is understandably alert to even subtle clues about the appropriateness or inappropriateness (or acceptability/unacceptability) of statements made during the interview. However the interviewer likewise responds to the applicant by probing further if dissatisfied with a reply, backing off if undue sensitivity is evidenced, and so on.

The dynamic nature of this interaction may well generate some degree of self-fulfilling prophecy. Each participant formulates initial impressions of the other. These initial impressions color their early behavior during the interview. This behavior, in turn, further reinforces the initial impression and leads to further continuation of similar behavior throughout the interview thereby generating evidence that the initial impression was correct. Thus, in analyzing differences between interviews in which applicants were hired and rejected, Anderson (1960) found that the interviewer talked more during the former and the interviewee was more hesitant in responding during the latter. One explanation is that the initial interpersonal impression set the tone. The interviewer's initially unfavorable impression caused him/her to be less verbal and the applicant to respond haltingly. Each one's behavior reinforced that of the other, leading to more of the same.

It is convenient to consider interview dynamics under two headings: participant characteristics, and process variables.

Participant characteristics

Certain participant characteristics are behavioral in nature; these include actions and statements as well as the attitudinal determinants of those actions and statements. Other characteristics—such as participant sex, race, age, and so on—while not behavioral may nonetheless influence the interview dynamics and outcomes. And to the extent such characteristics influence employment decisions *in the absence of demonstrated validity,* they exert adverse impact.

Arvey (1979) has reviewed the research concerning potential sources of unfair discrimination in employment interviewing and notes that there is cause for concern about the importance attached to certain interviewee characteristics. Younger applicants are often perceived more favorably than older ones. Similarly, males are often perceived more favorably than females, particularly for positions entailing historically male roles (Cohen & Bunker, 1975). Two other applicant characteristics—minority race and handicap—seem less to be systematically associated with unfavorable interviewer evaluations.

Two points are worth noting. First, fair employment practice does not automatically preclude all consideration of interviewee characteristics. Fair practice does require that selection standards relative to these characteristics meet the same test of job relatedness appropriate to any predictor. Thus the particular concern about age, sex, race, handicap, and so on, as determinants of interview outcomes is that such characteristics may be influential in the absence of appropriate demonstrations of their validity.

Second, the literature concerning potential systematic adverse effects of race and handicap is relatively sparse. Even accepting the available evidence at face value (that is, that these variables seem not to exert systematic adverse effects) does not remove these factors as potential sources of interviewer bias in individual cases.

Our concern about the potential invalidity of interviewee characteristics as predictors of job performance extends beyond the simple classification of persons by age, sex, and so on. Many factors indirectly reflect these classificatory variables through subtle interactions. As influences in the employment decision, information about arrest record, socioeconomic indicators (like home ownership, spouse's salary), marital status, child-care arrangements, and so on, selectively disadvantage one group or another. Hence the solicitation of such information is illegal unless supported by clear evidence of validity.

Process variables

Whereas we have thus far been concerned with the impact of specific interviewer and interviewee characteristics, we now turn to some studies more directly concerned with the interview as an interpersonal *process*.

The issue of structure. It has been suggested that the reliability—and hence the potential validity—of the selection interview is improved by imposing a degree of control, or structure, on the interaction (Latham et al., 1980).

In the extreme, the structured interview allows the interviewer little latitude; the questions and their sequence are predetermined and uniformly implemented for all applicants. An interview so highly structured is essentially an orally administered application form since the questions lending themselves to rigid sequencing are pretty much biographical. Highly structured interviews can be expected to be valid under essentially the same circumstances as are weighted application blanks.

What about the vast middle ground between extremely structured and totally uncontrolled, or free-wheeling, interviews? Whereas undue structure may obscure important interpersonal characteristics, some degree of standardization is indicated if we are to make fair comparisons between applicants interviewed at different times, perhaps under different physical circumstances, and sometimes by different interviewers.

The *patterned* interview is an attempt to strike such a middle ground. Here the interviewer asks a set of carefully worded questions in a predetermined sequence. The questions are designed to elicit evidence of such character traits as stability, industry, perseverance, and leadership. Furthermore, the interviewer is guided in appraising the applicant's qualifications in these respects (McMurry, 1947) or in transforming subjective impressions to numerical equivalents (Hovland & Wonderlic, 1939).

Indeed this latter aspect of patterned interviewing—that is, focusing the interviewer's evaluation of specific characteristics—may be more important than is the sequencing of questions. When left to their own devices, even experienced interviewers evaluating candidates for a relatively uncomplicated position on the basis of unambiguously presented cues have been found to weight the cues differently. This was demonstrated by requiring experienced interviewers to evaluate the credentials of each of 243 hypothetical applicants for a secretarial position (Valenzi & Andrews, 1973). The resumés were constructed by compiling all possible combinations of five different cues (typing proficiency, shorthand proficiency, previous experience, formal education, social skills) each at three different levels (low, middle, high). Not only did the interviewers disagree among themselves in weighting the five cues but, not surprisingly, their consequent evaluations of the likelihood of candidate success also differed appreciably.

Positive versus negative information. Given that most interviews elicit both positive and negative information about the candidate's suitability, what is the relative importance to interviewer judgment of these two types of information?

Relatively speaking, interviewers seem to be disproportionately influenced by negative information (Springbett, 1958). Either they assign an erroneously heavy weight to negative information (Miller and Rowe, 1967) or they weight negative information correctly but undervalue positive information (Hollman, 1972).

The general conclusion that negative information carries a disproportionate influence in interview decisions is tempered by at least three interactive variables: (a) the interviewer's expectations or preconceptions about the applicant, (b) the relative time during the interview at which the information surfaces, and (c) the interviewer's experience and knowledge of job requirements. Interviewers who are predisposed to expect the applicant to be of high quality tend to discount negative information elicited during the interview (London & Hakel, 1974). Further, negative information surfacing late in the interview has less impact than when it surfaces early (Bolster & Springbett, 1961). This is particularly the case when the early information has a positive tone.

Finally, the disproportionate influence of negative information or information elicited early in the interview is moderated by interviewer experience (Johns, 1975) and job knowledge (Peters & Terborg, 1975). Thus the case is clear for interviewer training calculated to provide the necessary interviewing experience, information about the job opening, sensitivity to positive as well as negative information elicited during the interview, and avoidance of inclinations to formulate premature judgments about the applicant.

Contrast effects. Interviews typically evaluate several applicants rather than a single applicant for a given position. This raises the possibility that evaluations of a particular interviewee may be influenced either positively or negatively by the interview performance of the immediately preceding applicant. Such a contrast effect would presumably benefit those interviewees who follow a particularly weak candidate and be detrimental to those following a particularly strong one. This possibility has been experimentally tested in a very limited way and with the general finding that although *statistically* significant contrast effects can be demonstrated, these effects have only limited *practical* significance for applicants who are either clearly qualified or clearly not qualified.

The typical research procedure requires interviewers to read and to evaluate a target resumé after examining other resumés which, unknown to the interviewer, are designed to establish an *expectation level*. The level of qualifications presented in both the target and preceding resumés is systematically varied to establish whether contrast effects exist at all and, if so, to help delimit the conditions under which they operate.

Minor contrast effects accounting for less than 2 percent of the variance of ratings of target resumés have been demonstrated with written resumés as the stimulus material (Hakel, Ohnesorge, & Dunnette, 1970). Even with videotapes of role-played interviews as the stimulus material, the contrast effect was still quite trivial for target applicants who were either very well qualified or very poorly qualified, although a marked contrast effect was obtained for target applicants who had intermediate qualifications (Wexley, Yukl, Kovacs, & Sanders, 1972).

The research on contrast effects is open to criticism because of its dependence upon artificial rather than real-life interview situations (Landy & Bates, 1973). Nevertheless, the data thus far available indicates that contrast effects may unintentionally lead interviewers to overestimate or underestimate the qualifications of those applicants who, by objective standards, have an average level of qualification. By one estimate (Wexley et al., 1972), contrast effect may account for as much as 80 percent of the variation in criterion ratings of average applicants when their interview follows those of several poorly qualified or several well-qualified applicants.

SUMMARY

Two types of predictors were discussed in this chapter: personal-history data (biodata), and interviews.

The rationale for using personal-history predictors in employment selection is that past and future behavior are correlated. Biodata have been successfully used to predict job performance in widely ranging positions.

Some type of application blank is commonly used to secure personal-history data. When used as a partial basis for employment selection, the application blank items must themselves be valid. Assuming that the item analysis establishes the item-validity of several such items, each can be weighted to reflect the character of the item-criterion relationship. Thereafter, the weighted application blank is treated similarly to other psychometric predictors.

The Biographical Information Blank (BIB) is an elaboration of the weighted application blank, but typically it is designed to yield several part-scores rather than a single overall score. BIB part-scores are based upon replies to homogeneous subsets (clusters or factors) of biographical items.

The unique feature of the interview as a selection device is its interpersonal character. Its pertinence to employment decisions requires evidence that such things as physical appearance and social behavior are critical job requirements. Assuming it is pertinent, the value of the interview rests upon the usual psychometric considerations (including reliability and validity).

In spite of the almost universal use of employment interviews, evidence concerning their validity is relatively sparse and largely negative. Furthermore, the level of inter-interviewer agreement (an index of reliability) tends generally to be unacceptably low for making individual predictions. Reliability (and hence, the potential validity) of the interview can be enhanced by (a) limiting the interview's scope to assessment in two areas—interpersonal behavior and job motivation, (b) standardizing the protocol so that interviewees are compared under essentially similar circumstances, (c) restricting predictions to specific aspects of job performance rather than attempting global predictions of likely "overall effectiveness", and (d) training the interviewers to be unbiased evaluators.

Certain participant characteristics and several process variables are potential sources of interviewer bias.

Any characteristic (sex, age, and so on) is a potential source of adverse impact. Such impact occurs whenever a personal characteristic influences the dynamics and outcomes of the interview in the absence of demonstrated validity. The concern for possible adverse impact extends beyond simple characteristics like age, sex, and race. Many other factors (like arrest record, marital status, and so on) may indirectly reflect these classificatory variables through subtle interactions.

Among the process variables considered as potential sources of bias were contrast effects and the relative weights given positive and negative information elicited during interviews.

Taken as a whole, the research on potential sources of interviewer bias emphasizes the need for interviewer training. One objective of such training is to help the interviewers acquire appropriate experience and skill (for example, how to put the applicant at ease; how to phrase probing questions). Additionally, training should encourage sensitivity to the positive as well as the negative information elicited during the interview, and prepare interviewers to resist inclinations to formulate premature judgments about applicants.

REFERENCES

Anderson, C. S.   The relation between speaking times and decision in the employment interview. *Journal of Applied Psychology,* 1960, *44,* 267–268.

Arvey, R.   Unfair discrimination in the employment interview: Legal and psychological aspects. *Psychological Bulletin,* 1979, *86,* 736–765.

Asher, J. J. The biographical item: Can it be improved? *Personnel Psychology*, 1972, *25*, 251–269.

Bellows, R. M., & Estep, M. F. *Employment psychology: The interview.* New York: Rinehart, 1954.

Bolster, B. F., & Springbett, B. M. The reaction of interviewers to favorable and unfavorable information. *Journal of Applied Psychology*, 1961, *45*, 97–103.

Cascio, W. F. Accuracy of verifiable biographical information blank responses. *Journal of Applied Psychology*, 1975, 60, 767–769.

Cascio, W. F. Turnover, biographical data, and fair employment practice. *Journal of Applied Psychology*, 1976, *61*, 576–580.

Cherry, R. L. Socioeconomic level and race as biographical moderators. *Dissertation abstracts international*, 1969, *30*, (4–B), 1967.

Cohen, S. L., & Bunker, K. A. Subtle effects of sex role stereotypes on recruiters' hiring decisions. *Journal of Applied Psychology*, 1975, *60*, 566–572.

Dunnette, M. D., & Maetzold, J. Use of a weighted application blank in hiring seasonal employees. *Journal of Applied Psychology*, 1955, *39*, 308–310.

England, G. W. *Development and use of weighted application blanks* (Rev. ed.). Minneapolis: University of Minnesota, Industrial Relations Center, 1971.

Fleishman, E. A., & Berniger, J. One way to reduce office turnover. *Personnel*, *1960*, *37*, 63–69.

Ghiselli, E. E. *The validity of occupational aptitude tests.* New York: Wiley, 1966.

Guion, R. M. Personnel selection. *Annual Review of Psychology*, 1967, *18*, 105–216.

Hakel, M., Ohnesorge, J. P., & Dunnette, M. D. Interviewer evaluations of job applicants' resumes as a function of the qualifications of the immediately preceding applicants. *Journal of Applied Psychology*, 1970, *54*, 27–30.

Henry, E. R. (Chm.) Research conference on the use of autobiographical data as psychological predictors. Greensboro, N.C.: The Richardson Foundation, 1965.

Hollman, T. D. Employment interviewers' errors in processing positive and negative information. *Journal of Applied Psychology*, 1972, *56*, 130–134.

Hovland, C. I., & Wonderlic, E. F. Prediction of success from a standardized interview. *Journal of Applied Psychology*, 1939, *33*, 537–546.

Johns, G. Effects of informational order and frequency of applicant evaluation upon linear information processing competence of interviewers. *Journal of Applied Psychology*, 1975, *60*, 427–433.

Kelly, E. L., Fiske, D. W. *The prediction of performance in clinical psychology.* Ann Arbor: University of Michigan Press, 1951.

Landy, F. J., & Bates, F. Another look at contrast effects in the employment interview. *Journal of Applied Psychology*, 1973, *58*, 141–144.

Latham, G. P., Saari, L. M., Pursell, E. D., & Campion, M. A. The situational interview. *Journal of Applied Psychology*, 1980, *65*, 422–427.

London, M., & Hakel, M. D. Effects of applicant stereotypes, order, and information on interview impressions. *Journal of Applied Psychology*, 1974, *59*, 157–162.

*Mayfield, E. C.   The selection interview: A reevaluation of published research. *Personnel Psychology,* 1964, *17,* 239–260.

McMurry, R. N.   Validating the patterned interview. *Personnel,* 1947, *23,* 270–271.

Meehl, P. E.   *Clinical versus statistical prediction.* Minneapolis: University of Minnesota Press, 1954.

Miller, J. W., & Rowe, P. N.   Influence of favorable and unfavorable information upon assessment decisions. *Journal of Applied Psychology,* 1967, *51,* 432–435.

Morrison, R. F., Owens, W. A., Glennon, J. R., & Albright, L. E.   Factored life history antecedants of industrial research performance. *Journal of Applied Psychology,* 1962, *46,* 281–284.

Mosél, J. N., & Cozan, L. W.   The accuracy of application blank work histories. *Journal of Applied Psychology,* 1952, *36,* 365–369.

Owens, W. A.   A quasi-actuarial basis for individual assessment. *American Psychologist,* 1971, *26,* 992–999.

Owens, W. A.   Biographical data. In M. D. Dunnette (Ed.), *Handbook of industrial and organizational psychology.* Chicago: Rand McNally, 1976, 609–650.

Owens, W. A., & Henry, E. R.   *Biographical data in industrial psychology: A review and evaluation.* Greensboro, N.C.: Richardson Foundation, 1966.

Owens, W. A., & Schoenfeldt, L. F.   Toward a classification of persons. *Journal of Applied Psychology Monographs,* 1979, *65,* 569–607.

Pace, L. A., & Schoenfeldt, L. F.   Legal concerns in the use of weighted applications. *Personnel Psychology,* 1977, *30,* 159–166.

Peters, L. H., & Terborg, J. R.   The effects of temporal placement of unfavorable information and of attitude similarity on personnel selection decisions. *Organizational Behavior and Human Performance,* 1975, *13,* 275–293.

Schmitt, N.   Social and situational determinants of interview decisions: Implications for the employment interview. *Personnel Psychology,* 1976, *29,* 79–101.

Schmuckler, E.   *Age differences in biographical inventories: A factor analytic study.* Greensboro, N.C.: The Creativity Research Institute, The Richardson Foundation, 1966.

Schoenfeldt, L. F.   Utilization of manpower: Development and evaluation of an assessment-classification model for matching individuals with jobs. *Journal of Applied Psychology,* 1974, *59,* 583–595.

Schoenfeldt, L. F.   *Use of non-test variables in admission, selection, and classification operations.* Symposium presented at the meeting of the American Psychological Association, Miami, September 1979.

Schuh, A. J.   The predictability of employee tenure: A review of the literature. *Personnel Psychology,* 1967, *20,* 133–152.

Schwab, D. P., & Oliver, R. L.   Predicting tenure with biographical data: Exhuming buried evidence. *Personnel Psychology,* 1974, *27,* 125–128.

Scollay, R. W.   Personal history data as a predictor of success. *Personnel Psychology,* 1957, *10,* 23–26.

Siegel, L.   A biographical inventory for students. *Journal of Applied Psychology,* 1956, *40,* 5–10.

Smith, W. J., Albright, L. E., Glennon, J. R., & Owens, W. A.   The prediction of research competence and creativity from personal history. *Journal of Applied Psychology*, 1961, *45*, 59–62.

Springbett, B. M.   Factors affecting the final decision in the employment interview. *Canadian Journal of Psychology*, 1958, *12*, 13–22.

Ulrich, L., & Trumbo, D.   The selection interview since 1949. *Psychological Bulletin*, 1965, *63*, 100–116.

Valenzi, E., & Andrews, I. R.   Individual differences in the decision process of employment interviewers. *Journal of Applied Psychology*, 1973, *58*, 49–53.

Wagner, R.   The employment interview: A critical review. *Personnel Psychology*, 1949, *2*, 17–46.

Wexley, K., Yukl, G., Kovacs, S., & Sanders, R.   Importance of contrast effects in employment decisions. *Journal of Applied Psychology*, 1972, *56*, 45–48.

chapter 9

Psychological Tests

The early history of psychology was rooted in psychometrics: that is, the measurement of individual differences. It is therefore not surprising that psychology and psychological testing are intimately associated in the public eye.

This is not to say that mankind waited until the late 19th century—when psychology evolved as a distinct discipline—before tests were advocated, invented, and used. Once man became aware of individual differences in performance—some persons being stronger, learning more rapidly, having a knack for artistic design, and so on—attempts to understand the origin of those differences and to make effective use of them was inevitable. Such awareness undoubtedly developed very early in human history.

An essential feature of a test is that it deliberately evokes an attribute. Thus it was only a small step from recognizing that individuals have unique patterns of strengths and weaknesses to deliberately creating circumstances to test them. All that was needed was the realization that individual differences could have functional significance: that society could make use of them. Plato, for example, clearly saw the occupational significance of individual differences in natural endowment, cautioning artisans to remain with the particular craft for which they were fitted, and suggesting the possibility that persons who were endowed with characteristics prerequisite to soldiering could be deliberately selected for such training.

As you are by now well aware, testing requires more than merely arranging circumstances to permit behavior to be displayed. The importance of making controlled and relevant observations of a representative sample of behavior under standardized conditions has been repeatedly emphasized in the preceding chapters. Also as we have discussed, particularly in Chapter 7, both the law and sound professional practice make identical requirements of *all* instruments and techniques generating results used to influence personnel decisions. Performance appraisals, interviews, and biodata forms are, from this perspective, psychological tests.

We are concerned here particularly with those devices that the public ordinarily regards as tests: The respondent answers a standardized set of questions, solves problems, and so on. The quality of performance on this set of questions or tasks is presumed to be generalizable; that is, the specific test questions are a *representative sample* of all of the questions that could have been asked.

Why make such generalizations? There are two basic reasons: evaluation and prediction. An *evaluation* is a statement about present conditions—the manager's level of effectiveness; the employee's skill as a computer programmer; your understanding and recall of particular course coverage; and so on. Tests as *predictors* use the evaluative information to forecast future behavior. Our discussion in this chapter is relevant to both objectives, although we somewhat emphasize the latter because of our overriding concern for employment selection.

The utilitarian distinction between evaluation and prediction is paralleled by the practical one of score interpretation. Test scores developed for evaluative purposes typically are relativistic; the person's performance is described in terms of some normative reference: for example, other students who are taking or have taken this course, or other employees doing essentially the same kind of work. Tests used exclusively for predictive applications may, but need not, have their scores referenced to some normative group. A more typical interpretation for prediction translates the scores into a dichotomous (hire/do not hire) or trichotomous (promote now/delay promotion and train further/delay promotion indefinitely) decision.

Finally, we do not differentiate in this chapter between tests used for *selection* and *placement*. The latter assumes that the organization can consider a particular applicant for more than one position opening, or an incumbent for more than one promotional opportunity. Differential placement seeks to effect the "best" match between individual qualifications and available openings. Thus differential placement is really a multiple selection effort. Several hiring (or promotional) decisions are made for each candidate.

HISTORY OF PSYCHOLOGICAL TESTING

We began by saying that the early history of psychometrics and the early history of scientific psychology were very much the same. Beginning in 1879 Wundt's laboratory (the first to study psychological phenomena) developed assorted physiologically based "mental tests" tapping such characteristics as reaction time, sensory acuity, and motor coordination. The presumption of the time was that such abilities would be found to correlate with learning ability. Although the presumption was not supported, the demonstration that behavioral elements could be measured in ways permitting comparisons between persons was an important step in psychometric technology.

Near the end of the 19th century Alfred Binet began to seek the correlates of scholastic learning ability in such cognitive areas as memory and comprehension. He was asked by the French government to identify children who would experience difficulty in school. Three aspects of the resulting first intelligence test (developed by Binet and co-worker Theodore Simon) deserve comment because of their powerful imprint upon the subsequent history of psychological testing.

First, the choice of tasks comprising the test was *empirically determined*. The test asked for performance on tasks similar to those actually required in school. The similarity between Binet's approach to identifying potential tasks as predictors of scholastic performance and the importance we now attach to job and task analysis preceding psychometric prediction is self-evident (Dunnette, 1976).

A second, insightful, contribution was Binet's assumption that the environment provides all children with essentially similar learning *opportunities*. Hence, any differences between them in performance on a set of tasks to which they have had similar exposure must reflect differences in learning ability. Given the relative homogeneity of that segment of French society sending its children to public schools at the turn of the century, the assumption made sense at the time. But this assumption fails in contemporary society. Differences in childrens' socioeconomic, ethnic, and racial backgrounds are paralleled by differences in learning opportunities afforded by these environments.

Finally, the *measure* of learning ability (the score) devised by Binet reflected a type of normative referrent. A "satisfactory" answer for children of a particular age was defined by the response quality of a normative group: that is, other youngsters of the same chronological age. It thus became possible to classify children with respect to this standard and to predict that those who fell below it would continue subsequently to experience scholastic difficulty. The original Binet test was quickly imported to the United States and revised by Lewis Terman of Stanford University.

The notion that psychological tests could forecast learning ability was not restricted to the classroom for long. The first textbook in industrial psychology (Munsterberg, 1913) discusses the use of tests for employee selection and placement. Just 10 years later Freyd (1923) published a three-part article laying out a thorough procedure for test construction, validation, and implementation which is as sensible today as when it was written. Freyd's sophistication is evident from his reference to such things as cost-effectiveness in deciding upon the department in which selection is to be attempted, job analysis as a precursor both to test and criterion development, and the potential usefulness as predictors of work samples and simulations. Further, he spoke of the necessity for periodic rechecks upon predictive validity.

The major event between Munsterberg's and Freyd's publications was, of course, World War I. This marked the first large-scale application of personnel selection and placement technology. Whereas the derivatives of the original Binet test were designed for individual administration, the war imposed a need for efficiently testing a large number of men. The result was the *Army Alpha* (and the *Army Beta* for illiterates). Both were general intelligence tests designed for group administration and were built upon the earlier efforts of Otis to produce a test suitable for industrial purposes. Almost 1.75 million men were tested and classified in less than two years (Uhlaner, 1977).

As is true of technology generally, the acceptance and implementation of developments in psychological testing required a "fit" with societal need. Enthusiasm for the potential of employment testing following World War I waned rapidly as experience confirmed that successful testing rested upon a sound (and costly) program of underlying research. Civilian modifications of the *Army Alpha* were no panacea for industrial selection. Thus, while certain large organizations (including Procter and Gamble and the Life Insurance Management Research Association) initiated substantial programs of selection research, employment testing generally languished until World War II.

This war again was accompanied by the urgent need to classify large numbers of recruits. With over 20 years intervening since the last such effort, the technology was considerably improved—particularly in the areas of criterion development, identification and measurement of specific aptitudes (as distinct from the more global general intelligence), and in further refinement of psychometric theory and related statistics.

Thereafter employment testing gained rapidly in acceptance, and commercial test publishing became big business. The American Psychological Association, the American Educational Research Association, and the National Council for Measurement in Psychology assumed joint responsibility in 1954 and again in 1974 for promulgating standards for designing and evaluating tests of all types—educational and clinical as well as industrial (APA, AERA, NCME, 1974).

As discussed in Chapter 7, enactment of the Civil Rights Act of 1964 and its implementation by EEOC and OFCC has caused a salutary renewal of attention to employment testing theory and practice, particularly as these relate to fair employment. We believe with Dunnette and Borman (1979) that the long overdue civil rights legislation emphasizes the conservation of human talent—an endeavor to which psychological testing is sympathetic rather than antagonistic. Employment testing, carefully conceived and implemented, is the best tool available to society for optimizing the balance between organizational needs to employ talented individuals and individuals' needs to utilize their talents effectively.

TEST STANDARDS AND ETHICS

How do we reconcile this favorable assessment of the promise of psychological tests with occasional evidence of public disenchantment with testing? The most recent such evidence is provided by advocates of so-called truth in testing legislation requiring disclosure, after test-administration of the questions and scoring key, as well as a copy of the subject's answer sheet, and validity statistics on the test. When New York State's legislature enacted the nation's first truth-in-testing law in 1979, the press generally hailed it as "about time!" (Truth in Testing, 1979). Although critics of testing have concentrated their attacks thus far on such educational tests as the SAT and LSAT (Nairn et al., 1980), their criticisms strike generally at the publishing industry and at the ethics of professional psychometricians. Earlier antagonists (for example, Gross, 1962; Whyte, 1956) were more patently critical of employment testing.

To state that there have been abuses of psychological testing by unethical nonprofessionals is merely to assert the obvious. This is somewhat abetted by a fairly widespread popular fascination with tests and some paranoia about decisions resting partly upon a relatively complex technology. The fascination leads otherwise hardheaded and sophisticated persons to view tests as almost magical sources of personal revelation. Managers who consider very carefully expenditures associated with new product development and distribution sometimes naively buy unvalidated personnel testing packages. The paranoia reflects a suspicion by the test-taker that evaluation necessarily infringes upon personal rights. When such suspicion is combined with misinformation (or incomplete information) about the way in which the test has been developed and is to be used, it can generate unwarranted criticism. (See, for example, ETS, 1980.)

Characteristics of useful tests

By this point in your reading you have a reasonably comprehensive notion about the characteristics differentiating carefully conceived tests from popularized pseudotests like those appearing in Sunday supplements and self-help books. These characteristics are ennumerated below by way of review:

1. The questions or items are carefully chosen to comprise an adequate (sufficiently large and representative) sample of behavior (knowledge, skill, and so on).
2. Test administration is standardized: that is, the conditions of administration (sequence in which the test is given, and so on) are uniform in order to permit meaningful comparisons between test-takers.
3. The test is reliable.
4. Test scores order persons along some kind of relevant scale. When used for evaluative purposes the raw scores are converted to norms providing a standard frame of reference for interpreting the raw scores. Although normative transformations are not required when tests are used solely for predictive purposes, the passing or critical score is empirically established.
5. The foregoing implies that there must be clear evidence of validity. Any assumptions about the underlying construct must be equally tenable for all test-takers and all tests. This requirement is especially critical to tests of mental ability which typically assume that all persons tested have been afforded equal opportunities to develop the sampled knowledges.

6. When used for predictive purposes, test validity further implies predictive *fairness*. Test scores must be shown to predict criterion performance without systematic adverse impact for any applicant subgroup.

The technical and ethical ramifications of these requirements have been comprehensively addressed in the latest revision by the Division of Industrial-Organizational Psychology of its *Principles for the Validation and Use of Personnel Selection Procedures* (1980). One objective of this statement is to protect the public by guiding the activities of professional psychologists and commercial test publishers. The ethical publisher is responsible for controlling test distribution to insure test availability only to professionally qualified users.

Who is qualified to purchase tests? A typical statement from one publisher's catalog reads: "Orders by private individuals having no professional or business responsibility for using tests cannot be honored—nor can tests be sold for self-guidance purposes." (SRA, 1978, p. 60.) Further restrictions on test sales are imposed by the *level* of test as defined by the American Psychological Association. This definition reflects the level of professional training and experience appropriately prerequisite to using various categories of tests.

CHOOSING TRIAL TESTS

Suppose there is reason to explore the possibility that testing may enhance employee selection in a particular organization. Although it would be possible to custom-build a test or battery for this purpose, the relative expense of doing so usually leads the investigator to seek potentially useful tests from those available in print.

The search for available tests must, of course, be preceded by a job analysis to give it direction. Once this has been accomplished, three major sources of information are available in the professional literature.

The first is descriptions of particular validation studies or summary reviews of validation efforts in similar situations—either by occupational area or by more specific performance-related characteristics. As you are by now well aware, such evidence does not insure that the test will be equally valid in another setting. However, it supports further study of the instrument as a trial predictor, particularly when the criteria are themselves sound. The most persuasive indications from the literature entail validations against multiple criteria (rather than a single global criterion) and work samples or performance records rather than supervisory ratings (Lent, Aurbach, & Levin, 1971).

Published reviews of specific tests are a second source of information. The key reference is Buros's *Mental Measurement Yearbooks* (MMYs). This series was initiated with the first MMY in 1938 and has been continuously updated since. The current edition (Buros, 1978) is the eighth. Each entry summarizes descriptive information (author, publisher, cost, time to administer, and so on) followed by critical reviews and a bibliography of pertinent publications.

A third source of information is the test *Manual* issued by the publisher. An adequate manual comprehensively describes the research underlying the test's development and standardization. Additionally, it details information about the logistics of test administration: the time required, populations for which it is suitable, and so on. Finally, the manual typically presents one or more sets of test norms.

NORMS

Test norms are derived by administering the instrument to normative groups and transforming the raw scores to an index of relative standing in the reference group. The reference groups for which a test has been normed may be classified by educational grade level, employment category (trainees, applicants, supervisors), race, sex, and so on.

The two most frequently reported normative transformations are percentiles and standard scores.

A percentile value indicates the percent of persons in the norms group earning at or below a particular raw score. Thus, if it has been determined that a raw score (number correct) of 35 on a computer-programmer aptitude test corresponds to the 84th percentile for programmer trainees, this signifies that 84 percent of the trainee norms group scored 35 or lower. Note the specificity of the norms group. Whereas a score of 35 may thus be interpreted as a high score when earned by a trainee, it would likely be transformed to a much lower percentile equivalent for a group of experienced programmers.

Standard scores indicate individual performance relative to the mean and standard deviation of the normative score distribution. The most obvious kind of standard score transforms raw scores to their equivalent in standard deviation units. Such z-scores are calculated by the formula

$$z = \frac{x - \bar{x}}{s_x}$$

If the mean $(\bar{x})$ test score in the trainee normative group were 30 with a standard deviation (s_x) of 5, a raw score of 35 would have a z-score equivalent of $+1.0$ (that is, it would fall at 1 standard deviation above the mean).

Some publishers set the normative group means and standard deviations to arbitrary values in order to facilitate standard score interpretation. Educational Testing Service, for example, sets the obtained mean to 500 and the obtained standard deviation to 100 for tests like the Graduate Record Examination. Hence a standard score of 600 on the GRE means the person tested has scored 1 standard deviation above the mean; 300 is 2 standard deviations below the mean; and so on.

FIGURE 9-1

Relationship between raw scores, percentiles, and standard scores (mean = 30; s = 5.0)

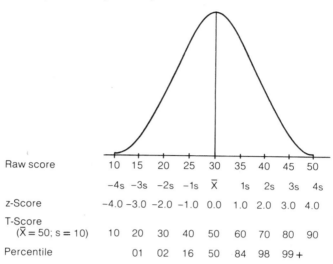

Raw score	10	15	20	25	30	35	40	45	50
	-4s	-3s	-2s	-1s	$\overline{X}$	1s	2s	3s	4s
z-Score	-4.0	-3.0	-2.0	-1.0	0.0	1.0	2.0	3.0	4.0
T-Score ($\overline{X}$ = 50; s = 10)	10	20	30	40	50	60	70	80	90
Percentile		01	02	16	50	84	98	99+	

The relationships between raw scores, percentiles, and several kinds of standard scores are illustrated in Figure 9–1. You will note one of the major advantages of standard scores over percentiles. Since the former are spaced equidistantly over the measurement continuum, they are amenable to the usual kinds of arithmetic operations required when tests are combined into batteries.

TYPES OF TESTS

It is convenient to classify tests by format and attributes measured.

Test formats

The classification by format emphasizes certain elements of test administration. Each format has certain general advantages and disadvantages, although some are more appropriate than others for organizational testing either because of economic considerations or because the particular attribute at issue can be more validly assessed using a particular format.

Individual versus group tests. Whereas group tests can be simultaneously administered to several persons, an individual test requires one examiner per test-taker. Recalling the history of psychological testing, the original Binet tests and their Stanford revisions were individual tests. The feasibility of group testing was demonstrated with the development during World War I of the *Army Alpha* and *Army Beta*.

The primary advantage of group testing is economy. Up to 500 men at a time were tested with the *Army Alpha* in a single 50 minute period. Assuming adequate testing facilities (including proctors) preemployment screening programs are considerably cheaper to implement using group instead of individual tests.

Nevertheless, the assessment of certain attributes may preclude group administration. This is particularly true in clinical and guidance testing where developing rapport and the ability to further probe test responses may be critically important.

There are two circumstances in organizational testing which may also call for individual rather than group test administration. The first is one in which the equipment required to assess the attribute is either so expensive to dupli-cate or automate for tracking tested performance that it is cheaper to admin-ister the test individually. This often occurs when testing motor skills. The second is where the behavioral process is more critical to the measured attribute than is the behavioral outcome. As we discuss later in this chapter, this sometimes is the case with managerial assessments. The actual solution to the problem may contribute little, if at all, to the score when the attributes being evaluated are such characteristics as interpersonal sensitivity. (Inter-personal interactions frequently present alternative potentially successful resolutions, depending upon *how* they are effected.)

Speed versus power tests.   A speed test has a fixed time limit which the respondent is not permitted to exceed even though, as is usually the case, the test is not completed. A power test is administered without a time limit or, at least, with a sufficiently generous limit to allow virtually everyone to finish.

The essential difference is that the score on a speed test reflects perfor-mance as a function of both accuracy and time; this is clearly important to certain skills like typing and most other tasks. Generally speaking, the items on a clerical speed test are sufficiently easy that most persons would answer all correctly, given sufficient time.

Paper-and-pencil versus performance tests.   Paper-and-pencil tests re-quire written replies, either marks on an answer sheet or narrative answers to written or orally presented questions. Performance tests require the ma-nipulation of physical objects. The distinction between the attributes mea-sured by these formats is illustrated by the difference between the written examination and road test required to be licensed as a driver.

A performance test requires apparatus—either real equipment, a simula-tion (for example, a flight simulator), or some other special apparatus for assessing a particular motor skill (like finger dexterity). Thus, performance tests are generally more expensive to administer, both because of the equip-ment cost and because relatively few persons can be tested simultaneously.

Attributes measured

We differentiate between three classes of tested attributes, each of which is discussed in more detail in the sections to follow:

Cognitive abilities: the present and likely future level of knowledge and problem-solving abilities.

Motor and physical abilities: the present and likely future level of muscular performance.

Affective attributes, including feelings, attitudes, interests, and personality.

The affective attributes comprise the emotional background influencing the quality of cognitive and motor performance under typical circumstances (Cronbach, 1970, p. 35). They determine how effectively or ineffectively we are likely to use our knowledges and skills.

The two remaining areas entail assessments both of present and likely future intellectual and motor behavior. Achievement and aptitude are subsumed under the cognitive abilities. Cleary et al. (1975) make a useful distinction between achievement and aptitude tests. *Achievement* tests assess learning over some specified period as a function of a particular course, curriculum, or training/educational program. *Aptitude* tests also assess learning but are intended to be used for predicting the likely level of future acquisition. Therefore, they assess learning which is the cumulative result of life experience to date rather than of a circumscribed instructional experience.

COGNITIVE ABILITIES

Tests in this area range from assessments of the most general kind of mental ability (intelligence) to extremely specific measures of task-relevant knowledge (for example, typing proficiency). We comment upon and describe only those tests of cognitive abilities that have the broadest application to employment testing.

General intellectual abilities

Tests of general ability are popularly regarded as likely predictors of job performance in diverse settings. In spite of the intuitive appeal of an "intelligence" test for employment selection, tests of general ability are neither what they seem to be, nor as broadly effective as their popularity would suggest.

We need first to clarify that intelligence is not a unitary construct. Although Binet's test yielded a single overall score, it was an omnibus test; that is, it sampled different abilities such as memory, attention, vocabulary, and arithmetic. The paper-and-pencil tests of "general intelligence" subsequently developed tend mostly to emphasize two areas: verbal fluency and numerical ability.

Probably the best known of the "general" intellectual measures is the *Otis Self-Administering Tests of Mental Ability* (1922–29) and its abbreviated cousin the *Personnel Test* (Wonderlic & Hovland, 1939; Wonderlic, 1945). The latter is published in several forms, takes only 12 minutes to administer, and consists of items selected from the *Otis* because they were found to differentiate between satisfactory and unsatisfactory employees.

As measures of cumulative attainments largely in the verbal and numerical areas, the *Otis* and *Wonderlic Personnel Test* are most valid for predicting performance in fields requiring those particular aptitudes. Thus, the tests tend to be most useful for predicting clerical performance although, even for these positions, variations in duties (hence, in personnel prerequisites) for say, accounting clerk, file clerk, and clerk-typist suggest that tests more narrowly targeted are likely to prove more valid.

Further, because the industrial versions of general intelligence tests are brief and limited in scope, they do not differentiate nearly as well at the upper intellectual levels as they do at the lower ones (Anastasi, 1976).

Specific cognitive abilities

Although Binet regarded intelligence as a composite of many abilities, the existence of multiple aptitudes was not demonstrated until after World War I. As concisely described by Dunnette (1976) subsequent theorizing about cognitive attributes went from identifying one (general intelligence) to a few (seven primary mental abilities for Thurstone, 1938) to many (120 hypothesized by Guilford, 1956)—and is now reversing direction from many back to a few.

A fairly recent review of the body of research spanning approximately 50 years (Ekstrom, 1973) supports a list of ten reasonably well-defined and independent cognitive factors. (See Figure 9–2.)

The actual number of factored (relatively discrete) mental abilities is less significant in the context of this discussion than is the identification of measurable abilities which have been found to be reasonably useful predictors of job performance. In this regard, Table 9–1 summarizes the median reported validities of several cognitive predictors against global performance ratings for four nonsupervisory job categories in the petroleum industry (Dunnette, 1972).

Note that for these jobs, at least, some of the factored abilities have little validity. Further, there seem to be distinct patterns of ability associated with overall performance ratings in each occupational area.

If you have examined Table 9–1 with particular care, you have observed that it includes a cognitive ability (mechanical) not cited in the presumably comprehensive list of cognitive factors (Figure 9–2). Mechanical abilities are measured by a composite of cognitive factors usually including mechanical reasoning (a variation of inductive reasoning) and spatial visualization, often supplemented by test components on number facility and mechanical knowledge.

It clearly is impossible, in this discussion, to sample particular tests measuring the more specific cognitive abilities comprehensively. We have

TABLE 9–1
Metal abilities as predictors of performance ratings; median validity coefficients

Cognitive ability	Occupational area			
	Operating and processing	Maintenance	Clerical	Quality control
General intelligence	.32	.20	.17	.24
Numerical ability	.19	.35	.12	.14
Verbal ability	—	.29	.22	.16
Mechanical ability	.20	.38	—	.18
Perceptual speed	—	.16	.15	—
Spatial relations	—	.24	.04	—

Source: After M. D. Dunnette, "Validity Study Results for Jobs Relevant to the Petroleum Refining Industry" (Washington, D.C.: American Petroleum Institute, 1972). Cited in Dunnette, ed., *Handbook of Industrial and Organizational Psychology*, p. 499. Copyright © 1976 by Rand McNally College Publishing Company. Adapted by permission of Houghton Mifflin Company.

FIGURE 9–2
Cognitive factors

1. *Flexibility and speed of closure.* Ability to "take in" a perceptual field, "fill in" unseen portions to form a meaningful whole, and keep the visual percept distinct from distracting background.

2. *Fluency.* Ability to rephrase ideas, generate new ideas, produce words fulfilling specific requirements independent of their meaning, and generate words from a restricted area of meaning.

3. *Inductive reasoning.* Ability to form and test hypotheses directed toward discovering and applying principles of relationship.

4. *Associative (rote) memory.* Ability to remember bits of unrelated material.

5. *Span memory.* Ability to recall a series of items perfectly for immediate reproduction after one presentation.

6. *Number facility.* Ability to rapidly manipulate numbers in arithmetic operations. (Note: this ability does not determine higher mathematical skills or complex mathematical reasoning ability.)

7. *Perceptual speed.* Speed in carrying out simple tasks involving visual perception: for example, finding hidden figures, making comparisons, and so on.

8. *Deductive reasoning.* Ability to reason from stated premises to their necessary conclusions.

9. *Spatial orientation and visualization.* Ability to manipulate visual percepts (to imagine changes in forms); to perceive spatial patterns, and to put together in visual imagination parts that are out of place in a visual pattern.

10. *Verbal comprehension.* Knowledge of words and their meanings; application of this knowledge in understanding connected discourse.

Source: After R. B. Ekstrom, "Cognitive Factors: Some Recent Literature" (Princeton, N.J.: Educational Testing Service, 1973), and M. D. Dunnette, "Abilities, Aptitudes, and Skills," in *Handbook of Industrial and Organizational Psychology,* ed. M. D. Dunnette (Chicago: Rand McNally, 1976).

elected to discuss a few illustrative tests and batteries in two widely tested areas—mechanical and clerical—and to comment briefly on multiple-aptitude batteries.

Mechanical ability and spatial ability.   We have already noted that mechanical ability typically is estimated from a combination of factored ability subtests and mechanical knowledge.

A widely used test of mechanical knowledge is the Bennett, Seashore, Wesman *Mechanical Reasoning Test* (1947). Its items tap understanding of mechanical principles and are similar to the illustration in Figure 9–3. This

FIGURE 9–3
Sample item from Form W, Bennett, Seashore, and Wesman Mechanical Reasoning Test

Which person has the heavier load? (If equal, mark C.)

Source: Reproduced by permission from the Differential Aptitude Tests. Copyright © 1980 The Psychological Corporation, New York, N.Y. All rights reserved.

paper-and-pencil test is rapidly administered and scored. The test has been validated for trade school applicants as well as applicants in fields like engineering.

The SRA Test of Mechanical Aptitude (1947), another paper-and-pencil test, covers three areas contributing to mechanical ability: mechanical knowledge, space relations, and shop arithmetic. Sample items of each type are shown in Figure 9–4. The total score on the three parts is taken as an index of mechanical aptitude. The manual advises that the investigator consider differentially weighting the part scores if the evidence from a particular validation effort supports this strategy. Thus, some mechanical positions may be more demanding of spatial visualization, others of arithmetic skill, and so on.

174

FIGURE 9–4
Illustrative sample questions: SRA Mechanical Aptitudes Test

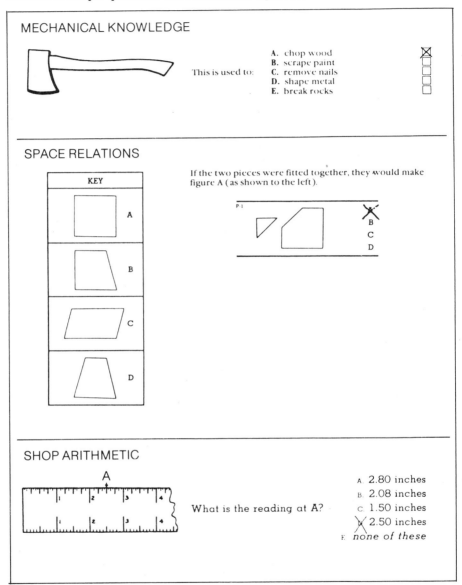

Source: From *SRA Mechanical Aptitudes Test,* Form AH. © 1947, Science Research Associates, Inc., Chicago. Reprinted by permission of the publisher.

Clerical abilities. The *Short Tests of Clerical Ability* (Palermo, 1960, 1973) comprise a battery of seven tests designed to predict successful performance in various office jobs. Norms are separately provided for applicants, employed minority and nonminority groups, and several occupational subgroups. Each of the tests is brief; six of the seven have five-minute time limits. The battery tests a mix of cognitive abilities and job-related knowledge.

Refer to Figure 9–2 and see if you can infer something about the likely composition of the STCA battery. (Its actual composition is shown in Figure 9–5).

Multiple aptitude batteries. As implied by the designation, multiple aptitude test batteries cover a wide range of cognitive abilities (and, in some cases, motor abilities) usually through a series of subtests. Since they provide very broad coverage, they offer the possibility for establishing differential validities for various positions in the same organization. Thus, their use may facilitate optimal placement when several openings exist. Because of the time and expense involved, they are generally used when testing employees who are being considered for promotion or further job-related training rather than for employment selection.

The cognitive abilities measured by multiple aptitude batteries (like the *General Aptitude Test Battery,* the *Differential Aptitude Tests,* and the *Flanagan Industrial Tests*) invariably cover the range described in Figure 9–2.

TESTS OF MOTOR AND PHYSICAL ABILITIES

Motor abilities include fine or gross muscular coordination, dexterity, and so on. *Physical* abilities entail characteristics like strength and stamina.

Most jobs make demands upon these abilities as well as cognitive abilities. However, the predictive usefulness of motor and physical tests typically is limited to jobs making substantial demands upon these abilities. The validity gains from supplementing cognitive ability tests with motor and physical tests are not otherwise sufficiently substantial to justify their cost. As we will see, most tests of motor ability require apparatus (that is, they are performance measures) and individual (rather than group) administration.

Motor abilities

Motor abilities are of two types: psychomotor and sensorimotor. Psychomotor responses entail muscular movement and control; sensorimotor responses entail psychomotor activity following receptor stimulation. Often, as when driving a car, performance is a function of both the operator's sensory abilities (for example, visual acuity, sensitivity to color changes) and psychomotor abilities. However, our discussion here is limited to the psychomotor components of such performance.

As with cognitive attributes testing, motor tests can be oriented toward evaluating present proficiency or forecasting future performance. The lan-

FIGURE 9–5
Short tests of clerical ability: Sample items

Sample Item
Coding

CODE 1	
plastic	25
rubber	12
china	18

CODE 2	
ball	P
doll	J
gun	Z

Column 1

plastic Ⓧ ⑫ ⑱
china ⑫ Ⓧ ㉕
rubber ㉕ Ⓧ ⑱

Column 2

doll Ⓩ Ⓟ Ⓧ
ball Ⓧ Ⓙ Ⓩ
gun Ⓙ Ⓧ Ⓟ

Sample Item
Checking

CORRECT LIST		LIST TO BE CHECKED		R	W
Sam J. Smith	15.06	R. A. Tomas	145.32	○	●
Tillie Smyth	36.50	Sam J. Smith	15.06	●	○
R. A. Thomas	145.32	Richard Young	230.42	○	●
Robert Williams	84.22	Tillie Smyth	36.50	●	○
Richard Young	203.42	Robert William	84.22	○	●

Sample Item
Filing

The list on the left side of each column is called the "Existing File." The list on the right side of each column is the material "To Be Filed." Following each name in the "To Be Filed" column are three numbered circles and one blank circle. You are to look at the name in the "To Be Filed" column and find the name in the "Existing File" which it should *follow*.

Existing File

1. Philip Jenkins
2. J. C. Kile
3. Thomas Morris Company
4. Paulson Company, Inc.
5. Sally White

To Be Filed

John Jones   Ⓧ ② ③

A. B. Reynolds   ① ② ③

Sample Item
Directions

First the examiner will read a list of company policies and office procedures of the kind that a new employee might be told. There will be *several* instructions on company benefits, *several* on *ways of seeking*... the blank back page. *The instructions will be read relatively quickly. You should concentrate on listening and take your notes as "memory aids."*

Days

	6	18	24	30	36
12 months employment	○	○	○	○	○
36 months employment	○	○	○	○	○
48 months employment	○	○	○	○	○
60 months employment	○	○	○	○	○

Sample Item
Arithmetic

                               NG

S1. 42 − 20 =   (40) (12) ⊗ (32)   ○

S2. 12 × 5 =   (36) (40) (48) (52)   ⊗

Sample Item
Business
Vocabulary

Duplicates of letters can be made by using _____

○ ink   ⊗ carbon paper   ○ second sheets   ○ bond paper

Sample Item
Language

Sentence	Kind of Error
The boy ran.	Wrong punctuation mark is used.
The boy ran	Punctuation mark is omitted.
The boy ran.	First "," in sentence is not needed.
She will go instead of me.	Word "instead" is misspelled.
Mr. smith will go.	Name "Smith" should be capitalized.
Mr. Smith went to the City.	Capital "C" in "city" is wrong.
He ain't been fair.	Grammatical error—"hasn't", not "ain't"
The devise is new.	Wrong word used—"device", not "devise"

Some sentences are correct and contain no errors. In other sentences, there may be several errors. For example.

A. This insurance give you coverege twenty four hours a day.   (0) (1) (2) ⊗ (4)

B. The sales for this month increased.   ⊗ (1) (2) (3) (4)

guage applied to cognitive tests usually differentiates between these objectives with the designations "achievement" and "aptitude." The parallel distinction for motor performance (Fleishman, 1966) is that between skill (the present level of task proficiency) and ability (physical talent prerequisite to learning skills). Thus, a person may presently be unskilled as a tennis player but have the requisite motor and physical abilities to profit from coaching.

E. A. Fleishman and his co-workers have been by far the most prolific investigators of motor performance, contributing both to the theory and practice of psychomotor testing. One major emphasis of this research has been to identify the fundamental motor abilities and ways of assessing them. Note the plural character of the preceding sentence. The evidence makes

FIGURE 9–6
Motor abilities

1. *Control precision.* Performance requiring finely controlled muscular movements; most critical when motor adjustments must be rapid but precise. *Example:* Moving a lever to a precise setting.
2. *Multi-limb coordination.* Ability to coordinate limb movement. *Examples:* Two-handed packing tasks; coordinating arm and leg movements when piloting a plane.
3. *Response orientation.* Choosing and making the correct movement in response to a stimulus. *Examples:* Evasive maneuvering; flicking a switch to "power down" following a warning signal.
4. *Reaction time.* Speed of response to a stimulus. *Example:* Elapsed time between hearing a smoke alarm and responding.
5. *Speed of arm movement.* Speed of gross arm movement when accuracy is not required. (Note: this does not correlate with reaction time.) *Example:* Using arms to rapidly sweep parts off the workbench and into a bin.
6. *Rate control.* Pursuing (and therefore anticipating changes in) a continuously moving target or object which changes speed and direction. *Example:* Antiaircraft gunnery.
7. *Manual dexterity.* Skillful, accurate, and rapid arm-hand movements when manipulating fairly large objects. *Example:* Gross assembly tasks.
8. *Finger dexterity.* Skillful and accurate movements of small objects, primarily using the fingers. *Example:* Precision placement of electronic components.
9. *Arm-hand steadiness.* Steady and precise arm-hand positioning where strength and speed are *not* at issue. Example: Threading a needle.
10. *Wrist-finger speed.* Rapid tapping movements involving the wrist and fingers. *Example:* Tapping a pencil within a relatively large circumscribed area.
11. *Aiming.* A narrow ability defined by tests requiring that dots be rapidly placed within circles.

Source: This work is an adaptation from E. A. Fleishman, "The Description and Prediction of Perceptual-Motor Skill Learning," in *Training Research and Education*, ed. R. Glaser. Published in 1962 by the University of Pittsburgh Press. Used by permission.

clear that there is an array of essentially independent motor abilities rather than a single overriding ability.

Fleishman's studies are largely factor analytic. The intercorrelation matrix of many separately taken measures—in this instance, of motor performance, is statistically examined for its underlying factor structure. This structure seeks to account for the obtained relationships between the various measures (that is, intercorrelations) with the smallest number of relatively independent explanatory concepts (factors).

Were there one overriding motor ability, this kind of analysis of the intercorrelations between motor test scores would result in just a single factor. As we have already indicated, this is not the case. After a series of studies involving devising motor tests, administering these along with other motor performance measures to groups of subjects, intercorrelating the scores, and factor analyzing the matrices, Fleishman identified 11 basic motor abilities (1962). (See Figure 9–6.)

At least some of the abilities listed in Figure 9–6 will look familiar. You read earlier (in Chapter 4) that seven of these abilities have been found, for all practical purposes, pretty much to account for industrial motor ability requirements: control precision, reaction time, speed of limb movement, manual dexerity, finger dexterity, arm-hand steadiness, and wrist-finger speed (Theologus & Fleishman, 1971).

Some psychomotor tests. The examples cited in Figure 9–6 suggest something of the range of tasks that might be developed to evaluate psychomotor abilities. You can envision an apparatus to measure control precision by requiring that dials or levers be precisely adjusted; multilimb coordination by a set-up requiring two hands simultaneously to adjust the location of a stylus; and so on.

Among the earliest of the tests for evaluating certain psychomotor abilities (manual and finger dexterity) were the *Crawford Small Parts Dexterity Test* (Crawford & Crawford, 1946) and the *Purdue Pegboard* (Tiffin, 1941). The former requires (*a*) inserting small pins into holes after which a collar is placed on each pin and (*b*) placing small screws by hand into threaded holes followed by using a screwdriver on each. The Purdue Pegboard taps gross dexterity by requiring pin placement in holes using each hand separately and then both together. Fine finger dexterity is measured by requiring collar and washer assemblies for each pin as it is placed.

Physical abilities

Following a research pattern similar to that employed for factoring motor abilities, Fleishman and his associates identified the nine relatively independent physical abilities (Fleishman, 1964) described in Figure 9–7 which is illustrated on the following page.

FIGURE 9–7
Physical abilities

1. *Static strength.* The maximum force that can be exerted against a fairly immovable or heavy object in order to life, push, or pull it. *Examples:* Lifting weights, pushing a wheelbarrow.

2. *Dynamic strength.* Power to repeatedly or continuously support or move the body's own weight. *Examples:* Pull-ups, climbing a ladder.

3. *Explosive strength.* Ability to mobilize energy for a burst of muscular effort. *Examples:* Throwing a shotput, relay sprints.

4. *Trunk strength.* Dynamic strength limited to the trunk (particulary abdominal) muscles. *Examples:* Sit-ups, repeated stooping.

5. *Extent flexibility.* Ability to flex or stretch the trunk and back muscles as far as possible in all directions. *Example:* Twisting and touching toes.

6. *Dynamic flexibility.* Ability to make repeated trunk and/or limb flexing movements; includes ability to recover from the strain of repeated flexing. *Examples:* Crawling, scraping paint.

7. *Gross body coordination.* Ability to coordinate actions while the body is in motion. *Example:* Jumping rope.

8. *Gross body equilibrium.* Ability to maintain balance without visual cues when equilibrium is temporarily lost or threatened. *Examples:* Walking a rail; walking on a wet surface.

9. *Stamina.* The ability to maintain physical activity entailing cardiovascular exertion over a prolonged period of time. *Example:* 600 yard run-walk.

Source: After G. C. Theologus, T. Ramasko, and E. A. Fleishman, *A Feasibility Study of Ability Dimensions for Classifying Human Tasks*, Tech. Rep. No. 5 (Washington, D.C.: American Institute for Research, 1970).

AFFECTIVE ATTRIBUTES

Although tests of mental ability are basic to any employment testing program, these predictors alone rarely yield validity coefficients above .40 to .50 (Ghiselli, 1973). When appropriate, the level of validity can be enhanced by supplementing the cognitive predictors with measures of motor and physical abilities.

Job performance involves a third set of factors—usually described as the "motivation" to perform at the level of one's abilities. Personality and interest inventories are sometimes explored as potential predictors of this intangible. For the most part these explorations have been rather unsuccessful (Guion & Gottier, 1965). Irrespective of their value for clinical evaluation and career counseling, their promise in employment psychology would seem to be much greater for evaluations as part of a management development program than it is for selection. A brief look at a small sample of instruments measuring affective attributes will help clarify certain properties—particularly transparency and unreliability—militating against validity for selection.

Personality inventories

These devices are: self-report questionnaires and projective measures.

Self-report questionnaires ask respondents to reply (agree-disagree; always-sometimes-rarely) to a series of potentially self-descriptive statements or phrases like:

I worry a good deal about my health.

I frequently have headaches.

I concentrate easily.

Although self-report questionnaires are easily administered and rapidly scored, applicants are understandably reluctant to admit to negative characteristics and are inclined to check only the positive ones in such a transparent format.

Projective techniques consist of relatively unstructured or ambiguous stimuli (for example, incomplete sentences and "ink blots") to which the respondent makes a free or unstructured response. The replies are assumed to be projections of thoughts, wishes, needs, and so on. Projectives are not transparent; it is difficult to fake replies when one is unsure of the "desired" response. However, their proper administration and interpretation is expensive because it requires individual testing by a highly experienced and skilled examiner. Furthermore, the reliability of interpretations with nonclinical populations is suspect.

Finally, in the absence of clearcut indications of validity, the administration of either type of personality inventory for employment selection can be construed as an unwarranted invasion of privacy.

Two self-report measures are cited below merely to give you an indication of the nature of these instruments.

Guilford-Zimmerman Temperament Survey (1949). This inventory yields scores on 10 bipolar personality traits which were established through factor analysis to be relatively homogeneous and independent.

G—General activity (drive) versus inactivity.

R—Self-restraint versus impulsivity.

A—Ascendance versus submissiveness.

S—Sociability versus shyness.

E—Emotional stability versus moodiness.

O—Objectivity versus hypersensitivity.

F—Friendliness versus criticalness.

T—Thoughtfulness (analytical) versus impulsivity.

P—Personal tolerance versus intolerance.

M—Masculinity versus femininity.

Minnesota Multiphasic Inventory. The MMPI, also a self-report inventory, consists of 550 statements scored for ten clinically significant scales (for example, "Hypochondria," "Paranoia"). The scales were empirically established from differences in item-response frequency obtained with clinical and nonclinical samples (Hathaway & McKinley, 1943). Additionally, the inventory contains separate scored scales for inferring whether the respondent replied truthfully and understood the instructions.

One difficulty with industrial applications of the MMPI is its clinical orientation. It was designed to help identify severely aberrant behavior of a type unlikely to be presented by job applicants.

Interest inventories

Interest inventories are widely used for career guidance. The two best known are the *Strong-Campbell Interest Inventory* (SCII) and the *Kuder Preference Record* (1953). The former is a revised edition (1974) of the earlier *Strong Vocational Interest Blank.*

Both inventories are backed by exceedingly comprehensive research programs for their intended purpose: that is, guidance. The SCII provides informative feedback concerning the similarity between the respondent's interests and those of persons engaged in various occupations. Additionally, it yields scores for broad occupational areas and several special scales including interest maturity and academic orientation.

The *Kuder* is conceptually different in that it was developed as a forced-choice (rather than checklist) inventory in an attempt to reduce the transparency of interest assessment. It yields scores only for such broad occupational areas as mechanical, clerical, and so on, although these have clear relevance to specific professions and vocations within each area.

JOB SAMPLES AND SIMULATIONS

This section considers what, at first glance, may appear to be two very different approaches to personnel evaluation. We discuss together procedures for testing applicants and incumbents at divergent occupational levels—from operations and maintenance to management. The element of cohesion for this section is one of rationale: the most valid index of future performance is a *measure* of present performance.

Heretofore this chapter has emphasized predictive validity: We have discussed tests permitting informed inferences about the level of likely job performance to be expected in the future. In contrast, job and task samples and simulations seek to measure that performance directly.

This difference is analogous to the alternatives of predicting a horse's speed in the fifth race from information about past performance under varying track conditions as opposed to actually clocking the speed as the race is run. Although a bettor has no choice, the trainer will opt for the measurement instead of the prediction every time. Similarly for job performance, carefully devised work samples almost always exhibit validity superior to that of tests designed to predict that performance (Dunnette & Borman, 1979).

Job samples as complex measures

As you know by now, actual job performance reflects the combined interaction of abilities (cognitive, motor, and physical), knowledge, skill, and such intangibles as *drive*. Measures of each of these contributing factors are fallible; and the combination of several such measures into a composite predictor battery enforces the identical (albeit optimal) weighting of each predictor component for all applicants.

Were we able to measure job performance directly we would, of course, bypass the entire issue of predictor fallibility. Further, the measure itself would reflect the synthesis of the abilities, skills, knowledges, and affective attributes operating for the particular person tested.

There are relatively few circumstances where an actual sample of job performance can be taken with applicants. Even trade tests (for example, of welding skill) do not sample actual on-the-job performance. And, as Dunnette (1976) points out, even when employment entails a probationary period before a final hiring decision is made, evaluations during that period tend more to emphasize such things as getting to work on time, listening to directions, and getting along with co-workers, than actual quality of job performance.

Although actual samples of complex job performance typically are unavailable for review in advance of committing to a hiring decision, two variations often *can* be made available: task samples and simulations. Task sampling entails identifying the critical components (tasks) of overall job performance and measuring proficiency in performing each component. Simulations, used when task performance cannot itself be sampled, entail assessments of behavior in situations modeled after reality.

We will discuss these two approaches separately, emphasizing the application of task sampling to employment selection and task simulation (through assessment centers) to managerial development. However, it must be clear at the outset that the success of such measures hinges not only on the psychometric properties of the instruments themselves, but also on the care taken in identifying the job's critical dimensions (tasks). In addition to emphasizing likely employee prerequisites (knowledges and abilities) the job analysis preceding these more direct measurement approaches must uncover the essential constituents of the job in ways that will permit their assessment (Schwartz, 1977).

Task sampling

Although involving only a small number of subjects ($n = 34$) the potential superiority of task sampling over aptitude testing was convincingly demonstrated in a study with maintenance mechanics (Campion, 1972). The investigator identified mechanical tasks that were independent of particular plant procedures, and therefore were appropriate for applicant testing. These tasks were incorporated into four standardized work sample exercises. Concurrent validities of the work sample tests were found to be superior to the validities of several aptitude tests, all of which were administered to a group of incumbents.

Job sample testing for selection clearly merits continued attention in spite of the time-consuming aspect of developing such tests. Job sample tests may not only be perceived as "more fair" by job candidates because of their clear face validity, but may generate less adverse impact than the more usual paper-and-pencil knowledge and ability tests (Schmidt et al., 1977).

Task simulations: Assessment centers

Since the assessment center was first developed in the military Office of Strategic Service to train spies in World War II, an estimated 200,000 managers in 1,000 U.S. corporations have been through a center at least once (Cascio & Silbey, 1979).

Strictly speaking, an assessment center is an approach to evaluative testing rather than a place. Its distinguishing features are : (a) involvement of a group of persons (assessors and assessees) who participate in most exercises either as an entire group or in smaller subgroups, (b) exercises which are standardized and for which there is a rational and/or empirical link to organizational behavior, (c) an emphasis upon "realistic" exercises; and (d) narrative, integrative performance summaries (rather than individual test scores) prepared by trained evaluators and covering such dimensions as human relations skills, persuasiveness, resistance to stress, and so on (Finkle, 1976).

Although usually used for managerial assessment in conjunction with management development programs, variations of the assessment center approach have also been reported for such other applications as estimating sales potential (Bray & Campbell, 1968). Nevertheless, the intent of the originators of the approach, and still its most typical application, is to predict the managerial effectiveness of incumbents with an eye both toward their future development and their differential placement (Bray, Campbell, & Grant, 1974).

Some simulation methods. The participant in an *in-basket exercise* is confronted with a hypothetical in-basket filled with realistically assorted items including memos, daily reports, computer printouts, social items, and so on. The task is to respond realistically and appropriately to each item. Response alternatives include referral, deferral, delegating, memo or letter writing, and others. After finishing the exercise, the person tested completes a form by justifying each action taken and each decision made.

In-basket responses are evaluated by trained assessors who evaluate such things as decisiveness, imagination, courteousness to subordinates, and so on. The technique has been found to tap three areas of behavior: (a) making versus deferring decisions and actions (b) high versus low work output rate, and (c) acting independently versus seeking advice and guidance from superiors (Frederickson, 1962).

In another simulation, the *leaderless group discussion,* a group of assessees (usually six) discusses and resolves a simulated problem involving, for example, a promotion decision, disciplinary situation, or possible financial expansion. Whereas supporting data are provided to all participants, alternative courses of action may not be specified. Also, the group members are not assigned particular roles; none, for example, is assigned to chair the group. The processes of interpersonal interaction among the group members are often more significant to the evaluation of their performance than is the actual solution or course of action finally endorsed by the group.

More structured simulations may require assessees to *role play* (for example, chair a labor-management arbitration meeting, interview a job applicant, give a talk on some subject) or to participate in management "games" in which teams must compete for access to limited materials, resources, and markets in order to show maximum profits.

Evaluation.   Some organizations adopt assessment-center techniques merely because they are in vogue, even though the techniques may be inappropriate to organizational goals and improperly implemented. The issue of faddishness aside, even the brief description above suggests that this approach is expensive. Furthermore, the usual psychometric considerations of reliability and validity are difficult to apply to these techniques both because of the global, narrative nature of the resulting assessment and because the validation criteria (like salary) may reflect the same subtle contaminents as do the predictors (general likability, appearance, and so on) (Klimaski & Strickland, 1977).

Is the financial investment in assessment centers worth it? Maybe. A cost-benefit analysis (Cascio & Silbey, 1979) finds the technique most useful when (a) job performance is poorly predicted by cheaper methods, (b) there is a large standard deviation in the criterion, and (c) the subject's work (like that of an executive) is very valuable, justifying the expense of even small increases in predictive validity. There seems no doubt that the use of assessment centers will increase in the future (Grant, 1980.) The challenge will be to incorporate simulations that are in fact linked to performance dimensions, and to continue research on standardizing the conditions for administering these exercises and interpreting the performance they evoke.

SUMMARY

We began this chapter by briefly tracing the history of psychological testing starting with Binet's contribution to individual intellectual assessment near the end of the 19th century. At the present time we regard employment testing, carefully conceived and implemented, as the best tool available to society for optimizing the balance between organizational needs to employ talented persons and individuals' needs to use their talents effectively.

It is convenient to classify tests by format and attribute measured.

The classification by format emphasizes certain elements of test administration: that is, individual or group administration, speed or power, paper-and-pencil or performance. Each format has advantages and disadvantages in particular applications.

We differentiated three classes of tested attributes: cognitive abilities, motor and physical abilities, and affective attributes.

Tests of cognitive abilities range from broad overall assessments of mental ability (intelligence) to extremely specific measures of task-relevant knowledge (for example, typing proficiency). Cognitive ability testing for employment selection and placement typically makes a differentiation between achievement and aptitude tests. Achievement tests assess learning over some specified period of time as a function of a particular course, curriculum, or training program. Aptitude tests assess learning as the cumulative result of life experiences to date from all sources. Thus, aptitude tests are regarded as the more useful predictors of the likely level of future acquisition.

Motor tests also are oriented both toward evaluating present proficiency (motor skill) or forecasting future performance (motor ability). Factor analysis has confirmed the existence of 11 relatively independent motor abilities (control precision, multi-limb coordination, response orientation, and so on).

In addition to cognitive and motor abilities, job performance reflects a third set of factors, usually described as the "motivation" to perform. Some evidence concerning this issue is provided by assessment in the affective domain: that is, personality, values, and interests.

Whereas assessments of cognitive, motor, and affective characteristics are useful for selection and placement to the extent that they have predictive validity, task sampling and simulation can sometimes provide more direct measures of performance. Task sampling entails assessments of proficiency in actually performing the several critical components of a job; simulations involve assessments of behavior in situations modeled after reality. For obvious reasons, both approaches are easier to implement with incumbents than job applicants.

The assessment-center approach to personnel evaluation was discussed as an interesting combination of more traditional testing and task simulation. The major application of this approach has been in the area of managerial assessment.

REFERENCES

American Psychological Association, American Educational Research Association, & National Council for Measurement in Psychology. *Standards for educational and psychological tests.* Washington, D.C.: APA, 1974.

American Psychological Association, Division of Industrial-Organizational Psychology. *Principles for the validation and use of personnel selection procedures* (2nd ed.) Berkeley, Calif.: Industrial-Organizational Psychologist, 1980.

Anastasi, A. *Psychological testing* (4th ed.). New York: Macmillan, 1976.

Bennett, G. K., Seashore, H. G., & Wesman, A. G. *Mechanical reasoning test.* New York: Psychological Corp., 1980

Bray, D. W., & Campbell, R. J. Selection of salesmen by means of an assessment center. *Journal of Applied Psychology,* 1968, *52,* 36–41.

Bray, D. W., Campbell, R. J., & Grant, D. L. *Formative years in business: A long term study of managerial lives.* New York: Wiley, 1974.

Buros, O. K. *The eighth mental measurement yearbook.* Highland Park, N.J.: Gryphon, 1978.

Campion, J. E. Work sampling for personnel selection. *Journal of Applied Psychology,* 1972, *56,* 40–44.

Cascio, W., & Silbey, V. Utility of the assessment center as a selection device. *Journal of Applied Psychology,* 1979, *64,* 107–118.

Cleary, T. A., Humphreys, L. G., Kendrick, S. A., & Wesman, A. Educational uses of tests with disadvantaged students. *American Psychologist,* 1975, *30,* 15–41.

Crawford, J. E., & Crawford, D. M. *Small parts dexterity test.* New York: Psychological Corporation, 1946.

Cronbach, L. J. *Essential of psychological testing* (3rd ed.). New York: Harper & Row, 1970.

Dunnette, M. D. *Validity study results for jobs relevant to the petroleum refining industry.* Washington, D.C.: American Petroleum Inst., 1972. (Cited in Dunnette, 1976.)

Dunnette, M. D. Abilities, aptitudes, and skills. In M. D. Dunnette (Ed.), *Handbook of industrial and organizational psychology.* Chicago: Rand McNally, 1976, 473–520.

Dunnette, M. D., & Borman, W. D. Personnel selection and classification systems. *Annual Review of Psychology,* 1979, *30,* 477–525.

Ekstrom, R. B. *Cognitive factors: Some recent literature.* Tech. Rep. No. 2, ONR contrast N 000 14-71-C-0117, NR 150–329. Princeton, N.J.: Educational Testing Service, 1973.

Educational Testing Service. *Test use and validity.* Princeton, N.J.: ETS, 1980.

Finkle, R. B. Managerial assessment centers. In M. D. Dunnette (Ed.), *Handbook of industrial and organizational psychology.* Chicago: Rand McNally, 1976, 861–888.

Fleishman, E. A. The description and prediction of perceptual-motor skill learning. In R. Glaser (Ed.), *Training research and education.* Pittsburgh: University of Pittsburgh Press, 1962.

Fleishman, E. A. *The structure and measurement of physical fitness.* Englewood Cliffs, N.J.: Prentice-Hall, 1964.

Fleishman, E. A. Human abilities and the acquisition of skill: Comment on Professor Jones' paper. In E. A. Bilodeau (Ed.), *Acquisition of skills.* New York: Academic Press, 1966.

Frederickson, N. Factors in in-basket performance. *Psychological monographs,* 1962, *76,* (22, Whole No. 541).

Freyd, M. Measurement in vocational selection: An outline of research procedure. *Journal of Personnel Research,* 1923, *2,* 215–249, 268–284, 377–385.

Ghiselli, E. E. The validity of aptitude tests in personnel selection. *Personnel Psychology,* 1973, *26,* 461–477.

Grant, D. Issues in personnel selection. *Professional Psychology,* 1980, *11,* 369–384.

Gross, M. L. *The brain watchers.* New York: Random House, 1962.

Guilford, J. P. The structure of intellect. *Psychological Bulletin,* 1956, *53,* 267–293.

Guilford, J. P., & Zimmerman, W. S. *The Guilford-Zimmerman temperament survey.* Beverly Hills, Calif.: Sheridan Supply, 1949.

Guion, R. M., & Gottier, R. F. Validity of personality measures in personnel selection. *Personnel Psychology,* 1965, *18,* 135–164.

Hathaway, S. R., & McKinley, J. C. *Minnesota multiphasic inventory.* New York: Psychological Corp., 1943.

Joint committee of APA, AERA, NCME. Technical recommendations for psychological tests and diagnostic techniques. *Psychological Bulletin,* 1954, *51,* 201–238.

Klimaski, R. J., & Strickland, W. J. Assessment centers—valid or merely prescient. *Personnel Psychology,* 1977, *30,* 353–361.

Kuder, G. F. *The preference record.* Chicago: Science Research Associates, 1953.

Lent, R. H., Aurbach, H. A., & Levin, L. S. Predictors, criteria, and significant results. *Personnel Psychology,* 1971, *24,* 519–533.

Munsterberg, H. *Psychology and industrial efficiency.* Boston: Houghton Mifflin, 1913.

Nairn, A., & Associates. *The reign of ETS: The corporation that makes up minds.* Washington, D.C.: 1980.

Otis, A. S. *Otis self-administering tests of mental ability.* Tarrytown-on-Hudson, N.Y.: World Book, 1922–29.

Palermo, J. M. *Short Tests of Clerical Abilities.* Chicago: SRA, 1960, 1973.

Schmidt, F. L., Greenthal, A. L., Hunter, J. E., Berner, J. G., & Seaton, F. W. Job samples versus paper-and-pencil trades and technical tests: Adverse impact and examinee attitudes. *Personnel Psychology,* 1977, *30,* 187–197.

Schwartz, D. J. A job sampling approach to merit system examining. *Personnel Psychology, 30,* 1977, 175–185.

Science Research Associates. *Mechanical Aptitudes Test.* Chicago: SRA, 1947, 1950.

Science Research Associates. *Validation: Procedures and Results. Part III: Supplemental Results* (3rd ed.). Chicago: SRA, 1973.

Science Research Associates. *Catalog for business.* Chicago: SRA, 1978.

Strong, E. K. Jr., & Campbell, D. P. *Strong-Campbell Interest Inventory* (Rev. ed.) Sanford, Calif.: Stanford University Press, 1974.

Theologus, G. C., & Fleishman, E. A. *Development of a taxonomy of human performance: Validation study of ability scales for classifying human tasks.* Tech. Rep. No. 10. Washington, D.C.: American Institutes for Research, 1971.

Theologus, G. C., Romasko, T., & Fleishman, E. A. *A feasibility study of ability dimensions for classifying human tasks*. Tech. Rep. No. 5. Washington, D.C.: American Institutes for Research, 1970.

Thurstone, L. L. *Primary mental abilities*. Chicago: University of Chicago Press, 1938.

Tiffin, J. *Purdue Pegboard*. Chicago: Science Research Associates, 1943.

Truth in testing. *New York Times* (Editorial), July 24, 1979, p. 48.

Uhlaner, J. E. *The research psychologist in the Army: 1917–1977*. Res. Rep. 1155 (rev.). Alexandria, Va.: U.S. Army Res. Inst. 1977.

Whyte, W. H. *The organization man*. New York: Simon and Schuster, 1956.

Wonderlic, E. F. *Personnel test*. Northfield, Ill.: 1945.

Wonderlic, E. F., & Hovland, C. I. The personnel test: A restandardized abridgement of the Otis S. A. test for business and industrial use. *Journal of Applied Psychology*, 1939, *23*, 685–702.

FACILITATING PERFORMANCE

part C

Selection and placement procedures seek to provide organizations with the best available human resources: that is, with those persons who have the knowledge, skills, ability, motivation, attitudes, and so on, to do their jobs satisfactorily. The remainder of this book is devoted to the broad issue of integrating people into jobs and organizations so that the total effort is maximally effective and rewarding.

Such integration is a process of dynamic adaptation. As you will read in Section Three, successful organizations both facilitate adaptation by their constituents (employees, management, and society) and themselves adapt to their constituents' objectives. The essence of an organization, as distinct from a collection of individuals, is that the members share common objectives and understandings.

SYSTEMS

Since we have several occasions in these chapters to refer to the systems concept, we introduce it here. A system is the broad designation applied to a cohesive package of events, materials, hardware, operations, and processes. At minimum, a system has inputs initiating its activity, and outputs—products, services, or signals. The systems with which we will be concerned have two additional elements: (a) controls and/or processors which regulate the sequence from input to output and (b) feedback which makes the system self-regulating.

Mechanical systems

Everyone is familiar with mechanical systems (like the one for a home freezer shown in Figure IIC–1). Once the thermostatic control is set to a particular temperature, the refrigerating motor will operate only when that temperature is exceeded. Note the self-regulatory nature of the system. The control continuously monitors freezer temperature. When the output causes the temperature to drop below the setting, the sensing unit signals the input source to shut down.

FIGURE IIC–1
Self regulating freezer system

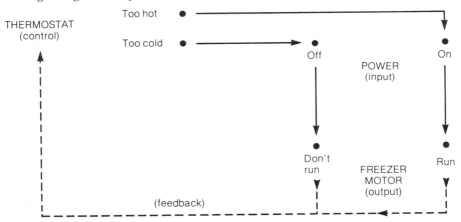

THERMOSTAT
(control)

Too hot

Too cold

Off

POWER
(input)

On

Don't
run

FREEZER
MOTOR
(output)

Run

(feedback)

Man-machine systems

Human functions can be conceptualized analagously. Our receptors (eyes, ears, and so on) provide inputs in the nature of information to be processed; the output is some kind of behavior; and the sequence from input to output is mediated by information-processing controls in the form of judgments, decisions, interpretations, and so on (see Figure IIC–2).

Finally, we can conceptualize man-machine systems; that is, systems in which the human organism is a subsystem functioning as the control point between mechanical inputs and outputs (see Figure IIC–3.)

FIGURE IIC–2

A human system: Maintaining driving speed at 55 miles per hour

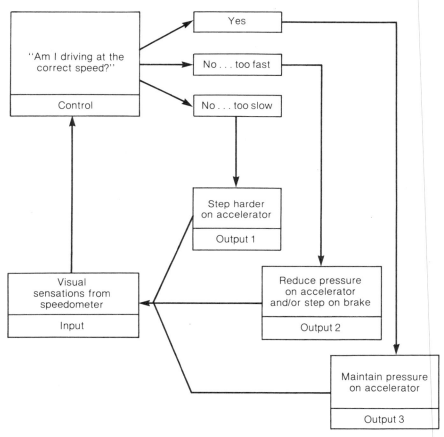

Source: L. Siegel and I. M. Lane, *Psychology in Industrial Organizations,* 3d ed. (Homewood, Ill.: Irwin, 1974), p. 272. © 1974 by Richard D. Irwin, Inc.

Organizations as systems

We have thus far discussed only very simple systems. Modern organizations are made up of systems within systems, each with hardware (that is, mechanical) subsystems and personnel (human) subsystems.

Before moving on to a comprehensive organizational perspective, we need first to consider the ways in which these subsystems interact with one another. In the following chapters, we are specifically concerned with the nature of the

FIGURE IIC–3

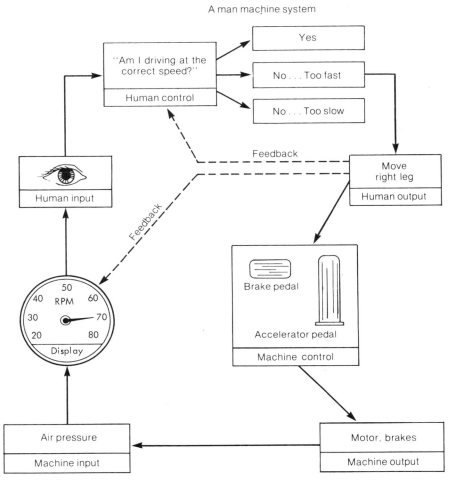

A man machine system

Source: L. Siegel and I. M. Lane, *Psychology in Industrial Organizations,* 3d ed. (Homewood, Ill.: Irwin, 1974), p. 272. © by Richard D. Irwin, Inc.

adaptation between employees and jobs. Even at this level, adaptation is a two-way street; people can be helped to adapt to their jobs, and jobs can be adapted to people. Chapter 10, Training, discusses the former. Job and task redesign, as one approach to the latter, is discussed in Chapter 11.

chapter 10

Training

Training is any organizational effort directed toward helping employees adapt to their jobs. The underlying psychological process is learning; hence training is the psychology of learning applied in an organizational context. Training programs may emphasize the acquisition of knowledge, skill, or attitudes; be directed toward newly hired employees or more senior ones; or teach specific skills prerequisite to an employee's present job assignment or a contemplated future assignment.

The distinction ordinarily made between training and education is one of breadth. Whereas education addresses the broad issues of personal growth and development, training is more narrowly focused on acquiring specific task-related skills. Although both may be encouraged by an organization, this chapter is restricted to training, and most particularly to the type of training conducted within the employing organization itself.

A SYSTEMS CONTEXT FOR TRAINING

Hinrichs (1976), among others, has suggested a systems viewpoint as one way of thinking about many of the issues in training. We have adopted a modified version of his approach (Figure 10–1) as the framework for this chapter. From this perspective, the training system is made up of three interactive levels or subsystems: (a) the individual trainee, (b) the training department responsible for conducting the programs, and (c) the organization within which the training department functions. To this may be added a fourth level: that is, the societal context in which the organization is embedded.

Our discussion in this chapter emphasizes only the two lower levels of the total training system; (a) the individual trainee and (b) the training department. Organizational considerations, including those relevant to training, are treated throughout Section Three. We need mention here only that an organization's executive managers make policy decisions directly relevant to the two lower training subsystems. Management determines, for example, that training is more or less cost-effective for the organization than are such

FIGURE 10–1
A systems view of training

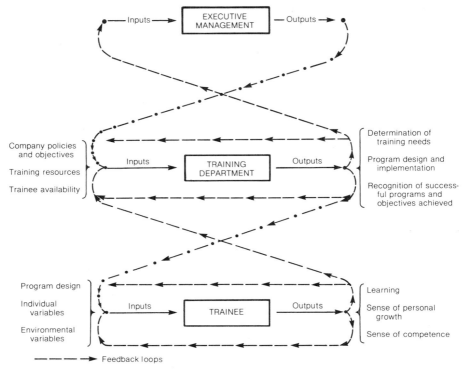

Source: After J. R. Hinrichs, "Personnel Training," in Dunnette, ed., *Handbook of Industrial and Organizational Psychology,* pp. 835, 845. Copyright © 1976 by Rand McNally College Publishing Company. Adapted by permission of Houghton Mifflin Company.

alternatives as intensified personnel recruitment, acquisition of already trained personnel through merger, and so on. When making such decisions, management relies partly upon feedback from the training department about the cost and effectiveness of its programs. This information is synthesized with feedback both from other organizational subsystems (for example, personnel, marketing) and from the macrosystem (the community).

These relationships are implied in Figure 10–1. Take a few moments now to examine that figure before reading further. Note especially:

1. The arrangement of the subsystems, each with their own inputs and outputs.
2. The self-regulating nature of each subsystem through feedback loops moderating the inputs on the basis of the outputs.
3. The self-regulating nature of the entire system through feedback loops traversing the different levels. Activities within the training department, for example, both influence and are influenced by what happens to individual trainees.

4. The different kinds of inputs and outcomes operating at the level of the individual trainee and the training department.

Note especially the possible trainee outcomes. The training objective most often emphasized is *learning* directed toward improved *job performance.* Although this emphasis on achievement (and the conditions facilitating it) is appropriate to our chapter, Figure 10–1 clarifies that there are also other kinds of training outcomes. These include the trainee's sense of personal growth and feelings of competence.

We call your attention to these satisfaction outcomes of training to make three points:

First, even a well designed and carefully implemented training program can fail if trainee motivation and ability are ignored. If the program is intended to teach supervisory skills, for example, the trainer had better be certain that this is something that the trainees wish to learn! Not everyone is interested in becoming a supervisor. Similarly, if the program is intended to train certain motor skills, one had better be certain that the trainees have the prerequisite motor abilities.

Second, optimally structured training programs are somewhat idiosyncratic to the learner. Each trainee brings unique needs into the program; a program that helps some achieve may not be similarly helpful to others of lesser or greater ability, lower or higher motivation, less or more self-confidence, and so on. Thus, particular instructional formats (like lectures and discussions) have been found to vary in effectiveness depending upon the trainee's prior experience with that format (Cronbach & Snow, 1977). Although evidence that acquisition is enhanced by matching learners to teaching strategies has been generated in educational settings (e.g., Siegel & Siegel, 1967), this issue has not been systematically explored in industrial settings. Nevertheless, we agree with a recent review of training strategies: "The use of randomly chosen abilities with whatever instructional technique happens to be available is not likely to produce any dividends" (Goldstein, 1980, p. 249).

Third, a training program's effectiveness is time-dependent. As shown in Figure 10–1, fluctuations in trainee availability and in the training department's resources can well dictate program modifications. Trainees may be of lower or higher quality now than formerly; the department's present operating budget may be tighter or looser than it was, and so on. To maintain itself as successful, a training program must have sufficient flexibility to adapt to changing circumstances.

ANALYZING TRAINING NEEDS

We begin by assuming that training has been organizationally accepted as a positive step toward improving employee performance in one or more departments or jobs. The first step now is to establish training objectives, that is, to decide which tasks, knowledges and attitudes need to be learned by which persons.

Although the importance of beginning with a systematic needs analysis has been recognized for over 20 years (McGehee & Thayer, 1961), training programs often are developed without this critical first step. Without a prior delineation of objectives, training may prove to be ineffectual or (worse still) to have negative consequences for performance; trainees can, in fact, be taught incorrect skills. Further, unless preceded by a needs analysis, it is impossible to make any evaluation of the program's effectiveness.

Components of needs analysis

The analysis of training needs usually proceeds at three levels: organizational, operational, and personal.

The issue at the *organizational* level is one of priorities. Given that training cannot be undertaken simultaneously for all employees, and may not even be indicated for many, organizational analysis seeks to identify the units in which the training need is most urgent. Its tools include manpower and skills inventories, the results of which are interpreted in the light of present and projected organizational requirements. Additional information is provided at this level by comparative evaluations of performance (including such things as safety record and absenteeism, as well as productivity) within the company's various departments and units. Once the most urgent training priorities are established, the needs analysis proceeds at the levels of operations and persons.

Operations analysis entails the systematic collection of data about jobs (and their constituent tasks) to determine what the employee must be helped to learn in order to perform effectively. This analysis is designed to yield four pieces of information critical to training program design:

1. Specified standards of acceptable job performance.
2. Identification of the task components which together comprise a "job."
3. Identification of the ways in which each of these components must be performed in order for the employee to meet or exceed the standards specified under (1) above.
4. Identification of the skills, knowledges, and attitudes prerequisite to performing each component satisfactorily. (McGehee & Thayer, 1961).

What the operations analysis seeks to accomplish for jobs and task clusters, *person analysis* attempts at the level of the individual employee. Does the employee meet the specified performance standards? If not, can the failure be attributed to inadequate performance on one or more of the task components? To an incomplete or erroneous understanding of organizational expectations relative to performance? To insufficient background skill or knowledge? Or to faulty attitudes and work habits?

Together, the operations and person analyses provide information necessary to decide who will be trained, the content of the training program, and the strategies for presenting that content. Decisions about strategy include issues such as where the training program will be conducted (some skills are better taught on the job, others in the classroom), what content will be included, and how that content will be sequenced.

Needs analysis in perspective

There are clear similarities between the kinds of data required for establishing training needs and those preliminary to I/O psychologists' activities in several other areas with which you are already familiar. Research to identify potential employment predictors and to develop performance criteria also begins with a comprehensive analysis of duties, responsibilities, and prerequisites to satisfactory performance. We made the point in Chapter 4, on job analysis, that a careful study of jobs, tasks, and personnel requirements is the indispensible foundation for personnel research.

This does not imply that the identical analysis will serve multiple ends. What was earlier described as job analysis has the relatively simple objective of identifying potentially useful selection requirements and/or signs of satisfactory job performance. A training-needs assessment must, in contrast, analyze tasks in ways prescribing appropriate training procedures.

This is more easily written than done. In order to be useful to training-program design, the statement of objectives must be highly specific. It is not useful, for example, to claim the objective of training a person to be a better manager; we need to identify the precise skills that make for effective management. Further, knowledge of the critical skills to be learned does not guarantee that these skills can be trained. Much about the teaching-learning process remains to be discovered. Finally, we sometimes gratuitously assume that training programs have content validity: that is, that skills developed through training are appropriate to performance on the job (Prien, 1977). The evidence does not always support the assumption, particularly for some of the more faddish management development programs.

PRINCIPLES OF LEARNING

We move on now to the level (in Figure 10–1) of the individual trainees. The inputs to learning are a combination of the strategies developed by the training department, organizational incentives (or disincentives) for learning, and such individual trainee characteristics as ability, motivation, and so on.

One way or another, training strategies provide trainees with opportunities to practice the skills being taught. And this is where you might expect the psychology of learning to make its greatest contribution.

What do psychologists have to say about the rules governing practice? Although they have a good deal to say about this matter, and can support a number of learning principles with evidence from the laboratory, these principles have less application to human learning in applied settings than those we discuss later as principles of *training*. The major reason for the discrepancy between the rather limited practical usefulness of principles of learning and the considerable evidence that they hold up in the laboratory is that laboratory controls are restrictive. Hence support for the power of the principles of learning comes from studies of relatively atypical behavior (like learning nonsense syllables) under atypical circumstances.

We discuss these principles briefly, and only as useful guides rather than as literal prescriptions for structuring the practice components of training.

Motivation

Other things being equal, highly motivated trainees progress more rapidly than poorly motivated ones. Some aspects of trainee motivation are outside of the trainer's control. Some employees, for example, may elect to participate in training as a break from their normal work routine. That issue aside, there are several things that can be done to enhance trainee motivation.

Trainees can be provided appropriate reinforcements for participating. These reinforcements can range from promotions and salary increases upon completing the program (fairly common for nonmanagerial employees) to verbal and/or written recognition for having completed another step in a career-development ladder (more common for managerial trainees). Since the power of the reinforcer depends upon the importance attached to it by the trainee, it is impossible to make blanket generalizations favoring one kind of reinforcer over another.

Motivation is also enhanced when the trainees are provided with reasonable short-term goals. Whereas the desired final performance involving relatively complex skills and knowledge may overwhelm the beginning trainee, frequent intermediate reinforcements for attaining subgoals encourage most persons.

It may prove helpful also to distribute (space out) practice sessions rather than massing them. People usually tire of practicing the same task for unduly long periods. Although there are no general rules for the optimal length of practice sessions devoted to a particular content, this is a researchable issue in the context of a particular training program. Further, trainee interest can often be enhanced by varying the content of successive training sessions. For example, practice on some physical skill can be interspersed between successive book-learning sessions. Such interspersed training activities need to be carefully chosen in order for them not to interfere with retention of prior learning.

Frequent feedback about the quality of performance (including knowledge of results on progress tests) has two kinds of beneficial effects—provided that it is done sensitively (the trainee is not embarrassed) and is accompanied by specific suggestions about the ways in which performance can be improved. One of these effects is motivational. The other is a more direct enhancement of skill development through helping the trainee to better organize what is being taught.

Organization of knowledge and skill

Practice does not always make perfect. Just ask a self-taught Sunday golfer!

In order for performance to improve, the skills must be practiced correctly. Thus, incorrect performance should be promptly called to the trainee's attention in a constructive manner, that is, accompanied by specific guidance for improvement. This implies close and conscientious supervision by the trainer. It also implies that the trainer is sufficiently knowledgable about the performance at issue to know what corrective action will have the most positive impact. In the case of teaching golf, when should "keeping the eye on the ball" be emphasized? When should the emphasis instead be on placement of the feet relative to the ball, gripping the club, the backswing, and so on?

When approaching a particular learning task, trainees learn different aspects of it at different times. This has been demonstrated, for example, during practice of discrimination reaction time (Fleishman & Hempel, 1955). Satisfactory performance of this task requires many of the abilities discussed in Chapter 9. However, as shown in Figure 10–2, different abilities are called into play at different stages of practice. Whereas spatial relations, for example, are very important to discrimination reaction time performance in the early practice sessions, it becomes progressively less so. Rate of movement, which is relatively unimportant in the early stages, becomes progressively more important to performance with further practice.

Transfer of training

The sole justification for training is that the newly learned skills will be transferred to the job. The underlying principle is a simple one: For behavior to transfer positively from one setting to another, that behavior should be perceived as equally appropriate to both settings. This means that training must be realistic; insofar as possible, trainees should solve real problems and work with real equipment (or with the closest and most realistic approximations possible).

However, there are other equally important but less well understood potential deterrents to transfer. Unless training is made an integral part of the total organizational system, and supervisors help shape the training program, the likelihood of positive transfer will be considerably reduced. The job supervisor and co-workers may not welcome new work procedures carried back to the job by a trainee (Allen & Silverzweig, 1976). Given a separa-

FIGURE 10–2
Relative contribution of ability factors to discrimination reaction time as training progresses

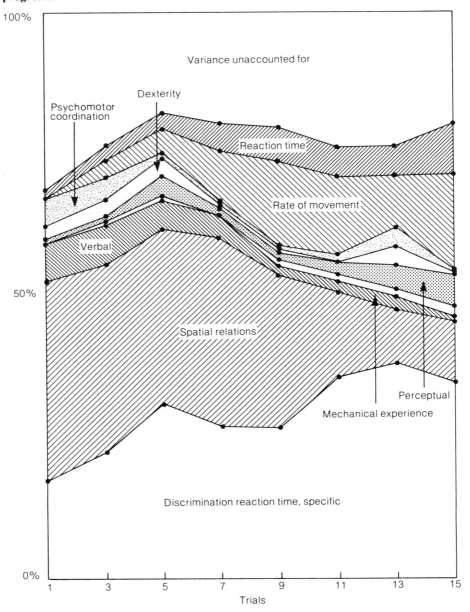

Note: Percentage of variance is represented by the shaded area for each factor.

Source: After E. A. Fleishman and W. E. Hempel, Jr., "The Relationship between Abilities and Improvement with Practice in a Visual Discrimination Task," *Journal of Experimental Psychology* 49 (1955), p. 308. Copyright 1955 by the American Psychological Association. Reprinted by permission.

tion of training and other organizational activities, supervisors may well feel that the training department does not really know conditions on the job and will covertly undo much that the training department has attempted to accomplish.

PRINCIPLES OF TRAINING

The principles discussed in the foregoing paragraphs apply to learners. The principles considered now operate at the level of the training department. These two sets of principles are qualitatively different: Principles of training are useful for designing strategies; principles of learning are helpful in guiding some of the details of implementing strategies for individual trainees.

Gagné (1962) first called attention to the need for principles of training and has continually contributed to this literature in highly significant ways. Based upon his work with the military, Gagné proposed the following two principles:

1. Any human task can be analyzed into distinctly separate component tasks (or subtasks).
2. These task components mediate final task performance; whereas their presence insures positive transfer to overall final performance, "their absence reduces such transfer to near zero."

From these two givens, Gagné proposed that training strategies be designed by (a) identifying the task components of the final performance, (b) building the program to insure the achievement of each subtask, and (c) arranging the total program in a sequence so that the acquisition of each component is facilitated by the components previously learned.

Irrespective of the particular strategy (lecture, role playing, etc.), Gagné (1977) maintains that complex learning must build upon the prior acquisition of simpler, subordinate skills. You cannot, for example, learn to find the hypotenuse of a right triangle without first learning such subordinate skills and concepts as the rules for squares and square roots, concepts of right angle, adjacent sides, and so on. Likewise, as he earlier (1962) pointed out, one cannot learn to troubleshoot electronic equipment without first knowing what tests to run (and in what order), what instruments to use for each test, how to interpret the instrument readings, and how to set up the test instruments in the first place.

Optimal sequencing is both a logical and an empirical issue. A careful task analysis may make clear that "it stands to reason" that the trainee must know X before Y can be learned. However the logic of content sequencing is less persuasive than an empirical demonstration of intertask transfer—actual evidence that knowing X does, in fact, help the trainee learn Y.

One interesting approach to laying the empirical foundation for sequencing begins by analyzing the subtask intercorrelations. Presumably, the higher the correlation between two tasks, the more they have in common. This analysis was conducted with pilot trainees for whom performance on the various training components (gunnery, navigation, and so on) was correlated (Bass & Vaughn, 1966). The authors suggest that the instructional sequence for future groups of trainees was improved by arranging the training schedule so that subtasks with the highest correlations were taught one after the other.

SOME SPECIFIC STRATEGIES

Training strategies seek to capitalize upon the principles of learning and of training. Campbell et al. (1970) have classified management training strategies into three categories: (1) simulation methods, (2) on-the-job training, and (3) information presentation techniques. These three categories serve to categorize all training strategies (including nonmanagerial) as well.

Simulation

The simulation procedures include several techniques with which you are already familiar from your reading of Chapter 9—role playing, in-basket, and so on. The difference when these are used in a training (rather than an assessment context) is that for training they are structured to teach new skills in addition to providing an evaluation of present skill level.

Information concerning the utility of most simulation strategies is sparse (Goldstein, 1980). We consider here two of the simulation procedures: one, behavior role modeling because it is relatively new, seems promising, and is appropriate to supervisory training; the other, machine simulation, because it has been a useful training strategy for quite a long time, and is more appropriate to nonsupervisory training.

Behavior role modeling (Goldstein & Sorcher, 1974) is a systematic approach to teaching the desired behavior by having trainees emulate a model. Unlike those strategies which attempt to train appropriate attitudes (for example, empathy), assuming that these will predispose the desired behavior, role modeling teaches the desired behavior, and assumes that the appropriate attitudes will follow when it becomes evident to the trainee that the newly learned behavior is utilitarian (Kraut, 1976).

Behavior modeling entails four steps:

1. The trainee learns some basic principle: for example, the importance of using follow-up probes during an interview.
2. Models of behavior correctly using the principle are observed (often by watching a film).
3. The trainee rehearses the desired behavior.
4. Once learned, the behavior is then carried from the training setting to the job.

Steps 3 and 4 are accomplished in the context of social reinforcement; that is, feedback from other trainees, the trainers, and ultimately, the job supervisor. Thus the trainee is somewhat relieved of the necessity for self-appraisal and correction; other persons serve these functions.

Judging from the published research, this strategy is most adapted to teaching supervisors interpersonal skills, and particularly skill in dealing with subordinates. Support for the usefulness of the procedure is provided by a study of front line supervisors, some of whom were randomly assigned to a behavior modeling program while the others comprised a control group (Latham & Saari, 1979). Those in the role-modeling program participated in nine weekly training sessions, each devoted to a particular supervisor-subordinate issue (like handling employee complaints). In comparison with the control group, trained supervisors were judged to perform better on a role-playing simulation three months after training, and scored higher on a test of supervisory skill administered six months after training. Furthermore, the beneficial effects transferred to the job and persevered, judging from the fact that performance evaluations one year after completing the program favored the behavior modeling group over the control group. As a clincher, these differences disappeared when the control group was subsequently given behavior role modeling training.

Mechanical simulations are especially useful to training motor skills (or a combination of motor and cognitive skills). This strategy is particularly attractive when training on real equipment poses dangers to the trainee and/or when the complexities of operating the actual equipment precludes isolating task components for training purposes. The primary applications of simulator training have been military, including aviation and astronautics.

The assumption, of course, is that skills learned during simulation will transfer to real task performance. Although plausible and generally accepted, such transfer has not generally been tested—perhaps because it seems self-evident. Issues related to simulation design for facilitating such transfer, including the optimal sequencing of the skills to be trained through simulation, also have not been sufficiently investigated (Miller, 1974).

The statement above should not be construed as invalidating mechanical simulation as a training strategy under appropriate circumstances. Trainees clearly can benefit from practicing skills in a protected environment. However, the very fact that the environment is protected (and the trainee is thereby sheltered from the potentially disasterous consequences of mistaken actions) constitutes a critically important difference between simulated performance and real-life performance. It is unlikely, for example, that pilot trainees in a simulator experience quite the same stress when confronted with an "emergency" as they would should they be confronted with the real thing.

On-the-job training

One of the concerns about simulation—transfer of learned skills to the actual job setting—is obviated by training directly on the job itself. Not surprisingly, some form of on-the-job instruction is the most widely used strategy for industrial training (Utgaard & Dawis, 1970). Often such training is supplemented by an initial orientation program and/or by relatively brief formal training to prepare the learner to better benefit from observing and working with a seasoned employee.

Apprenticeship, including elements of coaching by the master craftsman, is probably the oldest form of on-the-job training, and is still extensively used both to train trade and managerial skills. (For the latter, a more common designation than "apprentice" is administrative assistant or management training fellow.)

Other types of on-the-job training include job rotation (supervised experience in several departments, sections, or operations) and committee assignments (in which management trainees are assigned to actual problem-solving committees). Some on-the-job training is often incorporated into such other aspects of the total personnel program as performance appraisal by taking the occasion of providing performance feedback as an opportunity to also help the evaluatee learn new behavior calculated to lead to a more favorable appraisal during the next rating period.

The relative popularity of on-the-job training is easy to understand. Aside from bypassing the transferability issue, we note that this strategy (a) provides the new employee simultaneously with an opportunity to learn the necessary skills and to adapt to the physical and social work context, (b) usually is cheaper than other strategies, and (c) makes no distinction between theory and practice since principles and their application are simultaneously taught.

There also are a number of problems with the approach that may make it less attractive in certain circumstances than might first appear to be the case. We have already noted that some tasks cannot be taught on the job because of potential danger to the trainee (or to co-workers). Among other possible limitations of on-the-job training we include: (a) the fact that an employee performs the job effectively does not automatically qualify that employee as an effective teacher, (b) a possible tendency, given production pressures, to relegate the training function to secondary status and thereby to confront the trainee with a sink-or-swim atmosphere, and (c) the reality that trainees are often not integrated into the social and physical job context.

Information presentation

Whereas simulation and on-the-job training both emphasize having the trainee perform in some way, this third class of strategies is more cognitively focused. You have had first-hand experience with several of these procedures (lectures, discussions, films, TV, textbooks, and so on) which are passed over in this treatment. We will consider just one of the information presentation strategies: programmed (including computer-assisted) instruction.

Programmed instruction is really not very new (Pressey, 1926). In fact, it can be argued that all good instruction, regardless of the manner of presentation, is programmed in the sense that the material to be taught is organized, sequenced, and presented in bites calculated to maximize learning efficiency. However, programmed instruction has some other essential components. These include: (*a*) self-pacing whereby the rate at which the learner masters the material determines the rate at which new material is presented, (*b*) active participation by the learner, and (*c*) immediate feedback to the learner about the correctness or incorrectness of the response.

Computer-assisted instruction is a variation of programmed instruction whereby the trainee has an opportunity to interact with a more flexibly constructed program than can be presented in a written format. This is particularly useful, for example, for teaching something like diagnostic skills. The computer can be programmed to provide alternative questions and feedback contingent upon the trainee's previous responses. Contrary to the favorable impressions of programmed instruction held by many training directors, it is not markedly superior to other information dispensing procedures when the criterion is the amount of knowledge acquired or retained. However, it has been shown to save training time (Nash, Muczyk, & Vettori, 1971). Presumably, this advantage results from its self-pacing feature. Whereas a lecture, for example, must be paced to some hypothetical average learner, trainees can progress through programmed instruction (or written texts, for that matter) at their own pace.

A savings in training time is worthwhile provided that this gain is not excessively costly. One of the practical difficulties with programmed instruction (and even more so for computer-assisted instruction) is the expense of developing and pretesting effective programmed materials. Further, its use in training is limited to certain kinds of content. Even though we are not certain about what kinds of information are best conveyed by programmed instruction (Goldstein, 1980), there are several clues. This training strategy seems most suitable when the content is clear and the objectives are limited to developing cognitive rather than interpersonal skills (Hinrichs, 1976).

EVALUATING TRAINING PROGRAMS

In their review of training procedures, Campbell et al. (1970) identified no fewer than 22 different techniques appropriate to managerial training. With such an array of available strategies, we might hope for some systematic and rational basis for deciding in advance which one (or ones) are best suited to accomplishing particular ends.

Although choices are made, they do not often rest upon empirical evidence that one procedure is likely to be more effective than another! Instead, the choice usually follows anecdotal evidence ("so-and-so has used it and says it works") or the personal predispositions of the trainers.

Expert opinion

The opinions of training directors of large organizations are an indirect source of information about the perceived effectiveness of the various training strategies. A survey requested a sample of directors to evaluate the appropriateness of several strategies for attaining various training objectives (Carroll, Paine, & Ivancevich, 1972). Their mean rankings are shown in Table 10–1.

TABLE 10–1
Mean ranks assigned to alternative training methods for attaining various training objectives

Training method	Knowl-edge acqui-sition	Chang-ing atti-tudes	Prob-lem solv-ing	Inter-per-sonal skills	Trainee accep-tance	Knowl-edge reten-tion
Case study	2	4	1	4	2	2
Conference (discussion method)	3	3	4	3	1	5
Lecture (with questions)	9	8	9	8	8	8
Business games	6	5	2	5	3	6
Movie films	4	6	7	6	5	7
Programmed instruction	1	7	6	7	7	1
Role playing	7	2	3	2	4	4
Sensitivity training	8	1	5	1	6	3
TV lecture	5	9	8	9	9	9

Source: S. J. Carroll, Jr., F. T. Paine, and J. M. Ivancevich, "The Relative Effectiveness of Training Methods: Expert Opinion and Research," *Personnel Psychology* 25 (1970): p. 498.

You will note that many training methods considered effective for attaining certain objectives were considered ineffective for attaining others. For example, programmed instruction was ranked as superior to all other strategies for facilitating knowledge acquisition and retention, while it was ranked near the bottom for the other purposes.

We have already said that empirical studies do not support the superiority attributed by training directors to programmed instruction. In general, they probably tend, as in these rankings, to overestimate the value of participative strategies (including case study and role playing) and to underestimate the value of more traditional methods like the lecture. Lecture (including TV lectures) and discussion strategies are among the ones that have been most carefully analyzed for actual learning outcomes, at least in educational settings. Those results are more favorable to these somewhat traditional procedures than one would gather from the opinions summarized in Table 10–1 (Siegel & Macomber, 1960).

Empirical evaluations

Assessing the relative effectiveness of alternative training procedures is more difficult than might be supposed. The research issues are similar to those encountered in investigations of instructional procedures generally, and for clarity are discussed under two headings: (a) choosing appropriate criteria and (b) implementing evaluative designs.

Criteria. We have already discussed several considerations in identifying appropriate criteria (Chapter 5). We comment here just a little further on criterion issues specifically related to evaluating training programs.

The same criteria which are appropriate to some situations are inappropriate to others. We cannot speak of effectiveness without simultaneously asking, "Effective for *what* and for *whom?*" When evaluating training are we interested in some index of attitude change or performance while the trainee is in the program? Or are we interested in the impact of the training experience upon subsequent job performance? Or both? And suppose we demonstrate a desired impact for some trainee subgroups (say women) but not others? Is the program then to be judged a success or a failure?

Kirkpatrick (1959) has provided a helpful way of thinking about possible training criteria by identifying four criterion levels (two internal to the training program, and two extending beyond the program):

1. Reaction criteria—trainee impressions about the program (that is, whether or not they liked it, thought it was valuable, and so on).
2. Learning criteria—acquisition attributable to the program (evidenced, for example, on an achievement test).
3. Behavioral criteria—measures of performance on the job and subsequent to completion of the training program.
4. Results criteria—organizational impacts (like reduced turnover) of the training program.

Different elements of the organization will emphasize criteria at different levels. Management may be more interested in measures of overall organizational impact; training participants may be more concerned about what are cited above as reaction criteria, and so on. This matter is further complicated by the fact that each level itself is comprised of many different criteria. Thus we return to a point made earlier when we discussed criteria in the context of test validation: there is no single "best" criterion. Evaluations (whether of training or of employee performance) must proceed by using multiple criteria.

Further, even should hard evidence concerning the relative effectiveness of alternative strategies for attaining particular objectives be available, such evidence would not usually be the sole determinant of the choice among strategies. *Effectiveness,* however defined, would have to be weighed against such practical considerations as program cost (Mirabel, 1978) and available trainee time.

Implementing evaluative research. Research to evaluate a training program would appear to be relatively straightforward (assuming we have settled on the criteria). A model for such research might be to obtain pre- and posttraining performance measures for two groups of person: (1) a training group and (2) a control group (which has not taken the training). Assuming the persons are randomly assigned to these groups, observed differences in improvement scores should be attributable to the training.

However, there are complications. The fact that training (and evaluation) has been provided some employees may lead to performance improvements related more to motivational factors than to the program itself. (We are speaking here of the *Hawthorne Effect,* discussed more extensively in Chapter 12.) Similarly, the performance of employees deprived of the training by being assigned to the control group may deteriorate because they feel neglected (Hand & Slocum, 1972).

Finally, we note that several writers (e.g., Goldstein, 1980) have commented on the difficulty of isolating the effects of a training program from the effects of other simultaneously occuring organizational changes and programs.

TRAINING THE HARD-CORE UNEMPLOYED

Depending upon the economist, *full employment* in the United States is defined by an unemployment rate of 4.5 percent to 6.0 percent of eligible workers. This definition reflects society's acceptance that a large number of persons will never be integrated into the work force and therefore must become the responsibility of the social welfare system. Among these unemployables is the group designated *hard-core unemployed* (HCU).

The HCU ordinarily is defined by evidence of erratic work history, often filled with many short-term jobs, and unemployment for at least the previous six months. In terms of their characteristics, "The HCU are typically young, members of a minority group, lack a high school education, and are below a poverty level specified by the Department of Labor" (Goldstein, 1980).

The milieu of the 1960s, including enactment of Civil Rights legislation, encouraged attention to the issue of chronic unemployment with the hope of remediation. Buttressed by massive federal grants and contracts, a new industry directed toward training the HCU was created (Salipante & Goodman, 1976).

The original assumption was that the HCU member was defective, lacking the job skills, educational background, and middle-class values appropriate to stable employment. It followed that the solution was to correct these deficiencies through remedial education, specific job-skills training, and reorienting the trainee's values. By and large this approach has been judged unsuccessful. There is no clear evidence that it reduced turnover or chronic absenteeism for HCUs. Some of the issues will be clearer if you refer back to Figure 10–1. This figure has two implications specific to HCU trainees:

First, the type of training described above does not address issues of HCU trainee need-satisfaction. Mainstream employment, with its attendant restraints upon personal freedom, is not perceived as rewarding.

Second, this negative outcome can only be understood, and perhaps ameliorated, by considering the social and organizational context of which a systematic training program is but a small part. Such an examination suggests that the retention rate for HCU hires can be more effectively addressed through changed organizational practices than through training alone (Salipante & Goodman, 1976).

HCU as a cultural phenomenon

Given the biographical characteristics of the HCU population—minority status, low educational attainment, poverty—embedded within a society emphasizing the opposite as cultural values, psychological consequences are inevitable. These consequences coalesce into what has been labeled *ecosystem distrust* (Triandis et al., 1975): a basic distrust of people, their motives, and a rejection of authority including the system that authority represents.

Thus the ghetto culture reinforces values opposite to those reinforced by the larger society known to the white middle class. Self-esteem rests on factors other than holding a job. Indeed, assimilation into the system through job training may carry severe personal costs for the HCU trainee through peer pressure and family resentment (Shlensky, 1972). Seen from this perspective, the HCU trainee's chronic absenteeism and frequent turnover are seen both as a response to his/her anxiety over handling and keeping a job, and to cultural values and reinforcement.

The origins of this somewhat paradoxical conflict for HCU trainees are not difficult to comprehend intellectually, although a full appreciation of its more subtle ramifications may elude us. In contrast with blue-collar workers, the chronically unemployed feel powerless; they perceive that they are controlled by rather than controllers of their destiny (Searls et al., 1974).

Much of this feeling is justified, even though as a society we might wish otherwise. HCU trainees who are successfully inducted into the work force are brought in with low priority for retention when layoffs are required. The issue for the employer and co-workers is seniority. The dilemma is that the last-hired, first-fired principle protects employees whose service over the years is valued by the company, but at the expense of the more recently hired HCU trainees. From the latter's standpoint, job security is particularly ephemeral.

Implications

Although skills training is obviously required to break the HCU cycle, HCU trainees' needs in this regard are not markedly different from those of other unskilled job applicants. What does emerge from HCU research as a difference is a set of unique organizatio.ial implications. Of several factors investigated as potential predictors of HCU trainees' ability to retain jobs, only one was found to be a major correlate: the supportiveness of the organizational climate (Friedlander & Greenberg, 1971). Interestingly, the HCU trainees tended to perceive the organizational climate as much less favorable than did their supervisors. Among the factors contributing to organizational climate, Goodman and Salipante (1976; Salipante & Goodman, 1976) identify four (aside from the training program itself) as explaining the retention of HCU trainees: pay system, promotional opportunities, type of job held, and degree of counseling provided.

Clearly, supervisors who respond stereotypically to HCU workers by expecting absenteeism and tardiness contribute to self-fulfilling prophecies. This issue points up the need for training directed toward helping the supervisors (and the rest of the organization) adapt to the needs of the HCU!

Other required organizational adaptations are less amenable to training. If an organization is to recruit the HCU seriously, it has the responsibility for helping them deal effectively with several matters that may bear only indirectly on job performance but are critical to getting to work regularly and on time. The HCU have needs both for counseling and tangible support in such areas as housing, child-care, transportation, health care, and financial management. Unless they can be helped to solve the logistics of getting to work, caring for their children while they are there, and so on, the demands of regular work attendance are untenable.

Finally, certain issues of organizational climate may suggest that a particular organization, however well meaning, ought not attempt to recruit HCUs because the dice are loaded against success. Companies paying low entry wages or providing relatively few promotional opportunities are in this category. Turnover, in general, is higher when these circumstances prevail. It is perhaps for this reason that such companies attract workers from the HCU pool in the first place: their jobs do not appeal to workers who intend to remain. It is undoubtedly the reason that such job placements do not encourage the HCU to break their cycle of sporadic, short-term employment.

SUMMARY

Training is an organizational effort directed towards helping employees adapt to their jobs. This chapter emphasized particularly task-related skills training conducted within employing organizations themselves. A systems perspective helped to clarify two important issues in such programs: (1) More attention needs to be given to developing optimal training strategies for trainee subgroups. (2) Changing circumstances external to the training program itself may necessitate subsequent modifications of the training program.

The first step in initiating a training program is to assess training needs—

that is, to decide which tasks, knowledges, and attitudes need to be learned by which persons. The next step is to design the program to meet these needs.

One way or another, every strategy attempts to provide trainees with opportunities to practice the necessary skills. Although the several psychological principles or learnings, derived mainly from laboratory studies (often with infrahuman subjects), cannot be literally applied to industrial training, they provide some useful clues. Trainee motivation can be enhanced through providing appropriate reinforcement (largely through frequent performance feedback) and setting reasonable short-term goals. The practice itself must be closely supervised in order to insure that incorrect behavior is not acquired. And the training must be integrated into the total organizational structure to encourage positive transfer and acceptance of trained behavior in the work setting.

Irrespective of the training strategy (programmed instruction, lecture-discussion, and so on) the training effort must be structured to (a) teach each component of final task performance and (b) insure the attainment of each of these components or subtasks. Further, consideration must be given to sequencing the program's content so that each new component to be acquired builds upon the skills and knowledges previously learned.

Unfortunately, there is no body of empirical evidence clearly recommending one training strategy over another for accomplishing particular goals. The evaluative research in this area suffers, in part, because of difficulties associated with isolating the effects of a training program from the effects of other simultaneously occuring organizational changes, programs, and innovations.

The strategies whereby training can be accomplished were subsumed under three categories: (1) simulation methods (including behavior role modeling and mechanical simulation); (2) on-the-job training (including formal and informal apprenticeship, and job rotation); and (3) information-presentation techniques (lectures, discussions, programmed instruction, computer-assisted instruction, and so on).

Issues in training the hard-core-unemployed were discussed in the context of possible discrepancies between organizational and trainee objectives. The ghetto culture reinforces values different from those reinforced by the larger society known to the white middle class, thereby generating psychological conflicts for HCU trainees. In addition to providing skills training, organizations seriously intending to break the HCU cycle must adapt to the unique needs of these employees.

REFERENCES

Allen, R. F., & Silverzweig, S.   Group norms: Their influence on training effectiveness. In R. L. Craig, *Training and Development Handbook,* New York: McGraw-Hill, 1976, 1–12.

Bass, B. M., & Vaughn, J. A. *Training in industry: The management of learning.* Belmont, Calif.: Wadsworth, 1966.

Campbell, J. P., Dunnette, M. D., Lawler, E. E. III, & Weick, K. E., Jr. *Managerial behavior, performance, and effectiveness.* New York: McGraw-Hill, 1970.

Carroll, S. J., Jr., Paine, F. T., & Ivancevich, J. M. The relative effectiveness of training methods: Expert opinion and research. *Personnel Psychology,* 1972, *25,* 495–509.

Cronbach, L. J., & Snow, R. E. *Aptitudes and instructional methods.* New York: Irvington, 1977.

Fleishman, E. A., & Hempel, W. E., Jr. The relationship between abilities and improvement with practice in a visual discrimination task. *Journal of Experimental Psychology,* 1955, *49,* 301–312.

Friedlander, F., & Greenberg, S. Effect of job attitudes, training, and organizational climate on performance of the hard-core unemployed. *Journal of Applied Psychology,* 1971, *55,* 289–295.

Gagné, R. M. Military training and principles of learning. *American Psychologist,* 1962, *17,* 83:91.

Gagné, R. M. *Conditions of learning* (3rd ed.) New York: Holt, Rinehart & Winston, 1977.

Goldstein, I. L. Training in work organizations. *Annual Review of Psychology,* 1980, *31,* 229–272.

Goldstein, I. L., & Sorcher, M. *Changing supervisory behavior.* New York: Pergamon, 1974.

Goodman, P. S., & Salipante, P., Jr. Organizational rewards and retention of the hard-core unemployed. *Journal of Applied Psychology,* 1976, *61,* 12–21.

Goodman, P. S., Salipente, P., Jr., & Paransky, H. Hiring, training, and retraining the hard-core unemployed: A selected review. *Journal of Applied Psychology,* 1973, *58,* 23–33.

Hand, H. H., & Slocum, J. W., Jr. A longitudinal study of the effects of a human relations training program on management effectiveness. *Journal of Applied Psychology,* 1972, *56,* 412–417.

Hinrichs, J. R. Personnel training. In M. D. Dunnette (Ed.), *Handbook of industrial and organizational psychology.* Chicago: Rand McNally, 1976, 829–860.

Kirkpatrick, D. L. Techniques for evaluating training programs. *Journal of the American Society for Training Directors,* 1959, *13,* 3–9, 21–26.

Kraut, A. I. Developing managerial skills via modeling techniques—some positive research findings: A symposium. *Personnel Psychology,* 1976, *29,* 325–328.

Latham, G. P., & Saari, L. M. The application of social learning theory to training supervisors through behavioral modeling. *Journal of Applied Psychology,* 1979, *64,* 239–246.

McGehee, W., & Thayer, P. W. *Training in business and industry.* New York: Wiley, 1961.

Miller, G. G. *Some considerations in the design and utilization of simulators for technical training.* AFHRL Tech. Rep. 74–65, 1974, Texas.

Mirabel, T. E.   Forecasting future training costs. *Training Development Journal,* 1978, *32,* 78–87.

Nash, A. N., Muczyk, J. P., & Vettori, F. L.   The relative practical effectiveness of programmed instruction. *Personnel Psychology,* 1971, *24,* 397–418.

Pressey, S. L.   A simple apparatus which gives tests and scores—and teaches. *School and Society,* 1926, *23,* 373–376.

Prien, E. P.   The function of job analysis in content validation. *Personnel Psychology,* 1977, *30,* 167–174.

Salipante, P., Jr., and Goodman, P.   Training, counseling, and retention of the hard-core unemployed. *Journal of Applied Psychology,* 1976, *61,* 1–11.

Searls, D. J., Bravelt, G. N., & Miskimins, R. W.   Work values of the chronically unemployed. *Journal of Applied Psychology,* 1974, *59,* 93–95.

Shlensky, B. C.   Determinants of turnover in training programs for the disadvantaged. *Personnel Administration,* 1972, *35,* 53–61.

Siegel, L., & Macomber, F. G.   *Final report: The experimental study in instructional procedures.* Oxford, Ohio: Miami University, 1960.

Siegel, L., & Siegel, L. C.   A multivariate paradigm for educational research. *Psychological Bulletin,* 1967, *68,* 306–326.

Smith, P. B.   Why successful groups succeed: The implications of t-group research. In C. L. Cooper (Ed.), *Developing social skills in managers.* New York: Wiley.

Triandis, H. C., Felden, J., Weldon, D. E., & Harvey, W. M.   Ecosystem distrust and the hard-to-employ. *Journal of Applied Psychology,* 1975, *60,* 44–56.

Utgaard, S. B., & Dawis, R. V.   The most frequently used training techniques. *Training and Development Journal,* 1970, *24,* 40–43.

chapter 11

Human Factors in Performance

Training can encourage adaptations to work environments only to a point. Disregarding everything else potentially limiting human performance (like motivation, ability, skill, and so on), we are left with biological limitations as a bottom line.

The practical implications for task performance of these immutable limitations first became apparent to psychologists during World War II, with the attendant rapid development of high technology like radar, sonar, and increasingly complex aircraft. As F. V. Taylor neatly expressed it:

> Previous to this time (World War II) the only role played by psychologists relative to military mechanisms was that of doing research and giving advice on the selection and training of operators. However, very early in the war it became apparent that these Procrustean attempts to fit the man to the machine were not enough. Regardless of how much he could be stretched by training or pared down through selection, there were still many military equipments which the man just could not be moulded to fit. They required of him too many hands, too many feet, or in the case of some of the more complex devices, too many heads. (1957, p. 249).

Hence, psychologists joined with engineers, anatomists, physiologists, and others to create the then new field of human engineering (or engineering psychology) in order to effect better machine designs. As we have already noted when introducing this chapter and the preceding one on Training, the human operator thus was viewed as one of the elaborate components of a larger system.

In the early days of human engineering this larger system was conceptualized as a man-machine system; the emphasis was on equipment design and/or redesign in accordance with established psychological principles. These principles were derived mainly from work in experimental psychology on topics like sensation, perception, and cognition.

More recently, conceptualizations of systems including human beings as components have been enlarged to include the total environment, both mechanical and interpersonal, in which the systems operate, and all other factors impinging upon the quality of human performance. Thus, a fairly recent survey of the human-factors literature (Allusi & Morgan, 1976) cites applied research on such topics as environmental design (museums, hospitals, homes, offices), vibration and noise pollution, health-delivery systems, and prosthetic devices for amputees. The same review also cites basic (that is, nonapplied) research on the effects upon performance of factors like sleep deprivation, biological rhythms, drugs, pain, heat, cold, and infection.

Clearly, the concern for the role of human factors in performance has become very broad. It encompasses the implications of the way people function for designing the equipment they use and their living and working environments.

Our focus in this chapter is considerably narrower. We begin by discussing only selected potentially noxious features of the physical work environment and their impact upon selected aspects of job performance. Thereafter, we comment on human factors in establishing work and assignment schedules, including working hours, shift length, and assigned duties. Finally we consider human factors in equipment design: that is, engineering psychology.

Our emphasis throughout is on optimizing performance by encouraging maximum effective output (productivity and personal satisfactions) at minimum human cost (accidents, fatigue, and boredom).

PHYSICAL WORK ENVIRONMENT

No one takes issue with the desirability of providing pleasant working environments. Physically uncomfortable environments are undoubtedly partly responsible for lowered productivity, increased fatigue, and so on. Further, even when they produce no measurable adverse impact upon performance, noxious environments detract from the quality of work life.

The effects of certain noxious environments are more directly physical than psychological, and therefore are not our concern here. Thus, we do not discuss potentially life-threatening features like exposure to radioactivity, pollutants (like absbestos), or prolonged anoxia (oxygen deprivation). Neither do we discuss those conditions that, while not life threatening, nonetheless cause selective physiological damage, like hearing loss following prolonged exposure to noise. We take for granted that these and other hazards to health must be eliminated. The William-Steiger Occupational Safety and Health Act of 1970 (OSHA) was federally enacted to accomplish this.

But what of the more prosaic noxious aspects of the work environment, those that have an impact more on comfort than directly on health? Three widely investigated factors of this type are temperature, illumination, and the auditory environment (noise and music).

Research issues

Research on the impact of environmental manipulations poses several traps for the unsophisticated investigator. Thus many claims for supposed improvements in performance following a changed color scheme in the plant, piped music, and so on, are misleading. Features of the work environment interact with each other and with the larger life environment of which it is a part. A change in any one aspect can influence the others in subtle ways, sometimes unknown to the investigator.

Figure 11–1 clarifies some of these potential interactions. The arrows labeled A signify the reciprocal influences of the work environment upon

FIGURE 11–1
Environmental interactions influencing person-equipment performance

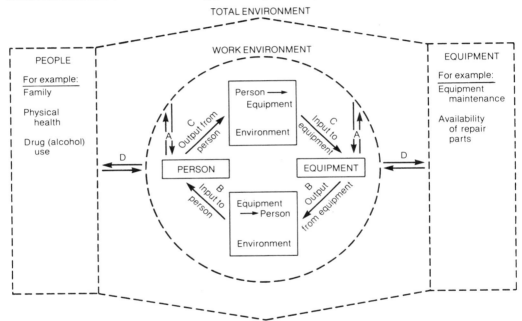

people and equipment. A noisy machine comprises part of the work environment of its operators; employees who form themselves into social cliques comprise part of the environment influencing the machine's efficiency; and so on. In addition, direct outputs from the equipment make up part of the personnel inputs (the arrows labeled B). Thus the equipment puts out dial readings, metal stampings, or typewriter copy which, in turn, influences the operator's next actions. Similarly, the arrows labeled C signify that the person's behavior (pressing keys, twisting knobs, moving controls, and so on) serves as a machine input. Finally, all of these interactions are subject to conditions external to the work environment (the arrows labeled D). Thus, the equipment's efficiency, irrespective of how well or poorly it is operated during working hours, is somewhat a function of the quality of routine maintenance and repairs. Likewise, irrespective of how well the equipment functions mechanically, the operator's efficiency in using it is potentially affected by a host of interpersonal and physical conditions—off-the-job conditions. Did the employee come to work following a breakfast-table argument, a restless night's sleep, a weekend drunk, and so on?

Because of the interdependence of all of these factors, we must be particularly alert to three potential sources of error when attempting to attribute changed performance to specific changes in the work environment.

First, any environmental manipulation may have secondary consequences that themselves influence performance. Suppose, for example, that in the interest of conserving energy a company adjusts its air-conditioning system, with a resulting slight increase in plant temperature and humidity. It would be tempting to interpret any subsequent production decline to the deleterious impact of this change upon employee comfort. On the evidence given, this might, but need not, be a correct interpretation. It is possible, instead, that the increased humidity caused more frequent mechanical malfunctions of moisture-sensitive equipment, thereby indirectly reducing productivity.

Second, identical environmental manipulations can have different effects depending upon employee attitudes associated with the change. If, as occurred in the Hawthorne studies (discussed in Chapter 13), employees interpret environmental changes as an expression of management's interest in their welfare, performance will improve—at least for some initial period. Thus, results on environmental changes must be interpreted cautiously. What superficially appears to be a behavioral change resulting from an environmental modification may, instead, reflect an attitudinal variable.

Third, we note that some of the initial impact (either positive or negative) of changes in the work environment may dissipate with time as employees adapt to the changed circumstances. All of us have had the experience of adjusting to noisy surroundings to the point where the "silence is deafening" when the noise stops. We likewise adapt to more favorable circumstances. The new employee lounge which evoked so much favorable notice when it was initially installed is soon taken for granted.

Adaptation raises two issues: (1) Since the long-term consequences of manipulations may be different from their short-term consequences, the investigator must not jump to conclusions from initial findings. (2) The adaptation process itself may entail unanticipated hidden costs. Although there may not be any long-term adverse effects upon production of, say, introducing a new piece of noisy equipment, the additional effort required to adapt to the increased noise level may divert employee attention, causing an increase in minor accidents, the incidence of stress-induced headaches and absenteeism, and so on.

In summary, it is very difficult to generalize from most studies of work environments. The effects of most environmental factors are conditioned by the nature of the work, employee characteristics (such as age), and all other features of the environment, both on and off the job. Thus, a noisy environment may not by itself have adverse effects. But when noise is combined with poor illumination, or is the setting for tasks requiring concentration, its effect may be deleterious. Likewise, music may improve the job satisfaction of employees engaged in monotonous, repetitive work but have little or no effect on people doing other kinds of tasks.

Research findings

It follows from the foregoing that we cannot offer simple-minded generalizations about optimal work environments. Those generalizations that can be made are self-evident: temperature can become so cold that the resulting numbness interferes with task performance requiring finger dexterity; noise can be so intense that it adversely affects tasks in which persons are required to communicate audibly with each other; and so on. Further, average tolerance levels specifying the minimum environmental conditions prerequisite to being able to see, hear, and move as required by various kinds of tasks have been developed. Although of great practical interest to engineers and others designing work settings, this information is not particularly interesting from a psychological standpoint.

Therefore, rather than review the voluminous literature on environmental variables like heat, noise, and illumination, we will quickly list five psychologically relevant conclusions and then will discuss arousal theory as an attempt to impose order on apparent chaos.

1. There are individual differences in responses to conditions of the work environment (as to all other conditions). Thus, preferred illumination levels are found to vary with age; people above age 35 prefer more reading light than younger persons (Feree & Rand, 1940). And some persons are apparently more sensitive than others to noise judging both from their complaints about it and its adverse affects upon performance (Weinstein, 1978).

2. Each environmental condition has several interactive dimensions which act jointly to determine the impact of the condition.

It is not just the heat, or just the humidity, but these two dimensions in concert with a third, air movement, that makes for climatic effects. The three together comprise effective temperature: how cool or warm it feels. Thus, with air movement at a minimum, a dry-bulb temperature of 90°F. at 10 percent humidity is as comfortable as a 75°F. reading at 100 percent humidity.

Likewise, intensity is not the only dimension of illumination. Other properties to be considered are glare, light reflectance of the work and surrounding surface, and spectral composition of the light.

Music has rhythm, beat, and character (pop, classical, rock, and so on). Further, it can be played continuously or intermittently. Noise also can vary both in continuity and character (loudness, pitch, tonal complexity).

Continuously presented stimuli are more likely to encourage adaptation than are intermittently presented stimuli. Thus, a particular noise exerts a greater adverse effect upon proficiency when it is intermittent than when it is continuous (Vernon & Warner, 1932), and when its loudness fluctuates rather than is constant (Teichner, Arees, & Reilly, 1963).

3.   Whether or not physical conditions of the environment adversely affect performance depends also upon the nature of the task.

Music may facilitate performance when the task is monotonous or otherwise does not absorb the employee's full attention (Smith, 1947). The potentially adverse affects of noise are conditioned by the level of stimulation provided by the task (that is, whether performance feedback is frequent or infrequent) and whether the task encourages or discourages alertness (Broadbent, 1954; Wilkinson, 1963).

4.   Even when noxious environmental conditions produce no performance decrement (or generate a temporary performance improvement) there may be a cost to the employee in increased effort. Such increased effort is not always manifested in obvious signs of fatigue, but often can be detected from physiological measures including muscle tension and central nervous system activity (McFarland, 1971).

5.   The multiple effect jointly exerted by two or more environmental factors may be quite different from the effect either exerts alone. Sometimes, the joint effect is additive or multiplicative. (Alcohol ingestion and sleep deprivation together cause greater performance deterioration than either alone.) For some other pairs of conditions the joint effect is less deleterious than that from each factor by itself. (For example, subjects who were deprived of sleep did better on a serial reaction task under noisy than quiet conditions; Wilkinson, 1963.)

Arousal theory

Research following the arousal hypothesis offers considerable promise for integrating the wealth of data on the effects of work environments upon performance.

Arousal refers to the organism's level of activation ranging from some very low level (like deep sleep) to some very high level (as, for example, during intense emotional experiences). Varying levels of arousal imply parallel variations in neural activity, particularly between the reticular formation and the cerbral cortex (Scott, 1966). The arousal hypothesis proposes that the organism's activation level influences the quality of task performance following a ∩-shaped function (Duffy, 1962) as shown in Figure 11–2. When arousal is very low, performance is poor. As the organism is further aroused to some optimum level, performance continues to improve. Additional increments in arousal beyond this optimal level are debilitating to performance.

The effects of environmental conditions upon performance are thus seen to be mediated by their effects upon arousal. Therefore, we first consider the link between the environment and arousal.

Arousal stimuli.   The stimuli to neural activity are both internal to the

FIGURE 11-2
The arousal hypothesis

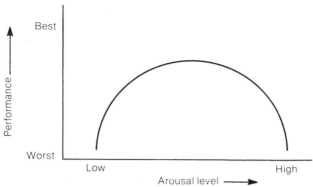

organism and external. Among the latter, Scott (1966) postulated such environmental factors as stimulus intensity, stimulus variety, and stimulus meaningfulness.

As applied to work, the person's activation level is thus seen to be influenced by perceived characteristics of the task (for example, whether or not it is interesting) and the environment in which the task is accomplished (noise, illumination, and so on). But much about such stimulus characteristics is idiosyncratic: tasks that are interesting to some people are dull to others; what are seen as noisy environments by some seem fairly quiet to others.

Arousal and performance. Much of the data on the effects of work environments on performance have been interpreted as supporting the arousal hypothesis. However, the hypothesis itself is somewhat seductive in that data can often be made to support it. If an environmental condition is found to improve performance, one can reason that the activation level is on the left side of the inverted-U. If performance is found to deteriorate following environmental change, one can similarly reason that the activation level has become too strong: that is, it has shifted to the right side of the inverted-U.

Furthermore, some obtained findings are very difficult to reconcile with the arousal hypothesis. One study, for example, (Wilkinson, R. T., Fox, R. H., Goldsmith, R., Hampton, I. F. G., & Lewis, H. E., 1964) studied performance on different tasks as a function of body temperature. Whereas a slight increase above normal body temperature interfered with performance, larger increases (and presumably greater arousal) improved performance.

Two modifications of the arousal hypothesis have been suggested, both incorporating the arousal hypothesis into the larger body of stress theory.

Stress and performance. In its most general use, stress is any condition that threatens the organism. We are here differentiating between a challenge and a threat. Challenges are presented by circumstances with which the organism feels it can cope; threats are presented by circumstances with

FIGURE 11–3
Performance as a function of arousal and task difficulty separately and in combination

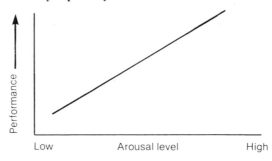

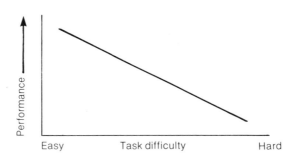

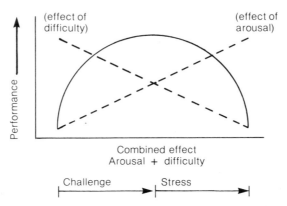

Source: J. E. McGrath, "Stress and Behavior in Organizations," in Dunnette, ed., *Handbook of Industrial and Organizational Psychology*, p. 1363. Copyright © 1976 by Rand McNally College Publishing Company. Adapted by permission of Houghton Mifflin Company.

which the organism feels it cannot cope. Thus, the determinants of whether or not stress will be experienced by a particular person in a given situation include (*a*) past experiences of success and failure in similar situations and (*b*) the expectation of likely success or failure in the present one (McGrath, 1970).

Up to a point, then, environmental conditions present challenges which the organism expects to be able to handle. Beyond that point, the conditions become stressful. The point where challenge becomes stress is the apex of the inverted-U in Figure 11–2.

Näätänen's (1973) modification of arousal theory holds that once conditions become stressful (rather than merely challenging), the organism is confronted with a secondary task: that of coping with the stress. The resulting performance decrement for the main task (the job) is caused by the fact that some of the energies formerly devoted to it now must be devoted instead to the task of coping.

McGrath (1976) reaches a similar conclusion through a different route. (See Figure 11–3). He reasons (from data obtained with Little League teams) that performance is a joint function of arousal and task difficulty. These factors have opposing effects: heightened arousal improves performance; increased task difficulty causes performance to deteriorate (Figure 11–3, A and B). Both variables, arousal and perceived difficulty, are incorporated into any task, with the combined impact shown in Figure 11–3 C. Using our earlier distinction between challenging and stressful circumstances, performance would be expected to deteriorate only when the arousal level is high and the task is perceived as relatively difficult.

WORK SCHEDULES AND ASSIGNMENTS

The five-day, 40-hour week with work beginning sometime between 7 o'clock and 9 o'clock A.M. and ending between 3 o'clock and 5 o'clock P.M., with a break for lunch, and assignment throughout the day to a particular job is pretty much the standard pattern of employment in the United States (though somewhat less so in cities). Although we tend to think of this pattern as most typical for hourly-paid shift workers in such industries as manufacturing and construction, it extends also to most salaried employees.

As you are well aware, this has not always been the pattern; a six-day, 48- to 52-hour (or longer) work week used to be standard. Further, variations in this pattern obviously must be implemented to meet the special requirements for double or triple shifts in round-the-clock organizations like hospitals or plants with operations that cannot be fully shut down.

Finally, you have undoubtedly read popularized accounts of attempts to manipulate the standard work schedule to a four-day 40-hour week, or daily work with flexible starting and ending times. Before commenting on these more recent variations and the general issue of work schedules, we must consider fatigue as the primary relevant human factor.

Fatigue

Although fatigue is not the sole factor limiting a person's productivity, it clearly has consequences for work, rest, and recreation.

Underlying mechanisms.   The mechanisms of fatigue are complex, entailing both physiological and psychological components. On the physiological side, prolonged muscular activity eventually produces biochemical changes including depletion of carbohydrate reserves and accumulation of lactic acid in the blood.

However, these biochemical changes correlate poorly with both the subjective experience of fatigue and measurable decrements in productivity. Thus, strong motivational pressures experienced, for example, during athletic competition, may reduce or virtually obliterate fatigue—both as a subjective feeling and as a factor impeding performance. Further, feelings of fatigue can be experienced without engaging in the heavy muscular activity ordinarily associated with these biochemical changes. Persons under continual emotional stress may become depressed (a kind of chronic fatigue) as a result of automatic nervous system and glandular activity, rather than muscle activity.

Finally, there is a clear subjective difference between fatigue following muscular exertion and mental fatigue or boredom. Although both may be accompanied by deteriorated performance, the former tends to generalize whereas the latter is highly specific. When we are fatigued we seek rest from all activity. When we are bored we seek relief only from the monotonous activity.

From a neurological standpoint, fatigue of all types seems to imply neurochemical mechanisms (constituting an inhibitory system) operating antagonistically to the arousal mechanisms discussed earlier (Grandjean, 1968).

It follows from the foregoing that there are several related kinds of fatigue, each with some capacity for "spilling over" to the other, all sharing common subjective components, but nonetheless somewhat distinguishable on the basis of etiology. Recognizing that such distinctions are extremely fuzzy, it is nevertheless convenient to differentiate (a) *emotional fatigue* resulting from exposure to intense stress, (b) *muscular fatigue* following prolonged and demanding physical activity, (c) *skills fatigue* for tasks requiring vigilance and attentiveness, and (d) *mental fatigue,* or boredom, emanating from monotonous activity.

We are primarily concerned with the performance consequences of the latter two: skills fatigue and boredom. These are chronic conditions in the sense that they are not relieved by rest or sleep, and have cumulative effects (McFarland, 1971). In contrast, fatigue resulting from hard physical activity is an acute condition which, though it interferes with efficiency, is temporary and effectively relieved by rest or sleep.

Fatigue and performance.   Bartlett (1951) introduced the concept of skill fatigue to help explain deteriorations of piloting performance. He had RAF pilots "fly" in a simulator for periods ranging from two hours upwards, until they were exhausted. As fatigue increased, the subjects unwittingly accepted progressively lower standards of accuracy and performance. Their range of attention became increasingly restricted; they became unable to interpret multiple instrument readings as parts of an overall portrayal of the way the entire airplane system was functioning.

The adverse impact of deteriorated skills can be demonstrated rather easily for tasks like piloting an airplane or driving a car; skills failure ultimately eventuates in an accident. Performance decrements associated with deteriorating skills on most jobs are more difficult to detect. McFarland (1971) suggests an approach to assessing skills fatigue by measuring (a) physiological signs of arousal and (b) evidence of spare mental capacity for coping with task demands that are peripheral to the central ones.

Both skills fatigue and boredom cause timing and vigilance to deteriorate. *Timing* calls for precise coordination of the type required to integrate behavioral elements into smoothly executed patterns, like swinging a golf club. *Vigilance* is alertness in monitoring and responding to critical stimuli. Most complex tasks, like automobile driving, require both. Timing is evidenced by smooth integration of the clutch and accelerator (assuming the car has a manual transmission). The vigilance tasks include continuous awareness of and responsiveness to road conditions, other traffic, pedestrians, signs and signals, the feel of the car, information provided by the dashboard instruments, and so on.

Although most tasks require some vigilance, it is central to effective performance on some jobs, like that of air traffic controllers at a busy airport. This job illustrates a kind of work requiring considerable skill with little margin for error, and where the implications of skills failure are especially disasterous. The combination of stresses thereby created for the controller increases the possibilities for "burnout" (that is, emotional fatigue). (Martindale, 1977.)

Scheduling variations

How does the work schedule affect fatigue and performance? We approach this question by considering three issues: (a) length of the work period, (b) shift schedules, and (c) task assignments.

We must emphasize that although it is convenient for us to consider scheduling issues as they relate to fatigue, we are not suggesting that modified scheduling is the only approach to fatigue reduction. Fatigue may also be reduced by changing jobs and tasks to better match employee characteristics (as discussed later under engineering psychology), and through improved selection, placement, and training. Since boredom is largely a matter of employee-task "fit" (in that not all employees regard the same tasks as monotonous), improved selection and placement is particularly important to controlling mental fatigue (P. C. Smith, 1955).

Length of work period.   Unfortunately, this issue is too often approached with misconceptions that appear on the surface to be reasonable. Managers sometimes express concern that shortened work periods will lower productivity and create social problems related to increases in available leisure time. Labor representatives, on the other hand, may press for shorter hours as a device for indirectly improving salaries and increasing the total number of available jobs.

Both viewpoints erroneously assume that productivity is a direct function of the amount of time spent at work. The evidence is to the contrary: Changes in work hours do not yield proportional changes in productivity.

It is helpful, in this regard, to distinguish between nominal and actual hours worked. Nominal hours are defined by the clock; the employee nominally is on the job between check-in and check-out time. However, some of this time is unproductive, both because of officially scheduled rest breaks and because of self-authorized rest periods. These unproductive interruptions of both types must be subtracted from nominal hours to yield actual hours. It has been found in general that increases in nominal hours decrease proportional actual hours of work, and vice versa.

It follows that overtime (except when infrequent and voluntary) is not likely to be cost-effective. Once having accepted the regular work period, whatever its length, as standard, employees will adjust their actual work time downward to compensate for a lengthened schedule. Actual productivity-per-nominal hour is lowered during both the overtime periods and those periods immediately preceding and following it. The combined effect of such lowered productivity plus the increased hourly costs of overtime (usually 1½ to 2 times the normal rate) is inefficiency. Except in unusual circumstances, the better solution is to add more employees or modify existing procedures and equipment.

The optimal length of the work week or workday is situational, depending upon task and employee characteristics. Although the 40-hour week is fairly standard in the United States at present, it is not similarly standard in other countries, has not always been the standard here, and undoubtedly will be reduced further both here and elsewhere in the future.

However, even when the 40-hour week is accepted as the norm, variations are possible. The one that has received the greatest attention in the popular press is the four-day 40-hour week. Ordinarily, the popular accounts are glowing, but supported by anecdotal reports rather than hard data.

Whereas this arrangement provides an additional leisure day, the increased potential for fatigue during a 10-hour work day is self-evident. Several studies of employees who have shifted to this schedule indicate that most of them like it, both initially and for a considerable period after the change is introduced. But there are "costs." Sixty-two percent of clerical and supervisory personnel is one study regarded the new schedule as "more tiring" (Goodale & Aagaard, 1975). Older workers, both in this study and another with pharmaceutical company employees (Nord & Costigan, 1973), held less favorable attitudes toward the change than did younger ones. We can infer that increased susceptibility to fatigue with age is one factor responsible for this finding. Another is that the younger workers reported that they were able to make more effective use of their increased leisure time.

The Nord and Costigan study also produced the interesting finding that although still favoring the change, workers on slower-paced (presumably more monotonous) jobs were less favorable one year after the change was instituted than they were at first. Judging from a third study (Ivancevich & Lyon, 1977), productivity increases for an initial period, but eventually returns to its original level.

Although all reports of experience with the four-day week confirm that employees tend to like it, additional research is specifically needed to clarify its limitations. There are clues that the nature of certain jobs (and the susceptibility of certain employees to fatigue) may contraindicate 10-hour workdays, even though the employees might claim to like the arrangement. There are also clues indicating the importance of helping some employees (particularly older males) to make effective use of the added nonworking day.

Another variation in work hours, still holding to the standard length work week as the norm, is flextime. Here the employees have some freedom in setting their starting and ending times. Obviously, such flexibility either is impossible or considerably limited for many types of jobs. This limitation applies, for example, when the work done by each employee depends upon that accomplished by another, or when customers or clients have to be served on some externally imposed schedule.

Assuming the hours can be flexibly arranged, one can guess that there would be some clear advantages to the employee. Rush-hour traffic could be avoided; other responsibilities, like child-care, could be more easily accomodated; and so on. Whether these assumed advantages have positive effects for increased job satisfaction and reduced turnover has not yet been investigated.

Shift scheduling. Human organisms are conditioned to a diurnal rhythm. This rhythm is a pattern of day/night variations in blood chemistry, glandular activity, and other bodily functions, which is learned through socially induced timetables for sleeping, eating, and so on. As we mature, the rhythm develops a degree of autonomy; we are accustomed to being awake and active at certain times and to sleeping at others.

You probably have experienced the implications of this rhythm following a flight to another time zone. Jet lag poses the same kind of problem as that presented by modifications of employee work-shift schedules. The modifications disrupt diurnal rhythm and, until the rhythm is restored through adaptation, they cause lost sleep and consequent fatigue. Reviewing a body of physiological research on the sleep-wakefulness cycle, Bloom (1961) concluded:

1. There are individual differences in the ability to adapt to shift changes. Therefore, persons should be selected for assignment to rotating shifts

on the basis of physiological indicators of diurnal flexibility (like body temperature adaptation as a sign of overall diurnal adaptation).
2. Shift changes should be instituted gradually, perhaps an hour at a time.
3. When possible, fixed shifts (requiring adaptation only once) are preferable to rotating shifts (requiring adaptation every time the shift is changed). If rotation is absolutely necessary, it should be infrequent and provide maximum time off between rotations to facilitate adaptation.
4. The graveyard shift (starting at midnight) is the most difficult one from the standpoint of maintaining vigilance. Therefore, shortening it would improve efficiency.

Besides disturbing the physiologically-based diurnal cycle, shift changes disrupt whatever prior social patterns the employee has established. These disruptions have clear negative implications for such things as family mealtimes, the parent's availability to play with the children, and so on. They also may contribute to sleep loss and fatigue as the shift worker tries to maintain established social and familial patterns in spite of the changed working hours.

Some workers apparently express preferences for every shift. The swing shift (starting at 4 o'clock or 5 o'clock P.M.) may meet the special needs of a student, for example. The night shift can be especially attractive to someone who is moonlighting. Obviously, it makes sense when possible to assign night shifts to those employees who prefer them. But there is mounting evidence that night shifts hold considerable potential for vigilance failures (and accidents) for all employees and therefore should be eliminated whenever possible (Wedderburn, 1975). Realizing that certain organizations must continue to function during the night, there is room for additional research particularly devoted to unique arrangements, including perhaps more frequent or better-timed breaks as well as shortened hours.

Task assignments. There is yet another type of possible modification: changing the work assignment. To the extent that boredom reflects the employee's perception that the job is insufficiently demanding or challenging, enlargement of the job's scope and responsibilities ought to be constructive.

The topic of job enlargement is discussed at length in Chapter 13 in the broader context of employee motivation and job satisfaction. Here we merely point out that it does not always have the anticipated effect. Although many employees give lip service to wanting more responsibility, they do not always accept it when offered. One possible explanation for this is that employees' attitudes toward tasks may be affected by broadly based cultural values (Hulin & Blood, 1968). Those workers who feel alienated from middle-class values (for example, blue-collar workers in urban locations) experience less rather than more satisfaction when their work assignment is made more complex.

As with all other possible modifications of the working conditions, the effectiveness of job enlargement is likely to be situationally conditioned by the particular tasks and employees.

ENGINEERING PSYCHOLOGY

We have thus far considered some of the implications of human factors for designing work environments and establishing work schedules. If you will turn back to Figure 11–1, you will note that our discussion has been restricted to the *Person* × *Environment* interactions shown by the left-hand arrows labeled *A*. We are ready now to consider some of the implications of human factors for equipment design: that is, the interactions labeled *B* and *C*. Those arrows in the figure imply three primary questions for engineering psychology:

1. On the basis of what is known about human behavior and equipment technology, which system functions ought to be allocated to people, and which ought to be allocated to machines?
2. Once this allocation is made, what are the optimal input modes for human operators? As shown by the *B* arrows in Figure 11–1, the equipment's outputs (including such things as dial readings, and auditory warning signals) comprise the operator's *inputs*. The person uses the information thereby conveyed to evaluate mechanical functions and decide on a next course of action.
3. What are the optimal *output* modes for the operator? People typically influence machine function by manipulating mechanical controls (like a steering wheel, throttle, or brake pedal).

The body of information reflecting sound research on these topics is vast, and only superficially touched in the following paragraphs. If you are interested in reading further in this area we call your attention particularly to surveys by Chapanis (1959, 1965b, 1976) and McCormick (1970).

Allocation of functions

There are many ways to design a person-equipment system. The number and complexity of mechanical components can be varied, as can the number of people in the system, and the functions performed by each person. Chapanis (1965a) notes two especially important points relative to the allocation of functions.

First, the allocation cannot be made solely on the basis of technological feasibility without regard also for important social, economic, and political values. The effects of technologically displaced employees are felt by families and communities. Thus, the social costs sometimes associated with automation may prove to be too large a price to pay for "progress." At the very least, automation frequently implies a need for employee retraining.

Second, assignments of functions must be continuously reevaluated. As technology advances, machines are made capable of performing functions not contemplated when the system was instituted. Book authorship is a case in point. These sentences were first written into a microcomputer programmed for word processing. Once entered, they were available in the computer's memory for the author to rework at will. When they were judged to be in final form, they were electronically printed by the same program. That printout was sent to the publisher without the traditional intervention of a typist. Word-processing equipment of all types has dramatically altered the duties and responsibilities of many office personnel.

The advantages of automation, besides convenience, are self-evident: machines are not subject to diurnal rhythms; they accomplish short-cycle repetitive tasks with no complaints about being bored; they are never late for work; and so on. Machines unquestionably can improve the quality of human worklife by relieving people of monotonous, fatiguing, or hazardous work. Are we as human beings then in danger of being relegated to the role of nonproductive consumer?

This seems most unlikely. Although tasks will undoubtedly continue to change, machines cannot replace the human organism's flexibility and judgment. The importance of these factors is nicely illustrated by a study of the reliability of navigational systems used for space exploration (Grodsky, 1962). As you know, critical mechanical systems are usually supported by one or more back-up systems designed to take over if the primary one fails. The investigator compared the reliability of various redundancies (that is, numbers of back-up systems) without any human operator with the reliability of a system with a human (but no mechanical) back-up. As shown in Figure 11–4, none of the totally mechanical systems (including one with four

FIGURE 11–4
Reliability of navigational back-up systems

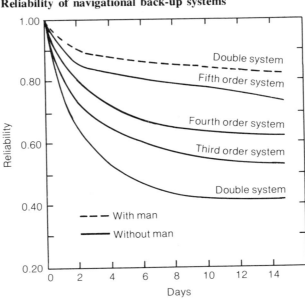

Source: M. A. Grodsky, "Risk and Reliability," *Aerospace Engineering 21,* no. 1, (1962): p. 30.

back-ups to the primary system) proved to be as reliable as a human being and a single mechanical system.

Inputs to people from machines

As we have noted, equipment communicates with an operator through some kind of display. Although any receptor organ could theoretically provide this input link, the two most commonly used modalities are vision and audition.

Choosing the modality. The potential number of visual and aural displays is vast. Visual displays can be made on TV screens, radarscopes, printed materials, and dials, to name a few. Similarly, aural communication devices include telephones, buzzers, gongs, and a host of others.

Chapanis (1976) has noted several circumstances influencing the relative appropriateness and efficiency of these two display modalities. Some of the major ones are summarized in Figure 11–5. As shown, there are two important factors to consider when choosing the input modality: the nature and content of the information to be communicated, and the general work environment.

Illustrative research on visual displays. We can only hint at the scope of research pertaining to the input side of the personnel subsystem component of person-machine systems. Since our intention is merely to illustrate something of the scope of this activity, we limit this discussion of visual input to some of the research that has been done on instrument arrangement and design. The general problem is to design instrument panels to provide several unambiguous bits of information simultaneously.

In order for the information to be conveyed unambiguously and grasped rapidly, interpretation of the instrument reading must be simplified. Consider the array of dials in a commercial-aircraft cockpit. The pilot's task in monitoring these instruments for abnormal signals is simplified by patterning the display (Woodson, 1954). This is accomplished by clustering instruments dealing with related functions and orienting the dials so that the normal pointer position is the same for each. Deviations from the normal thus can be quickly spotted.

It is impossible to cluster all of the instruments directly in front of the operator when the instrument panel is large and complex. Some instruments must be placed in the field of peripheral vision, where they are less likely to be as carefully monitored. Alternative arrangements of peripherally located instruments were investigated by comparing three conditions: (a) all instruments arranged vertically, (b) all arranged horizontally, and (c) mixed instrument arrangements—some vertical and some horizontal. The latter arrangement was found to facilitate the operator's accurate and rapid interpretation of peripherally placed inputs (Bauer, Cassatt, Corona, & Warhurst, 1966).

One last illustration further clarifies the scope of this research area. Assuming some kind of visual input is to be provided the operator, that input

FIGURE 11 –5
Appropriateness of display modalities

	Conditions favoring	
Factor considered	*Visual displays*	*Auditory communication*
A. The message:		
1. Complexity?	Complex or abstract (e.g., technical information); many displays to monitor	Simple
2. Length?	Long	Short
3. Content orientation?	Spatial (e.g., a map)	Temporal (e.g., signal to launch a missle)
4. Is further reference to message necessary?	Yes	No
5. Urgency, speed or attention— getting value?	Unimportant	Important (e.g., a horn signaling low altitude)
B. Work environment:		
1. Present over-load?	Already too many aural communications	Already too many visual displays
2. Suitability?	Too noisy for aural communication	Too dimly lit for visual display
3. Operator location?	Stationary	Moves around

Source: After A. Chapanis, "Engineering Psychology," in *Handbook of Industrial and Organizational Psychology*, ed. M. D. Dunnette (Chicago: Rand McNally, 1976), pp. 702–703.

can be provided in several ways: warning lights, moving dials, pointers, and so on. The general principle is to provide the type of visual indication of mechanical function most clearly related to the kind of use the operator must make of the information. Chapanis (1976) has summarized much of the research on the relative suitability of various types of indicators of mechanical function as shown in Figure 11–6.

Outputs from people to machines

After receiving and processing the information communicated from the equipment, the operator will ordinarily decide upon an appropriate course of

FIGURE 11–6
Suitability of three types of indicators

	Moving pointer	Moving scale	Counter
Quantitative reading: For exact numerical information; e.g., exact time to missile launch	+/− (fair or questionable)	+/− (fair or questionable)	+ (suitable)
Check reading: For "go - no go" signals; e.g., amount of fuel remaining in tank	+ (suitable)	− (not suitable)	− (not suitable)
Setting: For verification of mechanical setting; e.g., verifying an automotive cruise-control setting	+ (suitable)	+/− (fair or questionable)	+ (suitable)
Tracking: For information required to maintain continual and appropriate adjustments; e.g., a ship's compass	+ (suitable)	+/− (fair or questionable)	− (not suitable)

Source: After A. Chapanis, "Engineering Psychology," in Dunnette, ed., *Handbook of Industrial and Organizational Psychology*, p. 705. Copyright © 1976 by Rand McNally College Publishing Company. Adapted by permission of Houghton Mifflin Company.

action. Most often this action entails manipulating some kind of control knob, button, lever, and so on.

One of the earlier studies of errors attributable to control manipulations obtained information from critical incidents interviews. (The critical incidents interview, you will recall, asks respondents to provide detailed descriptions of an instance in which a certain kind of behavior—in this case, control error—critically affected the outcomes.) The investigators (Fitts & Jones, 1947) identified six kinds of control problems experienced by pilots: (1) *substitution errors* where one control was confused with another; (2) *control adjustment errors,* like setting a switch to the off position or a neutral position when the intention was to switch to on; (3) *forgetting errors,* including failure to use controls at the proper time; (4) *reversal errors,* that is, moving the control in the opposite of the direction required to produce the intended effect; (5) *unintentional activation* of controls; and (6) *inability to reach* the control.

Although these were identified as pilot control errors, it is clear that the same types of control problems can arise when operating a wide range of mechanical equipment. Considerable research has therefore been directed toward their amelioration by, for example, shaping control knobs tactually and visually to cue the operator concerning their function; arranging for controls so that the direction of their movement is logically related to their function; placing controls so that they can be easily reached; and so on.

Since the controls are themselves part of a total system, their design must also take into account several nonmechanical aspects of the system. The operator's digital and manual dexterity are affected by such things as heat and vibration; protective garments and safety devices can influence the ability to reach controls.

At least three factors must be considered in designing any control: (1) its operation must not require undue force or be incompatible with limitations imposed by the work environment; (2) it must be easily distinguishable from different controls which have other functions; and (3) it must be conceptually "sensible."

This last is particularly interesting to psychologists because of the cultural implications of what is sensible. It has been discovered, for example, that it is more natural for persons to respond to high tones by moving a switch up, and to low tones by moving it down (Simon, Mewaldt, Acosta, & Hu, 1976). And, based upon a host of earlier experiences, it is easiest for people to conceptualize a clockwise control movement as accelerating the machine's operation, and a counterclockwise movement as shutting it down. You can undoubtedly think of many other instances in which the direction of the control movement and the intended result seem to be so sensibly linked that they must not be violated by control design. There is one caution here: natural relationships between movements and expected outcomes are not universal. The author recalls some small difficulty initially experienced after arriving in Australia where it is natural to turn room lights on by depressing the wall switch!

SUMMARY

The concern for the role of human factors in performance has implications for equipment and task design and the environments in which work is performed. Only three aspects of this very broad topic were considered in this chapter: physical work environment, work and assignment schedules, and engineering psychology.

Our discussion of work environments considered only certain aspects having a potential impact upon comfort: temperature, illumination, noise, and music. Generalizations about these (and other) environmental influences must be made cautiously because environmental manipulations (a) may have secondary, and often unrecognized, consequences; (b) may have different effects depending upon employee attitudes towards the manipulation; and (c) have effects which often dissipate with time.

Arousal theory was presented as a framework for organizing apparent discrepancies in research findings concerning environmental impacts. The effects of environmental conditions upon performance are presumed to be mediated by their effects upon arousal: environmental stimuli generating too high a level of arousal cause performance to deteriorate. What makes for too high a level of arousal is an important, and still not satisfactorily resolved, research issue. We approach it here by differentiating between organismic challenges and stresses. The former produce facilitating levels of arousal; the latter are debilitating.

The second general topic treated in the chapter, work schedules and assignments, was considered in the context of two types of fatigue: skills fatigue, and mental fatigue (or boredom). Both cause timing and vigilance to deteriorate. The optimal length of the work week or workday is situational. The 40-hour work week is fairly standard in the United States at this time. It is not similarly standard in other countries, has not always been the standard here, and undoubtedly will be reduced further in the future.

One variation within the 40-hour workweek context is the four-day workweek. The nature of certain jobs (and the susceptibility of certain employees to fatigue) may contraindicate 10-hour workdays even though the affected employees might claim to like the arrangement. Another kind of variation discussed in the chapter is germane only to shift work. The implications of shift scheduling were discussed largely as a function of diurnal rhythm.

Three human-engineering issues were touched briefly in the chapter: (1) allocation of functions to people and to machines, (2) the nature of inputs to human operators, and (3) optimal output modes for operators.

REFERENCES

Allusi, E. A., & Morgan, B. B., Jr. Engineering psychology and human performance. *Annual Review of Psychology,* 1976, *27,* 305–330.

Bartlett, F. C. The bearing of experimental psychology upon human skilled performance. *British Journal of Industrial Psychology,* 1951, *8,* 209–217.

Bauer, R. W., Cassatt, R. K., Corona, B. M., & Warhurst, F., Jr. Panel layout for rectilinear instruments. *Human Factors,* 1966, *8,* 493–497.

Bloom, W. Shift work and the sleep-wakefulness cycle. *Personnel,* 1961, *38,* 24–31.

Broadbent, D. E. Some effects of noise on visual performance. *Journal of Experimental Psychology,* 1954, *6,* 1–5.

Broadbent, D. E. *Decision and stress.* New York: Academic Press, 1971.

Chapanis, A. *Research techniques in human engineering.* Baltimore: Johns Hopkins Press, 1959.

Chapanis, A. On the allocation of functions between men and machines. *Occupational Psychology,* 1965(a), *39,* 1–11.

Chapanis, A. *Man-machine engineering.* Monterey, Calif.: Brooks/Cole, 1965(b).

Chapanis, A. Engineering Psychology. In M. D. Dunnette (Ed.), *Handbook of industrial and organizational psychology.* Chicago: Rand McNally, 1976, 697–744.

Duffy, E. *Activation and behavior.* New York: Wiley, 1962.

Feree, C. E., & Rand, G. Work and its illumination. *Personnel Journal,* 1940, *19,* 55–64; 93–98.

Fitts, P. M., & Jones, R. E. *Analysis of factors contributing to 460 "pilot-error" experiences in operating aircraft controls.* Engr. Div., Air Materiel Command, Dayton, Ohio, Rept. No. TSEAA-694-12 (1947).

Goodale, J. G., & Aagaard, A. K. Factors relating to varying reactions to 4-day workweeks. *Journal of Applied Psychology,* 1975, *60,* 33–38.

Grandjean, E. Fatigue: Its physiological and psychological significance. *Ergonomics,* 1968, *11,* 427–436.

Grodsky, M. A. Risk and reliability. *Aerospace Engineering,* 1962, *21,* 21–33.

Hulin, C. L., & Blood, M. R. Job enlargement, individual differences, and worker responses. *Psychological Bulletin,* 1968, *69,* 41–55.

Ivancevich, J. M., & Lyon, H. L. The shortened workweek: A field experiment. *Journal of Applied Psychology,* 1977, *62,* 34–37.

Martindale, D. Sweaty palms in the control tower. *Psychology Today,* 1977, *9,* 71–75.

McCormick, E. J. *Human factors engineering* (3rd ed.) New York: McGraw-Hill, 1970.

McFarland, R. A. Understanding fatigue in modern life. *Ergonomics,* 1971, *14,* 1–10.

McGrath, J. E. Settings, measures, and themes: An integrative review of some research on social-psychological factors in stress. In J. E. McGrath (Ed.), *Social and psychological factors in stress.* New York: Holt, Rinehart & Winston, 1970.

McGrath, J. E. Stress and behavior in organizations. In M. D. Dunnette (Ed.), *Handbook of industrial and organizational psychology.* Chicago: Rand McNally, 1976, 1351–1395.

Näätänen, R. The inverted-U relationship between activation and performance: A critical review. In S. Kornblum (Ed.), *Attention and Performance IV.* New York: Academic Press, 1973.

Nord, W. R., & Costigan, R. Worker adjustment to the four-day week: a longitudinal study. *Journal of Applied Psychology,* 1973, *58,* 60–66.

Scott, W. E. Jr. Activation theory and task design. *Organizational Behavior and Human Performance,* 1966, *1,* 3–30.

Simon, J. R., Mewaldt, S. P., Acosta, E., & Hu, J. Processing auditory information. *Journal of Applied Psychology,* 1976, *61,* 354–358.

Smith, H. C. *Music in relation to employee attitudes, piece-work production, and industrial accidents.* Applied Psychology Monographs, No. 14, 1947.

Smith, P. C. The prediction of individual differences in susceptibility to industrial monotony. *Journal of Applied Psychology,* 1955, *39,* 322–329.

Taylor, F. V. Psychology and the design of machines. *American Psychologist,* 1957, *12,* 249–256.

Teichner, W. H., Arees, E., & Reilly, R. Noise and human performance: A psychophysiological approach. *Ergonomics,* 1963, *6,* 83–97.

Vernon, H. M., & Warner, C. G. Objective and subjective tests for noise. *Personnel Journal,* 1932, *11,* 141–149.

Wedderburn, A. A. I. *Studies of shiftwork in the steel industry.* Edinburgh: Heriot-Watt University, 1975.

Weinstein, N. D.   Individual differences in reactions to noise: A longitudinal study in a college dormitory, *Journal of Applied Psychology*, 1978, *63*, 458–466.

Wilkinson, R. T.   Interaction of noise with knowledge of results and sleep deprivation. *Journal of Experimental Psychology*, 1963, *66*, 332–337.

Wilkinson, R. T., Fox, R. H., Goldsmith, R., Hampton, I. F. G., & Lewis, H. E. Psychological and physiological responses to raised body temperature. *Journal of Applied Psychology*, 1964, *19*, 287–291.

Woodson, W. E.   *Human engineering guide for equipment designers*. Berkeley, Calif.: University of California Press, 1954.

section three

ORGANIZATIONAL PSYCHOLOGY

The previous section on personnel psychology was primarily concerned with the area of organizational entry. That is, personnel psychologists focus on attempting to bring into the organization those applicants who will be the most effective employees and then train them to perform their jobs to the best of their ability. However, even though the contributions of personnel psychologists are very substantial, I/O psychology has much more to contribute to organizations.

Section Three, Organizational Psychology, is primarily concerned with the area of organizational effectiveness. In an attempt to contribute to effectiveness, I/O psychologists study organizations from three increasingly broader perspectives: (1) the individual, (2) the group, and (3) the organization as a whole.

In Part A, Individual Variables, we will study the related topics of motivation (Chapter 12) and job satisfaction (Chapter 13).

While motivation has been the focus of considerable research in psychology, the study of work motivation is a much more recent development. Motivation can be defined as the process by which our behavior is initiated and directed. It will become evident as you read Chapter 12 that motivation is an exceedingly complex process. For one thing, motivation cannot be observed, it must be inferred. We present seven relatively complimentary theoretical perspectives to help you understand work motivation. Each of the theories has implications for maximizing employee motivation.

We next turn our attention to job satisfaction, a traditional area of concern for I/O psychologists. Most contemporary work emphasizes the intrinsic character of the work itself in relation to job satisfaction. Chapter 13 examines the relationship between job satisfaction and productivity, absenteeism, and turnover. You will probably be surprised by some of these findings. It also examines trends in job satisfaction over the past decades, and presents some of the major sources of dissatisfaction for various segments of our society (e.g., the young, women, and blacks).

In Part B, Individuals in Groups, we will study Group Behavior (Chapter 14) and Leadership (Chapter 15).

Group effort is a necessary and significant part of business and industry. Over 40 years ago, the Hawthorne researchers demonstrated the substantial influence of the work group on the behavior of individual employees. This finding was contrary to conventional wisdom at that time. Since then, research and theory have substantially refined our understanding of the importance of work groups for organizational effectiveness. Chapter 14 examines several aspects of work-group behavior including decision making and group norms.

As a society, we place much emphasis on the leader's responsibility for the effectiveness of group action. The earliest systematic leadership research sought unsuccessfully to identify the set of traits possessed by successful leaders. Since the traits approach was not productive, numerous other research strategies have been devised to help us understand leadership. As Chapter 15 indicates, recent efforts constantly emphasize the importance of situational factors for improving leader effectiveness.

In Part C, Organizational Dynamics, we will look at the big picture. Here we examine the broad perspective of organization theory, development, and change.

Chapter 16 begins with the classical theorists. Although these earlier views about organizational design have been criticized for neglecting peoples' needs, remnants of classical thinking still pervade many present-day organizations. We also discuss the several more-contemporary organizational theorists and contrast their position with those of the classicists.

Chapter 17 presents several technologies developed by practitioners who intervene in an attempt to increase the effectiveness of the whole organization. The field of organization development (OD) is relatively new; most OD technologies have been developed in the past two decades. OD is currently growing very rapidly as business and industry is increasingly becoming aware of the contributions of I/O psychologists in areas other than personnel psychology.

We conclude Section Three with Chapter 18 on Organization Change. The theories and research presented in the previous chapters must ultimately stand the test of successful application in organizations. Therefore, we examine two case histories of organization change, one a failure in a large university, the other a success in a manufacturing company, and present possible explanations for the differing outcomes.

We have tried in this section on organizational psychology to maintain a balance between theory and research. We hope that what is presented will help you understand organizational behavior and also be of practical value. Since organizational psychology is a considerably newer field than personnel psychology, much remains to be learned. Nevertheless, organizational psychology is a dynamic and growing area of study. We hope that we have captured some of that excitement in the following chapters.

INDIVIDUAL VARIABLES

part A

chapter 12

Motivational Theories

If you could go into most contemporary organizations and speak to the managers, you would probably hear comments from them like:

> "Some of my workers won't put out any extra effort when I need them to. They're just not motivated to do a good job. All they want is money and more money."

> "Most of the workers I've had to fire had the ability all right. They just didn't seem to want to work. They had bad attitudes."

> "If I could just find Tom's and Mary's hot buttons, then I'd know how to motivate them and get them to move their tails."

Furthermore, many industrial-organizational psychologists consulting for companies get asked questions like the two that follow.

> "Well, you're an expert, so tell me, what can I do to motivate my employees?"

> "Can you get me a test that will tell me which people want to work hard and which ones just want to goof off?"

Comments and questions like these reflect widespread concern with the topic of motivation.

Motivation can be defined as the process by which behavior is initiated and directed. The nature and strength of motivation cannot, of course, be directly observed. Motivation is inferred from behavior, which *is* observable. Thus, motivation is a construct which helps us understand and predict behavior.

This chapter summarizes seven of the most influential theories of work motivation. We can almost hear you saying "Seven different theories, why not present just one, the correct one?" It is simply not possible, at the present time, to have only one theory and to keep it within reasonable bounds (Campbell & Pritchard, 1976). The seven presented here are complementary rather than competitive.

CONTENT THEORIES

We consider first three content, or need, theories: the need-hierarchy theory, the ERG theory, and the two-factor theory. These theories share the belief that there exists some internal state of the individual called a need or motive. They focus on the variables which lead individuals to perform, to sustain, and to stop performing specific actions (Campbell, Dunnette, Lawler, & Weick, 1970).

Need-hierarchy theory

Maslow's (1954, 1965, 1970) need-hierarchy theory is probably the most widely known approach to individual work motivation. It is particularly popular in nonacademic settings.

Principles. Maslow postulates a continual state of striving as the normal human condition. Whenever one need is met, it is immediately replaced by another. This process of continual wanting motivates us from birth until death. He postulates five categories of needs: physiological, safety, social, esteem, and self-actualization. These needs are hierarchically arranged as shown in Figure 12–1.

FIGURE 12–1
Maslow's need hierarchy

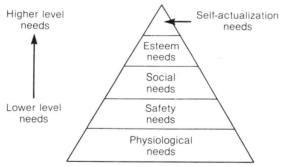

According to Maslow, individuals are motivated by the lowest, most basic, unsatisfied need in the hierarchy. Once a level of needs is satisfied, it no longer motivates behavior; hence, the next higher level in the hierarchy becomes dominant. Two levels of needs can operate at the same time, but the lower-level need is considered to be the more powerful motivator of behavior. Furthermore, Maslow stresses that the higher the level of a need, the less important it is for survival and the longer its gratification can be postponed. Moreover, he believes that the higher level needs are a more recent evolutionary development.

A description of the five sets of needs follows.

1. *Physiological needs.* The physiological needs (for example, for food and water) stand lowest in the hierarchy. However, they are preeminent in importance when thwarted. A person deprived of food or water is obviously not going to be concerned with satisfying a higher-level need such as that for status or personal recognition.

The placement of the physiological needs at the bottom of the hierarchy reflects Maslow's position that a satisfied need is not a motivator. Since the physiological needs are fairly well satisfied for most members of our society, these needs have little practical significance as motivators, and attention can be given to those needs at the next higher level.

2. *Safety needs.* These include the need for protection from physical danger and threat. Gratification of such needs clearly preoccupies the soldier in battle. Although the threat of physical danger is rarely present in everyday life, and therefore is not typically a powerful motivator, the need for psychological safety (that is, security) does have significant motivational consequences for large numbers of persons in our culture.

The need for security becomes especially important when people are in a dependent relationship in which they fear arbitrary action. The fear of such action characteristically has supported the efforts to organize labor and has motivated seniority provisions in virtually all union contracts.

3. *Social needs.* These needs include giving and receiving friendship, belonging, association, and love. Although aware of the social needs, managers often incorrectly assume that these needs conflict with the attainment of organizational goals and therefore may attempt to thwart their satisfaction (McGregor, 1960). As a result, the employee may become antagonistic and uncooperative.

4. *Esteem needs.* These needs stand at the next higher level and probably assume the greatest significance for both management and employees in contemporary organizational settings. The esteem needs are of two types:

a. Those related to self-esteem, including the needs for self-respect, self-confidence, and competence.
b. Those related to one's reputation, including the needs for recognition, appreciation, and status.

Unlike the lower-level needs, the esteem needs remain unsatisfied in typical organizations, particularly for employees below the supervisory level. It appears to us that many Americans may return home from their jobs every day feeling like an intelligent gorilla could have performed as well as they did. The simplification of many jobs in the interest of increased efficiency has the unfortunate consequence of blocking the satisfaction of some of the most important human needs. Of course, in times of widespread unemployment, even jobs that satisfy only the lower levels of needs become desirable because of the necessity to satisfy what are now more preeminent needs.

5. *Self-actualization needs.* The needs standing at the top of the hierarchy are those for self-actualization or self-fulfillment. These include the needs for being creative and fully realizing one's potential.

Relatively few jobs provide opportunities for self-actualization. Furthermore, the deprivation experienced at lower levels of the need hierarchy (particularly with reference to social and esteem needs) prevents most employees from attending to their need for self-fulfillment.

Research. Maslow's need-hierarchy theory was based primarily on his clinical observations rather than on empirical findings. Unfortunately, the amount of research testing the theory is still relatively scanty.

Porter (1964) has conducted research within the framework of Maslow's theory with 2,000 randomly selected managers belonging to the American Management Association. They each received a 13-item questionnaire which asked them to asess for each need (1) how much they had of it now, (2) how much there should be, and (3) how important it is. The results indicated that higher-level managers tended to place greater emphasis on the esteem needs and self-actualization than did lower- and middle-level managers but that there was no difference for the various managerial levels on the other three sets of needs (physiological, safety, and social). In addition, higher-level managers tended to rate the opportunity for personal growth, the authority connected with their position, and the opportunity to participate in goal setting as more important than did lower-level managers. A major contribution of this study is that it supported Maslow's contention that greater satisfaction of lower-level needs frees us to attend more to higher-level needs.

Most of the other research concerned with the need-hierarchy theory has provided findings that contradict important aspects of it (Wahba & Bridwell, 1976). For example, Lawler and Suttle (1972) tested several hypotheses related to Maslow's theory. Their research used the longitudinal approach, that is, their subjects were followed for a period of time. This enabled the researchers to study the behavior of individuals as they supposedly progressed up the motivational hierarchy. Their results provided no support for Maslow's notion of a five-level model. In addition, they found no support for the positions that (1) a highly satisfied need is no longer an important motivator of behavior and (2) a highly satisfied need in one category should result in the needs at the next higher level being more important.

Furthermore, Hall and Nougaim (1968) found that the more a need is satisfied the more important it becomes for an individual. For example, an individual made a suggestion at work that when implemented greatly reduced the amount of physical effort required daily by each of 100 workers including himself. As a result, he received recognition for his idea from both his fellow workers and management. This led to the worker thinking about other labor-saving ideas in an attempt to get more of the desired recognition. This finding is in direct opposition to the predictions of the need-hierarchy theory. In the past few years, there has been an absence of research on the need-hierarchy theory (Mitchell, 1979).

ERG theory

Alderfer's (1969, 1972) ERG theory is a modification and reformulation of Maslow's need-hierarchy approach.

Principles. Alderfer postulates that individuals have three sets of needs: existence needs (E), relatedness needs (R), and growth needs (G).

1. *Existence needs.* These are the needs for material substances such as the desire to have food, water, housing, money, furniture, and an automobile.
2. *Relatedness needs.* These are the needs to share one's thoughts and feelings with other people and to have them share these same things with you. Alderfer postulates that individuals desire to communicate openly with significant others in their life and to have meaningful relationships with family, friends, and co-workers.
3. *Growth needs.* These are the needs individuals have to develop their abilities to the fullest. This is akin to becoming the "best you" that you possibly can.

Alderfer states that the existence, relatedness, and growth needs lie on a concreteness continuum, with the existence needs being the most concrete and the growth needs being the least concrete. Thus, Alderfer arranges his needs on a continuum from the individual's perspective while Maslow arranges his needs on a continuum constructed from a social perspective. Basic postulates of the ERG theory are that (1) the more completely a more-concrete need is satisfied, the greater is the desire to satisfy the less-concrete needs and (2) the less completely a need is satisfied, the greater is the desire to have it satisfied.

Although Alderfer believes that there are three types of needs as compared to Maslow's five, the major difference between the two approaches is how an individual is theorized to move from one level of needs to another. According to Maslow, an individual moves up the need hierarchy when a lower-level need is satisfied. This process is referred to as "fulfillment-progression." Alderfer agrees that fulfillment-progression is important. However, he also feels that when the higher-level needs are not satisfied, the individual regresses and tries to gain additional gratification at the lower-level needs. This process is referred to as frustration-regression and it is a unique contribution of this theory.

Research. Alderfer's ERG theory is relatively new and there have been very few tests of its basic postulates. Alderfer's (1969, 1972) initial research on the theory, conducted in seven organizations with over 800 persons, provided mostly, but not entirely, positive findings. For example, he found support for the predicted positive correlation between satisfaction with the growth needs and the perceived importance of these needs in some types of organizations (fraternity houses and an adult T-group) but not in others (a bank and a manufacturing company). However, Wanous and Zwany (1977) did find considerable support for the basic parts of ERG theory. They found substantial evidence for the three dimensions of existence needs, relatedness needs, and growth needs. They also found that these needs were arranged hierarchically as Alderfer theorized.

Intuitively, the frustration-regression concept of ERG theory is very appealing and is an omission from the need-hierarchy theory. The concept of frustration-regression has interesting implications for motivating employees. It implies that motivation can be kept at a reasonable level for less challenging jobs, such as working on an assembly line, if more concrete needs, such as that for money, can be met. ERG theory currently awaits further empirical tests.

Two-factor theory

Herzberg's motivation-hygiene or two-factor theory (Herzberg, Mausner, & Snyderman, 1959; Herzberg, 1966) is similar in some respects to both Maslow's need-hierarchy theory and Alderfer's ERG theory. The two-factor theory relates to both motivation and job satisfaction. It has been placed here because this chapter focuses on theoretical approaches. However, due to its implications for job satisfaction (Chapter 13), you will be referred back to this section at the proper time. Herzberg's theory was an attempt to organize findings from an interviewing study conducted with 203 accountants and engineers (Herzberg et al., 1959). The researchers began by asking the interviewees to recall a time when they felt particularly good about their job. Subsequent probing sought to determine the reasons for the good feelings and their impact upon both job performance and overall sense of well-being. After a positive sequence of events was completed, the interview was repeated, but this time the workers were asked to describe events at work that resulted in negative feelings about their jobs. The interview was continued until a worker could think of no more sequences of events associated with increased or decreased job satisfaction.

Principles. Five factors, intrinsic to the job, stood out as the primary determiners of job satisfaction. They are:

1. Responsibility.
2. Advancement.
3. Work itself.
4. Achievement.
5. Recognition.

The first three were determined to be of greater importance for a lasting change of attitudes. These same five factors appeared very infrequently when the worker described events that resulted in job dissatisfaction.

Therefore, when one of these factors was present, workers were satisfied. However, when they were absent, the workers were not dissatisfied. Instead, they had neutral feelings. Herzberg named these five satisfier factors *motivators* since he claimed that when they were present they motivated an individual to be a high producer.

An entirely different set of factors was found to determine job dissatisfaction. The major dissatisfiers were factors extrinsic to the job itself. They are:

1. Company administration and policy.
2. Supervision.
3. Salary.
4. Interpersonal relations.
5. Working conditions.

Unlike the motivators, these dissatisfiers produced short-term changes in job attitudes and had no effect on employee motivation. These five factors were mentioned only infrequently when the workers discussed satisfying circumstances. Herzberg named these dissatisfiers *hygiene factors*.

Herzberg concluded that the factors involved in producing job satisfaction are separate and distinct from those leading to job dissatisfaction. In other words, semantics aside, job satisfaction and dissatisfaction are not opposites. Herzberg stresses that the opposite of job satisfaction is *no* job satisfaction while the opposite of job dissatisfaction is *no* job dissatisfaction. This elusive but key concept is depicted in Figure 12–2.

According to Herzberg, the motivator factors and hygiene factors are each presumed to reflect a different system of human needs. One need system is supposedly derived from the biological structure of human beings.

FIGURE 12–2
Schematic representation of the two-factor theory of job satisfaction

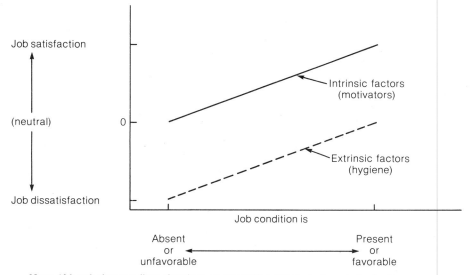

Note: Although shown as linear functions, no assumption of linearity is made by the theory.

This system is comprised of the primary drives (hunger and thirst, for example) plus all of the learned ones associated with these primary drives (for example, to earn money in order to buy food). The foundation of this need system is the biological drive to avoid pain and discomfort and it is reflected in the hygiene needs.

The other need system derives from peoples' unique ability to achieve and to grow. People need challenge, a sense of achievement, and a feeling of accomplishment in order to feel fulfilled and this is reflected in the motivator needs.

There are clear similarities between Herzberg's, Maslow's, and Alderfer's views of motivation. What Maslow classifies as the lower-level needs (physiological, safety, and social) are similar to Alderfer's existence and relatedness needs and to Herzberg's need to avoid unpleasantness. Similarly, Maslow's higher-level needs (esteem and self-actualization) correspond to Alderfer's growth needs and to Herzberg's need for achievement and growth.

Application. Herzberg's distinction between hygiene and motivator factors calls into question a number of current practices in contemporary organizations which tend to emphasize the hygiene factors. Herzberg does not deny the importance of these. On the contrary, he believes that failure to satisfy hygiene needs may generate considerable organizational distress. However, he sees as a frequent error the assumption that preventing dissatisfaction will automatically generate positive feelings with a resultant increase in motivation and productivity. According to Herzberg, satisfaction of hygiene needs leads only to a temporary absence of dissatisfaction. The hygiene demands including those of increased salary and fringe benefits, will tend to recur and escalate.

Therefore, Herzberg feels that it is especially important for organizations to recognize and respond to their employees' needs for personal growth. He claims that if organizations provide opportunities for employees to satisfy their motivator needs at work, positive motivation forces will be unleashed and this will lead to increases in productivity. Herzberg (1968) stresses that the way to satisfy the motivator needs at work is by job enrichment, a process by which jobs are made more meaningful. He claims that meaningful jobs enable people to experience feelings of pride and accomplishment in their work.

A few of the principles involved in job enrichment are:

1. Increasing the accountability of persons for their own work.
2. Granting additional authority to an employee.
3. Introducing new and more difficult tasks not previously handled (Herzberg, 1968).

The topic of job enrichment is further elaborated in Chapter 17.

Research. The motivation-hygiene theory has been responsible for giving direction to a tremendous amount of research. The evidence has been contradictory, sometimes supporting but generally refuting the theoretical propositions (King, 1970, Locke, 1976).

There has been much criticism of the methodology of the original research underlying the theory. For example, it has been suggested (Vroom, 1964) that the conclusions from the interviews were artifacts of the interview procedure. Attempts to replicate the original findings do, indeed, seem to indicate that whereas use of the original procedure tends to confirm the original findings, variations in the interview procedure generate nonsupportive findings (House & Wigdor, 1967). In particular, needs for salary and responsibility have, in Herzberg's terminology, power both as motivators and hygiene factors. It has been suggested that Herzberg's procedure prevented discovery of this dual action because of the tendency of people to attribute the causes of satisfying events to their own achievements on the job, and to attribute dissatisfying events to conditions beyond their control (that is, to the job environment) (Vroom, 1964; Wall, 1973).

In addition, the theory has been criticized on a number of logical and empirical grounds (Locke, 1976) including the imprecision of its formulation. For example, King (1970) notes that the statement of the theory is so ambiguous that five different versions of it have been explicitly stated or assumed by researchers. Moreover, Waters and Waters (1972) tested all five versions and found no support for any of them. Other researchers have reported equally damaging findings. As a result, there has been a dearth of recent research on the theory.

It is very difficult to asses the overall contribution of Herzberg's two-factor theory. On the positive side, the theory provides a framework for thinking about motivation and job satisfaction. The theory has stimulated an enormous amount of valuable research on these topics. Moreover, it suggests efforts toward job enrichment which is itself an appealing notion. While enrichment efforts have ensued from the theory, and thus must be counted as a contribution of Herzberg's work, job enrichment is neither synonymous with the two-factor theory nor a derivation of that theory alone. On the negative side, evidence has accumulated that some of its key positions are incorrect. For example, as previously indicated, salary and responsibility have power both as motivators and hygiene factors.

All of the need theories oversimplify the variables underlying human motivation. As a result, a second set of theories, process theories, developed in an attempt to represent the diversity and complexity of human motivation more adequately.

PROCESS THEORIES

The process theories are concerned with identifying and studying the processes that initiate, sustain, and terminate behavior.

Reinforcement theory—Operant conditioning

Reinforcement theory is based upon Skinner's (1953, 1969) operant-conditioning paradigm for learning. Although it is primarily based on research with animals, its principles for acquisition and extinction apply to much occurring in our everyday lives.

Principles. The theory has two basic sets of principles: those relating to the acquisition of correct responses and those relating to the extinction of incorrect responses.

Acquisition of a behavior requires its prior reinforcement. The reinforcement may be positive (a reward for making the desired response) or negative (removing an aversive stimulus when the desired response is made) but the organism must make the connection between its actions and their consequences. If the desired response is not in the organism's repertoire (and therefore unlikely to occur spontaneously), it must be shaped. Shaping occurs when responses which are approximations to the correct response are initially reinforced. Gradually, positive reinforcement is provided only when the approximated behavior becomes progressively refined until, finally, only the specific desired response (rather than an approximation) is reinforced.

Acquisition tends to occur most rapidly when reinforcement is continuous: that is, the correct response is rewarded after each occurrence. However, both life and the laboratory also provide partial reinforcement schedules, in which only some percentage of the correct responses are rewarded. Partial reinforcement leads to slower acquisition, but it has beneficial effects on extinction, as you will see shortly. Sometimes partial reinforcement is provided on a regularly-occurring (i.e., fixed) interval. Most American workers, for example, are paid on a fixed-interval schedule. They receive their salary (the reinforcement) on a regular periodic schedule (daily, weekly, etc.). The reinforcement is partial (rather than continuous) because it is meant to recognize satisfactory job performance throughout the pay period—not only on pay day. Ratio schedules are an alternative to interval schedules. Some workers are paid on the basis of the number of work units completed rather than for the length of time worked.

According to operant conditioning principles, responses that are not reinforced or punished will be extinguished. Skinner does not consider using punishment to be an effective way to eliminate an incorrect or undesirable response because of its undesirable side effects including anxiety and resentment. Moreover, punishment for an incorrect response does not necessarily clarify the nature of the desired response for the learner. Skinner states that incorrect responses should be ignored.

Learning that occurs under a continuous schedule of reinforcement extinguishes faster than that which occurs under a partial reinforcement schedule. An illustration of the resistance of behavior learned under partial reinforcement to extinction follows. You probably go to your mailbox every day to see if you have recieved any mail. However, most of us do not receive mail every day. Therefore, our response of looking for the mail is reinforced on a partial and not on a continuous schedule. Now, think of how many days of receiving no mail it would take before you completely stopped going to check your mail. Do you think you would stop if you did not receive any mail for 100 days? For 365 days? For three years? Rats and pigeons that learn under partial reinforcement schedules are like people in that they persist in making responses that are no longer being rewarded.

Application. Jablonsky and DeVries (1972) have specified certain managerial actions that should, based upon reinforcement theory, improve employee motivation:

1. Determine what the desired response is.
2. Clearly communicate this behavior to the employee.
3. Clearly communicate what rewards the employee will receive when the correct response occurs.
4. Give the reward only when the correct behavior is performed.
5. Reward the desired response as close to its occurrence as is practical.

Research. There have been hundreds of research studies using both animals and people that have validated the principles of operant conditioning. Presently, there are still very few well designed studies that have been concerned with the application of these principles in organizations (Mitchell, 1979; Schnier, 1974). However, the studies that have been completed clearly indicate that reinforcement increases performance. That is, most studies have demonstrated big performance differences between using a schedule of reinforcement versus not using one. However, the studies on the differences in performance between various schedules of reinforcement (e.g., ratio and interval) have yielded few differences in performance (Mitchell, 1979).

Furthermore, Mawhinney (1975) points out that there are inconsistencies in the definitions of basic terms across the various operant-conditioning studies and that there are even inconsistencies between how these terms have been used and Skinner's original definitions. These inconsistencies make comparisons of findings very difficult. One general criticism of reinforcement theory as a basis for managerial strategies is that it is a mechanistic theory derived from research with lower animals. Human beings reason and have a rich variety of feelings—both of which are largely ignored by reinforcement theorists. Locke (1977) makes the point that the apparent success of operant conditioning in modifying human behavior can be explained alternatively by such cognitive concepts as *expectancies* and *goals,* both of which credit the responding organism with intentionality.

The foregoing does not detract from the validity of operant-conditioning principles; behavior (including that of humans) is modified as the paradigm predicts. At issue, at least for higher organisms, is the role of cognition as a factor in that paradigm.

Thus, although Nord (1969) has been the leading proponent of organizational applications of operant-conditioning principles, he recognizes that many managers prefer those other motivational approaches that stress man's cognitive abilities as well as his striving for self-actualization. These other approaches are more concerned with the worth of the individual than is the reinforcement-theory approach.

Expectancy theory

The various expectancy theories (Georgeopolous, Mahoney, & Jones, 1957; Graen, 1969; Porter & Lawler, 1968; Vroom, 1964) have been the dominant approach to work motivation since Vroom's formulation. These theories have both a cognitive and a hedonistic orientation. Individuals are viewed as rational, calculating, and thoughtful entities who decide on which course of action to pursue and how much effort to expend. Peoples' decisions are supposedly based on their expectancies about the relative degree of pleasure and discomfort resulting from alternative courses of action. Expectancy theories state that individuals will select the course of action that they feel will maximize pleasure and minimize discomfort. Thus, the crucial aspect of the expectancy theories is that the selection of a course of action reflects the anticipated consequences of that action.

Although there are a number of expectancy theories with sometimes subtle differences between them in terms and concepts, their basic approaches are very similar. We have selected the Lawler (1971, 1973) modification of the Porter-Lawler (1968) expectancy-theory model to illustrate the group. This approach was selected because it (1) is the easiest one for us to present in detail, (2) demonstrates the level of sophistication of contemporary theorizing, (3) stimulates considerable current research, and (4) is among the most popular versions of the basic theory.

Principles. Lawler's model makes four assumptions.

1. People have preferences among the various outcomes that are potentially available to them. In other words, each alternative outcome has a valence (V), which refers to its attractiveness to the individual.
2. People have expectancies about the likelihood that their efforts (E) will lead to the intended behavioral performance (P). This is referred to as the $E \rightarrow P$ expectancy and will be discussed shortly in greater detail.
3. People have expectancies about the likelihood that certain outcomes (O) will follow from their performance (P). This is referred to as the $P \rightarrow O$ expectancy and will also be described in greater detail.
4. In any situation, the actions and the efforts associated with them that a person chooses to take are determined by the expectancies ($E \rightarrow P$, and $P \rightarrow O$) and the preferences that person has at that time.

In algebraic terms, Lawler's expectancy model states that people will behave in such a way as to maximize their score on the formula $\Sigma[(E \rightarrow P) \times \Sigma[(P \rightarrow O)(V)]]$. This formula may seem a little awesome right now but it should become intelligible after we look at each component separately within the framework of a realistic example.

Within a few weeks, you will probably be taking an exam in the course for which you are reading this book. We will use Lawler's model to help us determine how much effort you are going to put into studying for this exam.

One component of the formula is your $E \rightarrow P$ expectancy. As previously indicated, E represents effort or, in this example, the amount of time and energy you are going to put into studying for the exam. P represents performance or how many questions you will answer correctly on the exam. In most real-life situations, including your next exam, there is not a perfect correlation between your efforts and your performance. You probably have studied very hard and still performed poorly on a previous exam. Conversely, you have also probably hardly studied and performed very well. Lawler states that the greater the chance of effort leading to performance, the more likely you are to expend effort. Possible factors influencing the $E \rightarrow P$ expectancy in our illustration are your self-esteem or self-confidence, past experiences in similar situations, the actual present situation, and communication from others. The $E \rightarrow P$ expectancy is depicted in Figure 12–3. Con-

FIGURE 12–3
Determinants of $E \rightarrow P$ expectancies

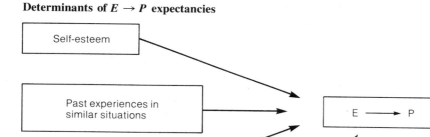

Source: From *Motivation in Work Organizations* by E. E. Lawler, III, p. 55. Copyright © 1973 by Wadsworth, Inc. Reprinted by permission of the publisher, Brooks/Cole Publishing Company, Monterey, California.

sider one of these variables: your past experiences in similar situations. Let us assume that you have had a previous course from the same instructor and when you studied hard you performed well. This should influence you to have higher $E \rightarrow P$ expectancies than if you had studied hard and recieved a poor grade.

A second major component in the formula is the $P \rightarrow O$ expectancy or the likelihood you attach to your performance (P) producing a specific outcome (O). In expectancy theory terms, P is referred to as a first-level outcome. It is a level of performance (e.g., score on the exam) but it does not directly meet one of your needs. Furthermore, O is referred to as a second-level outcome. Second-level outcomes are those that satisfy or fail to satisfy needs. An example of an O that may meet your needs is that if you perform well on the exam, this *may* influence your professor to write a letter of recommendation on your behalf to the graduate school of your choice.

However, real-life situations are usually very complex and performing well on the exam may have other consequences, some negative. For example, you may be taking this class with your fiancé who may study just as hard as you do but receive a poor grade. As you can well imagine, this may lead to an argument which could result in the frustration of some of your other needs.

There are many other potential second-level outcomes that may result from your performance on this exam. Each of these outcomes has, in your estimation, some probability of occurring. Lawler postulates that your past experiences in similar situations, the attractiveness of the outcome, your belief in internal versus external control, your $E \rightarrow P$ expectancies, the actual situation and the communications you receive from others influence your $P \rightarrow O$ expectancies. The relationship can be seen in Figure 12–4.

FIGURE 12–4
Determinants of $P \rightarrow O$ expectancies

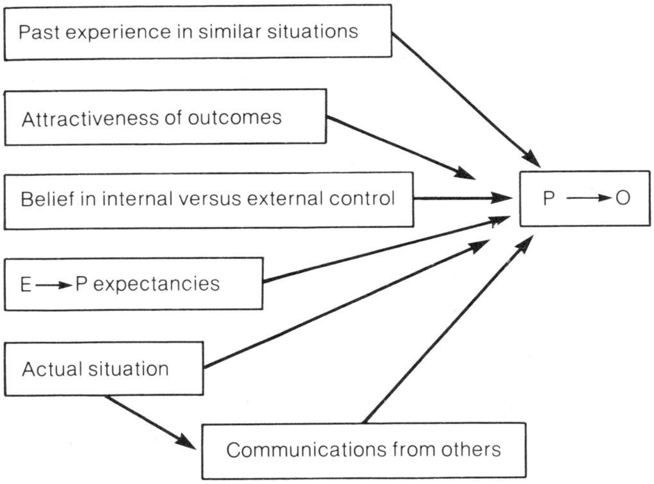

Source: From *Motivation in Work Organization,* by E. E. Lawler, III, p. 58. Copyright © 1973 by Wadsworth, Inc. Reprinted by permission of the publisher, Brooks/Cole Publishing Company, Monterey, California.

To illustrate the influence of these variables, we will use the variable, *belief in internal versus external control.* Some of us tend to believe that to a large extent our own actions determine what happens to us. This is referred to as *internal locus of control.* Others tend to feel that what happens to them is determined primarily by factors outside of their control (*external locus of control*). The more internal one's locus of control, the greater is the $P \rightarrow O$ expectancy. This is because you tend to feel that your performance will directly influence your outcomes.

A third component of Lawlers' formula is V, or valence, which reflects how you feel toward particular outcomes. Outcomes are positive if you prefer attaining them to not attaining them, negative if you prefer not attaining them, or neutral if you do not care. Valences vary from $+1$ to -1 with $+1$ being a maximally desirable outcome. For example, getting the letter of recommendation may be $+.7$ while aggravating your fiancé may be $-.3$.

There are also two summation symbols, Σ, in Lawler's formula. The first Σ indicates that an individual considers both the possibility of succeeding in accomplishing a desired level of P, and also failing to accomplish it. To illustrate, you may study very hard and not get a good grade. The second Σ indicates that you consider and evaluate all possible $P \rightarrow O$ expectancies. That is, you consider the possibilities of getting the letter of recommendation, aggravating your fiancé, and so on.

In conclusion, Lawler's model predicts that you will choose to behave in the manner that gives you the highest total motivational force. This force is determined by multiplying and summating the various components of the formula.

What all this means is that you evaluate different levels of effort (e.g., not studying at all, studying a little, studying a moderate amount, or studying a whole lot) based on your expectations about each one's outcome. You then select the effort level that does the best job of maximizing your pleasure and minimizing your discomfort.

We suggest that you go back to Figures 12–3 and 12–4 and determine, for each variable, how much it will influence your decision about the amount of effort you will expend studying for your next exam. Then, try to decide what you would do if you were an instructor committed to increasing the effort that students will put into the course.

An illustrative example.   The example used in the previous section was concerned with studying for an exam. However, expectancy theory was formulated to apply to motivational decisions in business and industry. The following illustration is concerned with a decision about how much effort to expend in a sales situation.

A saleswoman for a large drug corporation had to decide how hard to work during the next six months. She believed that if she worked very hard, that is, if she put in a lot of time in order to see many potential customers, she would almost definitely sell a lot of drugs (she had a high $E \rightarrow P$ expectancy).

She knew that if she sold a lot of drugs that this would increase her earnings, and she would probably gain the following additional benefits (positive valence outcomes): recognition from her regional manager, increased job security, and a new company car. However, she felt that increased effort at her job would probably cause her to lose some peer approval and would definitely reduce the time she could devote to her tennis game (negative valence outcomes). She believed the probability of all these positive and negative outcomes occurring was very high (high $P \rightarrow O$ expectancies). In addition, she needed to consider the possibility of expending a lot of effort and failing to sell additional drugs as well as various other effort levels besides a very high one. She decided to work very hard primarily because her need for money had a very high valence and was more important for her, at that time, than playing tennis, and so on.

Application. According to expectancy theory, if an organization is interested in motivating its employees, it should be concerned with raising the various components of the basic formula, that is $E \rightarrow P$, $P \rightarrow O$, and V.

Among the strategies an organization can employ in an attempt to raise the $E \rightarrow P$ expectancies are (1) assigning employees to jobs that are consistent with their abilities, (2) improving their training programs, and (3) redesigning the work set-up so as to maximize employee efficiency.

To help insure high $P \rightarrow O$ expectancies, the organization can (1) explain clearly to its employees in what ways superior performance leads to superior rewards. The organization also can (2) develop a valid program for evaluating employee performance and (3) then reward on some incentive-type system based on level of performance. A piece-rate system, in which an employee gets paid for each unit of work produced, is an example of a reward plan with a high $P \rightarrow O$ expectancy. The organization can also attempt to (4) reduce the negative consequences of high productivity by promising not to lay off employees and not to raise the performance level needed to earn a bonus when the level of production increases.

To raise the valence (V) component, the organization needs to become aware of the needs of each of its employees and how they want these satisfied. Once these are determined, then the employees can be rewarded on the basis of their actual needs rather than on management's guesses as to the hypothetical needs of the employees.

Research. Expectancy-theory predictions have been extensively studied. The reader interested in learning more about expectancy theory is referred to research reviews and critiques by Campbell and Pritchard (1976), House, Shapiro, and Wahba (1974), Locke (1975), Mitchell (1974), and Wahba and House (1974).

Most of the studies up to 1975 were correlational field studies using an across-subjects design. In these studies, the perceptions of $E \rightarrow P$, $P \rightarrow O$, and V were assessed for each individual by questionnaire and these scores or a combined score were correlated across subjects with various criteria including performance ratings. Overall, the results of the across-subjects research provided the theory with only modest support. (Campbell & Pritchard, 1976).

More recent expectancy-theory research has used a within-subjects design. Here, an attempt is made to identify for each subject the specific action or level of effort with the highest probability of occurrence. As a result, within-subjects research requires making especially careful assessments of $E \rightarrow P$, $P \rightarrow O$, V, and the criterion. However, the within-subjects line of research has improved the accuracy of predicting performance and therefore is replacing the between-subjects design for expectancy-theory research (Kopelman, 1977; Oldham, 1976).

Expectancy theory views people as calculating entities who rationally make decisions between alternative courses of action. However, as Locke (1975) indicates, there is evidence that the world is populated by individuals who act impulsively, irrationally, and neurotically. It seems that expectancy theory predictions should not hold for these individuals (Korman, 1977).

Furthermore, as Behling, Schriesheim, and Tolliver (1975) and Mitchell (1979) note, expectancy theory states that if people knew: (a) all the alternatives, (b) all the outcomes, (c) all the $P \rightarrow O$ expectancies, and (d) the V of all the outcomes, then they would use a complex formula to decide upon the best course of action. However, in reality, people do not know all of these things and do not use any complex formula in deciding what to do (Mitchell, 1979).

In summary, expectancy theory is on a more solid empirical base than the previously presented theories of employee motivation. Further refinements of expectancy theory can be expected to address themselves to the following issues.

1. The basic concepts of the theory ($E \rightarrow P, P \rightarrow O$, and V) are sound but the instruments currently available to assess the independent and dependent variables need to be improved (Campbell & Pritchard, 1976).
2. The theory is relatively new and continuously developing. Therefore, when additional refinements are made and incorrect concepts eliminated, the power of the approach will be increased (Campbell & Pritchard, 1976).
3. To repeat a previous point, many individuals tend to act irrationally, and behave in a manner inconsistent with the principles of hedonism. Therefore, the theory needs to be limited to some subset of individuals and does not apply equally well to everyone (Korman, 1977).

Campbell and Pritchard (1976) conclude that when all is said and done, the expectancy-theory approach will remain a powerful force in organizational psychology, even though its empirical base is not yet solid. Although this may be an optimistic viewpoint, we tend to agree with them, primarily because the logic of the expectancy-theory approach intuitively appears to be correct. Only time will tell if the needed refinements can be made to elevate the power of the theory.

Equity theory

Adams's (1965) equity theory is concerned with defining what individuals in our culture consider to be equitable (fair), and with their reactions to being in situations that they perceive as unfair.

Principles.   Adams theorizes that when individuals perform work in exchange for pay, they think about what they contribute to the job (inputs) and what they receive for working (outcomes). An input is defined as anything a worker perceives as deserving of a payoff. Examples of inputs are amount of education, number of hours worked, and previous job experiences. An outcome is defined as any factor the individual perceives to be a payoff for invested effort. These include pay, fringe benefits, and recognition.

The theory has four basic postulates:

1. Individuals strive to create and maintain a state of equity.
2. When a state of inequity is perceived, it creates tension which the individual is motivated to reduce or eliminate.
3. The greater the magnitude of the perceived inequity, the greater is the motivation to act to reduce the state of tension.
4. Individuals should perceive an unfavorable inequity (e.g., receiving too little pay) more readily than a favorable one (e.g., receiving too much pay).

According to the theory, a state of equity is defined by the following equation:

$$\frac{\text{Person's outcomes}}{\text{Person's inputs}} = \frac{\text{Other's outcomes}}{\text{Other's inputs}}$$

In this equation, *Person* is the individual with whom you are concerned, while *Other* is the referent for comparison. This equation states that equity exists whenever individuals perceive that the ratio of their own rewards (outcomes) to effort (inputs) equals the ratios for their comparison persons. On the other hand, a state of inequity exists whenever the two ratios are not equivalent.

We will use an example to help explain these basic concepts. Imagine that you work as a secretary in an office with another individual. As you perceive it, you have the higher inputs. You type faster, take shorthand better, and have worked for the company longer. However, the other person receives more money (higher outcomes) than you do. This situation makes you feel you are treated unfairly since you perceive your inputs are not being rewarded to the same degree as are the other secretary's. The theory predicts that you should attempt to eliminate the tension you feel as a result of the perceived inequity.

Equity theory suggests several alternative modes of inequity reduction. These include:

1. Reducing the quantity of your work.
2. Reducing the quality of your work.
3. Convincing your boss to give you a raise.
4. Quitting your job.
5. Selecting a different comparison person.
6. Distorting your inputs and/or outcomes as well as those of your comparison person.

Research. Two basic research paradigms have been used to test equity-theory predictions. In one, individuals are placed in an inequitable situation, and their reactions to it are observed. In most of these studies, students are hired to perform some work and they are either paid on an hourly or a piece-rate basis. Some subjects are induced to feel overpaid, others underpaid, and the rest equitably paid. The procedure used to induce feelings of overpayment includes telling the subjects that their qualifications are lower than the others who have been hired but that they, nevertheless, will be paid at the same rate.

The results of this body of research have been reviewed by Carrell and Dittrich (1978), Goodman (1977), Goodman and Friedman (1971). They strongly support equity-theory predictions when individuals are induced to feel underpaid. For example, hourly paid subjects who feel underpaid tend to produce fewer units of work and the quality of their output is lower than individuals who feel equitably paid. The results of the research on overpayment are not as clearcut. They tend to support equity theory predictions but only to a modest extent.

Recently, field studies have extended this line of research by investigating the reaction of employees to naturally occurring inequitable situations. Carrell's (1978) research indicates that employees do strive to reduce perceived inequities over time. Furthermore, Dittrich and Carrell (1979) found that employee perceptions about how equitably they were treated was a stronger predictor of absenteeism and turnover than were job satisfaction variables.

In the second research paradigm, individuals are given a choice between creating an equitable or an inequitable situation. These studies are generally conducted in the laboratory. In this research, individuals are given money to allocate to themselves and others after everybody has performed some work task. The results of this research offer strong support for equity theory. That is, most individuals tend to allocate the money based on input/outcome ratios. (Lane & Messé, 1971).

There is now considerable research support that indicates that people are motivated by considerations of equity. Unfortunately, it is not easy to apply these findings in organizational settings. The only way to determine if individuals feel equitably treated is to ask them and hope that they tell the truth.

Equity theory has been criticized because it is vague about certain concepts, such as which mode of inequity reduction an individual will employ and the manner in which a comparison person is chosen (Pritchard, 1969). This type of criticism indicates that the theory lacks precision in certain areas and this is a basic reason for the current difficulty in applying its principles.

However, Goodman (1974) has helped to identify three potential classes of referents (other, system, and self), that an individual may select when evaluating the fairness of pay. Equity theory is constantly developing and it may prove to be of considerable utility in the future.

Lawler (1968) indicates that equity theory and expectancy theory tend to make the same predictions and, as a result, there have been attempts to incorporate equity considerations within the expectancy-theory framework.

For example, Lawler (1973) uses equity in his model as a determinant of outcome valence (V).

Goal theory

Several of the theories thus far discussed assumed a relationship between intentions (goals) and behavior. Locke (1968, 1970) has proposed a cognitive model, referred to as *goal theory,* which attempts to explain this relationship.

Principles. The theory is relatively straightforward and simple. It is limited to conscious goal setting. Locke theorizes that clearly stated, specific, and difficult goals, if accepted, will result in higher performance than ambiguous, nonspecific, easily attainable goals, or no goals at all. Furthermore, Locke theorizes that goal setting mediates the effects on performance of feedback, participation, and incentives.

Application. Goal theory implies that goals should be set clearly and specifically at high but realistic levels. Although goal setting is practiced in many organizations, the implementation is often ineffective. Too often, goals are assumed by management to be understood and accepted by employees when, in fact, they have neither been explicitly stated nor accepted.

In an increasing number of organizations, goal setting is part of a comprehensive program referred to as management by objectives, or MBO (Drucker, 1954). MBO is widely used and it emphasizes joint manager-subordinate goal setting, establishment of action plans for goals, establishment of criteria for success, and periodic feedback sessions (Carroll & Tosi, 1973).

Research. Much of the initial research to test goal theory was conducted in the laboratory (e.g., Locke, Cartledge, & Knerr, 1970). These early studies were well controlled and they tended to provide strong support for the position that clear and specific difficult goals, when accepted, result in better performance than easy goals, nonspecific goals, or no goals. Further, additional corroboration of goal theory predictions has come from subsequent field (as well as laboratory) studies (Steers & Porter, 1974; Latham & Yukl, 1975).

Some of the more recent research on goal setting has been directed toward delineating circumstances which enhance or detract from the hypothesized beneficial effect of establishing a relatively difficult goal. For example, Erez (1977) found that providing knowledge of results on performance increases the benefits of goal setting, while Latham and Saari (1979) demonstrated the importance of supportive behavior by an authority figure when goals are set. Furthermore, Mossholder (1980) found that goal setting has positive effects for both boring and interesting jobs, but that with interesting jobs assigning difficult goals reduces task interest and persistence. Apparently, the theory's utility is enhanced by taking moderating circumstances into consideration.

One recent theoretical elaboration, the goal-setting process model (Yukl

& Latham, 1978), includes the factors of goal difficulty, goal acceptance, perceived goal instrumentality, employee participation, employee needs and traits, feedback, and employee performance. Some recent research has tested aspects of this extension of goal theory. For example, it has been found that when goal difficulty is held constant, assigned goals can be as effective if not more effective than participatively set goals (Dossett, Latham, & Mitchell, 1979). An important implication of this finding is that time can be saved by removing employee participation in goal-setting programs with minimal risk that this will cause deterioration in performance.

Goal theory, like equity theory, is based upon a solid intuitive base. The amount of research on goal theory during the past decade has been impressive. The theory has received considerable empirical support and refinement. Its usefulness for organizations should increase in the years ahead.

CONCLUSIONS

Let us review what we have already covered and try to reach some conclusions. The first three theories of motivation that were described, the content theories: need hierarchy, ERG, and two factor, were concerned with identifying and classifying the various needs of people. Despite these theoretical contributions, at the present time we do not have an idea of precisely how many different needs exist and likely never will.

Of the remaining four motivational theories, all of which are process theories, expectancy theory and reinforcement theory are the broadest in scope. The other two process theories—goal theory and equity theory—are substantially less inclusive.

It is evident that motivation is an exceedingly complex process. Therefore, we should not expect that any one theory will encompass all of its facets.

We know that many different factors motivate people and, moreover, that different factors may motivate individuals during various phases in their lives. This implies that the best way to motivate an individual is to find out what the individual wants and then try to provide these rewards contingent upon a specific level of job performance. This currently appears to be the wisest strategy for motivating an individual.

Two additional examples will be used to illustrate the point that you cannot motivate everybody by using the same strategy.

The first example is concerned with the use of monetary incentive plans. To simplify somewhat, these plans pay the worker more money for more production. Since everybody wants money, these plans are sure to be successful, aren't they? Well, the answer is no. There are proportionally fewer incentive plans today than there were several decades ago. Paying for productivity does not always lead to increased production. There are many good reasons for the decline in incentive plans, such as work-group and union pressures. Moreover, advocates of incentive plans state that the concept of the plans are good but that they have been implemented ineffectively. Even if one were to grant the validity of this defense, the fact remains that paying for productivity does not ensure it will occur. This seems to us to point to the complexity of work motivation.

Our second example is concerned with enriching jobs or making them more challenging. The advocates of job enrichment state that if jobs are made more stimulating, this will unleash positive motivational forces and lead to increased productivity and profits. This approach appears to be reasonable, and moreover, it is consistent with several motivational theories; therefore, how can it be incorrect? As Korman, Greenhaus, and Badin (1977) indicate in their review article, the research continues to show that a quality job possessing variety and responsibility is not equally satisfying to all workers.

In conclusion, despite the gaps in our present knowledge about work motivation, what appears even more striking is how much we have learned about the area during the last 20 years. We are now aware of the importance of (1) concerns with equity and (2) the benefits of accepted and high goal-setting levels. Moreover, we have five broad theoretical perspectives to guide our research efforts. The challenge to learn more about work motivation is very stimulating and this area will be the focus of the efforts of many industrial/organizational psychologists in the years ahead. From the amount of progress that has been made recently, we expect great strides in knowledge to occur during the next decade.

SUMMARY

Motivation can be defined as the process by which our behavior is initiated and directed. Motivation cannot be observed but must be inferred. There are currently a multitude of theories concerned with work motivation. The first three that were summarized—need hierarchy, ERG, and two factor—are referred to as content theories. The other theories—reinforcement, expectancy, equity, and goal—are process approaches.

Maslow's need-hierarchy theory states that people are never totally satisfied. When one need is met, another one appears to replace it. Maslow postulates that people have five categories of needs which are hierarchically arranged: physiological, safety, social, esteem, and self-actualization. According to Maslow, once a level of needs is satisfied, the next higher level in the hierarchy becomes prepotent.

Alderfer's ERG theory states that people have three sets of needs: existence, relatedness, and growth. Basic postulates of the theory are the more completely a more-concrete need is satisfied, the greater is the desire to satisfy the less-concrete needs, and the less completely a need is satisfied, the greater is the desire to have it satisfied. Alderfer agrees with Maslow that fulfillment-progress is important in moving from one level to another but he also stresses the importance of the frustration-regression process.

Herzberg's two-factor theory stresses that the factors that produce job satisfaction are separate and distinct from those that produce job dissatisfaction. The satisfier, or motivator, factors presumably reflect our need for growth while the dissatisfier, or hygiene, factors reflect our need to avoid pain. Job enrichment has developed from this theoretical background.

Skinner's reinforcement theory is concerned with the acquisition of correct responses and with the extinction of incorrect ones. Key concepts in reinforcement theory are shaping, and continuous and partial schedules of reinforcement. Reinforcement theory advocates rewarding correct responses and ignoring incorrect ones.

The various expectancy theories are currently the dominant approaches to work motivation. They presume a hedonistic and rational individual. The important building block concepts in Lawler's model are the effort → performance expectancy, the performance → outcome expectancy, and the valence of the outcome.

Adams's equity theory maintains that individuals strive to create and maintain a state of equity. When a state of inequity is perceived, this creates tension which the individual is motivated to reduce or eliminate. Furthermore, the greater the magnitude of the perceived inequity, the greater is the motivation to act to reduce the tension. According to the theory, a state of equity is defined by an equality between input-outcome ratios.

Locke's goal theory predicts that clear and specific difficult goals, if accepted, will result in higher performance than easy goals, nonspecific goals, or no goals at all. It also predicts that goal setting mediates the effects of feedback, participation, and incentives on performance.

The research support for these theories and their implications for organizations were described. The chapter concluded by stressing the complexity of work motivation and by indicating the large strides that have been made in the area during the past 20 years.

REFERENCES

Adams, J. S.   Inequity in social exchange. In L. Berkowitz (Ed.), *Advances in experimental social psychology* (Vol. 2). New York: Academic Press, 1965.

Alderfer, C. P.   An empirical test of a new theory of human needs. *Organizational Behavior and Human Performance,* 1969, *4,* 142–175.

Alderfer, C. P.   *Existence, relatedness, and growth: Human needs in organizational settings.* New York: Free Press, 1972.

Behling, O., Schriesheim, C., & Tolliver, J.   Alternatives to expectancy theory for work motivation. *Decision Sciences,* 1975, *6,* 449–461.

Campbell, J. P., Dunnette, M. D., Lawler, E. E., & Weick, K. E.   *Managerial behavior, performance, and effectiveness.* New York: McGraw-Hill, 1970.

Campbell, J. P., & Pritchard, R. D.   Motivation theory in industrial and organizational psychology. In M. D. Dunnette (Ed.). *Handbook of industrial and organizational psychology.* Chicago: Rand McNally, 1976.

Carrell, M. R.   A longitudinal field assessment of employee perceptions of equitable treatment. *Organizational Behavior and Human Performance*, 1978, *21*, 108–118.

Carrell, M. R., & Dittrich, J. E.   Equity theory: The recent literature, methodological considerations and new directions. *Academy of Management Review*, 1978, *3*, 202–210.

Carroll, S. J., & Tosi, H. L.   *Management by objectives: Applications and research.* New York: Macmillan, 1973.

Dittrich, J. E., & Carrell, M. R.   Organizational equity perceptions, employee job satisfaction, and departmental absence and turnover rates. *Organizational Behavior and Human Performance* 1979, *24*, 29–40.

Dossett, D. L., Latham, G. P., & Mitchell, T. R.   Effects of assigned versus participatively set goals, knowledge of results, and individual differences on employee behavior when goal difficulty is held constant. *Journal of Applied Psychology*, 1979, *34*, 291–298.

Drucker, P.   *The practice of management.* New York: Harper & Row, 1954.

Erez, M.   Feedback: A necessary condition for the goal setting-performance relationship. *Journal of Applied Psychology*, 1977, *62*, 624–627.

Georgeopoulos, B. S., Mahoney, G. M., & Jones, N. W.   A path-goal approach to productivity. *Journal of Applied Psychology*, 1957, *41*, 345–353.

Goodman, P. S.   An examination of referents used in the evaluation of pay. *Organizational Behavior and Human Performance*, 1974, *12*, 170–195.

Goodman, P. S.   Social comparison processes in organizations. In B. M. Staw & R. G. Salancik (Eds.), *New directions in organizational behavior.* Chicago: St. Clair Press, 1977.

Goodman, P. S., & Friedman, A.   Adams's theory of inequity. *Administrative Science Quarterly*, 1971, *16*, 271–288.

Graen, G.   Instrumentality theory of work motivation: Some experimental results and suggested modifications. *Journal of Applied Psychology Monograph*, 1969, *53*, 1–25.

Hall, D. T., & Nougaim, K. E.   An examination of Maslow's need hierarchy in an organizational setting. *Organizational Behavior and Human Performance*, 1968, *3*, 12–35.

Herzberg, F.   *Work and the nature of man.* Cleveland: World Press, 1966.

Herzberg, F.   One more time: How do you motivate employees? *Harvard Business Review*, 1968, *46*, 53–62.

Herzberg, F., Mausner, B., & Snyderman, B.   *The motivation to work.* New York: Wiley, 1959.

House, R. J., Shapiro, H. J., & Wahba, M. A.   Expectancy theory as a predictor of work behavior and attitudes: A reevaluation of empirical evidence. *Decision Sciences* 1974, *5*, 481–506.

House, R. J., & Wigdor, L. A.   Herzberg's dual factor theory of job satisfaction and motivation: A review of the evidence and a criticism. *Personnel Psychology*, 1967, *20*, 369–389.

Jablonsky, S. F., & DeVries, R.   Operant conditioning principles extrapolated to the theory of management. *Organizational Behavior and Human Performance*, 1972, *7*, 340–358.

King, N.   A clarification and evaluation of the two-factor theory of job satisfaction. *Psychological Bulletin,* 1970, *74,* 18–31.

Kopelman, R. E.   Across-individual, within-individual, and return on effort versions of expectancy theory. *Decision Sciences,* 1977, *8,* 651–662.

Korman, A. K.   *Organizational behavior.* Englewood Cliffs, N.J.: Prentice-Hall, 1977.

Korman, A. K., Greenhaus, J. H., & Badin, I. J.   Personnel attitudes and motivation. *Annual Review of Psychology,* 1977, *28,* 175–196.

Lane, I. M., & Messé, L. A.   Equity and the distribution of rewards. *Journal of Personality and Social Psychology,* 1971, *20,* 1–17.

Latham, G. P., & Saari, L. M.   Importance of supportive relationships in goal setting. *Journal of Applied Psychology,* 1979, *64,* 151–156.

Latham, G. P., & Yukl, G. A.   A review of research on the application of goal setting in organizations. *Academy of Management Journal,* 1975, *18,* 824–845.

Lawler, E. E.   Equity theory as a predictor of productivity and work quality. *Psychological Bulletin,* 1968, *70,* 596–610.

Lawler, E. E.   *Pay and organizational effectiveness: A psychological review.* New York: McGraw-Hill, 1971.

Lawler, E. E.   *Motivation in work organizations.* Monterey, Calif.: Brooks/Cole, 1973.

Lawler, E. E., & Suttle, J. L.   A causal correlational test of the need hierarchy concept. *Organizational Behavior and Human Performance,* 1972, *7,* 265–287.

Locke, E. A.   Toward a theory of task motivation and incentives. *Organizational Behavior and Human Performance,* 1968, *3,* 157–189.

Locke, E. A.   Job satisfaction and job performance: A theoretical analysis. *Organizational Behavior and Human Performance,* 1970, *5,* 484–500.

Locke, E. A.   Personnel attitudes and motivation. *Annual Review of Psychology,* 1975, *26,* 457–480.

Locke, E. A.   Nature and causes of job satisfaction. In M. D. Dunnette (Ed.), *Handbook of industrial and organizational psychology.* Chicago: Rand McNally, 1976.

Locke, E. A.   The myths of behavior mod in organizations. *Academy of Management Review,* 1977, *2,* 543–552.

Locke, E. A., Cartledge, N., & Knerr, C. S.   Studies of the relationship between satisfaction, goal setting, and performance. *Organizational Behavior and Human Performance* 1970, *5,* 474–485.

Maslow, A. H.   *Motivation and personality,* New York: Harper & Row, 1954.

Maslow, A. H.   *Eupsychian management.* Homewood, Ill: Irwin, 1965.

Maslow, A. H.   *Motivation and personality* (2nd ed.) New York: Harper & Row, 1970.

Mawhinney, T. C.   Operant terms and concepts in the description of individual work behavior: Some problems of interpretation, application, and evaluation. *Journal of Applied Psychology,* 1975, *60,* 704–712.

McGregor, D.   *The human side of enterprise.* New York: McGraw-Hill, 1960.

Mitchell, T. V.   Expectancy models of job satisfaction, occupational preference and effort: A theoretical, methodological and empirical appraisal. *Psychological Bulletin*, 1974, *81*, 1,053–1,077.

Mitchell, T. R. Organizational behavior. *Annual Review of Psychology*, 1979, *30*, 243–281.

Mossholder, K. W. Effects of externally mediated goal setting on intrinsic motivation: A laboratory experiment. *Journal of Applied Psychology*, 1980, *65*, 202–210.

Nord, W. Beyond the teaching machine: The neglected area of operant conditioning in the theory and practice of management. *Organizational Behavior and Human Performance*, 1969, *4*, 375–407.

Oldham, G. R. Organizational choice and some correlates of individual expectancies. *Decision Sciences*, 1976, *6*, 873–884.

Porter, L. W. *Organizational patterns of managerial job attitudes.* New York: American Foundation for Management Research, 1964.

Porter, L. W., & Lawler, E. E. *Managerial attitudes and performance.* Homewood, Ill.: Dorsey, 1968.

Pritchard, R. D. Equity theory: A review and critique. *Organizational Behavior and Human Performance*, 1969, *4*, 176–211.

Schnier, C. E. Behavior modification in management. *Academy of Management Journal*, 1974, *17*, 528–548.

Skinner, B. F. *Science and human behavior.* New York: McMillan, 1953.

Skinner, B. F. *Contingencies of reinforcement.* New York: Appleton-Century-Crofts, 1969.

Steers, R. M., & Porter, L. W. The role of task-goal attributes in employee performance. *Psychological Bulletin*, 1974, 81, 434–452.

Vroom, V. H. *Work and motivation,* New York: Wiley, 1964.

Wahba, M. A., & Bridwell, L. G. Maslow reconsidered: A review of research on the need hierarchy theory. *Organizational Behavior and Human Performance*, 1976, *15*, 212–240.

Wahba, M. A., & House, R. J. Expectancy theory in work and motivation: Some logical and methodological issues. *Human Relations*, 1974, *27*, 121–147.

Wall, T. D. Ego defensiveness as a determinant of reported differences in sources of job satisfaction and job dissatisfaction. *Journal of Applied Psychology*, 1973, *58*, 125–128.

Wanous, J. P., & Zwany, A. A cross sectional test of need hierarchy theory. *Organizational Behavior and Human Performance*, 1977, *18*, 78–97.

Waters, L. K., & Waters C. W. An empirical test of five versions of the two-factor theory of job satisfaction. *Organizational Behavior and Human Performance*, 1972, *7*, 18–24.

Yukl, G. A., & Latham, G. P. Interrelationships among employee participation, individual differences, goal difficulty, goal acceptance, instrumentality, and performance. *Personnel Psychology*, 1978, *31*, 305–324.

chapter 13

Job Satisfaction

Job-satisfaction research has been a part of the field of industrial psychology since the Hawthorne studies (described later) were initiated. Thousands of research articles on this topic have already been published, and it is likely that many more will follow. The interested reader is referred to four recent review articles for a more extensive treatment of job satisfaction issues than can be provided in this chapter: Berger and Cummings (1978); James and Jones (1976); Locke (1976); and Nord (1977).

No single definition of job satisfaction pleases all writers or investigators. For the purpose of this chapter, we accept Locke's definition (1976, p. 1319): job satisfaction is "the appraisal of one's job as attaining or allowing the attainment of one's important job values, providing these values are congruent with or help fulfill one's basic needs." In short, satisfied employees feel good about their job. Locke further notes that feelings related to job satisfaction/dissatisfaction tend more to reflect the employee's appraisal of job experiences in the present and past than expectations for the future.

A HISTORICAL OVERVIEW OF JOB SATISFACTION

Scientific management

During the first half of the 20th century, Taylor's (1911) theory of scientific management was extremely influential in the industrial community. Taylor's view of workers was very simplistic. He believed that every worker wanted money above all else and would work long and hard to obtain it.

One of the goals of scientific management was to make a significant improvement in the economic prosperity of both workers and management through increased productivity. Taylor felt that the burden for raising productivity rested with management. Its role was to design jobs that minimized employee fatigue and maximized efficiency. He believed that properly designed jobs would result in increased productivity, provided that workers were adequately compensated for their additional output. Paying for productivity was central to scientific management and it led to the installation of incentive pay plans throughout the United States. Taylor also believed that

271

employee satisfaction (as well as productivity) would improve when fatigue was decreased and pay increased.

The theory of scientific management generated substantial research activity in the United States, Great Britain, and Germany. These studies investigated environmental manipulations to reduce fatigue: for example, changing illumination, reducing noise, introducing music, and so on. Whereas the research emphasized productivity as the dependent variable, little attention was given to the impact of scientific-management principles upon job satisfaction.

The Hawthorne studies

The original study in this series was initiated in 1927 at the Hawthorne (Chicago) plant of the Western Electric Company. It was to have lasted for only one year and was conducted in the context of the theory of scientific management, which was extremely influential at the time (Roethlisberger & Dickson, 1939). The purpose was to investigate the relationship between the quality and quantity of illumination, worker fatigue, and industrial efficiency. This modestly conceived project eventuated in a 12-year comprehensive study now regarded as a classic research effort. Its findings were influential far beyond the investigators' initial expectations, even though the studies suffered from severe methodological deficiencies (Landsberger, 1958).

The Hawthorne studies were comprised of five major parts; two of the most important are considered in this chapter. (Another part, the Bank Wiring Room study, is discussed in the next chapter.)

Relay-assembly test room study. For this study, the researchers placed six female employees in a separate room away from the rest of the plant workers. The special test room was identical to their regular department except that a recording device was added to their equipment so that their productivity could be monitored constantly. In addition, a male observer was placed in the test room. His job was to keep records of what occurred in the room, including social interaction and significant bits of conversation.

There were four phases to this study over a two-year period. The first phase was an acclimatization one; the women were successfully transferred from the regular factory situation into the test room set-up, and became a social as well as a work group.

The second phase was comprised of four test periods each lasting, on the average, six weeks. During these test periods brief (5 and 10 minute) rest periods were introduced several times each day. The results indicated that average productivity increased substantially despite the reduction, due to the rest periods, in the actual number of hours worked.

During the third phase, the workweek was shortened from 48 hours to approximately 42 hours. Productivity again increased substantially. When asked to account for this increase, the women commented favorably on the absence of bosses and the opportunity they were given to set their own work pace. These results are particularly interesting in that freedom from excessive supervision was regarded by the subjects as more important than either the rest breaks or the shortened workweek.

Phase four was primarily a check on the validity of the previous findings. Several of the earlier test periods were replicated, including the initial one in which there were no rest breaks and the workweek was set at 48 hours. Production continued to rise. In fact, productivity under conditions like those before any modifications were introduced was now 22 percent above the initial output level.

The researchers concluded that the most important determiner of increased productivity was the change in supervision to a more permissive and democratic style. When the study was completed, the experimenters realized that they had not been investigating the effects of rest breaks and shortened workweeks on productivity. Instead, they had been studying the effects of the social situation on employee attitudes, like job satisfaction. The relay-assembly test room study clearly demonstrated the importance of the previously ignored factors of interpersonal relations and job attitudes.

Interviewing program. It was at this point that the investigators changed their focus from studying the impact of environmental manipulations to investigating employee attitudes, supervision, and morale. The central issue now became *human relations,* emphasizing the importance of human needs relating to interpersonal relationships. This decision to study employee attitudes and morale in a systematic manner significantly affected the subsequent development of industrial/organizational psychology.

The Hawthorne investigators initiated a massive interviewing program involving over 20,000 employees, each interviewed for an average of 90 minutes. The most important finding from the interviewing project was the discovery of the previously unsuspected importance of employee work groups. These informal clusters of workers were found to exert considerable control over the behavior, including productivity, of the individual group members.

Hoppock's research

Hoppock (1935) investigated the job satisfaction of workers in the small town of New Hope, Pennsylvania. Two of Hoppock's questionnaire items, and the results he obtained, are given in Table 13–1.

Note that in reply to item 1, 77 percent of the respondents indicated that they either liked, were enthusiastic about, or loved their jobs. The responses to item 2 reinforce the conclusion that the workers he surveyed derived considerable satisfaction from their jobs.

These results may seem somewhat surprising, since it is often assumed that workers typically are dissatisfied. It is interesting to note that the finding that most workers report reasonable levels of job satisfaction has been consistently replicated (Strauss, 1974).

TABLE 13–1
Responses in Hoppock's questionnaire

1. Choose ONE of the following statements which best tells how you like your job. Please place a check mark in front of that statement:

Response	*Percentage*
I hate it.	2
I dislike it.	1
I don't like it.	11
I am indifferent to it.	9
I like it.	63
I am enthusiastic about it.	9
I love it.	5
	101

2. Which gives you more satisfaction? (check one)

Response	*Percentage*
Your job.	66
The things you do in your spare time.	34
	100

Source: R. Hoppock, *Job Satisfaction* (New York: Harper & Row, 1935), pp. 250–252.

Hoppock also examined the relationship between the workers' job level and satisfaction. His results clearly indicated a positive correlation between the two.

THEORETICAL APPROACHES

Several of the theories presented in the previous chapter, especially the two-factor theory (Herzberg, Mausner, & Snyderman, 1959; Herzberg, 1966), equity theory (Adams, 1965), and the need-hierarchy theory (Maslow, 1970) have substantial implications for understanding job satisfaction. You may wish to review the presentation of these theories before proceeding further.

Three additional theoretical approaches will be presented here. Unfortunately, there is not yet substantial research support for any of these.

Discrepancy theory

Locke's (1969, 1976) discrepancy theory states that satisfaction or dissatisfaction with some aspect of a job reflects a dual value judgment: (1) the perceived *discrepancy* between what an individual wants and what is received, and (2) the *importance* of what is wanted to the individual. Overall job satisfaction for an individual is the sum of each of the aspects of job satisfaction multiplied by the importance of that aspect for that person. That is, for an individual, one aspect of a job (e.g., opportunities for advancement) may be much more important than other aspects (e.g., recognition). Therefore, for this person, advancement should be weighted higher than the amount of recognition received.

What determines whether a particular aspect of the job will be satisfying or dissatisfying? This, for Locke, is an individual matter hinging on the perceived congruence or discrepancy between desires and outcomes. Extra vacation time (an outcome) should enhance satisfaction for an employee who enjoys time off from work. However, the same amount of extra vacation time would be a source of dissatisfaction to another employee for whom leisure time is unpleasant. Similarly, overtime work (an outcome) will enhance or detract from satisfaction depending upon whether employees perceive it (and the additional income thereby provided) as compatible or incompatible with their desires.

Model of facet satisfaction

Lawler's (1973) model of facet satisfaction is closely related to equity theory (Adams, 1965). According to Lawler's model, individuals are satisfied with a particular facet of their job (e.g., co-workers, supervisors, pay) when the amount of the facet they perceive they should receive for performing their work equals the amount they perceive that they actually receive. In addition, if individuals perceive the amount they receive is greater than what is deserved, they should feel inequity and guilt. Finally, if they perceive they receive too little of the facet, the model predicts they should feel dissatisfied.

According to Lawler, the amount of a facet individuals perceive as appropriate depends on the individuals' perceived job inputs, the perceived job characteristics, and the perceived inputs and outcomes of those other people to whom the individuals compare themselves. Moreover, the amount of a facet individuals perceive they actually receive depends on the actual outcomes received and the perceived outcomes of the people to whom the individuals compare themselves. The model is summarized in Figure 13–1.

To determine a worker's level of job satisfaction, Lawler first weights each facet according to its importance for the individual, and then combines all the weighted facet-satisfaction scores into a single overall score. The idea of weighting aspects or facets of a job is common to both discrepancy theory and the model of facet satisfaction.

However, you may recall from our earlier discussion of differential versus uniform weighting of criterion components that the two procedures tend to generate about the same composite score. Thus, the measured level of overall job satisfaction with differential weighting is about the same as its level when the constituents are uniformly weighted (e.g., Ewen, 1967).

Opponent-process theory

Landy's (1978) opponent-process theory views job satisfaction from a substantially different perspective than the other approaches. This theory

FIGURE 13-1
Model of facet satisfaction

FIGURE 13-1
Model of facet satisfaction

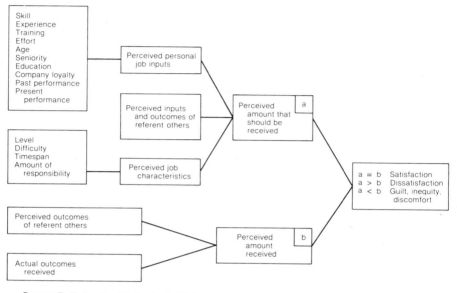

Source: E. E. Lawler, *Motivation in Work Organizations* (Monterey, Calif.: Brooks/Cole, 1973), p. 75.

emphasizes maintaining an emotional equilibrium. Since job satisfaction and dissatisfaction are seen as emotional states, the theory has implications for them.

Opponent-process theory assumes that extreme emotional states are not beneficial. Job satisfaction or dissatisfaction (and the associated emotions) trigger a physiological mechanism in the central nervous system which activates the opposite (opponent) emotion. It is hypothesized that this opponent emotion, although weaker than the original, lasts for a longer period of time.

Opponent-process theory states that when individuals receive rewards on their jobs they feel happy, but less so than they would feel if the opposite emotion were not activated. After a while, the happiness declines and eventually drops so much that the individual feels somewhat depressed before returning to a neutral emotional level. This occurs because the opponent emotion is presumed to have a more lasting effect than the original emotion.

For example, individuals might be expected to be extremely happy after they receive a pay raise. However, after a while the happiness with the amount of the raise probably decreases and later on the individuals may even become unhappy with the amount of the raise. Notice, the level of the pay raise did not change; it was the emotional response to the raise that changed.

Opponent-process theory has an important implication for measuring an individual's job satisfaction. Since the theory hypothesizes that an individual's job satisfaction varies substantially over time, it follows that job satisfaction measures should be taken periodically over appropriate time intervals and not just once.

COMPONENTS OF JOB SATISFACTION

Many factors (including security, pay, fringe benefits, supervision, working conditions, the intrinsic nature of the work, recognition, occupational level, vacation policies, decentralization of authority, and so on) have been investigated as possible determinants of satisfaction. We consider here just three: intrinsic aspects of the work itself, pay, and supervision.

Intrinsic features of the work

In reviewing the literature, Locke (1976) cites the following intrinsic features as being related to job satisfaction: variety, difficulty, amount of work, responsibility, autonomy, control over work methods, complexity, and creativity. While these are distinguishable intrinsic features of the work assignment, they share one common element—the level of mental challenge—which is currently believed to be an overriding intrinsic factor (Barnowe, Mangione, & Quinn, 1972). Unchallenging jobs are likely to generate boredom and uninvolvement. The converse, assuming the employee is appropriately challenged and therefore successful, results in commitment which is, of course, a primary management objective (Locke, 1976).

The concept of an appropriate challenge is an important one. A job demanding more ability (intellectual or physical) than the employee brings to it, or making personal demands that the employee cannot meet, generates frustration and, ultimately, job dissatisfaction (Chadwick-Jones, 1969).

The Job Diagnostic Survey. This questionnaire (Hackman & Oldham, 1975) evaluates five core (intrinsic) dimensions which have been shown to relate to job satisfaction across various occupations. Each dimension is clarified below:

1. Skill variety. This is the degree to which a job requires the employee to use a number of different talents in order to perform a variety of activities. The greater the skill variety, the less boring the job. Many assembly line jobs, for example, are low on this dimension.

2. Task identity. This is the degree to which a job requires doing a complete piece of work from beginning to end. Task identity is related to the perceived meaningfulness of one's work assignment. Thus, an employee who makes an entire piece of custom furniture from raw wood to finished product would experience considerable task identity.

3. Task significance. Tasks that are highly significant exert considerable impact upon the lives of other persons. Although there is a degree of relationship between this dimension and the one above, they are not identical. Given tasks of similar meaningfulness, some have more societal impact than

others. Physicians and lawyers probably are perceived as doing more significant work than taxi drivers.

4. Autonomy. This is the extent to which the job provides the employee with freedom, independence, and discretion in determining the procedures to be used. Occupations permitting a high level of autonomy enable persons to satisfy their higher-level needs (self-esteem, achievement, responsibility, and self-actualization).

5. Feedback provided by the job. A job high on this dimension has a built-in feedback feature which also operates to help satisfy higher-level needs since the worker does not need to rely upon some external referent (like the supervisor) for a performance evaluation.

While the research with the Job Diagnostic Survey indicates the importance to job satisfaction of these five core dimensions, some studies also indicate that individual personality characteristics mediate their impact. One, for example (Wanous, 1974), demonstrated that employees who have a strong work ethic reported greater satisfaction on jobs high on the dimensions of task identity, variety, and autonomy. In contrast, job satisfaction was not significantly related to any of the core dimensions for employees with a weak work ethic. (The moderator—*work ethic*—was defined as the belief that work makes one a better person, and that one's worth is related to job performance.)

Given the emphasis that contemporary theorizing about job satisfaction places on the importance of gratifying higher-level needs, we can anticipate future research to be directed toward learning more about the kinds of moderators that influence employee perceptions about their jobs.

Additional information relevant to intrinsic features of the work will be presented under the topic of job design in Chapter 17. A theoretical framework, the job-characteristics model (Hackman & Oldham, 1975), incorporating both the Job Diagnostic Survey and the five core dimensions, will be described at that time.

Pay

Several reviewers (Lawler, 1971; Nash & Carroll, 1975; Schwab & Wallace, 1974) evaluating the relatively large number of studies which have addressed the importance of pay as a determiner of job satisfaction conclude that psychologists have traditionally and erroneously minimized (or failed even to consider) its importance. This earlier neglect is being replaced by a much more active interest in the role of compensation. For example, Dyer and Theriault (1976) report that job satisfaction is a function of the absolute amount of pay received, the degree to which that pay meets employee expectations, and how it is administered.

One explanation of earlier reluctance by psychologists to investigate pay is that it is rather a complex issue. Money certainly means different things to different people. In addition to its obvious utility for satisfying Maslow's lower-level needs (food, housing) it can be a symbol of achievement, success, and recognition. Moreover, money may have secondary utility; the amount of salary earned can tangibly represent freedom to do what one wishes (take vacations, and so on).

Psychologists have only begun to investigate the implications of this complexity. Much of the recent research has been accomplished within the context of equity theory (Adams, 1965). You may recall that this theory maintains that we strive to maintain equitable situations. As applied to pay, it postulates that individuals receiving either too little or too much compensation should experience distress and dissatisfaction.

Laboratory studies of equity theory support postulates concerning underpayment. Persons who perceive themselves as earning less than they are worth express dissatisfaction and reduce their output, presumably to reestablish equity (Pritchard, Dunnette, & Jorgenson, 1972). However, the results for overpayment are not as clearcut (Campbell & Pritchard, 1976).

Field studies of equity theory are sparse. However, as we noted in Chapter 12, some research (Carrell, 1978; Dittrich & Carrell, 1979) supports the theory, particularly if we are willing to accept increased absenteeism as a behavioral index of job dissatisfaction.

Supervision

One of the more significant Hawthorne findings concerned the importance of developing a cooperative spirit between employees and supervisors. The quality of this relationship appears to generalize and to help create a favorable working climate (Roethlisberger & Dickson, 1939).

Chapter 15, Leadership, particularly addresses some of the subsequent research on organizational supervision. That research indicates only one leadership characteristic, consideration, that is consistently related to job satisfaction (Yukl, 1971). Employees prefer to work with considerate supervisors who are supportive, warm, and employee-centered rather than hostile, apathetic, and job-centered.

The relationship between other aspects of supervision and job satisfaction is less clear-cut. One frequently investigated supervisory variable is *supervisor's task orientation*. Some employees seem to prefer task-oriented supervisors whereas others seem to prefer less intensive supervision (Kerr, Schriesheim, Murphy, & Stogdill, 1974). The nature of the job setting has tentatively been identified as a moderator of this preference. Employees in ambiguous settings without clearly defined duties prefer task-oriented supervisors who will help them resolve the confusion. However, where the job demands are clearly defined and the employees are competent, they tend to prefer less structured supervision (House & Mitchell, 1974).

Locke (1970) has provided a theoretical framework for understanding employee satisfaction with supervision. He has identified two types of supervisor-subordinate relationships: functional and entity.

The functional relationship reflects the extent to which the supervisor helps the employee satisfy job values important to that employee. Recognizing the existence of individual differences, these functional relationships are contingent upon different objectives for different employees. For some it may entail interesting and challenging work; for others, promotions or pay raises, or verbal recognition, to name just a few.

The entity relationship is based on interpersonal attraction reflecting similar basic attitudes and values. Clearly one can like a supervisor personally (that is, a positive entity relationship) without a similarly gratifying functional relationship, and vice versa.

Locke (1976) hypothesizes that the greatest level of satisfaction with one's supervisor should occur when both types of relationship are positive, and he claims empirical support for this view.

MEASURING JOB SATISFACTION

We look briefly at the two basic approaches to evaluating job satisfaction: questionnaires and interviews.

Questionnaires

One characteristic of the early research on job satisfaction was that many investigators developed their own questionnaires for its assessment. This lack of uniformity made it very difficult to compare results across studies. Fortunately in more recent years, two questionnaires, the Job Descriptive Index (JDI) (Smith, Kendall & Hulin, 1969), and the Minnesota Satisfaction Questionnaire (MSQ) (Weiss, Dawis, England, & Lofquist, 1967), have become established as relatively standard assessment instruments. Of the two, the JDI has been somewhat the more dominant.

Job Descriptive Index. The JDI is a checklist containing items potentially descriptive of a job. Respondents mark "Y" for yes if the item describes their job, "N" for no if it does not, and "?" if they cannot decide. The checklist items are clustered into five sets, each of which is presented on a separate page: attitudes towards (a) work, (b) pay, (c) promotional opportunities, (d) supervision, and (e) co-workers. (Sample items are shown in Figure 13–2.) In addition to generating subscale scores, the JDI also generates an overall index of job satisfaction.

Since the JDI has been extensively used, norms reflecting such variables as age, sex, income, and educational level are available for comparative purposes. Two reasons for the widespread use of the JDI are ease of administration and speed of scoring. Moreover, it has been described as the most carefully constructed instrument for assessing job satisfaction (Vroom, 1964). It generates high split-half reliabilities (about .80); and retest reliability after a 16-month interval was shown to be .57 (Schneider & Dachler, 1978).

FIGURE 13–2
Sample items from the Job Description Index (each scale is presented on a separate page)*

Think of your present work. What is it like most of the time? In the blank beside each word given below, write

__Y__ for "Yes" if it describes your work
__N__ for "No" if it does NOT describe it
__?__ if you cannot decide

Work on present job

_____ Routine
_____ Satisfying
_____ Good
_____ On your feet

Think of the pay you get now. How well does each of the following words describe your present pay? In the blank beside each word, put

__Y__ if it describes your pay
__N__ if it does NOT describe it
__?__ if you cannot decide

Present pay

_____ Income adequate for normal expenses
_____ Insecure
_____ Less than I deserve
_____ Highly paid

Think of the opportunities or promotion that you have now. How well does each of the following words describe these? In the blank beside each word put

__Y__ for "Yes" if it describes your opportunities for promotion
__N__ for "No" if it does NOT describe them
__?__ if you cannot decide

Opportunities for promotion

_____ Promotion on ability
_____ Dead-end job
_____ Unfair promotion policy
_____ Regular promotions

Think of the kind of supervision that you get on your job. How well does each of the following words describe this supervision? In the blank beside each word below, put

__Y__ if it describes the supervision you get on your job
__N__ if it does NOT describe it
__?__ if you cannot decide

Supervision on present job

_____ Impolite
_____ Praises good work
_____ Influential
_____ Doesn't supervise enough

Think of the majority of the people that you work with now or the people you meet in connection with your work. How well does each of the following words describe these people? In the blank beside each word below, put

__Y__ if it describes the people you work with
__N__ if it does NOT describe them
__?__ if you cannot decide

People on your present job

_____ Boring
_____ Responsible
_____ Intelligent
_____ Talk too much

* The Job descriptive Index is copyrighted by Bowling Green State University. The complete forms, scoring key, instructions, and norms can be obtained from Dr. Patricia C. Smith, Department of Psychology, Bowling Green State University, Bowling Green, Ohio 43403.

Minnesota Satisfaction Questionnaire. The MSQ consists of a set of Likert rating scales using five-point continuation (ranging from "very dissatisfied" through "neither dissatisfied nor satisfied" to "very satisfied"). The basic MSQ contains 100 items pertaining to work, like those illustrated in Figure 13–3. A short form, consisting of only 20 items, is also available.

The long version of the MSQ generates information on 20 separate scales measuring both intrinsic and extrinsic components of job satisfaction. The

FIGURE 13–3
Sample items from the Minnesota Satisfaction Questionnaire

On my present job, this is how I feel about	Very dissat- isfied	Dissat- isfied	Neutral	Satis- fied	Very satis- fied
1. Being able to keep busy all the time	____	____	____	____	____
2. The chance to work alone on the job	____	____	____	____	____
3. The chance to do different things from time to time	____	____	____	____	____
4. The chance to be somebody in the community	____	____	____	____	____
5. The way my boss handles his men	____	____	____	____	____
6. The competence of my super- visor making decisions	____	____	____	____	____
7. The way my job provides for steady employment	____	____	____	____	____
8. My pay and the amount of work I do	____	____	____	____	____
9. The chances for advance- ment on this job	____	____	____	____	____
10. The working conditions	____	____	____	____	____
11. The way my co-workers get along with each other	____	____	____	____	____
12. The feeling of accomplish- ment I get from the job	____	____	____	____	____

Source: D. J. Weiss, R. V. Dawis, G. W. England, and L. H. Lofquist, *Manual for the Minnesota Satisfaction Questionnaire; Minnesota Studies in Vocational Rehabilitation* (Minneapolis: University of Minnesota, Vocational Psychology Research, 1967). © Copyright 1967, Vocational Psychology Research, University of Minnesota. Reproduced by permission.

MSQ also yields an overall general satisfaction score which can be compared with norms developed for several occupational groups.

Interviews

Interviews have not been used as frequently as questionnaires for assessing job satisfaction for reasons with which you are already familiar. As noted in Chapter 7, interviewing is relatively expensive and generates subjective information, the interpretation of which can be difficult and the validity of which may be suspect. These difficulties are surmountable, given a sound interviewer-training program, which itself can be very costly.

Despite these drawbacks, the interview has some distinct advantages for job satisfaction research. (In this regard, you will recall the powerful influence exerted by the interview findings from the Hawthorne studies). One clear advantage is in the potential depth of information generated from interviews, and the opportunity they afford to clarify the kinds of misunderstandings and ambiguities that sometimes crop up in questionnaires.

Many organizations routinely use exit interviews for employees who have decided to terminate. The purpose is to explore the reasons for leaving, including specific sources of dissatisfaction. Whereas this information is clearly important to management, the validity of exit-interview data has been questioned. One study (Lefkowitz & Katz, 1969) determined that 59 percent of a sample of women who had quit their jobs gave a different reason for leaving during the exit interview and on a follow-up questionnaire six months later. Moreover, all of the employees who said during the interview that they were leaving "for no specific reason" gave a specific one on the follow-up survey.

Obviously the sources of job satisfaction are often personal and emotionally sensitive. This may argue for using questionnaires, because anonymity is thereby preserved. However, the interview's unique potential for exploring such issues in depth commends it—provided that a climate of honesty and openness can be established.

CONSEQUENCES OF JOB SATISFACTION AND DISSATISFACTION

In the years since the Hawthorne researches, the general issue of the behavioral consequences of job satisfaction and dissatisfaction has been extensively studied. As you will read shortly, some of the findings are probably contrary to your commonsense expectations.

Effects on productivity

The initial thinking, based upon common sense, was that productivity could be raised by improving job satisfaction. Perhaps surprisingly, the data are consistent in refuting this view. The relationship between job satisfaction and productivity is a slight one indeed (Brayfield & Crockett, 1955; Vroom, 1964). The median correlation reported in Vroom's review of a large number of studies was only .14. Although these comprehensive reviews are now somewhat dated, there is no recent evidence to challenge their conclusion. Although a relationship is consistently obtained, its magnitude is low (Organ, 1977a).

Why is this relationship, which stands to reason, not higher? Part of the explanation may simply be that productivity is influenced by so many moderating factors in addition to job satisfaction (Schwab & Cummings, 1970). For example, even if an employee were highly satisfied with the job and therefore wished to be highly productive, the level of productivity actually manifest might be limited by such things as ability, level of skill, or counter-productive work-group pressures.

An interesting aspect of current thinking about the relationship is that job satisfaction may be a consequence of, rather than the cause of, productivity level (Locke, 1976; Organ, 1977a). Locke theorizes that high satisfaction results from high productivity that (a) is congruent with the employee's important job values (e.g., for recognition) and (b) does not entail such high cost (for example, in fatigue, marital problems, and so on) that the overall consequences are viewed as negative.

In the same vein, Lawler and Porter (1967) expect high productivity to cause increased job satisfaction only when employees perceive that both the intrinsic rewards (e.g., sense of achievement) and extrinsic rewards (e.g., pay) they receive are fair and associated with superior performance. If the employee does not perceive that intrinsic and extrinsic rewards are associated with performance, then increases in performance will not be correlated with increases in satisfaction. The proposed relationship is depicted in Figure 13–4.

FIGURE 13–4
Model of the relationship between performance and satisfaction

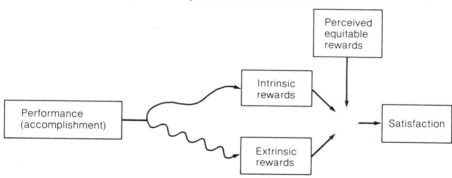

Source: E. E. Lawler and L. W. Porter, "The Effect of Performance on Satisfaction," *Industrial Relations*, 7 (1967): p. 23.

The evidence in support of the contention that productivity causes job satisfaction is equivocal (for example, Kopelman, 1975; Pritchard, 1973).

Perhaps the best we can do with this issue for now is to bypass the cause-effect question by viewing job satisfaction and productivity as separate outcomes of employee-job interactions the nature of which are not yet clearly understood.

Effects on absenteeism and turnover

Reviews of earlier studies (Brayfield & Crockett, 1955; Herzberg, Mausner, Peterson, & Capwell, 1957; Vroom, 1964) uniformly concluded that satisfied workers were less likely than unsatisfied ones to be absent or quit. More recent work has questioned this conclusion.

Porter and Steers (1973) conclude that absenteeism and turnover are qualitatively different types of responses. Of the two, absenteeism is the more spontaneous and therefore less likely to reflect job dissatisfaction. Because of the potentially severe economic consequences of quitting one's job, however, they regard turnover as more directly related to job dissatisfaction. Further reviewing the presumed absenteeism-dissatisfaction relationship, Nicholson, Brown, and Chadwick-Jones concluded (1976) that the studies purporting to find the relationship were flawed, either in experimental design or data analysis. Conducting their own study with 1,200 employees from 16 organizations, these authors found no relationship between job satisfaction and absenteeism. Although not specifically at issue here, they did find that older workers were less likely than younger ones to have unexplained absences (Nicholson et al., 1977).

Two different models, one on the relationship between absenteeism and satisfaction (Steers & Rhodes, 1978) and one on the relationship between turnover and satisfaction (Mobley, Horner, & Hollingworth, 1978) have recently been proposed. Both posit a more indirect and complex relationship than earlier investigators assumed.

The Steers and Rhodes model is shown in Figure 13–5. They attribute attendance behavior (the opposite of absenteeism) to two factors: attendance motivation and the ability to attend. They believe attendance motivation to be influenced by job satisfaction in combination with other internal and external pressures to come to work. Although this model awaits further empirical validation, it makes sense.

The Mobley, Horner, and Hollingworth turnover model is shown in Figure 13–6. They suggest that after an employee becomes dissatisfied several other stages occur (e.g., thinking of quitting), before a decision to quit is made. They tested parts of this model in a hospital using questionnaire responses by 203 employees. In support of their model, they found evidence to indicate that the level of job satisfaction correlated with thoughts of quitting, and that intentions to quit were correlated with actually quitting.

Effects on health

There is some evidence of a relationship between job satisfaction and both physical and mental health. One 15-year longitudinal study (Palmore, 1969) correlated initial measures of several physical and attitudinal variables with a follow-up criterion designated the *longevity quotient*. (This quotient was the ratio of life span following the original physical examination to actuarial predictions of life expectancy.) The initial measure of job satisfaction proved to be an even better predictor of longevity than either the initial measure of physical health or the use of tobacco.

Emphasizing the negative, several other studies have demonstrated a rela-

FIGURE 13–5
Major influences on employee attendance

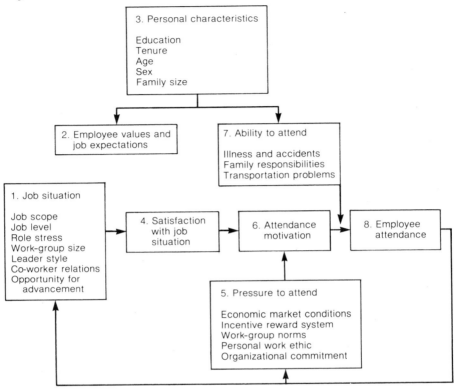

Source: R. M. Steers and S. R. Rhodes, "Major Influences on Employee Attendance: A Process Model," *Journal of Applied Psychology,* 63 (1978): p. 393.

tionship between job dissatisfaction and physical malaise including heart disease (Jenkins, 1971), fatigue, headaches, and illness (Burke, 1969).

A most comprehensive study of mental health and job satisfaction was made by Kornhauser (1965). Mental health scores were obtained from structured interviews with over 400 skilled and unskilled automotive craftsmen. These scores were found to be related both to the level of job satisfaction and to occupational level. One of the most significant findings was that for all occupational levels, the employees' perception that their job required making effective use of their abilities (a form of self-actualization) was associated with high mental health scores.

Although it is clear that job satisfaction and health are related, the causal link in the relationship is, of course, speculative. Equally plausible are hypotheses that satisfaction enhances the level of physical and mental function, and that satisfaction is itself a sign of health. Further, these hypotheses are

FIGURE 13–6
Intermediate steps in the employee withdrawal decision process

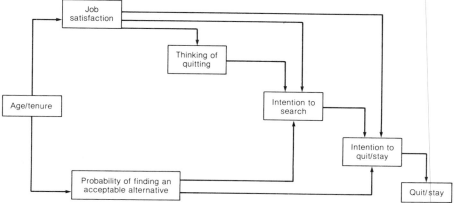

Source: W. H. Mobley, S. O. Horner, and A. T. Hollingworth, "An Evaluation of Precursors of Hospital Employee Turnover," *Journal of Applied Psychology,* 63 (1978): p. 410.

not mutually exclusive. The level of job satisfaction and of health are likely to be mutually reinforcing so that a deterioration of either can have adverse effects upon the other.

As important as job satisfaction is to feelings of well-being, it would be a mistake to conclude from the foregoing that feelings of satisfaction with one's job are necessarily central to well-being. Work is only one part of life, and therefore only one of several potential sources of gratification for most people. Other potential sources of gratification include interpersonal relationships (for example, as a parent, spouse, friend, and so on) and nonoccupational attainments (hobbies, organizations, and so on). We discuss later some evidence indicating that the relative importance of one's perceptions about the work role as a component of overall satisfaction with life may be diminishing (London, Crandall, & Seals, 1977).

SOCIETAL TRENDS

In spite of employment in a new, attractive factory, almost 8,000 youthful workers struck General Motors. The issue was not a demand for higher wages or increased retirement benefits. The strikers sought a voice in managing this fastest moving assembly line in the world (Sheppard & Herrick, 1972). This incident dramatically called attention to the work place as a mirror of changes occurring elsewhere in society.

HEW Task Force report

Many of these changes were addressed in the widely quoted report *Work in America* (HEW Special Task Force, 1973). This report, prepared for the

Secretary of Health, Education, and Welfare, summarizes hundreds of studies of American workers and job settings.

The report concluded that there is great disenchantment in our society with work and with traditional work-values. Although acknowledging that 80 percent to 90 percent of the Gallup poll respondents reply affirmatively to the question, "Is your work satisfying?" the report makes the point that the question is itself superficial. A contrary picture results from analyzing replies to more probing questions like "What type of work would you try to get into if you could start all over again?" Only 43 percent of white-collar workers (including professionals) and 24 percent of blue-collar workers replied that they would remain in their present occupation (Kahn, 1972).

Further, given a hypothetical 26-hour day, only one-in-five nonprofessional workers said they would devote the additional two hours to work-related activities (Wilensky, 1966).

The Special Task Force cites what it considers to be the two major reasons for dissatisfaction in the American work force: (1) the continuing, but no longer functional, influence of Taylor's scientific management philosophy and (2) diminishing opportunities to become one's own boss.

Outdated scientific management. We earlier noted Taylor's profound influence upon management philosophy at the beginning of this century. His approach was widely embraced because it generally resulted in substantial productivity increases.

The Task Force maintains that the Taylor philosophy continues to influence management practice and job design at a time when it is no longer appropriate. The average educational level of employees has improved during the last half century from about the 9th grade to the 12th grade. The prevailing literacy rate has been much improved. As a result, where economic survival was a primary motivator for employees at the beginning of the century, our societal expectations now include moderate affluence as part of the "good life." Given changes like these, the perpetuation of Taylor's influence has resulted in too many jobs that are oversimplified, inappropriately fragmented, and on which performance is too closely supervised.

Diminished opportunities for self-employment. The report also concludes that the American dream of self-made success reflecting individual initiative and resourcefulness is now mostly a myth. The trend throughout the century has been toward employment by large corporations and government. As "little cogs in big wheels" many employees feel alienated, powerless, and isolated (Blauner, 1964).

Special issues

The Task Force report painted with a broad brush in making its case for widespread and significant levels of job dissatisfaction. The reality may not be quite as dismal. Indeed, the most recent and comprehensive review of the job satisfaction surveys, conducted from 1972 to 1978 at the National Opinion Research Center, concluded there were no substantial decreases in over-all levels of job satisfaction during this period (Weaver, 1980). In addition, job satisfaction surveys conducted at Sears Roebuck over the past 25 years indicate only a slight decline in the prevailing level of job satisfaction (Smith, Scott, & Hulin, 1977). However, data on group trends tend to obscure impor-tant moderators. It may well be the case that while older employees have maintained a relatively constant level of job satisfaction, the average level has declined somewhat because a proportionately greater number of younger employees now are in the work force (Organ, 1977b).

Irrespective of the issue of the absolute magnitude of the decline in job-satisfaction level, there is little doubt that particular societal subgroups ex-perience unique problems as members of the work force. Some of these are considered below with the understanding, of course, that it is impossible to make statements applying with equal validity to all members of any group.

Blue-collar workers. The expression "blue collar blues" has been used to summarize the feelings of manufacturing and construction laborers (Shep-pard & Herrick, 1972). A primary reason for the "blues" is perceived immo-bility; many workers are frustrated by the lack of opportunity for promotion to more prestigious employment. The aspiration is not to do the job well for its own sake, but to be promoted out of having to continue doing the job!

Why has mobility become such an issue? Improved technology undoubt-edly has contributed; the worker as artisan has often been replaced by the worker as an extension of a piece of mechanical equipment.

The media have also contributed, both by perpetuating stereotypes (for example, the lazy plumber, the insensitive "hard hat") and by pressing values incorporating affluence, status, and personal freedom. Actually, blue-collar workers do not participate in the realization of these attainments. They lack certain white-collar "privileges"; it is difficult, for example, for a factory worker to arrange to handle necessary personal chores—like getting the car repaired or getting a haircut—during working hours. Seventy percent will never receive a pension from an employer-based plan; and 40 percent ac-cumulate no sick leave (HEW Special Task Force, 1973). Not surprisingly, many feel that the system does not deliver to them what it maintains is rightfully theirs.

Young workers. Over 25 percent of the work force is under age 30. In many ways, this group shares certain values with its older counterpart. A meaningful career is still regarded by the majority of youth as an important part of life (Yankelovich, 1972), and the work ethic of youth may be even stronger than that of their parents' generation (Buchholz, 1978).

But along with these traditionally respected attitudes towards work, American youth have been acquiring new cultural values which shape the way in which they attain the more traditional ones (Heller & Clark, 1976; Yankelovich, 1978). One such addition is a concern for self-actualization in all areas of life, including work. This concern exerted a powerful influence even in the short span of time between the late 1960s and the early 1970s. The percentage of college students indicating that they did not mind the prospect of being bossed dropped from 56 to 36; endorsement of the notion that "hard work pays off" dropped from 70 percent to 30 percent (Yankelovich, 1974). Over roughly the same period of time, the importance of money and security as factors in career choice was greatly overshadowed by "having a challenging job" (Kahn, 1972).

Two points seem clear. First, younger workers are every bit as committed to deriving gratification through work and to doing a good job as their older counterparts; but they demand challenge, stimulation, and an appropriate degree of autonomy from the job. Second, the job market has not, thus far, been especially responsive to these demands. This conclusion follows from the results of recent national surveys of over 4,700 respondents (Weaver, 1980) indicating that there still exists a positive correlation between age and level of job satisfaction.

Minority employees. One third of America's minority work force is unemployed, irregularly employed, or simply out of the job market. Another third holds relatively menial employment (HEW Special Task Force, 1973). We need not here belabor the issue of discrimination in employment; that has already been extensively discussed earlier (Chapter 5). In general, black employees tend to feel exploited and seek redress through a more active voice in managerial decision making (Buchholz, 1978).

Not surprisingly, job satisfaction is considerably lower among blacks than among whites (Weaver, 1980). In a very real sense, job satisfaction for blacks in contemporary society defers to the more basic issue of gaining employment. For many older black workers at least, job satisfaction is viewed in terms of employment versus no employment (Kahn, 1972).

Women. Over half the women between ages 18 and 65 are in the work force; about 90 percent will hold a job outside their home at some time during their lives (U.S. Department of Labor, 1971). Women more than men feel that their jobs exploit them (Buchholz, 1978). However, the overall level of job satisfaction of employed women is similar to that of employed men (Weaver, 1980).

Some future directions

In critically reviewing the entire area of job satisfaction research, Nord (1977) makes the point that while much has thus far been learned, further progress is hampered by three crucial but unrecognized assumptions.

First, researchers have rather uncritically accepted the view of organization decision makers to delegate job satisfaction to a secondary role in relation to economic factors.

Second, investigators generally assume that work is, or should be, a central life interest. Therefore they have pressed effort to promote job involvement in spite of considerable evidence that many employees are not interested in having their jobs enriched.

Finally, studies have tended to emphasize the human organism's competitiveness to the relative neglect of our cooperative potential.

Nord (1977) suggests that psychological research on job satisfaction has been unduly guided by managerial philosophies and views, as evidenced by these implicit assumptions. He regards their reconsideration as imperative for future progress in our understanding of job satisfaction.

We believe Nord is on target, and anticipate that he has identified the direction to be taken by the next cycle of job satisfaction studies. Some important issues for future job satisfaction research include investigating job satisfaction in worker-owned firms, a more thorough study of the relevance of job satisfaction to overall life satisfaction, and a determination of the importance of improved job satisfaction to the profit picture of organizations.

SUMMARY

Job satisfaction occurs when an individual subjectively appraises his/her current job situation and has a positive or pleasurable emotional response. Based on a historical perspective, Taylor's (1911) theory of scientific management has been extremely influential. Taylor believed that when fatigue was reduced and pay increased, management would have satisfied workers who would be highly productive. The Hawthorne studies, beginning in 1927, are regarded as a classic research effort, although many methodological deficiencies can now be identified. The Relay-Assembly Test Room study demonstrated to the researchers the importance of interpersonal relationships, supervision, and job attitudes for industry. Level of production was demonstrated not to be solely determined by environmental factors such as illumination. These findings were at variance with some of the managerial assumptions at that time (e.g., scientific management). Hoppock's research in the 1930s demonstrated that most employees are satisfied with their jobs and that there is a positive correlation between job level and job satisfaction.

Three theoretical approaches to job satisfaction were presented. Locke's discrepancy theory emphasizes the perceived discrepancy between what an individual wants and what is received, and the importance of what is wanted to the individual. Lawler's model of facet satisfaction is closely related to equity theory. According to the model, individuals are satisfied with a particular facet of their job when the amount of the facet they perceive they deserve for performing their work equals the amount they perceive that they actually receive for performing it. To determine overall job satisfaction, each facet is weighted according to its importance and then these scores are combined into a single overall score. Landy's opponent-process theory states that whenever we are satisfied or dissatisfied with our job, there is a physiological mechanism that is triggered which attempts to keep our emotional response under control.

Contemporary research and thinking emphasizes the importance of the job itself to job satisfaction. One attribute of the job especially important to job satisfaction is mental challenge. The *Job Diagnostic Survey* measures five dimensions of jobs that are important to job satisfaction. They are skill variety, task identity, task significance, autonomy, and feedback from the job itself. Pay is another aspect of a job that is related to job satisfaction. A good deal of the recent research on pay has been conducted within the framework of equity theory. The quality of supervision is also related to job satisfaction. The only leadership characteristic consistently related to job satisfaction is consideration.

Research has indicated that there is only a slight positive relationship between job satisfaction and productivity. Current theorizing tends to view job satisfaction as a consequence of productivity and not vice versa, although the evidence in support of this view is far from conclusive. Recent research has failed to find a significant relationship between the level of job satisfaction and the amount of absenteeism. There is some evidence to indicate that individuals with high job satisfaction are physically and mentally healthier than those with low job satisfaction.

Two questionnaires, the *Job Descriptive Index* (JDI) and the *Minnesota Satisfaction Questionnaire* (MSQ), are widely used for assessing job satisfaction. The JDI measures satisfaction with work, pay, opportunities for promotion, supervision, and people. Interviews have also been used to assess job satisfaction. Some reasons that interviews have not been used as extensively as questionnaires are their greater cost, potential for subjectivity, and potential for low inter-interviewer reliability.

The book *Work in America* concludes that there is some dissatisfaction in our society with work. However, the overall level of job dissatisfaction did not decrease substantially during the 1970s. Two reasons for job dissatisfaction are greatly simplified jobs and diminishing opportunities to be one's own boss. Blue-collar workers tend to be dissatisfied with their work because of a perceived lack of upward mobility, a lowering of their status as a result of technology, and rising expectations. Young workers tend to be dissatisfied because of a change in their cultural values. They have become more interested in self-fulfillment and job challenge and less interested in money and security. The problem of job discrimination is very important to women and blacks. Both groups feel more exploited at work than do white males and, as a result, both want more of a voice in decision making to help overcome these feelings.

REFERENCES

Adams, J. S. Inequity in social exchange. In L. Berkowitz (Ed.), *Advances in experimental social psychology* (Vol. 2). New York: Academic Press, 1965.

Barnowe, J. T., Mangione, T. W., & Quinn, R. P. The relative importance of job facets as indicated by an empirically derived model of job satisfaction. Unpublished report, Survey Research Center, University of Michigan, 1972.

Berger, C. J., & Cummings, L. L.   Organization structure, attitudes and behaviors. In B. Staw (Ed.), *Research in organizational behavior* (Vol. 1). Greenwich, Conn.: JAI Press, 1978.

Blauner, R.   *Alienation and freedom: The factory worker and his industry.* Chicago: University of Chicago Press, 1964.

Brayfield, A. H., & Crockett, W. H.   Employee attitudes and employee performance. *Psychological Bulletin,* 1955, *52,* 396–424.

Buchholz, R. A.   An empirical study of contemporary beliefs about work in American society. *Journal of Applied Psychology,* 1978, *63,* 219–227.

Burke, R. J.   Occupational and life strains, satisfaction, and mental health. *Journal of Business Administration,* 1969, *1,* 35–41.

Campbell, J. P., & Pritchard, R. D.   Motivation theory in industrial and organizational psychology. In M. Dunnette (Ed.), *Handbook of industrial and organizational psychology.* Chicago: Rand McNally, 1976.

Carrell, M. R.   A longitudinal field assessment of employee perceptions of equitable treatment. *Organizational Behavior and Human Performance,* 1978, *21,* 108–118.

Chadwick-Jones, J. K.   *Automation and behaviour.* New York: Wiley, 1969.

Dittrich, J. E., & Carrell, M. R.   Organizational equity perceptions, employee job satisfaction, and departmental absence and turnover rates. *Organizational Behavior and Human Performance,* 1979, *24,* 29–40.

Dyer, L., & Theriault, R.   The determinants of pay satisfaction. *Journal of Applied Psychology,* 1976, *61,* 596–604.

Ewen, R. B.   Weighting components of job satisfaction. *Journal of Applied Psychology,* 1967, *51,* 68–73.

Hackman, J. R., & Oldham, G. R.   Development of the Job Diagnostic Survey. *Journal of Applied Psychology,* 1975, *60,* 159–170.

Heller, F. A., & Clark, A. W.   Personnel development. *Annual Review of Psychology,* 1976, *27,* 405–435.

Herzberg, F.   *Work and the nature of man.* Cleveland: World Press, 1966.

Herzberg, F., Mausner, B., Peterson, R. O., & Capwell, D. F.   *Job attitudes: Review of research and opinion.* Pittsburgh: Pittsburgh Psychological Services, 1957.

Herzberg, F., Mausner, B., & Snyderman, B. B.   *The motivation to work.* New York: Wiley, 1959.

HEW Special Task Force.   *Work in America.* Cambridge, Mass.: MIT Press, 1973.

Hoppock, R.   *Job satisfaction.* New York: Harper & Row, 1935.

House, R. J., & Mitchell, T. R.   Path-goal theory of leadership. *Contemporary Business,* 1974, *3,* 81–98.

Jenkins, D. C.   Psychologic and social precursors of coronary disease (II). *New England Journal of Medicine,* 1971, *284,* 307–317.

James, L. R., & Jones, A. P.   Organizational structure: A review of structural dimensions and their conceptual relationships with individual attitudes and behavior. *Organizational Behavior and Human Performance,* 1976, *16,* 74–113.

Kahn, R. L.   The meaning of work: Interpretation and proposals for measurement. In A. A. Campbell & P. E. Converse (Eds.), *The human meaning of social change.* New York: Russell Sage Foundation, 1972.

Kerr, S., Schriesheim, C. A., Murphy, C. J., & Stogdill, R. M.   Toward a contingency theory of leadership based on the consideration and initiating structure literature. *Organizational Behavior and Human Performance*, 1974, *13*, 17–30.

Kopelman, R. E. Organizational control system responsiveness and work motivation. *Proceedings of the Academy of Management National Meetings*, 1975, 125–127.

Kornhauser, A. *Mental health of the industrial worker*. New York: Wiley, 1965.

Landsberger, H. A. *Hawthorne revisited: Management and the worker: its critics and developments in human relations in industry*. Ithaca, N.Y.: New York School of Industrial and Labor Relations, 1958.

Landy, F. J. An opponent process theory of job satisfaction. *Journal of Applied Psychology*, 1978, *63*, 533–547.

Lawler, E. E. *Pay and organization effectiveness*. New York: McGraw-Hill, 1971.

Lawler, E. E. *Motivation in work organizations*. Monterey, Calif.: Brooks/Cole, 1973.

Lawler, E. E., & Porter, L. W. The effect of performance on satisfaction. *Industrial Relations*, 1967, *7*, 20–28.

Lefkowitz, J., & Katz, M. L. Validity of exit interviews. *Personnel Psychology*, 1969, *22*, 445–455.

Locke, E. A. What is job satisfaction? *Organizational Behavior and Human Performance*, 1969, *4*, 309–336.

Locke, E. A. Job satisfaction and job performance: A theoretical analysis. *Organizational Behavior and Human Performance*, 1970, *5*, 484–500.

Locke, E. A. Nature and causes of job satisfaction. In M. D. Dunnette (Ed.), *Handbook of industrial and organizational psychology*. Chicago: Rand McNally, 1976.

London, M., Crandall, R., & Seals, G. W. The contribution of job and leisure satisfaction to the quality of life. *Journal of Applied Psychology*, 1977, *62*, 328–334.

Maslow, A. H. *Motivation and personality* (2nd ed.). New York: Harper & Row, 1970.

Mobley, W. H., Horner, S. O., & Hollingworth, A. T. An evaluation of precursors of hospital employee turnover. *Journal of Applied Psychology*, 1978, *63*, 408–414.

Nash, A. N., & Carroll, S. J., Jr. *The management of compensation*. Monterey, Calif.: Brooks/Cole, 1975.

Nicholson, N., Brown, C. A., & Chadwick-Jones, J. K. Absence from work and job satisfaction. *Journal of Applied Psychology*, 1976, *61*, 728–737.

Nicholson, N., Brown, C. A., & Chadwick-Jones, J. K. Absence from work and personal characteristics. *Journal of Applied Psychology*, 1977, *62*, 319–327.

Nord, W. R. Job satisfaction reconsidered. *American Psychologist*, 1977, *22*, 1026–1035.

Organ, D. W. A reappraisal and reinterpretation of the satisfaction causes performance hypotheses. *Academy of Management Review*, 1977, *2*, 46–53. (a)

Organ, D. W. Inferences about trends in labor force satisfaction: A causal correlational analysis. *Academy of Management Journal*, 1977, *20*, 510–519. (b)

Palmore, E. Predicting longevity: A follow-up controlling for age. *The Gerontologist,* 1969, *9,* 247–250.

Porter, L. W., & Steers, R. M. Organizational work and personal factors in employee turnover and absenteeism. *Psychological Bulletin,* 1973, *80,* 151–176.

Pritchard, R. D. Effects of varying performance-pay instrumentalities on the relationship between performance and satisfaction. *Journal of Applied Psychology,* 1973, *58,* 122–125.

Pritchard, R. D., Dunnette, M. D., & Jorgenson, D. O. Effects of perceptions of equity and inequity on worker performance and satisfaction. *Journal of Applied Psychology,* 1972, *56,* 75–94.

Roethlisberger, F. W., & Dickson, W. J. *Management and the worker.* Cambridge: Harvard University Press, 1939.

Schneider, B., & Dachler, H. P. A note on the stability of the Job Description Index. *Journal of Applied Psychology,* 1978, *63,* 650–653.

Schwab, D. P., & Cummings, L. L. Theories of performance and satisfaction: A review. *Industrial Relations,* 1970, *9,* 408–430.

Schwab, D. P., & Wallace, M. J., Jr. Correlates of employee satisfaction with pay. *Industrial Relations,* 1974, *13,* 78–89.

Sheppard, H. L., & Herrick, N. Q. *Where have all the robots gone? Worker dissatisfaction in the '70's.* New York: Free Press, 1972.

Smith, F. J., Scott, K. D., & Hulin, C. L. Trends in job-related attitudes of management and professional employees. *Academy of Management Journal,* 1977, *20,* 454–460.

Smith, P. C., Kendall, L. M., & Hulin, C. L. *The measurement of satisfaction in work and retirement.* Chicago: Rand McNally, 1969.

Steers, R. M., & Rhodes, S. R. Major influences on employee attendance: A process model. *Journal of Applied Psychology,* 1978, *63,* 391–407.

Strauss, G. Job satisfaction, motivation and job design. In G. Strauss, R. Miles, C. Snow, & A. Tannenbaum (Eds.), *Organizational behavior: Research issues.* Madison: University of Wisconsin, Industrial Relations Research Service, 1974.

Taylor, F. W. *The principles of scientific management.* New York: Harper & Bros., 1911.

U. S. Department of Labor. *Myths and reality.* April 1971.

Vroom, V. H. *Work and motivation.* New York: Wiley, 1964.

Wanous, J. P. A causal correlational analysis of the job satisfaction and performance relationship. *Journal of Applied Psychology,* 1974, *59,* 139–144.

Weaver, C. N. Job satisfaction in the United States in the 1970's. *Journal of Applied Psychology,* 1980, *65,* 364–367.

Weiss, D. J., Dawis, R. V., England, G. W., & Lofquist, L. H. *Manual for the Minnesota Satisfaction Questionnaire; Minnesota studies in vocational rehabilitation.* Vocational Psychology Research, University of Minnesota, 1967.

Wilensky, H. Work as a social problem. In H. S. Becker (Ed.), *Social problems: A modern approach.* New York: Wiley, 1966.

Yankelovich, D. *The changing values on campus: Political and personal attitudes on campus.* New York: Washington Square Press, 1972.

Yankelovich, D. The new psychological contracts of work. *Psychology Today,* May 1978, *11,* 46–50.

Yankelovich, D. Turbulence in the working world: Angry workers, happy grads. *Psychology Today,* December 1974, *8,* 80–89.

Yukl, G. A. Toward a behavioral theory of leadership. *Organizational Behavior and Human Performance,* 1971, *6,* 414–440.

INDIVIDUALS IN GROUPS

part **B**

chapter 14

Group Behavior

Group decision making and problem solving are held in low esteem by American folklore proclaiming: "A camel is a horse designed by a committee" and "A committee is comprised of the incompetent led by the uninformed."

Such whimsy aside, it is clear that group endeavor is a necessary and significant aspect of American industry. The highly skilled craftsman working alone and completing a product from raw material to finished result has been replaced by work groups and assembly-line technology. This is particularly true, of course, when an end product (like an automobile) requires such diverse and highly specialized skills that the manufacturing process exceeds the reasonable capabilities of a single worker.

Group effort is also important at managerial levels. Almost all organizations have a standing committee system with most important decisions made in committee meetings. Each participant contributes his/her particular expertise to the management group's solution of complex problems.

Before describing the contemporary research and theorizing on group functioning, we will review two classic pieces of research concerned with groups: The Bank Wiring Observation Room study of the Hawthorne researches and the Tavistock Institute Coal Mining study.

TWO CLASSIC STUDIES

Bank wiring observation room study

In the previous chapter, we summarized the Hawthorne researches (Roethlisberger & Dickson, 1939). However, we indicated that one part of that research, the Bank Wiring Observation Room study (BWOR), would be described in the present chapter because of its particular relevance to understanding group processes.

As indicated in the previous chapter, the most important finding from the interviewing program of the Hawthorne researches in terms of understanding industrial behavior, was the discovery of the previously unsuspected importance of employee work groups. As a result, the BWOR study was designed to investigate the impact of informal employee social structure.

Procedure. This study involved a detailed investigation of a work group under as nearly normal everyday working conditions as possible. Although no experimental manipulations such as illumination changes were performed, one change from normal working conditions was required: The workers were moved from the plant into an experimental room. This was done because previous findings had demonstrated that it was infeasible to conduct research in the plant itself where rivalries tended to develop between the "special" research group and the rest of the employees. These rivalries and jealousies interfered both with the research efforts and with the normal work routine. In spite of this change in work setting, attempts were made to make the work situation in the experimental room as realistic as possible.

In addition, an observer was placed in the room. He was instructed to avoid any supervisory or leadership activities and against violating any employee confidences. The primary task for the observer was to determine how both the formal and informal social group functioned. Further, he was instructed to assess the interrelationships between these two types of groups. Data recorded by the observer were supplemented by those obtained by an interviewer who remained outside the test room. The general plan was for the observer to record actual behavior and for the interviewer to uncover the reasons for that behavior.

During the first week the artificiality of the work setting, including the presence of the observer, itself appeared to influence the workers' behavior. The men worked constantly and were suspicious of the observer. Shortly, however, they appeared to return to their more usual work routine: They took frequent rest breaks and violated several company policies. After a month, the researchers were confident that the work group was operating in its usual manner. The observations in the BWOR continued for approximately seven months.

Division of work. Fourteen men worked in the BWOR. Nine were wiremen, three were soldermen, and two were inspectors. These men made parts of switches for telephone equipment. Wiring and soldering required different lengths of time. One solderer could solder the connections made by about three wiremen. As a result, the men were divided into soldering units. Two inspectors could handle the work of all the men. The arrangement of these formal work groups is shown in Figure 14–1.

The wiremen worked on two kinds of switches for the telephone equipment: connectors and selectors. The method of wiring was the same for both types of switches and the differences between them were very small. The men in the front of the room (W_1, W_2, W_3, W_4, W_5, W_6, S_1, S_2, and I_1) worked on connectors while the men in the back (W_7, W_8, W_9, S_4, and I_3) worked on selectors.

The social organization in the BWOR. Although the 14 men in the test room felt an identity as a group, two smaller cliques, or informal work groups, developed. The men in the front of the room, clique A, consisted of

FIGURE 14–1
The formal work groups in the bank wiring room

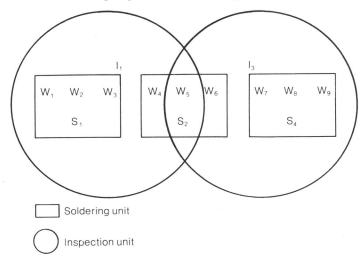

Source: From *The Human Group* by George C. Homans, p. 56, copyright 1950 by Harcourt Brace Jovanovich, Inc., N.Y. Copyright 1978 by G. C. Homans. Reproduced by permission of the publisher.

W_1, W_3, W_4, S_1, and I_1. W_2 participated in the games that the clique played but he rarely participated in the conversation. The men in the back of the room, clique B, consisted of W_7, W_8, W_9, and S_4. W_6 joked around quite a lot with the men in clique B but at times he was excluded from their activities. W_5, S_2, and I_3 did not participate in the activities of either clique. These social relationships are summarized in Figure 14–2.

Men within a clique tended to help each other on the job when it became necessary and they occasionally traded jobs with each other. The men within

FIGURE 14–2
The informal work groups in the bank wiring room

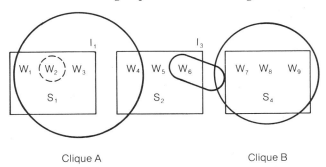

Source: F. J. Roethlisberger and W. J. Dickson, *Management and the Worker* (Cambridge, Mass.: Harvard University Press, 1939), p. 509. Reprinted by permission.

a clique tended to become friends and they also played games together during breaks at work.

Results. There were two major findings from this study: (1) informal social groups were found to exert considerable influence on the behavior of the men; and (2) the men often violated company rules on important issues.

The results clearly indicated that the informal work groups strictly enforced certain rules, or norms, of their own even when these conflicted with established company policy. These norms defined proper behavior in the work group. Thus, although the men were capable of higher productivity, they established and enforced a norm of 6,000 units per day as *fair* production. If any employee attempted to "bust the rate" by producing more than this number in order to receive more pay, strong informal pressures were brought to bear against him by the rest of the work group which perceived rate-busting as a serious threat. They feared that if production became too great, fewer employees would be needed and some employees would be fired. It is interesting to note that a chiseler (a person who produced less than the standard) was subjected to the same kind of peer group pressures as a rate-buster.

The group was found to have several norms relating to its supervisor. One forbade squealing or telling the supervisor anything that might hurt one of the men in the group. Another governed the supervisor's behavior by providing social sanctions if he acted officiously or attempted to take advantage of his position of authority. The men were able to put sufficient pressure on one supervisor to cause him to request a transfer.

The observer also noted that the men broke company policy on a number of significant issues. For example, they frequently traded jobs thereby reducing the boredom and increasing opportunities for socialization. Company rules prohibited job trading because each man was trained only for his own job and was presumed to be unqualified for another one. The men also violated company policy by reporting uniform productivity each day whereas, in reality, their daily output rate showed considerable variation. Since such a violation required supervisory complicity, it is clear that the supervisors also violated company regulations.

The Tavistock Institute coal mining study

The Tavistock Institute of London, England, engaged in the late 1940s in a study of the effects of changes in coal-mining procedures (Trist & Bamforth, 1951). The procedure entailed individual and group interviews conducted over a two-year period. The approximately 20 miners interviewed performed different coal mining jobs and had all been employed in the industry for a considerable time. Representatives of various levels of management were also interviewed.

The short wall method. Coal mining procedures had remained essentially unchanged for a very long time until mechanized equipment was introduced in the 1940s. The premechanized, short wall method relied upon small work groups working autonomously at the coal face. Each work group was comprised of a highly skilled leader, his mate, and several unskilled laborers who removed the coal in tubs. The size of the work groups varied from two to eight men. The leader negotiated a contract with the mine management for a piece of the mine. Management bought the coal mined by the group but exercised no supervisory function.

Each work group was responsible for the entire coal mining task. The leader and his mate performed the many complex and highly skilled operations that were required. Although the equipment was simple, the tasks were varied and the men considered themselves artisans.

The choice of work mates was obviously of crucial importance. This choice was made by the leader—a highly skilled and respected man in the community. Once a work group was formed, the relationships among its members tended to become stable and long lasting. When a man was injured or killed, the other group members typically cared for his family. The powerful interpersonal bonds between the work group members were often reinforced by composing the groups on kinship lines.

These autonomous closely knit work groups were remarkably adaptive to the mining environment. Mining was accurately perceived by the men as a dangerous occupation; they reported that the fear of death and the extreme darkness of the mine made the work environment a source of constant anxiety. The close relationships between the men helped them overcome their fears. The importance to the men of this group function was considerable.

The short wall method encouraged conflict between the various work groups about the availability of tubs for moving the coal. These tubs were always in short supply and many rather unethical practices were followed by each work group in its attempt to have access to as many tubs as it needed. This interteam conflict, which sometimes spilled over from the mine into the community, tended to increase intragroup loyalty and cohesion.

A type of graft developed in this mining environment. The leader often paid off a mine official in order to secure a prime section of the mine for his work group: that is, one in which the coal was reputed to be soft and easy to work. The mining community was rough and tough; the short wall system of mining was well suited to the general environment.

The long wall method. The coal-mining industry was nationalized in the 1940s, and the engineering consultants suggested the installation of mechanical coal-cutting equipment and automatic conveyors. Consequently, coal mining became technologically more complex. Whereas the earlier procedures emphasized human effort, the newer ones emphasized mechanical effort. Mechanization made possible the working of a single large face of the mine.

The new procedure, referred to as the long wall method, resulted in the creation of a work relationship very different from that associated with the earlier procedures. The artisan relationship between a skilled leader and his mate assisted by one or more laborers was not compatible with the new job demands. The need arose for a work unit somewhat analogous in size and complexity to a small factory department. The basic unit became a work group of 40–50 men and their supervisors.

The long wall method divided the work into a standard series of constituent and sequential operations. The work groups were spread over approximately 200 yards in a mining tunnel approximately 2 yards wide and 1 yard high. Production engineers wrote the simple equation: 200 tons of coal mined daily equals 40 men over 200 yards over 24 hours. Things did not turn out to be that simple.

Trist and Bamforth (1951) stated:

> Anyone who has listened to the talk of the older miners who have experienced in their own worklives the changeover to the long wall cannot fail to be impressed by the confused mourning for the past that still goes on in them together with a dismay over the present coloured by despair and indignation (p. 10).

A primary reason for the morale decrease following institution of the long wall mining system was that this system eliminated the close-knit work group. No comparable social structure emerged to help the men cope with their psychological and emotional problems.

Changes other than those of morale were also apparent. Productivity decreased considerably. The men replaced their former norm of high productivity with a lower standard. Whereas externally imposed supervision was unnecessary under the short wall method, it became critical with the new system. Unfortunately, effective supervision was essentially impossible with the long wall; the men were spread out too far to supervise effectively, and combined with the darkness in the mine, they were able to do much as they pleased. Absenteeism increased and contributed further to decreased productivity.

Conclusions. Trist and Bamforth interpreted their observations psychologically. They attributed the production decreases to the workers losing their sense of meaning in life. Withdrawal in its many forms characterized the miners' behavior.

The results of this research indicate that changes that are technologically advantageous may prove to be harmful to an organization whenever such changes ignore human needs. Moreover, the results of the Tavistock Institute study replicated an important finding of the BWOR study, in particular, and the entire Hawthorne researches in general: the importance both to morale and productivity of the work group.

GROUPS IN ORGANIZATIONS

The two previous studies illustrate many important characteristics of group behavior. Three of these, formal and informal groups, norms, and cohesion have been singled out for further description.

Formal and informal groups

Organizations strive to attain goals. In order to reach these goals, certain tasks must be performed. As a result, the employees of the organization are assigned to specific duties and responsibilities. This process leads to the creation of formal work groups: that is, legitimate subunits (departments, sections, etc.) that have been created to help achieve organizational goals.

There are two types of formal groups. The first type of formal group, the *command* group, is defined by the organization chart. It consists of a supervisor and all the subordinates who report to him. The second type of formal group, the *task* group, consists of employees who temporarily work together at the request of management in order to complete a particular project. Once this project is finished, the group is disbanded and the employees return to their full-time regular assignment (Sayles, 1957). (Figure 14–1 portrays the formal work groups in the Bank Wiring Room.)

In addition to these formal work groups, organizations also have informal groups which the employees create for themselves. Informal groups are also of two types: friendship groups and interest groups. A *friendship* group is a collection of workers who share common characteristics (like age) or activities off the job (such as hobbies or political beliefs). Friendship groups often extend their interactions beyond working hours.

Persons comprising an *interest* group interact to achieve some goal of their own rather than an organizational goal (Sayles, 1957). For example, bakery employees might join together to demand improved working conditions. (Figure 14–2 portrays the informal work groups in the Bank Wiring Room.)

Informal groups can have a very important impact in organizations. They can provide employees with stimulating conversation, valued friendships, information on many topics, emotional support, help in performing the job, and job security. The Tavistock Institute Coal Mining Study dramatically illustrated the importance of informal work groups. In the short wall mining system, the informal and formal work groups were identical. This is not the usual state of affairs. However, this arrangement enabled the coal to be mined effectively and it also met the social, emotional, and security needs of the men. When the long wall system was installed, new formal work groups were created. Because no parallel informal group structure emerged to meet the needs of the miners, the long wall system encountered serious difficulties.

Both formal and informal groups frequently regulate the social and task behavior of their members by enforcing rules of conduct (group norms).

Group norms

A group norm is an agreement among the members of a group concerning their individual behavior (Litterer, 1973). The group establishes its norms gradually, and usually only for behaviors which most members consider important (Thibaut & Kelley, 1959). Furthermore, the norms are often applied differently to various group members. That is, higher status members of the group are frequently given more leeway to deviate from the exact letter of the rule than are lower status members.

The range of norms that groups enforce are almost limitless. You will recall that two such group norms were developed by employees in the Bank Wiring Room: output restriction, and not squealing on co-workers.

Most members accept their group's norms and behave accordingly. In some instances, the behavior specified by the group is inconsistent with the attitudes or beliefs of one or more group members. When this occurs, there are two conditions required for individual members to comply with the group norm. They are:

1. The pressure to conform must be strong enough to be experienced by the target individual.
2. The target individual must value the rewards given by the group sufficiently to be guided by its wishes rather than his own inclinations (Hackman, 1976).

The process of norm formulation and enforcement can be so subtle that the affected persons may not even be consciously aware that their behavior is being modified (Machotka, 1964). However, in many instances the pressures to comply are far from subtle. In the Bank Wiring Room, the men "binged" (forceful punches to the arm) a co-worker who they felt was producing too much work. Not surprisingly, the binging tended to produce quick restriction of output from the men who were busting the normative rate of production.

A second example of the pressures toward compliance that can be brought upon members of the group follows:

> At a large birthday party for his wife, Robert Kennedy, the Attorney General, who had been constantly informed about the Cuban invasion plan, took Schlesinger aside, and asked him why he was opposed. The President's brother listened coldly and then said, "You may be right or you may be wrong, but the President has his mind made up. Don't push it any further. Now is the time for everyone to help him all they can" (Janis, 1972, pp. 41–42).

Schlesinger subsequently wrote:

> In the months after the Bay of Pigs, I bitterly reproached myself for having kept so silent during those crucial discussions in the Cabinet Room, though my feelings of guilt were tempered by the knowledge that a course of objection would have accomplished little save to gain me a name as a nuisance. I can only explain my failure to do more than raise a few questions by reporting that one's impulse to blow the whistle on this nonsense was simply undone by the circumstances of the discussion (1965, p. 255).

From these two quotes, it is easy to see why Arthur Schlesinger did not press his objections to the Bay of Pigs invasion. Among the pressures experienced in this type of situation is the pressure to conform. Nonconformity leads to rejection by group members and eventual expulsion from the group.

The behavior of most of the members of Nixon's administration with respect to the Watergate conspiracy and coverup can be explained in terms of the norm to protect the President at all costs. The Watergate hearings confirmed both the intensity of the pressures to conform to this norm and the power of the norm for influencing behavior.

Cohesion

Cohesive work groups are characterized by a high degree of mutual esteem and friendship. The greater the cohesion, the greater is the individual member's resolve to remain active and resistant to leaving (Seashore, 1954).

What factors affect cohesion? Three such factors are group size, perceived management pressure, and member interdependence. The relationship between group size and cohesion tends to be inverse (Seashore, 1954), presumably because it is more difficult for members of larger groups to interact and communicate. The relationship to perceived management pressure is direct: that is, the greater the perceived pressure from supervisors, the more likely the workers are to become unified and cohesive as a means of reducing this external threat. Similarily, the more interdependent the individuals (for accomplishing their task goals and satisfying their social, emotional, and economic needs) the greater is the possibility that the forces for cohesion will arise.

Seashore (1954) investigated the relationship between work-group cohesion and productivity in 228 industrial work groups with interesting results. He found that the level of cohesion taken by itself, did not predict productivity. Some cohesive work groups demonstrated high productivity, others had low productivity. A key variable found to interact with cohesion was the group perception of management and the company. When this perception was unfavorable, the noncohesive groups produced best. When management was perceived positively, the cohesive groups were the most productive. These findings corroborate those from the Hawthorne studies.

However, a second finding of the research was that noncohesive work groups produce less than cohesive work groups that perceive company management and goals as supportive. That is, Seashore found that cohesive work groups may work toward accomplishing the goals of the organization. This replicated the findings of the Hawthorne researchers with respect to the Relay Assembly Test Room study (described in Chapter 13). In that research, the women operators formed a cohesive team whose norm was high production.

Taken together, these results indicate that the degree of cohesion determines the amount of group influence but not whether it is beneficial or detrimental to the organization. Rather, the specific norms set by the work group determine the direction of group influence, that is, whether the group will work to benefit or harm the organization.

A THEORY OF GROUP INFLUENCE

The other people with whom an individual interacts can influence how that person thinks, feels, and behaves. Two examples—the Hawthorne researches and the Tavistock Institute Coal Mining Study—have already been presented to illustrate the importance of co-workers' influence on employee behavior and attitudes. Why is it that groups seem to have such a substantial impact on the behavior and attitudes of individuals? Until recently, there was no theory specifically formulated to help us answer this question for individuals in organizational settings. This omission from the organizational literature has been removed by Hackman (1976). A brief summary of his theoretical position follows.

Basic concepts

The two core concepts of Hackman's theory are ambient stimuli and discretionary stimuli.

Ambient stimuli. The stimuli which are potentially available to all of the members of a group but not to outsiders are referred to as *ambient* stimuli. Ambient stimuli pervade the group, and group members are exposed to them as a regular part of their organizational activities. Examples of ambient stimulus sources are the other people in the group, the task materials, and the working conditions.

Discretionary stimuli. Other stimuli are made available to individual group members selectively at the wishes or discretion of the other group members. These stimuli are referred to as *discretionary* stimuli. Discretionary stimuli include direct messages of disapproval or approval, and instructions about appropriate behavior. The discretionary stimuli provided to an individual vary with that person's behavior and characteristics, the characteristics of the group, and its norms.

The impact of ambient stimuli

Hackman states that, unfortunately, organizational psychologists have overlooked ambient stimuli and have focused upon discretionary stimuli. However, ambient stimuli can have a substantial impact on the informational and affective states of the group members.

Informational impact. People spend a substantial part of their lives in groups and tend to believe because of past experience that they are adept at determining what kinds of potential satisfactions a group offers. Hence, groups are evaluated as potentially providing: (1) meaningful friendships, (2) hostile and destructive feedback, (3) sexual "action," and (4) help in advancing one's job skills. Such evaluations provide information about the group (or at least assumptions about the group) and our behavior is guided accordingly.

Affective impact.   In addition to providing information, ambient stimuli may arouse emotional states. Thus, you probably would have very different emotional responses upon entering a fancy restaurant and a university classroom. Presumably, affective states become conditioned to ambient stimuli on the basis of past experience (McClelland, 1951).

The more positive the individual's response to the ambient stimuli in a group, the more likely he/she is to be attracted to the group and to try to become an accepted member of it.

The impact of discretionary stimuli

Discretionary stimuli can also influence the group member's informational and affective states.

Informational impact.   Because organizations and jobs are often very complex, employees who rely solely upon their own senses and experiences to gain information frequently obtain incomplete and/or inaccurate impressions. This is particularly the case with new employees who have not yet had any opportunity to make first-hand observations. The new employee often depends upon the work group to provide information about employer and co-worker expectations. The more complex the job, the more likely it is that the new employee will rely upon the work group to provide information.

Whether or not the group does so is discretionary with the group itself. It may elect, for example, to ignore a new member's requests for information or, worse yet, deliberately provide incorrect or misleading information. By providing or withholding discretionary stimuli, the work group has the power to socialize and educate its members and to produce uniformity on certain issues (e.g., level of output) and diversity on others (e.g., status hierarchies within the group).

Affective impact.   After reviewing the literature, Hackman concludes that when the group is important to an individual member, it often has considerable impact on that member's attitudes, feelings, preferences, and so on. For example, in a now-classic piece of research, Newcomb (1952) found that the political orientation of students at Bennington College became substantially more liberal if they accepted their fellow students and faculty members as their reference group.

Even though the discretionary stimuli responsible for influencing the affective states of members are controlled by the group, the resulting changes often occur without the individual's awareness. Thus, if a group were to set out to deliberately control the attitudes of those members who depended on the group for personal satisfactions, the amount of change realized could be very large (Hackman, 1976).

Group influence on individual performance

Hackman theorizes that through the combination of ambient and discretionary stimuli, groups control work behavior in four important ways. They influence:

1. The amount of effort members exert.
2. The work procedures.
3. The worker's level of knowledge and skills.
4. The level of psychological arousal experienced on the job.

Furthermore, he also theorizes that most of the variation in individual worker behavior, with respect to areas such as level of productivity, is a result of differences in these four group influences.

Admittedly, the current level of research support for this theorizing is somewhat meagre. However, Hackman's approach appears to offer a needed framework for future research about the influence of groups in organizations.

GROUP PROBLEM SOLVING

For the remainder of this chapter we have singled out for more intensive discussion one particular group function: problem solving (including decision making). Although some organizational structures permit some kinds of decisions to be made unilaterally (usually by the chief executive officer), most decisions are made in groups in which informational and affective inputs are pooled and responsibility for the interpretations and conclusions is shared.

It has been estimated that middle-level managers spend about 35 percent of their time in meetings while top management is in meetings almost 50 percent of the time. Furthermore, taking into account that most organizations involve virtually all employees in at least some meetings, approximately 10 percent of the personnel budget of a company is spent on individuals while they are in meetings (Doyle & Strauss, 1976).

It is a reasonable assumption that an organization's success relates to its ability to solve its present problems and to avert potential ones through conducting effective group problem-solving meetings. Therefore, it is somewhat surprising to find that until recently this topic had not been the subject of widespread psychological research. As described in the following sections, we have relatively few insights into group problem solving.

Dimensions of effective decisions

The literature on problem solving focuses on two dimensions of effective decisions: solution quality and solution acceptance. *Solution quality* refers to the adequacy of the solution in terms of the objective facts of the problem;

solution acceptance refers to the members' motivation to carry out the decision. (Maier, 1963). Most problem-solving groups focus upon quality; acceptance is generally either ignored or relegated to a less important role. To the extent this occurs, Maier maintains that the implementation of the decision will fail. The solution may be a good one, but if the members do not accept it, they will either deliberately or inadvertently sabotage it.

With respect to solution quality, Maier and Maier (1957) found that a developmental discussion technique whereby the group makes its decision following a systematic analysis of the issue, results in higher quality decisions than does a free type of discussion. Maier and Solem (1962) demonstrated that decision-making quality could be improved by procedures that delay immediate selection of a solution and cause the group to examine numerous alternatives more carefully. Furthermore, Hoffman and Maier (1961) found that groups of people heterogeneous with respect to personality were superior in solving problems to groups of people with homogeneous personalities, probably because the points of view are most diverse in a heterogeneous group.

The research on solution acceptance has repeatedly demonstrated that satisfaction with the solution is strongly correlated with the group members' perception of their personal influence in shaping the solution selected by the group (e.g., Hoffman, Burke, & Maier, 1965).

Stages in decision making

Groups go through a sequence of stages when solving a problem entailing a decision: the problem must be diagnosed, alternative solutions generated and evaluated, leading ultimately to selection and implementation of the preferred solution. The most significant research on all aspects of this sequence has been conducted by Maier (1970). Most of the following description is based upon his work.

Diagnosing the problem. You can't begin to solve a problem until you know what it is. This initial diagnostic phase can be extremely difficult to complete successfully. Potential diagnostic errors include confusing the symptoms of the problem with its causes, and treating opinions as if they were facts. Moreover, it is important that the group does not begin generating and evaluating solutions until the diagnosis phase is complete.

Generating potential solutions. The goal of this phase is to obtain as many solutions as possible. This can be impeded if group members are hesitant to say anything that may make them look silly or if there is premature evaluation of potential solutions. To overcome these problems and others, Osborn (1957) developed the technique of brainstorming. When a group brainstorms a problem, they typically adhere to four rules:

1. Criticism of any kind is prohibited.
2. Group members are encouraged to think of wild or outlandish solutions.

3. Quantity of ideas is emphasized. The greater the number of possible solutions suggested, the greater the likelihood of good ones.
4. Group members are encouraged to improve upon the suggestions of other group members and thus to combine or chain ideas.

Brainstorming is widely used to encourage idea generation. However, even with it there can still be considerable inhibition on the part of group members. Moreover, there is substantial research that suggests that for producing both unique and high-quality ideas, the combined efforts of individuals working alone is superior to the ideas generated by brainstorming groups (Dunnette, Campbell, & Jaastad, 1963).

Evaluating alternative solutions. At this stage, each of the proposed solutions is evaluated. The advantages and disadvantages of all the potential solutions are listed. It is important that each solution be given a fair evaluation and not dismissed by one or more comments such as "won't work." It is also important that the side effects of each solution be discussed. That is, a potential solution may create as many other problems as it solves. Some mistakes that are made at this stage include attacking the individual who suggested the solution instead of his idea, and selecting a solution before evaluating all the possible alternatives.

Selecting a solution. After the solutions are evaluated, the group must select the one that they feel is the best. Occasionally, in the process of evaluation, everything indicates that one of the potential solutions is clearly the best. However, unanimous agreement rarely occurs and usually there are several different solutions that appear to be good. There are several procedures that a group may then use to select one solution.

1. Authoritative decision making. Sometimes one person, the chairperson or whoever is in authority, makes the final decision. Although this approach is very quick, the solution quality depends entirely upon how well this one person gathered all the relevant information. Further, it is difficult to see how such unilateral decision making can generate maximum solution acceptance which, you will recall, is prerequisite to implementing a decision.

2. Minority decision making. Occasionally two or three members can "railroad" a decision. They do this by not allowing the opposition an adequate opportunity to express its views. For example, after two people who are in agreement speak, one may turn to the group and say, "Well, we are all in agreement so let us go ahead and implement this idea." Dissenters may remain silent in the often erroneous belief that they are alone, or at least in the minority. Here again, solution acceptance is apt to be minimal.

3. Majority rule. The most common approach to decision making in our culture is through a majority vote or less formal expression of majority sentiment. One of the potential difficulties, in spite of its democratic appeal, is that a vote creates winners and losers. As Schein (1969) indicates, the minority members often feel that there was insufficient time for discussion and, as a result, their point was not fully understood. Further, voting en-

courages coalitions. The losing coalition can often hinder the implementation process while it regroups for the next round.

4. Consensus. Schein (1969) defines consensus as a state of affairs where communication is open and the group climate is supportive. The members each feel that they have had a fair chance to influence the decision. Operationally, consensus can be defined by the fact that those members who do not agree with the group's decision nevertheless understand it clearly and are prepared to support it.

Since the process of reaching consensus involves every participant, this approach should generate the highest level of solution acceptance. Nevertheless, consensus is a time-consuming decision strategy requiring high participant commitment to solving the problem. Therefore, it is not appropriate to circumstances in which solution time is critical (e.g., emergencies).

Implementing the solution. Two major kinds of difficulties can arise even when implementing solutions for which there is high acceptance by the group. One source of difficulty is procedural: no decision has been made on *when* to start the implementation, or *who* is to do what, or *how* implementation is to occur, or *where* it should begin. Some individual or group of individuals needs to be responsible for ensuring that the process of implementation proceeds effectively.

A second kind of impediment to implementation results from discontinuity between the level at which the decision is made and that at which it must be implemented. The fact that management, for example, has reached consensus and made a decision which has high acceptance for them does not imply acceptance also by the line supervisor who, although not a decision-making participant, is supposed to follow through. When implementers cannot participate directly in the decision-making process, they must be involved in such other ways as periodic staff meetings and individual conferences.

Finally, plans for evaluation should be incorporated into any decision-implementation program. Again, for the evaluative findings to be accepted, the group should decide what data need to be collected, who will make the evaluation, and when it will be made.

Strategies

Certain strategies have been found to enhance both solution quality and solution acceptance. These strategies, which are applicable at all stages of decision making, are designed to enhance two types of functions within the group: task and maintenance functions (Schein, 1969). We have taken our description of task and maintenance functions in groups largely from the classic article by Benne and Sheats (1948).

Task functions. The major task functions are: initiating, opinion seeking, opinion giving, information seeking, information giving, clarifying, elaborating, and summarizing.

Initiating occurs when someone in the group states the problem to be solved, the goals of the meeting, and sets a time limit. Initiating often is performed by the individual who called the group together.

In order for a group to make progress, some individuals must state their *opinions* and provide facts. In addition, it is beneficial if some individuals seek the facts and opinions from the other group members. Some groups appoint a task leader, that is, an individual who is responsible for seeing that each of the task functions occurs and that enough time is spent on each function.

Clarifying and *elaborating* are also crucial for group effectiveness. Clarifying ensures that the communications of individual group members are understood by the other members and may stimulate the thinking of the other group members. *Summarizing* includes a review of points that have already been made so that the group doesn't lose sight of some important issue when making its decision. Some groups appoint an official summarizer who takes notes on a blackboard or flip chart so there is a written record of ideas available for review.

Maintenance functions. Whereas the task functions relate directly to the cognitive aspects of decision making, effective groups also attend to such maintenance functions as paying attention to the feelings of the individual group members, improving interpersonal relationships, and reducing destructive conflict between group members (Schein, 1969). Four maintenance activities facilitating these functions are gatekeeping, encouraging, harmonizing, and compromising.

Gatekeeping ensures that members who have an idea get a chance to express it. Sometimes when one individual talks in a group, others interrupt. After one or two such episodes, some individuals choose to remain silent. The gatekeeper intrudes at such times, *encouraging* persons who may feel cut off to express their views.

Harmonizing and *compromising* are two maintenance devices that can be used to reduce destructive conflict in a group. However, it is not desirable to smooth over all differences between group members. Frequently a confrontation of opposing viewpoints is beneficial to making progress on solving a problem. Therefore, it takes considerable skill on the part of group members to know when harmonizing and compromising will be productive and when they will be counter productive.

Difficulties

Although the traditional face-to-face approach of group-problem solving is widely used, it has numerous potential difficulties. A few of these are that the traditional approach:

1. Is susceptible to a vocal minority overpowering a less assertive majority.
2. Is susceptible to individuals arguing and competing with each other to get their way.

3. May interfere with the generation of ideas because the constant discussion allows little time for thought.
4. Requires all the members to be physically present at the same time and place.

Two nontraditional approaches

Our discussion thus far has emphasized what can be regarded as the "traditional face-to-face interaction" approach to group problem solving. The group as a whole proceeds through a sequence of fairly rigid steps from problem diagnosis to solution implementation. This approach emphasizes face-to-face interactions among the group members at every stage.

Recent efforts to encourage effective group problem solving deemphasize the importance of such direct face-to-face interactions and are designed to reduce or eliminate some of the difficulties of the traditional approach. Two of these approaches, considered here, are the nominal group technique (NGT) and the delphi technique.

The nominal group technique (NGT) (Delbecq, Van de Ven, & Gustafson, 1974) relies upon a combination of individual (rather than group) brainstorming, followed by limited discussion and a secret ballot. The format is as follows: (1) Individual members first silently and independently generate their ideas on a problem in writing. (2) This period of silent writing is followed by a recorded round-robin procedure in which each group member, in turn, presents one of his ideas to the group without any discussion. The ideas are summarized in a brief phase and are written on a board so that they are visible to all. (3) After all the ideas have been presented, they are discussed for the purposes of clarification and evaluation. (4) The meeting concludes with a silent independent voting by individuals using either a ranking or a rating procedure. The group decision is the pooled outcome of the individual votes.

Unlike NGT which entails some amount of face-to-face interaction, the delphi technique pools independently formed judgments by persons who do not participate in any interactive discussion (Dalkey, 1968, 1969). This approach begins when a questionnaire designed to obtain information on a topic or problem is mailed to a group of respondents who are anonymous to one another. The respondents independently generate their ideas in answering the questionnaire which they then return. The responses are summarized in a report which is sent back to the respondent group. They evaluate the report and answer questions about it. Generally, the respondents vote independently by ranking the ideas included in the report. Finally, a summary and feedback report is then developed and sent to the group members.

How effective are the nominal group and delphi techniques when compared to the more traditional interacting groups? There is some evidence (Van de Ven and Delbecq, 1971; 1974) that both nontraditional techniques are superior to the traditional one, in terms of quantity of ideas generated and the perceived level of satisfaction of the group members with the decision.

By this stage in your study of behavior you know that such broad generalizations derived from gross comparisons between procedures are subject to potentially moderating influences. Thus, while the nontraditional procedures may, in general, be superior (at least with respect to the criteria used by Van de Ven and Delbecq) specific circumstances (or other criteria) may support a preference for face-to-face interactions among group members while they solve problems.

Two such moderating variables, for example, are the participants' (a) level of sophistication concerning the problem and (b) willingness to participate in open discussion of it. Under such circumstances, the NGT at least is not superior to the traditional one (Green, 1975). Future research on traditional versus nonparticipative techniques will undoubtedly be directed toward further clarifying for whom, what kinds of problems, and under which circumstances, each technique works best.

Toward a theoretical integration

It is evident that much of the writing about group problem solving to date involves suggestions for managing groups engaged in solving problems. These suggestions make sense; and they have been found, through experience, to work. However, the entire issue lacks the theoretical foundation necessary to allow us to understand group processes in problem solving.

A step in this direction is Hoffman's (1979) valence model, on the basis of which he attempts to integrate findings from a 15-year series of investigations of problem solving in face-to-face groups.

Valence. The use of the valence notion to represent the perceived attractiveness (or unattractiveness) of behavioral outcomes was introduced by Lewin (1935). Objectives, goals, or outcomes carry either a positive or negative valence depending upon whether the respondent perceives them as attractive (desirable, worth pursuing, etc.) or unattractive. While two or more objectives can each carry positive or negative valences, the relative strengths of those valences will determine a person's course of action. Lewin used the notion to explain, among other things, how a person resolves conflicts, that is, selects a particular course of action from among two or more alternatives. In the I/O context, Vroom (1964) used the same concept to help explain issues related to job satisfaction and position choices (e.g., quitting one job to take another).

Hoffman's application of valence to group problem solving is as follows:

1. Valence is the degree of acceptability a solution has for an individual or a group. Positive valence indicates the solution is acceptable and negative valence indicates it is unacceptable.

2. A solution to be adopted by a group must acquire more positive valence (support) than some minimal value.
3. When this level of support has been achieved, resistance to that solution disappears or becomes relatively small.
4. Then the group focuses upon providing additional justification for adopting that solution.
5. When this occurs, the search for, or the thorough discussion of, alternative solutions is inhibited.
6. Member acceptance of the solution that is chosen will be high only if the member's individual valence (support) for the solution is substantially above some minimum threshold value.

The hierarchical model. In order to integrate substantial past research on the concept of valence with other group problem-solving studies, Hoffman (1979) has presented the beginnings of a hierarchical model of group problem solving. He posits three dimensions as important for understanding group problem solving: (1) task versus maintenance processes, (2) explicit versus implicit levels of functioning, and (3) normative versus localized behavior.

You are already familiar with the first of these dimensions. The group can focus on solving the problem (task orientation) or need satisfaction for its members (maintenance orientation). As you will recall, both are important, but work towards different ends. Hoffman makes the point that *both* orientations may be required to encourage individuals to modify their position. A task orientation (e.g., presenting rational arguments in support of a solution) without maintenance processes designed to meet members' needs for involvement, recognition, participation, and so on may not succeed in effecting a consensus.

With respect to the second dimension of the model (explicit versus implicit), Hoffman points out that matters remaining at an implicit (covert) level are open to different interpretations.

Finally, when the procedures of a group become sufficiently explicit that they are also shared by all those in the group, they take on a normative stature. That is, they become rules and procedures accepted by the group. This contrasts with other occasions when certain matters of the group are perceived uniquely and, as a result, they are localized within an individual or a few individuals in the group.

We agree with Hoffman that this theoretical formulation is in its beginning stage. It will be modified by future research results. However, it does provide a theoretical basis for understanding and conducting group problem-solving research.

SUMMARY

The Bank Wiring Observation Room study of the Hawthorne researches entailed a detailed investigation of a work group under as nearly normal working conditions as possible. There were two major findings from this study: (1) the informal social groups were found to exert considerable influence on the behavior of the men and (2) the men frequently violated company rules on important issues.

The Tavistock Institute Coal Mining study investigated the effects of a change in English coal mining procedures. Before the change, coal was mined using the short wall method. Small autonomous work groups (two to eight men) mined the coal. These closely knit work groups helped the workers cope with the problem of fear that is part of the mining profession. An engineering study indicated that mining would be more efficient if mechanical equipment was installed. The suggestion was followed and the long wall method of mining was initiated. This method increased the work group size to about 40. The stable social relationships between workers that were present in the short wall method now disappeared. Production decreased and absenteeism increased as a result of these new mining procedures. These results are attributed to the workers losing a sense of meaning in their life because of the break-up of their closely knit work groups.

Formal work groups can be defined as legitimate subunits of the organization that have been created to help achieve organizational goals. Informal groups do not arise as a result of deliberate design but rather they evolve naturally. Informal work groups can provide employees with conversation, friendship, information, and help in performing the job.

A group norm is an agreement among the members of a group concerning how they should behave. Most group members tend to behave in accordance with the norms that the group establishes. The process of norm formulation and enforcement can be so subtle that the individual is not even aware that his/her behavior is being modified.

Group cohesion is the degree of attraction of the members of a group in terms of the strength of forces on the individual group members to remain active in the group and to resist leaving it. Factors influencing the degree of cohesion present in a work group include its size, managerial pressure, and the degree of dependence of the work group members upon each other.

There are two basic concepts in Hackman's (1976) theory about the effects of groups on individuals in organizations: ambient stimuli and discretionary stimuli. Ambient stimuli are those that are potentially available to all of the members of a group and not to outsiders. Discretionary stimuli are made available to individual group members at the wishes of other group members. Both ambient and discretionary stimuli can have an informational and an affective impact. Hackman theorizes that most of the variation in individual worker behavior occurs as a result of group influence on (1) the amount of effort an individual worker exerts, (2) the procedures that a worker utilizes, (3) the knowledge and skills of the worker, and (4) the psychological arousal of the worker. He theorizes that these four variables are influenced by the ambient and discretionary stimuli present in the work group.

The two dimensions of effective decisions are solution quality and solution acceptance. The stages of effective problem solving are diagnosis, generating potential solutions, evaluating solutions, selecting a solution, and implementation. The process of brainstorming is often used in generating solutions. Four procedures for selecting a solution are authoritative decision making, minority decision making, majority decision making, and consensus. If a group is to function effectively, both task and maintenance activities must be handled properly. Task functions include initiating, opinion giving and seeking, information giving and seeking, clarifying, elaborating, and summarizing. Maintenance functions include gatekeeping, encouraging, harmonizing, and compromising.

Recently attention has focused on two nontraditional problem solving techniques: NGT and delphi. NGT is characterized by: silent generation of ideas, listing of ideas, discussion of ideas, and silent voting to rank the ideas. Delphi is characterized by mailing questionnaires to people who do not meet, first to collect the ideas and then to rank them.

Valence is the degree of acceptability a solution has for an individual or a group. A solution to be adopted by a group must acquire some minimal level of positive valence (support). When this level of support has been achieved, resistance to that solution tends to disappear or become small.

Hoffman's hierarchical model of problem solving posits three dimensions as important to understanding group problem solving: (1) task versus maintenance processes, (2) explicit versus implicit levels of functioning, and (3) normative versus localized behavior. This model may prove helpful to researchers concerned with group problem solving.

REFERENCES

Benne, K. D., & Sheats, P. Functional roles of group members. *Journal of Social Issues,* 1948, *2,* 42–47.

Dalkey, N. C. *Experiment in group prediction.* Santa Monica, Calif.: RAND Corp., 1968.

Dalkey, N. C. *The delphi method: An experimental study of group opinion.* Santa Monica, Calif.: RAND Corp., 1969.

Delbecq, A. L., Van de Ven, A. H., & Gustafson, D. H. *Group decision making techniques in problem solving.* Chicago: Scott Foresman, 1974.

Doyle, M., & Straus, D. *How to make meetings work.* Ridgefield, Conn.: Wyden, 1976.

Dunnette, M. D., Campbell, J. P., & Jaastad, K. The effect of group participation on brainstorming effectiveness for two industrial samples. *Journal of Applied Psychology,* 1963, *47,* 30–37.

Green, T. B. An empirical analysis of nominal and interacting groups. *Academy of Management Journal,* 1975, *18,* 63–73.

Hackman, J. R. Group influences on individuals. In M. D. Dunnette (Ed.), *Handbook of industrial and organizational psychology.* Chicago: Rand McNally, 1976.

Hoffman, L. R., Burke, R. J., & Maier, N. R. F. Participation, influence, and satisfaction among members of problem-solving groups. *Psychological Reports,* 1965, *16,* 661–667.

Hoffman, L. R. *The group problem solving process: Studies of a valence model.* New York: Praeger, 1979.

Hoffman, L. R., & Maier, N. R. F. Quality and acceptance of problem solutions by members of homogeneous and heterogeneous groups. *Journal of Abnormal and Social Psychology,* 1961, *62,* 401–407.

Homans, G. C. *The human group.* New York: Harcourt, Brace, & World, 1950.

Janis, I. L. *Victims of groupthink: A psychological study of foreign-policy decisions and fiascoes.* New York: Houghton Mifflin, 1972.

Lewin, K. *A dynamic theory of personality* (K. E. Zener & D. K. Adams Trans). New York: McGraw-Hill, 1935.

Litterer, J. A. *The analysis of organizations.* New York: Wiley, 1973.

Machotka, O. *The unconscious in social relations.* New York: Philosophical Library, 1964.

Maier, N. R. F. *Problem-solving discussions and conferences: Leadership methods and skills.* New York: McGraw-Hill, 1963.

Maier, N. R. F. *Problem solving and creativity in individuals and groups.* Belmont, Calif.: Brooks/Cole, 1970.

Maier, N. R. F., & Maier, A. R. An experimental test of the effects of "developmental" vs. "free" discussion on the quality of group decision. *Journal of Applied Psychology,* 1957, *41,* 320–323.

Maier, N. R. F., & Solem, A. R. Improving solutions by turning choice situations into problems. *Personnel Psychology,* 1962, *15,* 151–157.

McClelland, D. C. *Personality.* New York: Sloane, 1951.

Newcomb, T. M. Attitude development as a function of reference groups: The Bennington study. In C. C. Swanson, T. M. Newcomb, & E. L. Hartley (Eds)., *Readings in social psychology.* New York: Holt, Rinehart & Winston, 1952.

Osborn, H. F. *Applied imagination.* New York: Scribners, 1957.

Roethlisberger, F. W., & Dickson, W. J. *Management and the worker.* Cambridge, Mass.: Harvard University Press, 1939.

Sayles, L. R. Research in industrial human relations. *Industrial Relations Research Association.* New York: Harper & Row, 1957.

Schein, E. *Process consultation: Its role in organization development.* Reading, Mass.: Addison-Wesley, 1969.

Schlesinger, A. M. *1,000 days.* Boston: Houghton Mifflin, 1965.

Seashore, S. *Group cohesiveness in the industrial work group.* Ann Arbor: Institute for Social Research, University of Michigan, 1954.

Thibaut, J. W., & Kelley, H. H. *The social psychology of groups.* New York: Wiley, 1959.

Trist, E. L., & Bamforth, K. W. Some social and psychological consequences of the long wall method of coal-getting. *Human Relations,* 1951, *4,* 1–38.

Van de Ven, A. H., & Delbecq, A. L. Nominal versus interacting group processes for committee decision-making effectiveness. *Academy of Management Journal,* 1971, *14,* 203–212.

Van de Ven, A. H., & Delbecq, A. L.   The effectiveness of nominal, delphi, and interacting group decision making processes. *Academy of Management Journal,* 1974, *17,* 605–621.

Vroom, V. H.   *Work and motivation.* New York: Wiley, 1964.

chapter 15

Leadership

It follows from the preceding chapter that groups need leaders in order to effectively accomplish their assignments. It is possible, of course, to conceptualize a "leaderless" group; indeed, as you will see in our discussion of sensitivity training (Chapter 17), T-groups are convened without leaders. Even in this artificial circumstance, one or more leaders eventually emerge as the group matures.

As a society, we place much emphasis on the leader's responsibility for group action. As college football coaches know only too well, we tend to credit the leader when the group succeeds, and to hold the leader personally responsible when it fails.

This chapter samples an enormous body of research on leadership. Because the several directions taken by this research impinge upon one another, any topical organization is bound to be somewhat unsatisfactory. It is important that you recognize that we have created somewhat artificial distinctions in order to facilitate the discussion, and that research findings under one heading have implications also for topics emphasized under another.

The chapter is divided into three major sections concerned with leadership. They are, respectively, (a) determinants, (b) dimensions, and (c) strategies.

The first substantive section, "Leadership Determinants," emphasizes studies of leaders as persons. We ask here not only whether leaders are "born" or "made," but whether it is possible to predict whether and under which circumstances a prospective leader will function most effectively? The primary practical implications of this section are for leader selection and placement.

The third section ("Strategies") emphasizes some of the alternative courses of action open to leaders in various circumstances. A primary practical implication of this section is leadership training.

The intermediate section, "Leadership Dimensions," is a theoretical bridge between the research emphasizing the analysis of leaders and the research emphasizing leadership strategies.

LEADERSHIP DETERMINANTS

The earliest systematic research sought to identify a set of personal characteristics (that is, traits) inevitably linked to leadership. By and large, this search proved not to be fruitful; leaders in different kinds of situations possess quite different characteristics.

Thus, the research with potential application to leadership selection (or the early identification of managerial talent) shifted to a situational orientation. Instead of asking, "What kinds of personal and physical characteristics predict leadership?", the question has become, "Under *which* circumstances will *what* kind of person be an effective leader?"

This section briefly examines the traits approach (now largely of historic interest) and extensively examines Fiedler's contingency model to illustrate a highly contemporary situational approach.

The search for traits

The traits approach assumed that "great men" or "natural leaders" are endowed with certain characteristics predisposing their effective leadership in widely ranging situations. The search for leadership traits, essentially involving comparisons between the characteristics of successful leaders with those of unsuccessful ones and nonleaders, pretty much ended in the 1950s after repeatedly generating negative results (Mann, 1959). There seem not to be personal or physical characteristics predisposing persons toward generalizable kinds of leadership. That is, a leader in one group is a follower in another.

This conclusion does not invalidate attempts to identify certain *learned skills* and *acquired drives* that may be associated with leadership in circumscribed situations. Ghiselli (1971) has taken precisely this approach to understanding some of the factors underlying managerial talent. Comparing successful managers with successful nonmanagers, he reports that the former scored higher on tests of supervisory skill and verbal/symbolic ability and the need for self-actualization. None of these are traits (in the sense of genetically determined predispositions). Further, there is no implication that successful managers are also successful as leaders in nonmanagerial settings.

Fiedler's contingency model

We next examine Fiedler's (1967) situationally-based model of the determinants of leader behavior. This model resulted from, and in turn has stimulated, a stream of research for almost two decades.

The basic proposition is a simple one: Effective leadership is a joint function of characteristics of the leader and features of the situation. The tasks for the model builder are to discover (*a*) which leader characteristics are important, (*b*) which situational factors potentially condition leadership behavior, and (*c*) how these two sets of variables interact.

Leader characteristics. One source of continuing criticism of Fiedler's model (Schriesheim & Kerr, 1977) is its definition of leader characteristics in terms of a score earned on a particular instrument (rather than in terms of some conceptually meaningful framework).

The instrument Fiedler uses is the *least preferred co-worker* (LPC) scale. Fiedler's logic is that the leader's characterization of persons with whom it is especially difficult to work reveals valuable information about the leader. The respondent is asked to recall all present and past co-workers, to choose the one with whom it was most difficult to work, and to rate this "least preferred co-worker" using a series of bipolar adjectives, some of which are presented in Figure 15–1.

The scoring scheme translates these ratings into an LPC index for the *respondent*. A high LPC leader is one who describes his least preferred co-worker in generally positive terms; a low LPC leader tends to describe his least preferred co-worker in generally negative terms.

What does the LPC score tell us about the leader's characteristics? Fiedler (1978) concludes that low LPC leaders are basically more concerned with task activities than interpersonal relations while high LPC leaders have the converse concerns.

The implication (Vroom, 1976) is that low LPC leaders generalize from a subordinate's poor task performance to a negative evaluation of that subordinate's personal characteristics. High LPC leaders, however, make an important distinction between the two.

Situational factors. The initial focus of Fiedler's research program was validating the LPC. To this end, he investigated the relationship between the leader's LPC score and objective measures of his/her group's performance in such diverse settings as boards of directors, steel-mill crews, basketball teams, and army tank crews.

The initial research results were confusing. The correlations between LPC and group effectiveness were in some cases significantly positive (e.g., boards of directors) and in other cases significantly negative (e.g., steel-mill crews).

Fiedler reasoned that he might be obtaining inconsistent results because of differences between the several groups. He conceptualized these possible differences in terms of three situational factors: (1) leader-member relations, (2) task structure, and (3) leader-position power.

1. Leader-member relations. This is the degree to which group members like and trust and, therefore, are willing to follow their leader. According to the contingency model, the better the leader-member relations, the more favorable the situation is to the leader.

2. Task structure. This is the extent to which the group's task can be spelled out step-by-step and performed according to a standard or well-

FIGURE 15–1

Sample Instructions and Items from Fiedler's LPC Scale Instructions:

Throughout your life you will have worked in many groups with a wide variety of different people—on your job, in social groups, in church organizations, in volunteer groups, on athletic teams, and in many other situations. Some of your co-workers may have been very easy to work with in attaining the group's goals, while others were less so.

Think of all the people with whom you have ever worked, and then think of the person with whom you could work least well. He or she may be someone with whom you work now or with whom you have worked in the past. This does not have to be the person you liked least well, but should be the person with whom you had the most difficulty getting a job done, the one individual with whom you could work least well.

Describe this person on the scale which follows by placing an "X" in the appropriate space. The scale consists of pairs of words which are opposite in meaning.

Friendly	8	7	6	5	4	3	2	1	Unfriendly
Rejecting	1	2	3	4	5	6	7	8	Accepting
Tense	1	2	3	4	5	6	7	8	Relaxed
Distant	1	2	3	4	5	6	7	8	Close
Cold	1	2	3	4	5	6	7	8	Warm
Supportive	8	7	6	5	4	3	2	1	Hostile
Boring	1	2	3	4	5	6	7	8	Interesting
Quarrelsome	1	2	3	4	5	6	7	8	Harmonious
Gloomy	1	2	3	4	5	6	7	8	Cheerful
Open	8	7	6	5	4	3	2	1	Guarded
Backbiting	1	2	3	4	5	6	7	8	Loyal
Untrustworthy	1	2	3	4	5	6	7	8	Trustworthy
Considerate	8	7	6	5	4	3	2	1	Inconsiderate

Source: F. E. Fiedler, M. M. Chemers, and L. Mahar, *Improving Leadership Effectiveness: The Leader Match Concept* (New York: Wiley), pp. 6–8. Copyright © 1976 by John Wiley & Sons, Inc. Reprinted by permission.

defined procedure. According to the contingency model, the more highly structured the task is, the more favorable it is to the leader.

3. Leader-position power. This is the power inherent in the leader's position including the freedom to hire, fire, promote, or demote. As you would expect, the model posits that the stronger the leader's position power the more favorable the situation is to the leader.

After conceptualizing these three situational factors Fiedler chose to dichotomize them for the purpose of his model. From that point on, he referred to leader-member relations as either good (+) or relatively poor (−), tasks as either structured (+) or unstructured (−), and leader-position power as either strong (+) or weak (−). As shown in Figure 15–2, there are thus

FIGURE 15–2
A model for the classification of group task situations: Fiedler's octants

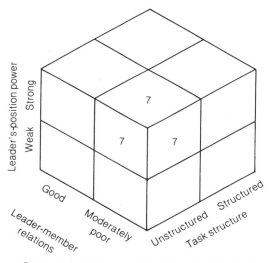

Source: Adapted by permission from Fred E. Fiedler, "Engineering the Job to Fit the Manager", The *Harvard Business Review,* September–October 1965, p. 117. Copyright © 1965 by the President and Fellows of Harvard College; all rights reserved.

eight different combinations of the situational factors relevant to this model. Cell 7, for example, schematically represents a situation in which leader-member relations are relatively poor, the task is unstructured, and the leader's position carries with it strong power.

The model. Fiedler plotted the obtained correlations from past studies between LPC scores and group performance measures for each cell (octant) with results as shown in Figure 15–3. When the results were plotted, many apparent inconsistencies in the relationship between a leader's LPC score and that group's effectiveness now seemed to be comprehensible.

FIGURE 15–3
Fiedler's contingency model: Correlations between leader's LPC scores and group effectiveness for each octant

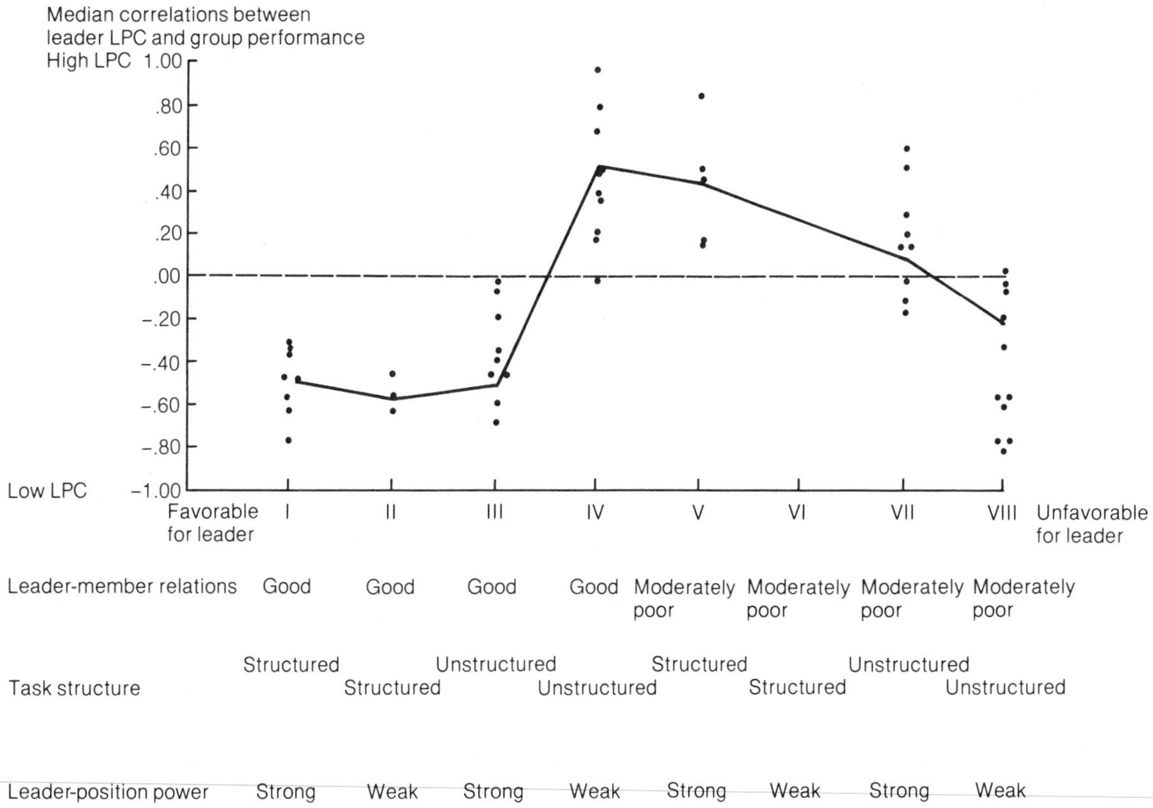

Median correlations between
leader LPC and group performance
High LPC 1.00

.80

.60

.40

.20

.00

-.20

-.40

-.60

-.80

Low LPC -1.00

	I	II	III	IV	V	VI	VII	VIII
Favorable for leader								Unfavorable for leader
Leader-member relations	Good	Good	Good	Good	Moderately poor	Moderately poor	Moderately poor	Moderately poor
Task structure	Structured	Structured	Unstructured	Unstructured	Structured	Structured	Unstructured	Unstructured
Leader-position power	Strong	Weak	Strong	Weak	Strong	Weak	Strong	Weak

Source: F. E. Fiedler, *A Theory of Leadership Effectiveness* (New York: McGraw-Hill, 1967), p. 146.

As Figure 15–3 indicates, where the situation was favorable to the leader (left side of the figure), the most effective leaders were found to have been task oriented (i.e., low LPC score). This was indicated by the strong negative correlations between LPC and group performance. However, in moderately favorable situations (middle of the figure), effective leaders had a high LPC (i.e., they had an interpersonal rather than a task-oriented emphasis). This was reflected in the moderately high positive correlation between leader's LPC score and group performance. Finally, in situations unfavorable to leadership (right side of the figure) effective leaders again were those with lower LPC scores. This was indicated by a moderate negative correlation on the figure between LPC and group performance.

Fiedler uses this figure to generate his contingency model of leadership. It states that the effectiveness of a leader is contingent upon the leader's characteristics (LPC score) and the degree of favorableness of the situation. The major predictions of the model are:

1. Low LPC leaders will be more effective in situations that are both very favorable and very unfavorable to the leader than in situations of intermediate favorability.
2. High LPC leaders will be more effective in situations of moderate favorability than in situations at either extreme.

Implications of the model. Assuming the model is accurate, it has implications for both selecting and training leaders and for "organizational engineering." For *selection,* one needs first to determine whether or not the group is receptive to receiving direction through leadership. Armed with this information, the LPC becomes the selection instrument. The person with the appropriately high or low LPC score, depending upon the situation favorability, will, when selected, provide the optimal match for the group (Fiedler, 1971).

Training, of course, works the other way around. Given a particular group with a leader, the group's effectiveness can be improved either through training the leader to adopt the style appropriate to that group's needs or by training the leader to understand and change the situation in which he/she is functioning. Since Fiedler believes a leader's style is relatively unchangeable, he developed a self-paced program, *Leader Match* (Fiedler, Chemers, & Mahar, 1976), to train leaders to diagnose the situation and perhaps to alter it to fit their own style.

Their book, *Improving Leadership Effectiveness: The Leader Match Concept,* a self-teaching guide, contains a description of the contingency model. It also has a copy of the LPC scale which leaders take and score for themselves. The leader is then presented with a series of cases which contain questions. If the individual gives an incorrect response, the principle needed to answer the question correctly is explained. These situations are designed to teach an individual how to apply the contingency model in real life situations. The book generally takes less than four hours to complete.

The idea of altering the work situation to meet the style of the leader is referred to as "organizational engineering" (Fiedler, 1967), For example, a high LPC leader's environment could be altered to the most favorable situation for him/her, that is Octant IV. As indicated in Figure 15–3, a high LPC leader should be most effective when leader-member relations are good, the task is unstructured, and the leader's-position power is weak.

   Research. The development of the model was preceded by considerable research. As previously indicated, it resulted from an attempt to "make sense" out of data, especially those presented in Figure 15–3.

   But beyond merely explaining the data preceding its formulation, the model predicts optimal circumstances for exercising leadership by particular kinds of leaders. How accurate are these predictions?

   The evidence has been prolific and contradictory (Mitchell, 1979); the associated debate has been lengthy and, sometimes, heated.

   A laboratory study by Chemers and Skrzypek (1972), that used all of the octants, gave strong support for the contingency model. On the other hand, a laboratory study by Vecchio (1977) that also used all the octants failed to find support for the model. Fiedler (1978) responded by labeling Vecchio's procedure "curious," seemingly implying it was not a valid test of his model. A recent literature review by Schriesheim and Kerr (1977) is extremely critical of the model. However, Fiedler (1977) believes he has rebutted their criticism.

   A full summary of this controversy and its ramifications is beyond the scope of this book. One area of disagreement will serve to illustrate. Graen, Alvares, Orris, and Martella (1970) and Schriesheim and Kerr (1977) criticize Fiedler for using nonsignificant correlational data to support the contingency model. As previously described, the contingency model predicts positive correlations between LPC and group effectiveness in some octants and negative correlations between these two variables in other octants. However, the theory does not explicitly predict whether the correlations will be statistically significant. Graen et al. claim that finding a nonsignificant small correlation in the predicted direction is not meaningful support for the model. Instead, they classify such results as merely chance findings. Fiedler's (1978) reply is that the model has repeatedly proved through the years that it has predictive power and that numerous nonsignificant correlations in the predicted direction add up to substantial support.

   Barrow's (1977) review of the literature is the most consistent with our position. He concludes that although the model has received considerable support, it may need to be revised or expanded for the following reasons:

1. Behaviors exhibited by low LPC leaders are often the opposite of what the model predicts.
2. The use of procedures or criteria other than that employed by Fiedler often results in findings inconsistent with the model.
3. The contingency model is not flexible enough for the incorporation of new variables.

The more critical reviews of the literature (e.g., Schriesheim & Kerr, 1977) seem to imply that the theory is useless and should be discarded. This position seems too harsh. Whereas the contingency model may not be the ultimate in leadership theory, its general emphasis upon situational factors in interaction with leader characteristics makes sense. Some of the key variables may yet be missing, and our understanding of the action of the others may need further refinement, but additional research along these lines seems clearly to be warranted (Konar-Goldband, Rice, & Monkarsh, 1979).

LEADERSHIP DIMENSIONS

Having discussed some of the earliest (trait) and most recent (contingency) attempts to find bases for identifying and selecting leaders, we change focus now both historically and with respect to content.

Leadership *behavior* (as distinct from the personal and/or situational determinants) has long been a productive research area. This research essentially was begun in the 1950s at Ohio State University when it became clear that the trait approach was not particularly fruitful. It has continued unabated since.

Ohio State studies

This series of studies began by developing and classifying over 1,800 observationally derived statements describing leader behavior. The statements were classified into ten broad categories of leader behavior (e.g., communication, domination, evaluation). The list of statements was then used as a checklist for describing leader behavior in different kinds of organizations (e.g., educational, military, business, and industrial). By submitting these data to factor analysis (described in Chapter 9) it was discovered that two factors (rather than the ten originally hypothesized) accounted for most of the variance. These two factors, or *dimensions* of leader behavior, were designated *consideration* and *initiating structure* (Fleishman, 1953).

The dimension consideration reflects the degree to which the supervisor's behavior indicates respect for subordinates' ideas, mutual trust, and warmth. A considerate leader is concerned with subordinates' needs and feelings, and, therefore, encourages effective two-way communication, subordinate participation in decision making, and good rapport.

The second dimension, initiating structure, relates to the leader's role in facilitating task attainment. Supervisors high on this dimension define both their role and those of their subordinates with respect to organizational goal attainment. Therefore, they are disposed to assign tasks, plan ahead, push for high productivity and quality output, communicate information, maintain definite standards of performance, try out new ideas, and define the procedures to be used in getting things done.

Measurement.   There are two approaches to measuring a leader's behavior relative to the dimensions of consideration and initiating structure. One is a questionnaire by which subordinates evaluate their supervisor; the other is an inventory administered to the supervisor himself (or herself).

The subordinate-rating form is *The Leader Behavior Description Questionnaire* (LBDQ) originally developed by Hemphill and Coons (1957) and applied primarily in military settings. The LBDQ has since been modified for use in industrial organizations (Stogdill, 1974). Affirmative responses to the following two questionnaire items contribute to the supervisor's consideration score:

He/she expresses appreciation when one of us does a good job.

He/she puts suggestions that are made by foremen under him (her) into operation.

Similarly, affirmative responses to the following two items are scored as part of the scale, *initiating structure:*

He/she offers new approaches to problems.

He/she insists that foremen follow standard ways of doing things in every detail.

The alternative approach, testing the supervisor directly, is accomplished by the *Leadership Opinion Questionnaire* (LOQ) developed by Fleishman (1957). The respondent describes how he/she thinks he/she *should* behave relative to supervisory actions.

Since the two dimensions measured by these instruments were identified by factor analysis, they should presumably be independent of each other: that is, a supervisor could score high on either, neither, or both. This is indeed the case with the LOQ; most studies using it report essentially zero correlations between the two dimensions. However, most researchers using the LBDQ found a significant positive relationship between scores on consideration and scores on initiating structure (Weissenberg & Kavanaugh, 1972). Although the dimensions themselves may be independent, it seems that subordinates' evaluations of their supervisor with respect to either dimension is contaminated by their evaluation of the other.

Research.   There have been dozens of studies concerned with the dimensions of leadership behavior. Most have replicated the findings of the initial Ohio State researchers (e.g., Fleishman, Harris, & Burtt, 1955). Their results tend to indicate that a very large proportion of the variance in leadership behavior (about 80 percent) is accounted for by "consideration" and "initiating structure." Vroom (1976) provides an excellent brief review of these research findings. Some of the major conclusions follow.

1.   Leaders who are high on consideration tend to have subordinates who are more satisfied with them than those who are low on consideration

(Fleishman, Harris, & Burtt, 1955; Fleishman, 1973). This is by far the most consistent finding in the literature on these two dimensions of leadership.

2. Leaders who are high on consideration tend to have subordinates who are likely to have fewer absences (Fleishman, Harris, & Burtt, 1955).

3. Consideration and initiating structure interact in determining both grievance and turnover rates (Fleishman & Harris, 1962) as shown in Figure 15–4.

FIGURE 15–4
Interaction of consideration and initiating
structure as joint determinants of grievance rate

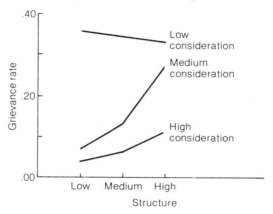

Source: E. A. Fleishman and E. F. Harris, "Patterns of Leadership Behavior Related to Employee Turnover and Grievance," *Personnel Psychology,* 15 (1962): p. 50.

Note the elevated employee grievance rate when supervisors are low on consideration and the correspondingly low grievance rate when supervisors are highly considerate. These conclusions also hold true irrespective of the supervisor's score for initiating structure. However, notice the effect of structure for supervisors who are mid-range in consideration. When the supervisor is semi-considerate, the grievance rate is a function of structure: Those low on initiating structure generate a low grievance rate, whereas, those high on initiating structure generate a high grievance rate.

Thus, although initiation of structure *may* contribute to an elevated grievance rate, *it need not.* The determining factor is the interpersonal atmosphere in which the direction and structure are provided.

4. The relationship between consideration and rated leader effectiveness varies with the research population. For example, a negative correlation was reported for air-crew commanders in combat (Halpin & Winer, 1957), while a positive relationship was found for managers and office staff in an industrial organization (Graen, Dansereau, & Minami, 1972).

These last two studies point to some of the recent thinking in this research area. There is beginning to be an awareness that the effects of high and low scores on these two dimensions may be mediated by situational factors. Kerr, Schriesheim, Murphy, and Stogdill (1974) have suggested several situational factors that may influence the effects of these dimensions. These situational variables have been placed in one of three categories: subordinate characteristics (e.g., competence, experience), supervisor characteristics (e.g., upward influence), and task characteristics (e.g., time urgency, ambiguity, physical danger). Two of their propositions based on these situational considerations are:

1. The greater the support shown by higher management for considerate behavior, the stronger the positive relationship between consideration scores and subordinate satisfaction.
2. The greater the stress on a job, the more likely it is that subordinates will be satisfied with a leader high on initiating structure.

Partial evidence for these propositions is provided by a recent demonstration (O'Reilly & Roberts, 1978) that there are some situations (e.g., low supervisor influence, low subordinate mobility aspirations) that act to counteract the otherwise positive correlations between the two leadership dimensions and subordinate attitudes and performance.

Thus, the initial Ohio State studies identified consideration and initiating structure as dimensions of leader behavior which, in turn, influence subordinate behavior in important ways. However, later research demonstrated that the "most appropriate" or "most effective" leadership style—whether considerate or structured or both—is influenced by such other organizational factors as the particular kind of job being supervised and the general managerial viewpoint.

This conclusion sounds very much like the general philosophy underlying Fiedler's contingency model; and in historical context it is. However, Fiedler's characterizations of leaders in terms of their LPC scores are somewhat different from their *behavioral* characterizations in terms of consideration and initiating structure. We look to further research and theory to clarify both the differences and similarities between these approaches.

We look to other research and theory also to provide us with an understanding of why the dimensions of consideration and initiating structure consistently emerged as the key dimensions of leader behavior and not some others.

As you will see shortly, path-goal theory, presented next, also makes substantial use of these two dimensions.

Path-goal theory

The proponents of this situational theory (Evans, 1970; House, 1971; House & Dessler, 1974; House & Mitchell, 1974) argue that leadership is the process of *motivating* subordinates. Therefore, to be effective, the leader must adopt whatever approach will accomplish this. Instead of hypothesizing about the overall effectiveness of polar styles (like consideration and initiating structure), the theory hypothesizes about the relative appropriateness of different styles to different subordinates and circumstances.

The path-goal theory of leadership is an outgrowth of the expectancy theory of motivation (described in Chapter 12). The three major components of expectancy theory are (*a*) effort→ performance expectancy, (*b*) performance → outcome expectancy, and (*c*) valence. In general terms, according to path-goal theory, one role of the leader is to increase these three components for each subordinate. Both path-goal theory and expectancy theory agree that when these components are increased, subordinate motivation will also increase.

Theoretical propositions. More specifically, in its current form, path-goal theory has two basic propositions:

1. The leader functions to increase subordinate motivation. Since motivation is a matter of goal satisfaction, effective leadership has three components. The leader should:
   a. Arrange circumstances to make available the appropriate incentives (that is, incentives appropriate to the individual subordinate).
   b. Make the receipt of these desired outcomes contingent upon satisfactory task performance. (Job performance, thus, is the path to goal attainment.)
   c. Facilitate the subordinate's progress along this path (through coaching and guidance).
2. The motivational impact of specific leader behaviors is determined by the situation in which the leader functions.

House and Dessler (1974) have identified two classes of situational variables, (*a*) subordinate characteristics and (*b*) environmental forces, which are hypothesized to influence the extent to which subordinate motivation can be increased by leader behavior. Subordinate characteristics considered important include ability, authoritarianism, and need for affiliation, while the environmental forces include the nature of the task, the formal authority system of the organization, and the primary work group.

Early versions of the theory included both subordinate job performance and overall job satisfaction as dependent variables. The current version has dropped them because the present moderators do not enable them to be predicted accurately. Instead, path-goal theory now focuses on the specific psychological states of subordinates which are hypothesized to have a significant effect on their motivation. These psychological states include expectancies, the perceived degree of role clarity, and intrinsic and extrinsic job satisfaction.

Figure 15–5 schematically diagrams the path-goal viewpoint. The possible interactions are simplified for the figure by showing the effects of only four

FIGURE 15–5
Schematic representation of path-goal theory

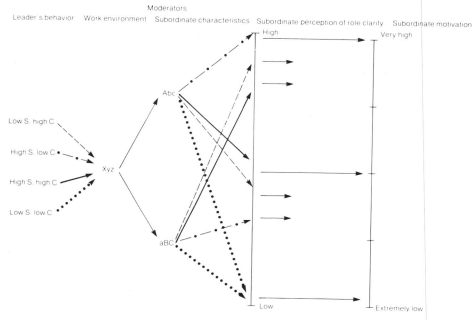

extreme patterns of leader behavior (*C* is *consideration; S* is *initiating struc-ture*), in a single work environment, upon two different subordinates. These limited circumstances potentially produce eight different levels of perceived-role clarity and, in turn, eight corresponding levels of motivation.

The figure deals with two subordinates, *Abc* and *aBC*. Of the two assume that Abc is the more authoritarian and aBC has the greater need for affiliation. The various leadership styles differentially affect these two subordinates' perceptions of their roles as shown by the pairs of similarly marked arrows. Both employees feel unsure of their role (and are poorly motivated) with a supervisor who is low on both structure and consideration. However, whereas employee Abc develops the clearest role perception (and is most highly motivated) by a high-S, low-C supervisor, employee aBC develops the clearest role perception (and is most highly motivated) by a high-C, low-S supervisor. Other leadership styles generate intermediate levels of motivation by these two employees.

Research. Typical path-goal research investigates the relationship between the two Ohio State leadership dimensions of consideration and initiating structure as measured by the *Leader Behavior Description Questionnaire—Form XII* (Stogdill, 1963) and subordinate satisfaction, performance, expectancies, and role clarity. The environmental forces and subordinate characteristics are included as moderator variables in these studies.

Mitchell's recent review (1979) indicates there is some support for basic path-goal positions. For example, Miles and Petty (1977) found that high-C generally leads to high subordinate satisfaction and that high-S can create tension when consideration is low. Furthermore, Downey, Sheridan, and Slocum (1975, 1976) found some support for the path-goal position that consideration is most helpful in structured situations and less helpful in unstructured ones, but no support for the position that high-S will lead to greater satisfaction when tasks are ambiguous or stressful than when they are highly structured and well defined.

Mitchell concludes that the research findings provide stronger support for path-goal predictions about consideration than about initiating structure and stronger support for predictions about satisfaction than about performance. Research published since the review generally supports these conclusions (Greene, 1979). However, some of Greene's results, especially with respect to role clarity, were inconsistent with path-goal predictions. Greene concludes, and we agree, that path-goal theory shows promise but requires further refinement before it can generate specific strategies telling leaders how to act with particular subordinates under particular circumstances. In order to accomplish this, future path-goal research needs to employ designs that are capable of evaluating questions of causation.

LEADERSHIP STRATEGIES: A PRESCRIPTIVE MODEL

On the basis of what is now known about leadership, what can the I/O psychologist say to a manager or supervisor about strategies of effective leadership? How can this information be put into practice?

The clear, but somewhat unsatisfying generalization in the world of applied leadership is, "It depends." It depends upon *who* is being supervised, to do *what,* under what *circumstances.* In a very real sense, the leader may have to play multiple roles, acting in different ways at different times and/or for various subordinates.

This very point of view—that leaders and subordinates exert reciprocal influences upon each other—is the thesis of the *vertical dyad* model (Graen, 1976; Graen & Cashman, 1975). The leader is here perceived as entering into a dyadic (two-person) relationship with each subordinate. Each dyad requires a certain amount of accommodation. The leader's effectiveness is thus seen to depend upon his/her flexibility in perceiving and adapting to subordinate characteristics (Graen & Schiemann, 1978).

To permit more specificity in outlining leader strategies, we need to limit some of the potential variations in circumstances, people, and tasks. Therefore, we address the remainder of this discussion to strategies of leadership for a particular purpose: that is, to involve subordinates in the decision-making process. The evidence that the effectiveness of such "participative" decision making is situational (Vroom, 1976) led Vroom and Yetton (1973) to formulate their prescriptive or normative model of leadership. This model prescribes the particular courses of action to be taken by leaders under particular circumstances.

The model begins by classifying the strategies available to a leader for encouraging group participation in decision making. It then outlines a set of rules specifying the circumstances under which each strategy will be maximally effective.

Taxonomy of strategies

Vroom and Yetton conceive of three primary classes of strategies: autocratic (A), consultative (C), and group (G). Although these strategies may each require the leader to act with some measure of consideration and structure initiation, the autocratic strategy allows the leader most clearly to initiate structure and the consultative strategy capitalizes most heavily on the dimension consideration. These basic strategies, with their variations, are described in Table 15–1.

Rules for selecting the strategy

Vroom and Yetton's model is designed to help a leader make a rational choice from among the alternative decision-making strategies. They see

TABLE 15–1
Decision processes for groups: A taxonomy

AI	You solve the problem or make the decision yourself using the information available to you at the present time.
AII	You obtain any necessary information from subordinates, then decide on a solution to the problem yourself. You may or may not tell subordinates the purpose of your questions or give information about the problem or decision you are working on. The input provided by them is clearly in response to your request for specific information. They do not play a role in the definition of the problem or in generating or evaluating alternative solutions.
CI	You share the problem with the relevant subordinates individually, getting their ideas and suggestions without bringing them together as a group. Then *you* make the decision. This decision may or may not reflect your subordinates' influence.
CII	You share the problem with your subordinates in a group meeting. In this meeting you obtain their ideas and suggestions. Then, *you* make the decision, which may or may not reflect your subordinates' influence.
GII	You share the problem with your subordinates as a group. Together you generate and evaluate alternatives and attempt to reach agreement (consensus) on a solution. Your role is much like that of chairman, coordinating the discussion, keeping it focused on the problem, and making sure that the critical issues are discussed. You can provide the group with information or ideas that you have but you do not try to "press" them to adopt "your" solution and are willing to accept and implement any solution that has the support of the entire group.

Source: V. H. Vroom and A. C. Jago, "On the Validity of the Vroom-Yetton Model," *Journal of Applied Psychology*, 63: p. 152. Copyright 1978 by the American Psychological Association. Reprinted by permission.

three classes of outcomes which influence the ultimate effectiveness of a decision, two of which (solution quality and solution acceptance) are already familiar to you from your reading of Chapter 14.

1. The *quality* or rationality of the decision.
2. The *commitment* or acceptance of subordinates to execute the decision effectively.
3. The *amount of time* required to make the decision.

Vroom and Yetton have developed seven rules for selecting a strategy, three which protect decision quality and four which promote acceptance by subordinates (see Table 15–2). Although there are no rules for the time dimension, this variable plays a significant role at a later stage in the model.

Applying the rules

Vroom and Yetton have developed questions and a flow chart to help a manager apply these rules to a particular situation. These questions and the flow chart are given in Figure 15–6.

The manager starts at the left hand side of the flow chart and works toward the right. Depending upon the answer to Question A, the flow chart directs the manager either to Question D or Question B, and so on, ultimately reaching one of 18 possible terminal points. The number at this terminal point indicates which of the decision strategies apply to the particular situation.

As shown in Figure 15–6, the flow chart sometimes terminates in more than one feasible strategy. This is where the time variable becomes important. The alternative to be selected in such cases is the one that minimizes the time expended. This is referred to as the *minimum man-hours rule*. When a choice between strategies is permitted, applying this rule leads to selecting the most autocratic (and, therefore, the least participative) procedure. Thus, for problem type 14, CII would be selected since consultation is generally faster than group decisions. The minimum man-hours rule tends to emphasize short-run consequences (Vroom, 1976). The benefits of utilizing a long-term approach that emphasizes participative decision making without minimizing decision time has also been suggested (Vroom & Jago, 1974).

The example given in Figure 15–7 illustrates how the normative model can be applied to a specific case.

Research

Thousands of managers have been presented with standardized problems and asked what methods (e.g., AI, CII) they would use to solve them. The major finding from this line of research is that there is a much larger proportion of managers who change their methods to fit the demands of the situation than there are managers who apply one style to fit all situations (Vroom

TABLE 15–2
Rules underlying the normative model

Rules to protect the quality of the decision

1. The leader information rule:
    If the quality of the decision is important and the leader does not possess enough information or expertise to solve the problem by himself, then AI is eliminated from the feasible set.

2. The goal congruence rule:
    If the quality of the decision is important and subordinates are not likely to pursue the organization goals in their efforts to solve this problem, then GII is eliminated from the feasible set.

3. The unstructured problem rule:
    In decisions in which the quality of the decision is important, if the leader lacks the necessary information or expertise to solve the problem by himself, and if the problem is unstructured, the method of solving the problem should provide for interaction among subordinates likely to possess relevant information. Accordingly, AI, AII, and CI are eliminated from the feasible set.

Rules to protect the acceptance of the decision

4. The acceptance rule:
    If the acceptance of the decision by subordinates is critical to effective implementation and if it is not certain that an autocratic decision will be accepted, AI and AII are eliminated from the feasible set.

5. The conflict rule:
    If the acceptance of the decision is critical, an autocratic decision is not certain to be accepted and disagreement among subordinates in methods of attaining the organizational goal is likely, the methods used in solving the problem should enable those in disagreement to resolve their differences with full knowledge of the problem. Accordingly, under these conditions, AI, AII, and CI, which permit no interaction among subordinates and therefore provide no opportunity for those in conflict to resolve their differences, are eliminated from the feasible set. Their use runs the risk of leaving some of the subordinates with less than the needed commitment to the final decision.

6. The fairness rule:
    If the quality of the decision is unimportant but acceptance of the decision is critical and not certain to result from an autocratic decision, it is important that the decision process used generate the needed acceptance. The decision process used should permit the subordinates to interact with one another and negotiate over the fair method of resolving any differences with full responsibility on them for determining what is fair and equitable. Accordingly, under these circumstances, AI, AII, CI, and CII are eliminated from the feasible set.

7. The acceptance priority rule:
    If acceptance is critical, not certain to result from an autocratic decision, and if subordinates are motivated to pursue the organizational goals represented in the problem, then methods that provide equal partnership in the decision-making process can provide greater acceptance without risking decision quality. Accordingly, AI, AII, CI, and CII are eliminated from the feasible set.

Note: See Table 15–1 for a description of AI, AII, CI, CII, and GII.
Source: V. H. Vroom and A. C. Jago, "On the Validity of the Vroom-Yetton Model," *Journal of Applied Psychology* 63 (1978): p. 153.

FIGURE 15-6
Decision-process flow chart for group problems

A. Is there a quality requirement such that one solution is likely to be more rational than another?
B. Do I have sufficient information to make a high-quality decision?
C. Is the problem structured?
D. Is acceptance of decision by subordinates critical to effective implementation?
E. If I were to make the decision by myself, is it reasonably certain that it would be accepted by my subordinates?
F. Do subordinates share the organizational goals to be attained in solving this problem?
G. Is conflict among subordinates likely in preferred solutions?
H. Do subordinates have sufficient information to make a high-quality decision?

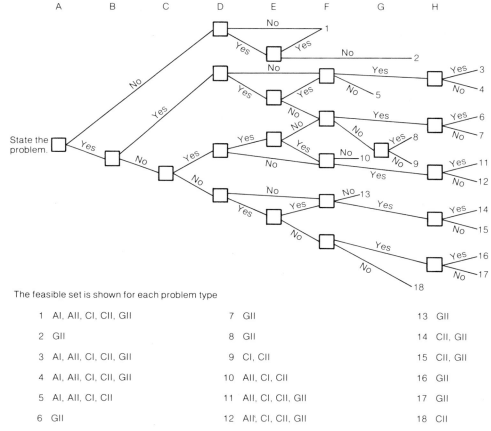

The feasible set is shown for each problem type

1 AI, AII, CI, CII, GII	7 GII	13 GII
2 GII	8 GII	14 CII, GII
3 AI, AII, CI, CII, GII	9 CI, CII	15 CII, GII
4 AI, AII, CI, CII, GII	10 AII, CI, CII	16 GII
5 AI, AII, CI, CII	11 AII, CI, CII, GII	17 GII
6 GII	12 AII, CI, CII, GII	18 CII

FIGURE 15–7
Application of the normative model to a case

You are the head of a staff unit reporting to the vice president of finance. He has asked you to provide a report on the firm's current portfolio including recommendations for changes in the selection criteria currently employed. Doubts have been raised about the efficiency of the existing system in the current market conditions, and there is considerable dissatisfaction with prevailing rates of return.

You plan to write the report, but at the moment you are quite perplexed about the approach to take. Your own specialty is the bond market, and it is clear to you that a detailed knowledge of the equity market, which you lack, would greatly enhance the value of the report. Fortunately, four members of your staff are specialists in different segments of the equity market. Together, they possess a vast amount of knowledge about the intricacies of investment. However, they seldom agree on the best way to achieve anything when it comes to the stock market. While they are obviously conscientious and knowledgeable, as well as concerned with the welfare of the organization, they have major differences when it comes to investment philosophy and strategy.

You have six weeks before the report is due. You have already begun to familiarize yourself with the firm's current portfolio and have been provided by management with a specific set of constraints that any portfolio must satisfy. Your immediate problem is to come up with some alternatives to the firm's present practices and select the most promising for detailed analysis in your report.

Analysis based on Figure 15–6

Question A (quality?)—Yes
Question B (leader's information?)—No
Question C (structured?)—No
Question D (acceptance?)—No
Question F (goals?)—Yes
Question H (subordinates' information?)—Yes

     Problem type—14
     Feasible set—CII, GII
     Minimum man-hours solution—CII

Source: Reprinted from *Leadership and Decision Making* by Victor H. Vroom and Philip W. Yetton, pp. 42–43, by permission of the University of Pittsburgh Press. © 1973 by University of Pittsburgh.

& Yetton, 1973). Thus, as Vroom and Yetton contend, it makes more sense to talk about participative and autocratic *situations* rather than participative and autocratic *managers*.

More recently (Vroom & Jago, 1978), 96 managers were first taught the different decision strategies. After this, they were asked to describe two problem-solving situations they faced on their jobs, one handled successfully, the other unsuccessfully. Each manager specified the decision strategy used for each problem and rated the overall effectiveness of the outcome.

The managers were then taught how to apply the prescriptive model to analyze their problems so that they could determine whether they did or did not solve the problems as the model suggests. Comparing the strategy actually used with that prescribed by the model supported the model's validity.

Those problems which the managers regarded as successfully handled frequently had been resolved using the strategy suggested by the model. Conversely, those situations which the managers felt were handled unsuccessfully were shown, through this postmortem analysis, largely to have employed the wrong strategy. Furthermore, Jago and Vroom (1980), using this same data, concluded that the normative model explains more variance in decision criteria than alternative models.

Assuming the model is valid, can managers be trained through analyzing cases to apply the appropriate strategy to real situations? This question has thus far been addressed only indirectly. Managers have been found to respond to written problem cases in much the same way that they have responded to similar situations in real life (Jago & Vroom, 1978). A direct test of transfer from case analysis and training to managerial behavior on the job is still needed.

Concluding note

The prescriptive model is the closest approximation to a coherent, trainable set of strategies whereby leaders can deal effectively with one of their major functions: decision making. Vroom and Yetton have packaged into their model many of the elements considered by leadership theorists to be important. The strategies reflect the two major leadership dimensions. Strategies are matched to circumstances, taking into account such factors as subordinate acceptance of organizational goals and features of the work group environment (cohesion, relevant information available to the participants). Also, the model recognizes the need to optimize performance outcomes (quality, acceptance, cost-effectiveness as reflected in time).

The model was not intended to (and does not) prescribe strategies for accomplishing leadership functions other than decision making. Without minimizing the importance of this particular leadership role, we must be clear that effective leadership also entails such things as scheduling, planning, encouraging and evaluating performance, developing subordinates' skills, resolving interpersonal conflicts, and so on. However, research on leadership is thriving (Mitchell, 1979). Further refinements in the theories described in this chapter combined with new information yet to be generated will, we expect, permit further clarification of effective leadership strategies.

BY WAY OF INTEGRATION: A BACKWARD GLANCE

A pause to take stock of where we have come thus far is in order before moving on to the next cluster of chapters on Organizational Dynamics. Chapters 12 through 15 have approached Organizational Psychology first from the perspective of the individual participant (Chapters 12 and 13), and then from the perspective of groups of individuals (Chapters 14 and 15). We began by discussing motivation and job satisfaction as individual variables, and followed those chapters with ones on group behavior and leadership. Our present concern for leadership allows us to call attention to some of the threads which have permeated the discussion thus far.

Leadership and motivation. As you have seen, the path-goal theory of leadership regards as effective those leader behaviors which increase subordinate motivation. Therefore it is not surprising that this theory grew out of the expectancy theory of motivation. One of the leader's roles, in path-goal terms, is to increase the three major components of individual motivation (using the expectancy theory framework): $E \rightarrow P$, $P \rightarrow O$, and valence.

Although the connections are perhaps less obvious, all of the motivational theories presented in Chapter 12 have implications for leader behavior. Goal theory, for example, implies that performance goals must be clearly and specifically established at high but acceptable levels in order to maximize motivation and performance. Who is to be responsible for setting goals in this fashion and insuring their acceptance? There is evidence (already cited) that the leader can contribute constructively and effectively to this process. Furthermore, as was noted in Chapter 12, supportive behavior by the supervisor is critical to goal attainment once the goals have been established.

Leadership and job satisfaction. The relationship between leader behavior, employee productivity, and employee attitudes was a major finding of the early Hawthorne studies. The consistent body of evidence accumulated thereafter has led every job-satisfaction theorist to include leadership (and supervision) as critical determinants of satisfaction and dissatisfaction. Furthermore, two dimensions of leadership—consideration and initiating structure—have been demonstrated to be especially critical to employee attitudes. Employees prefer to work with considerate supervisors who are supportive and employee-centered (as opposed to hostile and job-centered). Both high-consideration supervisors and low-structure supervisors have lower turnover and grievance rates than do their opposing counterparts.

Leadership and group behavior. When a team performs poorly the baseball manager or football coach is fired. As a society, we hold the leader responsible for the quality of subordinate performance.

There is good reason for doing so. Think back to the discussion of the Tavistock Institute coal mining study (Chapter 14). When coal was mined using the short wall method requiring that leaders select their work mates, productivity and satisfaction were high. However, following institution of the long wall method, which drastically altered the quality of supervisor-subordinate relationships, productivity and satisfaction plummeted.

As we noted in the discussion of group problem solving, some person or persons generally need to take leadership responsibilities in order to insure the group's success. The leader facilitates effective performance of both task and maintenance activities, and timely as well as successful implementation of the group's solution once it is developed.

SUMMARY

As a society, we place much emphasis on the leader's responsibility for group action. The earliest systematic research sought to identify a set of traits inevitably linked to successful leadership. This line of research was not particularly fruitful; leaders in different kinds of situations possess quite different characteristics.

This realization led Fiedler to develop his contingency model of leadership. The basic proposition of the model is that effective leadership is a joint function of a leadership characteristic (least preferred co-worker score—LPC) and situational characteristics (leader-member relations, task structure, and leader-position power). The major predictions of the contingency model are: (1) Low-LPC leaders will be more effective in situations that are both very favorable and unfavorable to the leader in terms of the situational characteristics. (2) High-LPC leaders will be more effective in situations of moderate favorability than in situations of either high or low favorability. Fiedler and his associates have developed a training program, *Leader Match,* to help apply the contingency model. The research on the model has created a heated debate. It seems reasonable to conclude that there is substantial research support for the contingency model but that it may need to be revised or expanded.

The Ohio State leadership studies demonstrate that there are two basic dimensions of leadership behavior: consideration and initiating structure. Consideration reflects the degree to which a leader's behavior indicates respect for subordinates' ideas, mutual respect, and warmth. Initiating structure reflects the degree to which supervisors are likely to define both their role and those of their subordinates with respect to organizational goal attainment. The research on these two dimensions tends to show that they account for a large proportion of the variance in leadership behavior. It also tends to indicate that high-consideration supervisors have subordinates who are more satisfied and less likely to be absent. Not surprisingly, recent research has indicated that high and low scores on these two dimensions may be mediated by situational factors.

Path-goal theory has two basic propositions: (1) The leader functions to increase subordinate motivation and job satisfaction. (2) The motivational impact of specific leader behaviors (e.g., consideration and structure initiation) is determined by the situation in which the leader functions. Two classes of situational variables, subordinate characteristics and environmental forces, are hypothesized to influence the extent to which subordinate motivation can be increased by leader behavior. The research findings on the path-goal theory provide stronger support for predictions about consideration than about initiating structure and stronger support for predictions about satisfaction than about performance.

Vroom and Yetton's normative model is designed to help a leader make a rational decision about which of the alternative decision-making methods is best suited to the demands of the situation. The model identifies three classes of outcomes which influence the ultimate effectiveness of a decision: quality, acceptance, and amount of time. They have developed seven rules for leaders to follow to protect both the quality and acceptance of a decision, and a flow chart to help apply these rules to a particular problem situation. The initial research on the normative model is encouraging.

The chapter concluded by integrating the content of this chapter with that presented in the previous three chapters.

REFERENCES

Barrow, J. C.   The variables of leadership: A review and conceptual framework. *Academy of Management Review,* 1977, *2,* 231–251.

Chemers, M. M., & Skrzypek, G. J.   An experimental test of the contingency model of leadership effectiveness. *Journal of Personality and Social Psychology,* 1972, *24,* 172–177.

Downey, H. K., Sheridan, J. E., & Slocum, J. W.   Analysis of relationships among leader behavior, subordinate job performance and satisfaction: A path-goal approach. *Academy of Management Journal,* 1975, *18,* 253–262.

Downey, H. K., Sheridan, J. E., & Slocum, J. W.   The path-goal theory of leadership: A longitudinal analysis. *Organizational Behavior and Human Performance,* 1976, *16,* 156–176.

Evans, M. G.   The effects of supervisory behavior on the path-goal relationship. *Organizational Behavior and Human Performance,* 1970, *5,* 277–298.

Fiedler, F. E.   *A theory of leadership effectiveness.* New York: McGraw-Hill, 1967.

Fiedler, F. E.   *Leadership.* Morristown, N.J.: General Learning Press, 1971.

Fiedler, F. E.   A rejoinder to Schriesheim and Kerr's premature obituary of the contingency model. In J. G. Hunt & L. L. Larson (Eds.), *Leadership: The cutting edge.* Carbondale: Southern Illinois University Press, 1977.

Fiedler, F. E.   The contingency model and the dynamics of the leadership process. In L. Berkowitz (Ed.), *Advances in experimental social psychology* (Vol. 11). New York: Academic Press, 1978.

Fiedler, F. E., Chemers, M. M., & Mahar, L.   *Improving leadership effectiveness: The leader match concept.* New York: Wiley, 1976.

Fleishman, E. A.   The description of supervisory behavior. *Journal of Applied Psychology,* 1953, *38,* 1–6.

Fleishman, E. A.   The leadership opinion questionnaire. In R. M. Stogdill & A. E. Coons (Eds.), *Leader behavior: Its description and measurement.* Columbus: Bureau of Business Research, Ohio State University, 1957.

Fleishman, E. A.   Twenty years of consideration and structure. In E. A. Fleishman & J. G. Hunt (Eds.), *Current developments in the study of leadership.* Carbondale: Southern Illinois University Press, 1973.

Fleishman, E. A., & Harris, E. F.   Patterns of leadership behavior related to employee turnover and grievance. *Personnel Psychology,* 1962, *15,* 43–56.

Fleishman, E. A., Harris, E. F., & Burtt, H. E.   *Leadership and supervision in industry.* Columbus: Ohio State University, Personnel Relations Board, 1955.

Ghiselli, E. E. *Explorations in managerial talent.* Pacific Palisades, Calif.: Goodyear, 1971.

Graen, G. Role making processes within complex organizations. In M. D. Dunnette (Ed.), *Handbook of industrial and organizational psychology.* Chicago: Rand McNally, 1976.

Graen, G., Alvares, K. M., Orris, J., & Martella, J. Contingency model of leadership effectiveness: Antecedent and evidential results. *Psychological Bulletin,* 1970, *74,* 285–296.

Graen, G., & Cashman, J. F. A role making model of leadership in formal organizations: A developmental approach. In J. G. Hunt & L. L. Larson (Eds.), *Leadership frontiers.* Carbondale: Southern Illinois University Press, 1975.

Graen, G., Dansereau, F., & Minami, R. Dysfunctional leadership styles. *Organizational Behavior and Human Performance,* 1972, *7,* 216–236.

Graen, G., & Schiemann, W. Leader member agreement: A vertical dyad linkage approach. *Journal of Applied Psychology,* 1978 *63,* 206–212.

Greene, C. N. Questions of causation in the path-goal theory of leadership. *Academy of Management Journal,* 1979, *22,* 21–41.

Halpin, A. W., & Winer, B. J. A factorial study of the leader behavior descriptions. In R. M. Stogdill & A. E. Coons (Eds.), *Leader behavior: Its description and measurement.* Columbus: Ohio State University, Bureau of Business Research, 1957.

Hemphill, J. K., & Coons, A. E. Development of the leader behavior description questionnaire. In R. M. Stogdill & A. E. Coons (Eds.), *Leader behavior: Its description and measurement.* Columbus: Ohio State University, Bureau of Business Research, 1957.

House, R. J. A path-goal theory of leadership effectiveness. *Administrative Science Quarterly,* 1971, *16,* 321–338.

House, R. J., & Dessler, G. The path-goal theory of leadership: Some post hoc and a priori tests. In J. G. Hunt & L. L. Larson (Eds.), *Contingency approaches to leadership.* Carbondale: Southern Illinois University Press, 1974.

House, R. J., & Mitchell, T. R. Path-goal theory of leadership. *Journal of Contemporary Business,* 1974, *3,* 81–97.

Jago, A. G., & Vroom, V. H. Predicting leader behavior from a measure of behavioral intent. *Academy of Management Journal,* 1978, *21,* 715–722.

Jago, A. G., & Vroom, V. H. An evaluation of two alternatives to the Vroom/Yetton normative model. *Academy of Management Journal,* 1980, *23,* 347–354.

Kerr, S., Schriesheim, C. A., Murphy, C. J., & Stogdill, R. M. Toward a contingency theory of leadership based upon consideration and initiating structure literature. *Organizational Behavior and Human Performance,* 1974, *12,* 62–82.

Konar-Goldband, E., Rice, R. W., & Monkarsh, W. Time-phased interrelationships of group atmosphere, group performance, and leader style. *Journal of Applied Psychology,* 1979, *64,* 401–409.

Mann, R. D. A review of the relationships between personality and performance in small groups. *Psychological Bulletin,* 1959, *56,* 241–270.

Miles, R. H., & Petty, M. M. Leader effectiveness in small bureaucracies. *Academy of Management Journal,* 1977, *20,* 238–250.

Mitchell, T. R.   Organizational behavior. *Annual Review of Psychology,* 1979, *30,* 243–281.

O'Reilly, C. A., & Roberts, K. H.   Supervisor influence and subordinate mobility aspirations as moderators of consideration and initiating structure. *Journal of Applied Psychology,* 1978, *63,* 96–102.

Schriesheim, C. A., & Kerr, S.   Theories and measures of leadership: A critical appraisal of current and future directions. In J. G. Hunt & L. L. Larson (Eds.), *Leadership: The cutting edge.* Carbondale: Southern Illinois University Press, 1977.

Stogdill, R. M.   *Manual for the Leader Behavior Description Questionnaire—Form XII.* Columbus: Ohio State University, Bureau of Business Research, 1963.

Stogdill, R. M.   *Handbook of leadership.* New York: Free Press, 1974.

Vecchio, R. P.   An empirical examination of the validity of Fiedler's model of leadership effectiveness. *Organizational Behavior and Human Performance,* 1977, *19,* 180–206.

Vroom, V. H.   Leadership. In M. D. Dunnette (Ed.), *Handbook of industrial and organizational psychology.* Chicago: Rand McNally, 1976.

Vroom, V. H., & Jago, A. G.   Decision making as a social process: Normative and descriptive models of leader behavior. *Decision Sciences,* 1974, *5,* 743–769.

Vroom, V. H., & Jago, A. G.   On the validity of the Vroom-Yetton Model. *Journal of Applied Psychology,* 1978, *63,* 151–162.

Vroom, V. H., & Yetton, P. W.   *Leadership and decision making.* Pittsburgh, Pa.: University of Pittsburgh Press, 1973.

Weissenberg, P., & Kavanaugh, M.   The independence of initiating structure and consideration: A review of the evidence. *Personnel Psychology,* 1972, *25,* 119–130.

ORGANIZATIONAL DYNAMICS

part C

chapter 16

Organizational Theories

In contemporary American society, large organizations such as the federal government, the AFL–CIO, General Motors, and Exxon have a profound influence on our daily lives. Modern civilization seems to require extremely large numbers of people working together to produce our goods and services. The dominance of large organizations is a relatively recent historical development, occurring during this century.

The present chapter focuses on two broad theoretical approaches to understanding organizations: the classical and the modern. These two approaches are very different in emphasis. Their differences will become apparent when you have completed reading the following descriptions.

CLASSICAL THEORY

During the first half of the 20th century, several authors including Taylor (1911), Fayol (1929), Mooney and Reiley (1939), and Weber (1947), presented their principles and theories of how organizations should be designed in order to function efficiently and effectively. Although these theorists lived in different parts of the world, the principles of organization they advocated were so similar in many respects that their basic approach is now referred to as classical organization theory.

Four basic concepts of classical theory are: (*a*) division of work, (*b*) delegation of authority, (*c*) chain of command, and (*d*) span of control. Each of these is an integral part of contemporary organizations and must be understood before one can begin to comprehend how they operate.

Division of work

Organizations typically are divided into departments (like marketing, advertising, human resources, accounting, and so on), each with specified areas of responsibility. It is up to the department heads and their subordinates to complete tasks assigned to their department. In order to achieve a coordinated and effective group effort, the department heads organize their teams by dividing them into levels and functions.

The division into levels is referred to as the *scalar process* and is depicted in Figure 16–1. The term scalar process comes from the scale of authority and responsibility that is created. Figure 16–1 depicts a department with three levels: head, supervisory, and employee. Heads of departments have more authority and responsibility than their supervisors, who correspondingly have more authority and responsibility than their employees.

FIGURE 16–1
Division of work into levels: The scalar process

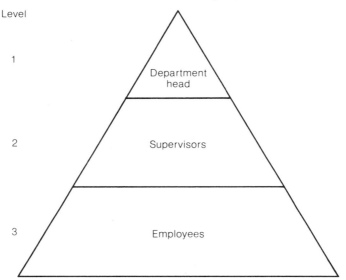

Not only is the department scaled into levels, but the work being performed is divided into different kinds of duties. This is referred to as functionalization or specialization and is depicted in Figure 16–2. This figure indicates that there are eight employees in the department, each assigned a specific job.

A simple sports illustration classifies the distinction between scalar process levels and functionalization. On a baseball team the difference between

FIGURE 16–2
Division of work into duties: Functionalization

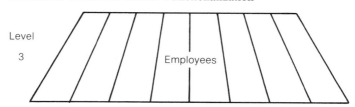

the manager, the coaches, and the players is scalar while the difference between the pitcher, shortstop, left fielder, and catcher is functional. Therefore, in Figure 16–1, the top level could represent the manager of the team, the second level the coaches, and the lowest level the players. Similarly, in Figure 16–2, the eight boxes could represent the first baseman, second baseman, shortstop, and so on.

Figure 16–3 is a chart of a typical department in an organization. It combines both the scalar process and functionalization. If the department manager is operating effectively, all the work has been allocated and assignments do not overlap.

FIGURE 16–3
A departmental chart

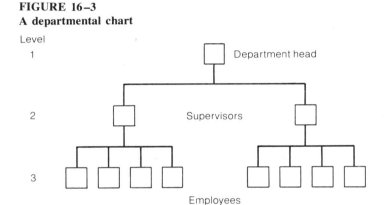

Delegation of authority

In the department depicted in Figure 16–3, the head delegates assignments, responsibilities, and duties to each of the supervisors who in turn delegate to each of their employees. By delegating to the supervisors, the department heads can accomplish things that they do not personally have the time or energy to complete.

Since department heads retain the ultimate responsibility for performance, fear of subordinate failure makes delegation very difficult for many managers. However, the reality of managing requires delegation, hence the primary source of management failure is either insufficient or inappropriate delegation.

Classical organization theory assumes that the person doing the delegating will also lay out specific guidelines, rules, and procedures for the subordinates to follow. Little freedom of action is left to the subordinates.

Chain of command

The hierarchy of levels in scalar structures implies a chain of command. There are typically seven levels in the chain of command: board of directors, president, vice president, division manager, unit manager, first-level supervisor, and operator. The chain of command influences patterns of relationships, by imparting social status, power, and authority.

Span of control

Span of control is the number of subordinates a manager supervises. As far back as Moses in the Old Testament, there was a realization that there is a limit to the number of subordinates a manager can handle effectively. The typical span of control in contemporary organizations is between 5 and 15 subordinates, but in some industries a span as large as 100 exists. Some factors that influence the optimum span of control are the similarity of the tasks, the proximity of the workers, and the type of technology employed.

Figure 16-4 depicts two organizations, each with 37 employees. One has a maximum span of control of six individuals while the other has a maximum span of three. The smaller the span of control, the greater the number of levels the organization tends to have and the taller it becomes. Conversely, with a greater span of control, there are fewer levels and consequently the organization becomes flatter. For example, in Figure 16-4, organization A has six levels in its hierarchy while organization B has only three levels.

A tall organizational structure encourages closer cooperation and control because each manager works with only a few people. However, the number of levels a communication must travel is great, thereby increasing the probability of misunderstandings and misinterpretations. Conversely, a flatter structure permits a simpler communication chain, but the manager has so many subordinates to supervise that he cannot spend much time with any individual. Whereas classical theorists sought to find the ideal span of control, we now recognize that its optimum size depends on many other organizational and individual variables.

For example, Woodward's (1965) research investigated the relationship between the type of production technology employed and several characteristics of organizations, including span of control. She classified the organizations into three categories based on the production technology employed. The results of her research, with respect to span of control are summarized in Table 16-1. The *job-order production* firms produced custom-made articles or small batches of a specialty product according to the specifications of the customer. The *mass production* firms made large batches of a standardized product on an assembly line. The *process production* firms were characterized by highly automated, continuous-flow production of substances such as gases or liquid chemicals. Table 16-1 indicates substantial differences in both the chief executive's span of control and the first-line supervisor's span of control, based on the category of production technology employed. Woodward's findings also indicated that the most successful firms in each category tended to have spans of control close to the

FIGURE 16–4
Span of control in two organizations employing 37 individuals

A. Maximum span of control is 3 employees

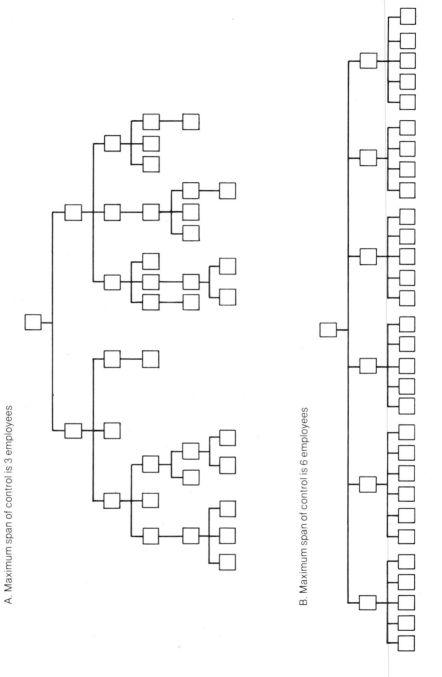

B. Maximum span of control is 6 employees

TABLE 16–1
Relationship between span of control and production technology

	Job-order production firms	Mass production firms	Process production firms
Median span of control of chief executives	4	7	10
Median span of control of first-line supervisors	23	48	15

Source: J. Woodward, *Industrial Organization: Theory and Practice* (New York: Oxford University Press, 1965).

medians indicated in Table 16–1 while the least successful firms tended to depart more from those medians.

Critique

Although the above brief description does not do justice to the richness of classical organization theory, it does cover the highlights and allows us to point out certain weaknesses and omissions.

Bennis (1959) summed up the overriding deficiency of classical theory: It designs organizations without regard to people. The classicists created beautiful structures that would appear to function perfectly in an environmental vacuum. Furthermore, the classical principles are presented as pronouncements although they lack an empirical foundation (Simon, 1945).

Argyris (1970) sees the following consequences of classically designed organizations for lower-level employees:

1. The perception that few of their abilities will be used.
2. A tendency to experience a sense of dependence upon their supervisors.
3. A tendency to manifest a low degree of responsibility because of their realization that someone else will tell them what to do, how well to do it, when to do it, etc.
4. High levels of absenteeism, turnover, anger toward the top, and trade unionism.

He also presented the consequences of classically designed organizations for managerial level employees. They are a low level of:

1. Openness to new ideas, feelings, and values.
2. Experimenting and risk taking.
3. Receiving and giving nonevaluative feedback.

Although classical theory seems now to rest on an extremely simplistic view of human behavior, we note that information recently acquired about motivation, job satisfaction, cognition, leadership, and so on was not avail-

able to them (March & Simon, 1958). Further, they could not possibly anticipate the degree of influence presently exerted upon organizations by such
external forces as regulatory agencies and consumer groups.

MODERN THEORIES

Contemporary theorists stress the importance of the individual and as a
result are more humanistic in their approach than were the classicists. Motivation, leadership, and job satisfaction are important concepts to a contemporary theorist.

We present summaries of three representative approaches: McGregor,
Likert, and Lawrence and Lorsch.

McGregor: Theory X and Theory Y

McGregor published his major work *The Human Side of Enterprise* in
1960. In it, McGregor presents two sets of managerial assumptions, Theory
X and Theory Y. As you will shortly see, these two sets of assumptions are at
opposite ends of a continuum. Unfortunately, many have misinterpreted
McGregor's writings as indicating that these are the only possible sets of
managerial assumptions (McGregor, 1967).

Theory X: The traditional view of direction and control. McGregor indicates that there is one set of managerial assumptions about workers that is so
pervasive that it underlies most supervisory actions. This set of assumptions
is seen as being consistent with the principles of classical organization
theory. McGregor calls these assumptions Theory X and he refers to managers who act consistently with them as Theory X managers. Although it is
doubtful that many managers would agree that they subscribe to these assumptions, McGregor claims that most employees feel that they are supervised by individuals who are Theory X in approach. The three Theory X
assumptions are (McGregor, 1960, pp. 33–35):

1. "The average human being has an inherent dislike of work and will
avoid it if he can." McGregor maintains that the stress placed by management on a "fair day's work" and the evils of output restriction reflect the
underlying belief that the average worker is lazy and therefore tries to work
as little as possible. Theory X managers perceive that the evidence for this
assumption is overwhelming.

2. "Because of this human characteristic of dislike of work, most people
must be coerced, controlled, directed, threatened with punishment to get
them to put forth adequate effort toward the achievement of organizational
objectives." Theory X managers feel that the promise of reward is not sufficiently strong to overcome the fundamental dislike of work. Hence the threat
of a punishment, such as that of employment termination, is necessary to
achieve reasonable levels of productivity.

3. "The average human being prefers to be directed, wishes to avoid responsibility, has relatively little ambition, wants security above all." This viewpoint assumes the mediocrity of the masses; Theory X managers bemoan the low quality of their workers.

Theory X managers focus on the reinforcements provided through wages and job tenure, both of which relate only to the workers' physiological and safety needs. You may recall from Chapter 12 that Maslow's need-hierarchy theory states that once these lower-level needs are satisfied, the social and egoistic needs assume added importance. However, Theory X managers tend to minimize these higher-level needs and provide little opportunity for them to be satisfied on the job.

McGregor addresses a classic counterargument sometimes made by management. This argument states that it is virtually impossible to gratify higher-level needs (such as status or personal recognition) for most employees on their job because they are unwilling to work efficiently. In McGregor's view, when employees are reluctant to cooperate with management in the attainment of organizational goals, this reluctance is attributable to management rather than employee deficiencies. He points out that the rewards offered by Theory X managers (pay, fringe benefits, and so on) are useful to workers only when they leave their jobs and go home. Wages or medical benefits are useless to an employee while he is on the job. Therefore, it is reasonable to expect that by thwarting ego needs, work is perceived as a source of punishment rather than reward. To the extent that work is perceived as an evil that must be endured to provide for subsequent pleasures *off* the job, it is not surprising that some workers attempt to do as little of it as they can.

McGregor acknowledges that this analysis of management may appear unduly harsh and that the lot of the industrial employee has been greatly improved during the 20th century. Management has become more humanitarian and equitable. However, he insists that this has been done without any fundamental change in management's assumptions about the wants and needs of its employees. He stresses that a different set of assumptions about workers must replace Theory X if present conditions are to be improved further.

Theory Y: The integration of individual and organizational goals. McGregor designates a contrasting managerial philosophy as Theory Y. The six Theory Y assumptions are based on Maslow's need-hierarchy theory of motivation (McGregor, 1960, pp. 47–48):

1. "The expenditure of physical and mental effort in work is as natural as play or rest." This assumption implies that people do not inherently dislike work. Rather, depending upon conditions over which management has control, work may be perceived as satisfying and voluntarily performed or dissatisfying and avoided whenever possible.

2. "External control and the threat of punishment are not the only means for bringing about effort toward organizational objectives. Man will

exercise self-direction and self-control in the service of objectives to which he is committed."

3. "Committment to objectives is a function of the rewards associated with their achievement." If the rewards provided at work result in the satisfaction of the egoistic and self-fulfillment needs, then the workers will direct their efforts toward organizational objectives.

4. "The average human being learns, under proper conditions, not only to accept but to seek responsibility."

5. "The capacity to exercise a relatively high degree of imagination, ingenuity, and creativity in the solution of organizational problems is widely, not narrowly distributed in the population."

6. "Under the conditions of modern industrial life, the intellectual potentialities of the average human being are only partially utilized."

These assumptions have very different implications for management than do those of Theory X. Theory Y implies that collaboration between labor and management is possible, while Theory X assumptions offer management an easy rationalization for organizational failures.

The central principle of organization derived from Theory X is the scalar principle: that is, direction and control through the use of authority. In contrast, the central principle derived from Theory Y is *integration:* that is, the creation of conditions such that organizational members can best achieve their own goals through helping the organization realize its objectives. The principle of integration implies that an organization will be more effective in achieving its economic objectives if it makes significant adjustments to the needs and goals of its members.

Putting Theory Y into practice. The Scanlon Plan is the most widely known organizational strategy for attaining integration between organizational and employee needs. The plan devised by Scanlon, an associate of McGregor, implements a philosophy of management consistent with Theory Y and the principle of integration (Lesieur, 1958). The two important features of this plan are cost-reduction sharing and effective participation.

Improvements in organizational effectiveness and consequent economic gain resulting from employee suggestions are shared with the employees. The method for *sharing cost-reduction savings* requires the development of a ratio between the organization's total manpower costs and a measure of output, like total sales. This ratio is derived after considerable study and is generally unique to that particular organization. Improvement of the ratio, representing an economic gain to the organization, is shared with the employees on a monthly basis.

Taken alone, the cost-reduction sharing feature of the Scanlon Plan is simply a form of incentive or profit sharing. The distinctive feature of the plan is that it provides, in addition, a mechanism whereby all the organizational members can contribute to organizational efficiency. In so doing, it provides opportunities for all the members to satisfy their higher-level needs through efforts directed toward organizational (rather than external) objectives.

Effective participation is implemented through a committee structure with representation from all organizational groups and levels. The function of these committees is to discuss and critically evaluate all suggestions for improving the organizational effectiveness ratio. Membership is rotated, thereby giving everyone in the organization a chance to serve as a committee member. Departmental committees of workers and lower-level supervisors have the authority to immediately implement ideas appropriate to their level. Suggestions which have broad organizational implications are referred to higher-level screening committees consisting of representatives of both workers and management. Minutes of all meetings are kept to insure that ideas are never lost and that the screening committee is aware of the actions taken throughout the organization.

McGregor claims that in Scanlon Plan companies participation is significantly greater than that obtained from conventional suggestion plans. He attributes this to the absence of impersonal suggestion boxes and remote committees evaluating worker ideas. In the Scanlon Plan, individuals present their ideas in their own work setting or at a screening committee meeting. Then, in the individual's presence, the idea is discussed and evaluated. If the idea is accepted, the individual is reinforced for the contribution to the company. If not, the individual is often encouraged to seek help from others in the company in order to improve the original idea. McGregor claims that in a Scanlon Plan company a climate is created which encourages individuals to work together to develop ideas rather than one which encourages secrecy to prevent someone from stealing the idea and getting the reward for himself/herself. Individuals are encouraged to cooperate rather than compete for monetary rewards. The economic gains from an employee's suggestions are shared with other employees while providing the worker with considerable satisfaction of social and ego needs.

Evaluation. McGregor's contributions to the field of organizational psychology are those of a formulator of theory and not those of a validator of theory. He did not empirically test his theoretical positions. Despite the absence of strong research support for McGregor's theories, he has had a significant impact on contemporary management thought. *The Human Side of Enterprise* has been credited with helping turn management thinking around in the last two decades toward a more humanistic viewpoint. Furthermore, McGregor is credited with being the first to identify the dichotomy between the modern organization theory viewpoint (Theory Y) and the classical approach (Theory X).

The one derivative of his writing that has been subjected to research is the Scanlon Plan. Much of the early research purporting to demonstrate favorable organizational outcomes following the plan's installation has been criticized methodologically (Frost, Wakeley, & Ruh, 1974). However, a recently conducted analysis is very supportive (White, 1979). White conducted his research in 23 companies, 12 of which had abandoned the plan, presumably because they regarded it as unsuccessful. Based upon his data and that collected in previous evaluative studies, he concludes that the Scanlon Plan succeeds in organizations with Theory Y rather than Theory X orientations.

Likert: Four-system organizational typology

Likert served as the director of the University of Michigan's Institute of Social Research for over 25 years. Since the late 1940s, the institute has conducted numerous studies that have contrasted the best and poorest units within an organization with respect to such variables as leadership style, communication, and group process. Although the institute's program is still active, two major works summarize its research and provide a theoretical integration: *New Patterns of Management* (Likert, 1961) and *The Human Organization* (Likert, 1967).

The empirical bases.   The theoretical formulations follow from two lines of research which we will describe separately. The first consists of studies of specific variables (for example, communication and employee loyalty in the organization context). The second derives from analysis of the results of large-scale administrations of an attitude survey, the *Survey of Organizations.*

Two representative studies will serve to indicate something of the scope and direction taken in research on specific organizational variables, one on superior-subordinate communication, and the other on work-group loyalty.

The first was a study of perceived communication patterns in a public utility company (Mann, cited in Likert, 1961) that generated the results shown in Table 16–2. This table reveals marked discrepancies between supervisors' and subordinates' perceptions about the effectiveness of the

TABLE 16–2
Extent to which superiors and subordinates agree as to whether superiors tell subordinates in advance about changes

Always tell subordinates in advance about changes which will affect them or their	Top staff says as to own behavior	Foremen say about top staff's behavior	Foremen say as to own behavior	Men say about foremen's behavior
work	70% ⎫	27% ⎫	40% ⎫	22% ⎫
Nearly always tell subordinates	30 ⎭ 100%	36 ⎭ 63%	52 ⎭ 92%	25 ⎭ 47%
More often than not tell ...	—	18	2	13
Occasionally tell	—	15	5	28
Seldom tell	—	4	1	12

Source: R. Likert, *New Patterns of Management* (New York: McGraw-Hill, 1961), p. 52. Reprinted by permission.

communication process; the former perceived the communication process as more effective than the latter. Such findings are probably not unique to this particular company.

The second study tested, and refuted, a proposition derived from Theory X assumptions which suggest a fundamental schism between loyalty to the work group and loyalty to the organization. As shown in Figure 16–5, closely

FIGURE 16–5
Relationship between peer-group loyalty and attitude toward superior

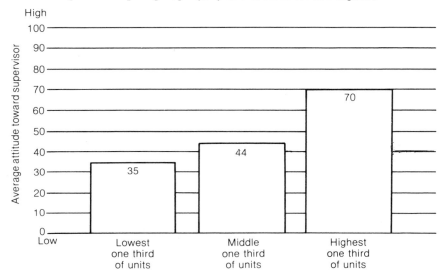

Units grouped by peer-group loyalty score

Source: R. Likert, *New Patterns of Management* (New York: McGraw-Hill, 1961), p. 33. Reprinted by permission.

knit industrial work groups (high peer-group loyalty) tend to hold more favorable attitudes toward their supervisor than do work groups with low peer loyalty (Seashore, 1954). Instead of banding together in opposition to the supervisor, as suggested by the assumptions of Theory X, closely knit work groups are likely to perceive their boss and presumably, the organization in which they work more favorably.

The periodically updated *Survey of Organizations* form has been administered during the last decade to tens of thousands of employees. Results from these administrations furnished much of the data which led to the development of Likert's organizational typology. Three sample items and a portion of the instructions are reproduced in Figure 16–6.

Organizational typology. Based on both types of research described above, Likert has classified organizations into four categories for theoretical purposes: System 1 (exploitative authoritative), System 2 (benevolent au-

FIGURE 16–6
Sample survey feedback questionnaire items

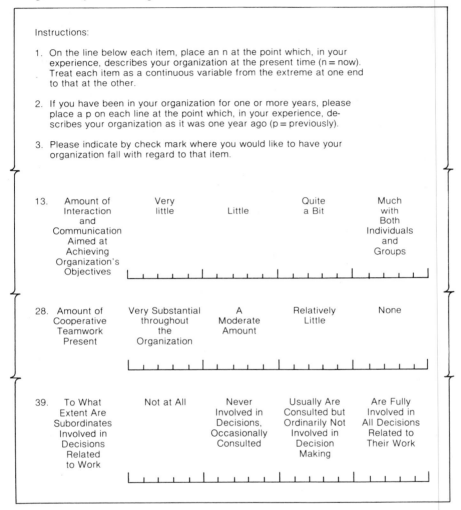

Instructions:

1. On the line below each item, place an n at the point which, in your experience, describes your organization at the present time (n = now). Treat each item as a continuous variable from the extreme at one end to that at the other.

2. If you have been in your organization for one or more years, please place a p on each line at the point which, in your experience, describes your organization as it was one year ago (p = previously).

3. Please indicate by check mark where you would like to have your organization fall with regard to that item.

13. Amount of Interaction and Communication Aimed at Achieving Organization's Objectives

| Very little | Little | Quite a Bit | Much with Both Individuals and Groups |

28. Amount of Cooperative Teamwork Present

| Very Substantial throughout the Organization | A Moderate Amount | Relatively Little | None |

39. To What Extent Are Subordinates Involved in Decisions Related to Work

| Not at All | Never Involved in Decisions, Occasionally Consulted | Usually Are Consulted but Ordinarily Not Involved in Decision Making | Are Fully Involved in All Decisions Related to Their Work |

Source: Adapted from R. Likert, *The Human Organization* (New York: McGraw-Hill, 1967), pp. 197–211. Reprinted by permission.

thoritative), System 3 (consultative) and System 4 (participative group) Table 16–2 summarizes some of the essential distinctions between these four systems of organization. As shown in this table, System 1 organizations have a Theory X orientation while System 4 organizations have a Theory Y orientation. Likert's System 2 and 3 organizations lie somewhere in between on a Theory X-Theory Y continuum. Table 16–3 summarizes Likert's description of the four systems and his expectations for the quality of performance in each one. These expectations were developed from empirical research.

TABLE 16–3
Organizational and performance characteristics of different management systems based on a comparative analysis

Operating characteristics	System of organization			
	Exploitative authoritative (System 1)	*Benevolent authoritative (System 2)*	*Consultative (System 3)*	*Participative group (System 4)*
1. Character of motivational forces				
a. Underlying motives tapped	Physical security, economic security, and some use of the desire for status	Economic and occasionally ego motives	Economic, ego, and other major motives	Full use of economic, ego, and all other major motives
b. Kind of attitudes developed toward organization and its goals	Attitudes usually are hostile and counter to organization's goals	Attitudes are sometimes hostile and counter to organization's goals and are sometimes favorable to these goals	Attitudes may be hostile but more often are favorable and support behavior implementing organization's goals	Attitudes generally are strongly favorable and provide powerful stimulation to behavior implementing organization's goals
2. Character of communication process				
a. Amount of interaction and communication aimed at achieving organizational objectives	Very little	Little	Quite a bit	Much with both individuals and groups

3. Character of decision making				
a. At what levels in organization are decisions formally made?	Bulk of decisions at top of organization	Policy at top, many decisions within prescribed framework made at lower levels	Broad policy and general decisions at top, more specific decisions at lower levels	Decision making widely done throughout organization, although well-integrated through linking processes provided by overlapping groups
4. Character of interaction-influence process				
a. Amount of cooperative teamwork	None	Virtually none	A moderate amount	Very substantial amount throughout the organization
5. Performance characteristics				
a. Productivity	Mediocre	Fair to good	Good	Excellent
b. Excessive absence and turnover	Tends to be high when people are free to move	Moderately high when people are free to move	Moderate	Low

Source: Adapted from R. Likert, *New Patterns of Management* (New York: McGraw-Hill, 1961), pp. 223–233. Reprinted by permission.

However, this research has not been sufficiently comprehensive to accept the expectations as statements of fact.

System 4 organizations. It is clear from Table 16–3 that Likert believes that System 4 is the most effective organizational system. He regards three principles as fundamental to the development and maintenance of such participative organizations: (1) supportive relationships, (2) group decision making, and (3) high performance goals.

System 4 organizations genuinely attempt to insure *supportive interpersonal interactions* among their members. Such supportive interactions enhance each organizational member's sense of personal worth and add importance to the attainment of organizational goals (Likert, 1961). Although this principle can be used to guide all interpersonal relationships within an organization, its application is especially crucial in superior-subordinate relationships. The supervisor can encourage employee commitment to organizational objectives by enhancing the latter's sense of individual contribution to the successful attainment of organizational goals. As noted by Likert, this principle can only be implemented with regard for the employee's values, expectations, and background. The entire notion of *support* rests upon a perceptual phenomenon reflecting these values and expectations. What is viewed by one employee as supportive may well be viewed by another as punitive. Differences in background variables may generate a considerable discrepancy between what the supervisor perceives as supportive and what the employee perceives as supportive. This is perhaps most evident in, but certainly not limited to, instances where the supervisory-subordinate relationship involves persons of different races, sexes, vastly different educational backgrounds, and so on.

We have already noted (Table 16–3) differences in decision making and interaction patterns within the four organizational systems posited by Likert. These differences are further clarified in Figure 16–7 which schematically summarizes interactions with two different organizational structures. The man-to-man model shown in that figure is the traditional one characteristic of System 1 and System 2 organizations. This is essentially a hierarchical, or chain-of-command structure with progressive delegation of authority to successively lower levels of the organizational hierarchy.

In contrast, a group pattern of organization (Figure 16–7B) involves subordinates at each level of the organizational hierarchy in making and implementing the decisions that affect their own work group. Obviously, some mechanism is required to ensure coordination of the decisions and efforts of each of these work groups toward the attainment of *organizational* goals. This mechanism is provided by the "linking-pin" structure (see Figure 16–8) suggested for System 4 organizations. Each linking pin is both a supervisor of one work group and a subordinate in another (next higher level) work group. Linking-pin individuals are thus the key persons insuring adequate communication throughout the organization and, while representing their subordinates, are fully accountable to their supervisor for the effectiveness of decisions made and their execution within the group.

FIGURE 16–7
Man-to-man and group patterns of organization

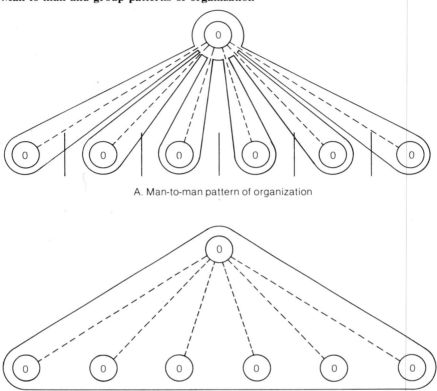

A. Man-to-man pattern of organization

B. Group pattern of organization

Source: R. Likert, *New Patterns of Management* (New York: McGraw-Hill, 1961), p. 107. Reprinted by permission.

The third fundamental principle of System 4 organization is that it *expects high levels of performance* from its members. This expectation must not be management's expectation alone; all employees at all levels must share and be committed to the goal of high performance. Likert (1967) postulates that this shared expectation of superior performance will follow from the development of supportive relationships and the involvement of the group members in decisions affecting them.

Evaluation.   Likert's theoretical views are much more heavily grounded in empirical research than McGregor's. However, support for many of his key positions is minimal. For example, Table 16–3 states that a System 4 organization is characterized by high productivity and low absenteeism and turnover while the opposite is true of a System 1 organization. The primary support for this position is a study by Marrow, Bowers, and Seashore (1967) which is described in detail in Chapter 18. In this research, a financially

FIGURE 16–8
The linking pin

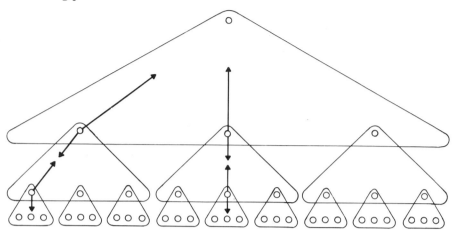

Arrows indicate the linking pin function

Source: R. Likert, *New Patterns of Management* (New York: McGraw-Hill, 1961), p. 113. Reprinted by permission.

distressed authoratative organization was transformed in two years into a profitable consultative one. However, the change in managerial style and philosophy was only one of a series of major organizational changes occurring at about the same time (e.g., improved selection and training, altered work procedures). Exactly what part the change in managerial systems played is difficult to assess, although it appears to have been considerable.

However, seemingly contrary to Likert's theoretical views, there exist scores of large, relatively authoritarian, U.S. corporations that are extremely successful. In addition, there are some participative organizations that have gone bankrupt. Therefore, even with support from the Marrow, Bowers, and Seashore study, much more research is needed to evaluate the validity of Likert's theoretical positions.

The above paragraphs were not intended to minimize Likert's contribution. He has provided organizational psychology with a much-needed, broad theoretical framework within which research can be integrated and understood. Many of his concepts such as linking pin and supportive relationships are now established parts of modern organization theory and the Institute for Social Research's *Survey of Organizations* which he helped develop, has been used extensively for research and improving organizational effectiveness.

Lawrence and Lorsch: Contingency theory

Lawrence and Lorsch (1969) proposed a contingency theory of organizational design that is based on their own findings and those of their predecessors in the area of comparative organizational structure (e.g., Burns & Stalker, 1961; Woodward, 1965). Before describing contingency theory, a review of previous findings will be presented. Burns and Stalker (1961) studied 20 organizations whose products and services were very different from each other. They found two basic types of organization structure, "mechanistic" and "organic," which in their pure form are postulated to be end points on a continuum.

The *mechanistic* structure was found in organizations that operated in a relatively stable external environment. Mechanistic organizations were characterized by well-defined procedures, rules, and roles, vertical communication, small span of control, top management control, clear job descriptions, and a high degree of task specialization. Therefore, these organizations closely followed the prescriptions of the classical organization theorists.

Organic organizations were found where there were less stable environmental conditions. These organizations were characterized by more open and less rigid systems. There was more lateral communication, and larger spans of control. Leadership and decision-making responsibilities were not as centered at the top, and more emphasis was placed on reaching consensus and using consultative management.

Woodward's (1965) research (parts of which were described previously) builds nicely on the work of Burns and Stalker. She found that successful mass-production firms tended to have mechanistic structures consistent with classical organization theory prescriptions while successful job-order production firms tended to have more open and flexible organic structures.

Premises.   Lawrence and Lorsch's contingency theory is based upon three premises:

1.   There is no one best way to design an organization.
2.   The design of an organization must fit its environment.
3.   The needs of the individuals in the organization are satisfied better to the degree that the organization is properly designed.

In contrast with the early classical emphasis on developing the one "best" structure, Lawrence and Lorsch seek to describe the form of organizational structure for a particular type of company or industry that would help it to maximize its ability to cope with a changing environment. They stress that the ideal structure for an organization changes over time in response to changing environmental conditions. This approach is a contingency theory because the optimal organizational structure is presumed to be contingent upon environmental factors.

Basic theoretical concepts.   Lawrence and Lorsch's theory has two basic theoretical concepts: differentiation and integration.

Differentiation is defined as the difference in cognitive and emotional orientations of the managers in the various parts of the organization. The dimensions of differentiation include:

1. *Formality of structure.* The extent to which an organization's subunits have different rules and procedures.
2. *Interpersonal orientation.* The degree of concern about people as opposed to tasks in various parts of the organization.
3. *Time orientation.* How quickly different units of the organization need to react to environmental pressures.
4. *Goal orientation.* The degree of similarity in goals of the various subunits of the organization.

Integration is defined as the quality of the state of collaboration among the subunits of an organization that are required to work closely together because of environmental demands. That is, integration is the degree of cooperation and coordination that is required. The greater the interdependence of the subunits, the more integration is required.

In order to achieve integration, the conflicts between departments that have been caused by differentiation must be resolved. The higher the level of differentiation, the more difficult integration is to achieve. This is because subunits with different goals, time orientations, etc., naturally find it more difficult to coordinate their efforts.

Lawrence and Lorsch theorize that different environmental conditions require different levels of differentiation and integration. More specifically, they theorize that in highly dynamic environments, organizational effectiveness requires a high degree of both differentiation and integration. However, in relatively stable fields, effective organizations require less differentiation but still need a high level of integration.

From this, it follows that it is precisely the organizations that require high differentiation that, at the same time, also require high integration. Therefore, some organizations must work extremely hard to attain high levels of both of these antagonistic processes if they are to be successful in their fluid environments.

Research. In their research, Lawrence and Lorsch studied a total of ten organizations in three different industries: plastics, containers, and packaged foods. These particular industries were chosen because they fell at diverse points on an environmental stability continuum. The container industry was in a relatively stable unchanging environment, while the plastics industry was in a highly volatile, quickly changing external environment. The packaged-foods industry fell approximately in the middle of this continuum.

Interviews and questionnaires were employed to obtain information from various managerial levels about the structure of the organization, its environment, and its degree of success in its field. The findings are complex, and will be presented in two sections.

1. *Organizational effectiveness and environmental fit.* The results in this area were highly supportive of the theoretical predictions. Of the six organizations in the highly unstable environment of the plastics industry, two were very successful, two moderately successful, and the remaining two were

poor performers. As predicted, the two highly successful organizations were found to have the highest degrees of both differentiation and integration while the two poorest performers were lowest on both of these dimensions. The two companies in the container industry, characterized by a stable environment, were direct competitors. As predicted, the more successful organization had a higher degree of integration but both had about equal levels of differentiation. The results in the packaged-food organizations were not totally clearcut, but were supportive of the theory. The higher-performing organization had higher levels of both differentiation and integration.

2. *Characteristics of successful organizations.* Lawrence and Lorsch found that successful organizations in stable environments used fewer and more conventional strategies to achieve integration than successful organizations in fluid environments. For example, the most frequently used integration strategy in the container industry was the conventional strategy of direct managerial contact. This is a reasonable finding, since the container industry requires a relatively low level of differentiation. Therefore, managers in different divisions can communicate relatively easily since their orientations are quite similar.

In fluid environments, direct managerial contact is not as beneficial because the degree of required differentiation is very high. Thus, organizations in the plastics industry use other mechanisms, some unconventional, to supplement direct managerial contact. Some organizations utilize an individual or a group of individuals to integrate the various divisions of the organization, such as production, sales, and research. Successful integrators were found to be individuals who are able to keep a balance between the orientations of different divisions. Moreover, the successful integrators tended to rely on their competence and expertise while the unsuccessful integrators tended to rely on the power of their position in the organization.

An important aspect of the integrator's success was the mode of conflict-resolution employed. Some integrators used the confrontation or problem solving approach in which organization members are encouraged to openly exchange ideas and information. When this mode is used, the goal is to reach the best solution for the entire organization.

A second mode of conflict resolution is referred to as *smoothing,* an attempt to sweep the problem under the rug. This is not an ideal long-range solution. Since the problem is not solved (and infrequently disappears), it often becomes worse.

A third mode that was employed is forcing a solution through *edicting.* This occurs when one side in a dispute tries to get a superior to make a decision, or an edict, in its favor. Edicting creates separate winners and losers. Not surprisingly, the losers frequently are not committed to carrying out the decision that was imposed on them.

Lawrence and Lorsch found that high-performing organizations tended to prefer the problem-solving, confrontation strategy, while low-performing organizations tended to prefer the less effective smoothing strategy the most, and the edicting strategy only as a last resort.

Huse (1980) has summarized and reviewed most of the recent research on contingency theory. He cites ten research studies that have been performed in various parts of the world in different types of organizations (e.g., large corporations, school systems). The results of this research, taken as a whole, strongly support the contingency theory approach.

For example, Beer (1971) performed an organization-change intervention based on contingency theory. After conducting a six-month diagnosis of a division in an organization, Beer concluded that the problem was poor organization design. The organization existed in a highly unstable environment but was attempting to use classical organizational principles to achieve the needed integration. Beer recommended that the organization structure needed to be changed to fit the environment better. Individuals were selected and trained to be integrators, and project teams were established in order to push the decision-making level down to conform to the Lawrence and Lorsch model. Several different types of training sessions were required to make the transition in the organization work smoothly.

Follow-up procedures were used to evaluate the success of the intervention. Pre- and postmeasures revealed greater use of the confrontation strategy and less use of smoothing. As a result, there was greater commitment to the decisions that were made. In addition, almost twice as many new products were introduced in the year following the intervention as during the year preceding it.

Evaluation. Contingency theory is substantially different from both classical organization theory and the other contemporary approaches in that it posits that there is no one best organization structure. The classicists stressed that rigid rules and bureaucratic structures were best while the modern theorists have emphasized that participative decision making is the best approach. Contingency theory advocates that a fit between the organization and its environment is the best approach to organization design.

As indicated, there is already considerable research support for Lawrence and Lorsch's theory. However, while the support is impressive, the theory is far from being verified. For one thing, the model has been used primarily to analyze the effectiveness of existing organizations. However, as Huse (1980) indicates, not enough work has been performed on (1) *changing* organizations to fit the model and then examining the effects of such changes and (2) *designing* new organizations and then evaluating their effectiveness. Despite these gaps in knowledge at the present time, Lawrence and Lorsch's contingency theory provides the field with an extremely useful framework in which to diagnose and change orientations.

A review of modern organization theory

While classical organization theory has been criticized for designing organizations without regard to people, the modern theorists have also had their share of criticism. For example, Bennis (1959) described the modern theorists as those who studied individuals without organizations. That is, he believed that too great an emphasis was placed on individual needs and not enough on organizational needs. As a result, modern theorists have been described as being too humanistic.

March and Simon (1958) state that the modern theorists have placed a great emphasis on the individual's ability to feel but have minimized his ability to think. Modern theorists have tended to be almost as rigid in their approach to organization design as the classicists were. It is just that newer principles such as supportive relationships and participative decision making have replaced older approaches such as the scalar principle.

These criticisms of the modern theorists are least applicable to Lawrence and Lorsch's contingency theory. Perhaps their approach, or one yet to be developed, will become a basis for integrating the material about organizations summarized in the previous chapters.

The field of organization theory is still in its infancy. While it is beginning to grow in sophistication and beginning to acquire the needed data base, it still has a long way to go.

SUMMARY

Classical organization theorists stress the importance of four concepts—division of work, delegation of authority, chain of command, and span of control. In classical theories, department heads organize their teams by dividing them into levels and functions. The division into levels is called the scalar process while the division into functions is called specialization. Delegation is the assignment of duties, responsibility, and authority to another individual. Classicists emphasize that delegated problems must be solved within strict guidelines which leave little latitude to the subordinate. The hierarchy of levels in an organization results in a chain of command which influences patterns of relationships, and gives social status and power. The span of control is the number of subordinates a manager supervises. Classical theorists were interested in determining the best span of control for organizations. The classicists have been criticized for designing organizations without regard to people's needs. They appear to have created beautiful structures that work perfectly on paper but have considerably more difficulty in changing environmental conditions.

Modern organization theories developed largely as a reaction to the classical approach. Modern theories stress the importance of the individual and such concepts as motivation, leadership, and group processes.

McGregor presented two antagonistic sets of managerial assumptions: Theory X and Theory Y. The Theory X approach, referred to as the traditional view of direction and control, stresses that individuals dislike work and must be coerced to perform it. McGregor claims most contemporary managers are Theory X in approach. Theory X managers focus on salary and job security. The central principle of Theory X is the scalar principle that advocates the use of authority as a means of control. Theory Y, referred to as the integration of individual and organization goals, stresses that work is natural and can be a source of satisfaction if it allows individuals to satisfy their own needs on the job. The central principle of Theory Y is integration which is the creation of conditions such that organization members can best attain their own goals by directing their efforts toward the success of the enterprise. The Scanlon Plan, which is based on cost-reduction sharing and effective participation is the most well-known strategy for attaining integration.

Based largely upon an empirical foundation generated by researchers at the University of Michigan's Institute for Social Research, Likert has classified organizations into a four-system typology. A System 1, or exploitative-authoritative organization, has a Theory X orientation while a System 4, or participative organization, has a Theory Y approach. System 2 and 3 organizations lie on a continuum between these two extremes. System 4 organizations are typified by supportive relationships, group decision making, linking pins, and high performance expectations. Likert theorizes that System 4 organizations should have the highest productivity and the lowest absenteeism and turnover. There is only a very modest amount of research to support this theorizing.

Lawrence and Lorsch's contingency theory is based upon three principles: (1) There is no one best way to design an organization. (2) The design of an organization must fit its environment. (3) The needs of the individuals in the organization are satisfied better to the degree that the organization is properly designed. They describe organizations in terms of two basic concepts: differentiation and integration. Differentiation is the difference in cognitive and emotional orientation among managers in various parts of the organization. Integration is the degree of cooperation and coordination required within the organization. Lawrence and Lorsch theorize that different environmental conditions require different levels of differentiation and integration. For example, they state that in fluid environments high degrees of both differentiation and integration are required but in stable environments less differentiation is necessary. There is a considerable amount of research support for the contingency theory.

REFERENCES

Argyris, C. *Intervention theory and method: A behavioral science view.* Reading, Mass.: Addison-Wesley, 1970.

Beer, M. Organizational diagnosis, an anatomy of poor integration. Paper presented at the meeting of the American Psychological Association. Washington, D.C., 1971.

Bennis, W. G. Leadership theory and administrative behavior: The problem of authority. *Administrative Science Quarterly,* 1959, *4,* 259–301.

Burns, T., & Stalker, G. M. *The management of innovation*. London: Tavistock, 1961.

Fayol, H. *General and industrial management* (J. A. Conbrough, Trans.). Geneva: International Management Institute, 1929.

Frost, C. F., Wakeley, J. H., & Ruh, R. A. *The Scanlon Plan for organization development: Identity, participation, and equity*. East Lansing: Michigan State University Press, 1974.

Huse, E. F. *Organization development and change* (2nd ed.). St. Paul: West, 1980.

Lawrence, P. R., & Lorsch, J. *Organization and environment: Managing differentiation and integration*. Homewood, Ill.: Irwin, 1969.

Lesieur, F. (Ed.). *The Scanlon Plan*. New York: Wiley, 1958.

Likert, R. *New patterns of management*. New York: McGraw-Hill, 1961.

Likert, R. *The human organization*. New York: McGraw-Hill, 1967.

March, J. G., & Simon, H. A. *Organizations*. New York: Wiley, 1958.

Marrow, A., Bowers, D. G., & Seashore, S. E. *Management by participation*. New York: Harper & Row, 1967.

McGregor, D. *The human side of enterprise*. New York: McGraw-Hill, 1960.

McGregor, D. *The professional manager*. New York: McGraw-Hill, 1967.

Mooney, J. D., & Reiley, A. C. *Onward industry*. New York: Harper, 1939.

Seashore, S. E. *Group cohesiveness in the industrial work group*. Ann Arbor, Mich.: Institute for Social Research, 1954.

Simon, H. A. *Administrative behavior*. New York: Macmillan, 1945.

Taylor, F. W. *The principles of scientific management*. New York: Harper & Bros., 1911.

Weber, M. *The theory of social and economic organization* (A. M. Henderson & T. Parsons, Trans.). New York: Oxford University Press, 1947.

White, J. K. The Scanlon Plan: Causes, and correlates of success. *Academy of Management Journal*, 1979, *22*, 292–312.

Woodward, J. *Industrial organization: Theory and practice*. New York: Oxford University Press, 1965.

chapter 17

Organization Development Technologies

Organizations have short- and long-range goals. Under the management of an executive team, the strengths of an organization are mobilized and directed toward attaining these objectives.

As behavioral scientists began intervening in organizations, they started to develop techniques for helping the total organization overcome impediments to goal attainment. These techniques, although sometimes based on previous theory and research, more generally reflected attempts by creative practitioners to solve organization problems (Beer, 1976). The initial efforts of these pioneering practitioners were received very favorably by organizational decision makers and led to further interventions by applied behavioral scientists. As a result, there now exists a considerable variety of technologies, largely developed within the past 15 years, for intervening in, changing, and developing organizations. This led to the creation of a new field within I/O psychology called *organization development* (OD).

WHAT IS OD?

OD has been defined in several ways. The most frequently cited definition is that *OD* "is an effort (1) *planned,* (2) *organization-wide,* and (3) *managed* from the top, to (4) increase *organization effectiveness* and *health* through (5) *planned interventions* in the organization's 'processes' using *behavioral-science* knowledge" (Beckhard, 1969, p. 9).

Beer and Huse (1972) are critical of the ideas that OD must be planned and managed from the top. While they agree that, at least, top management should not be opposed to OD, they maintain that OD cannot be so thoroughly planned that a complete blueprint is laid out in advance. A definition more compatible with this view is:

"Organization development is concerned with the deliberate, reasoned, introduction, establishment, reinforcement, and spread of change for the purpose of improving an organization's effectiveness and health" (original source unknown, cited in Huse, 1980, p. 23).

TABLE 17–1
Some principles underlying OD

Principles regarding individuals

1. Individuals have needs for personal growth and development. These needs are most likely to be satisfied in a supportive and challenging environment.
2. Most workers are underutilized and are capable of taking on more responsibility for their own actions and of making a greater contribution to organizational goals than is permitted in most organizational environments. Therefore, the job design, managerial assumptions, or other factors frequently *demotivate* individuals in formal organizations.

Principles regarding people in groups

1. Groups are highly important to people, and most people satisfy their needs within groups, especially the work group. The work group includes both peers and the supervisor and is highly influential on the individual within the group.
2. Work groups, as such, are essentially neutral. Depending on its nature, the group can be either helpful or harmful to the organization.
3. Work groups can greatly increase their effectiveness in attaining individual needs and organizational requirements by working together collaboratively. In order for a group to increase its effectiveness, the formal leader cannot exercise all of the leadership functions at all times and in all circumstances. Group members can become more effective in assisting one another.

Principles regarding people in organizations

1. Since the organization is a system, changes in one subsystem (social, technological, or managerial) will affect other subsystems.
2. Most people have feelings and attitudes which affect their behavior, but the culture of the organization tends to suppress the expression of these feelings and attitudes. When feelings are suppressed, problem solving, job satisfaction, and personal growth are adversely affected.
3. In most organizations, the level of interpersonal support, trust, and cooperation is much lower than is desirable and necessary.
4. Although win-lose strategies can be appropriate in some situations, many win-lose situations are dysfunctional to both employees and the organization.
5. Many personality clashes between individuals or groups are functions of organizational design rather than of the individuals involved.
6. When feelings are seen as important data, additional avenues for improved leadership, communications, goal setting, intergroup collaboration, and job satisfaction are opened up.
7. Shifting the emphasis of conflict resolution from edicting or smoothing to open discussion of ideas facilitates both personal growth and the accomplishment of organizational goals.
8. Organizational structure and the design of jobs can be modified to more effectively meet the needs of the individual, the group, and the organization.

Source: Reproduced by permission from *Organizational Development and Change,* second edition, pp. 29–30, by Edgar F. Huse, Copyright © 1980, West Publishing Company. All rights reserved.

In this definition, *effectiveness* refers to setting and attaining appropriate goals in an environment that is changing, while *health* refers to the motivation, utilization, and integration of the human resources within the organization.

Finally, Lundberg (1974) has suggested the simplest way of describing OD. He states that OD promotes asking two questions—"Where are we now?" and "Where would we like to be?"—and that it offers a number of ways in which members can move their organizations toward the desired state.

Although these three definitions are somewhat different, they all have in common that OD: (*a*) is a process for change and (*b*) can be beneficial both to the organization and its members. As we will see shortly, there are several very different OD technologies, but all are consistent with these definitions.

Since the field of OD draws heavily on the areas of motivation theory, personality theory, leadership theory, and organization theory, it is based on a number of their principles, which are summarized in Table 17–1 on the preceding page. Many of these principles follow from the material presented in earlier chapters.

AN EXAMPLE OF OD

The following case history based upon one of the author's experience illustrates many of the characteristics of an OD intervention.

The executive director of a metropolitan hospital retired and the board of directors hired a replacement to manage the hospital. Soon after starting on the job, the new executive director realized that there were organizational problems within the hospital. Whereas he envisioned a structure similar to that depicted on the organization chart, with four relatively coequal division directors, he found an organization dominated entirely by the director of nursing.

The new executive director attempted to restore a balance between the divisions by reducing the power of the director of nursing. He was unsuccessful in his attempt and, as a result, he terminated her employment.

He subsequently actively recruited throughout the country for a top-notch director of nursing, and hired one after screening numerous applicants. This woman was selected both because of her personal compatibility with the executive director and her high level of nursing expertise.

In an attempt to reduce the power of the position of the director of nursing, the executive director created five new positions, called *coordinators*. The coordinators were directly subordinate to the director of nursing on the hospital's organization chart, but each was responsible for certain functions formerly allocated to the director. Five head nurses with considerable experience and respect throughout the hospital were promoted to these new positions.

Two years later, the original imbalance of power within the hospital was remedied. The four division directors got along and worked together very well. However, another problem surfaced: the morale within the nursing division appeared to be poor. Turnover was very high and rumblings of dissatisfaction were continually reaching the executive director. Aside from the high financial cost of the turnover, there were times when there were insufficient nursing personnel to provide a satisfactory level of patient care.

This problem was sufficiently serious that the executive director of the hospital and the director of nursing jointly decided outside intervention was needed. They felt they did not possess the skills necessary either to diagnose or correct the problems in the nursing division. An organizational psychologist was consulted.

Although he felt that it would be desirable to work also with the hospital's other divisions, he determined that nursing was almost autonomous. Thus, he felt that improvements in this one division would make an important contribution to raising the level of patient care within the hospital.

The consultant began by having individual interviews with the executive director, the director of nursing, and the five coordinators. He found them all in essential agreement and this gave him a clear understanding of the situation. The consultant determined that when the coordinators were promoted to this position, they were told to be "managers of their head nurses." However, no one explained what this meant or provided any training for them.

As you might expect, there were no adequate job descriptions for the position. This entire situation left the coordinators immensely frustrated.

The consultant also interviewed the head nurses in groups, with all the head nurses under each coordinator being interviewed together. These meetings initially were ventilation sessions.

The head nurses wanted to meet with all the coordinators to "let them have it." After discussing the potential benefits and risks of a joint meeting with all the nurses involved, everyone agreed it was desirable and it was arranged.

Prior to this meeting, the consultant conducted several sessions with the coordinators and the director of nursing as a group, and with the 15 head nurses as a group. The consultant stressed the importance of making the upcoming joint meeting a constructive one instead of merely a gripe session. To help accomplish this goal, he presented and demonstrated principles of effective group communication and problem solving. The joint meeting took place only after the groups had practiced these techniques through solving actual hospital problems.

This two-hour meeting proved to be extremely productive. Many problems and misunderstandings were cleared up and a constructive climate was achieved. Group-problem-solving meetings were then set up on a once to twice a month schedule for each coordinator-head nurse team. The several problems that surfaced in these sessions were largely solved by the nursing staff itself. The OD consultant led the first few meetings and then assumed a much more unobtrusive role as different nurses were trained to conduct the meetings. These problem-solving meetings were evaluated periodically and continued for about two years.

Occurring simultaneously with the group-problem-solving meetings was a project to write job descriptions for the nursing staff. Under the supervision of the nursing director and with input from the consultant, first job descriptions and then performance standards were established. These job descriptions enabled the coordinators to learn their role within the hospital and greatly reduced their frustrations and the dissatisfaction of the head nurses. The performance standards enabled all the nurses to obtain meaningful feedback on their performance.

In order to determine the effectiveness of the intervention, four different types of criterion measures were obtained: (1) The amount of turnover was calculated periodically. (2) An attitude survey was constructed and administered periodically to all nurses. (3) The patients were sent a survey after they left the hospital in order to determine their perceptions of the quality of care they received. (4) The physicians were surveyed to determine the level of patient care delivered. The four measures showed considerable improvement over the two years.

The success of the nursing intervention was well received throughout the hospital. As a result, all the directors of divisions and the executive director requested additional services from the consultant. They wanted to know what the consultant could do for the hospital as a whole. In order to determine this, the consultant interviewed all the directors and many other management personnel before making several recommendations for further OD. These recommendations were fully discussed and then several were implemented with some major modifications suggested by the management staff. First, an attitude-survey program was designed and implemented throughout the hospital. The survey was used as a vehicle to assess the internal health of the hospital as an organization, and to pinpoint current and potential problem areas. This survey program revealed several problem areas for which intervention programs were designed. In addition, a management training program was installed to develop the supervisory talent of the staff. Both of these programs continued for several years. As a result of the OD intervention, the hospital continually developed and matured as an organization.

OD TECHNOLOGIES

As you will see shortly, several OD technologies were used to implement the illustrative intervention. Many such technologies are available to the practitioner and researcher. As a result, there have been several recent attempts to classify them (Blake & Mouton, 1976; Bowers, Franklin, & Pecorella, 1975; French & Bell, 1978; Harrison, 1970; White & Mitchell, 1976).

We have selected White and Mitchell's (1976) OD model as a way to conceptualize the approaches to OD. Their model classifies intervention technologies on three dimensions: recipient of change, level of expected change, and the relationships involved in change. Their model is depicted in Figure 17–1.

FIGURE 17–1
White and Mitchell's model for classifying OD intervention technologies

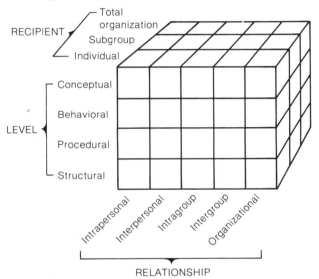

The model is meant to encompass all possible OD technologies. We have selected for discussion only a representative sample of six. A seventh OD technology, the Scanlon Plan, was presented in Chapter 16. Two excellent and comprehensive descriptions of the full range of possible approaches are provided by French and Bell (1978) and Huse (1980).

Laboratory training—sensitivity training

Sensitivity training, or as it is frequently called, *laboratory training* or *T-groups,* is the forerunner of contemporary OD technologies. T-groups were developed by Lewin, Bradford, Benne, and Lippitt and the pioneering sessions were sponsored by the National Training Laboratory (NTL) and conducted in Bethel, Maine, in 1947. Laboratory training is still in use although its popularity is declining in favor of alternative OD technologies.

Description. Laboratory training is difficult to describe because of the many procedural variations employed by different trainers. The following summary is based upon Campbell and Dunnette's (1968) effort to extract common procedural elements.

The heart of laboratory training is the T-group usually comprised of 10 to 15 persons confronted by an unstructured activity. Typically, no topics for discussion and no specific tasks are planned for the group. A trainer is usually present, but he/she tends to reject the leadership role. The trainer may set limits on the length of the meeting and state the objective of the group as "enhancing the understanding of one's own and others' behavior."

T-groups emphasize the "here and now." That is, the behavior displayed in the group by its members is the object of study and discussion. Whereas T-groups explore the feelings and emotions of members at the instant they occur, they tend to reject consideration of past behavior and future problems along with the feelings and emotions associated with these past and future events.

The session is usually initiated with a brief statement by the trainer who then falls silent and, as a rule, refuses to guide the group. The vacuum of silence is often filled with feelings of frustration and hostility. Eventually one or more of the group members attempt to assume leadership and give direction to the group's activity. These attempts become the issue for group study with the objective of enhancing each member's understanding of how he/she affects and is affected by the others in the group.

Given the unstructured group as the primary vehicle and the behavior emitted as the principal topic of conversation, the group's success depends almost entirely on the feedback process. Each participant is encouraged to tell the others how their behavior is seen and interpreted and to describe the feelings generated.

Two elements are considered necessary for the feedback process to be successful. First, a certain amount of anxiety or tension must be generated. Anxiety is generally evoked in the T-group sessions when a participant discovers that his/her previous methods of interaction do not suffice in this new situation. The second prerequisite to effective feedback has been termed *psychological safety* (Schein & Bennis, 1965). A group member must feel that the others in the group will act in a supportive and nonevaluative way when the individual is revealing himself/herself.

The trainer's behavior is crucial to the group's ability to learn to give constructive feedback and to promote psychological support. The trainer serves as a model for the participants to imitate. He/she absorbs feelings of hostility without acting aggressively or becoming defensive. The trainer provides feedback to others and is open and honest in expressing his/her own feelings.

The following is a brief episode from a laboratory training session.

At the fifth meeting the group's feelings about its own progress became the initial focus of discussion. The "talkers" participated as usual, conversation shifting rapidly from one point to another. Dissatisfaction was mounting, expressed through loud, snide remarks by some and through apathy by others.

George Franklin appeared particularly disturbed. Finally pounding the table, he exclaimed, "I don't know what is going on here! I should be paid for listening to this drivel? I'm getting just a bit sick of wasting my time here. If the profs don't put out—I quit!" George was pleased; he was angry, and he had said so. As he sat back in his chair, he felt he had the group behind him. He felt he had the guts to say what most of the others were thinking! Some members of the group applauded loudly, but others showed obvious disapproval. They wondered why George was excited over so insignificant an issue, why he hadn't done something constructive rather than just sounding off as usual. Why, they wondered, did he say their comments were "drivel"?

George Franklin became the focus of discussion. "What do you mean, George, by saying this nonsense?" "What do you expect, a neat set of rules to meet all your problems?" George was getting uncomfortable. These were questions difficult for him to answer. Gradually he began to realize that a large part of the group disagreed with him; then he began to wonder why. He was learning something about people he hadn't known before. "How does it feel, George, to have people disagree with you when you thought you had them behind you?"

Bob White was first annoyed with George and now with the discussion. He was getting tense, a bit shaky perhaps. Bob didn't like anybody to get a raw deal, and he felt that George was getting it. At first Bob tried to minimize George's outburst and then he suggested that the group get on to the real issues; but the group continued to focus on George. Finally Bob said, "Why don't you leave George alone and stop picking on him. We're not getting anywhere this way."

With the help of the leaders, the group focused on Bob. "What do you mean, 'picking' on him? Why, Bob, have you tried to change the discussion?" "Why are you so protective of George?" Bob began to realize that the group wanted to focus on George; he also saw that George didn't think he was being picked on, but felt he was learning something about himself and how others reacted to him. "Why do I always get upset," Bob began to wonder, "when people start to look at each other? Why do I feel sort of sick when people get angry at each other?" . . . Now Bob was learning something about how people saw him, while gaining some insight into his own behavior (Tannenbaum, Weschler, & Massarik, 1961, p. 123).

Laboratory training originally utilized *stranger groups,* that is, participants who did not work for the same organization or know each other beforehand. However, these trainees tended to experience difficulties in the "back-home" situation. When persons returned from the T-group experience, their fellow workers frequently did not understand or appreciate their different behavior patterns. As a result, they often put pressure on them to go back to being their old selves. These difficulties led to the creation of *cousin groups,* composed of individuals from the same organization but working for different supervisors, and *family groups,* supervisors and their subordinates, in an attempt to increase transfer back to the parent organization. These procedures were improvements in that the participants received support and encouragement from some of their co-workers for their newly learned behavior patterns. However, as OD matured, it became clear that a greater impact could be realized by working with the whole organization rather than with isolated individuals or groups. This realization led to the development of newer OD technologies as described later in this chapter.

Goals. After an extensive review of the literature, Campbell and Dunnette (1968) described some of the goals of sensitivity training as follows:

1. To increase self-insight and self-awareness concerning one's own behavior and its impact in a social situation. To learn how other people perceive and interpret one's behavior.
2. To increase one's sensitivity to the behavior of others. To increase one's empathy, that is, the ability to infer accurately what other people are feeling.
3. To increase awareness and understanding of the processes that inhibit and facilitate group function.

Research and critique. The three major review articles on laboratory training (Buchanan, 1969; Campbell & Dunnette, 1968; House, 1967) were published well over a decade ago. However, the conclusions reached by the authors are still valid (Beer, 1976). The reviewers concluded that one group of evaluative studies indicates some support for the position that the participants' self-perceptions improve after attending laboratory training. That is, the participant's "real self" and "ideal self" move closer to each other after attending T-group sessions. Another group of studies tend to indicate that T-groups do induce some behavior change in the back-home setting. Increased flexibility and awareness, greater tolerance of differences, better listening, and less dependence on others are among the changes that have been reported to occur. Beer (1976) and Huse (1980) conclude that the research findings, taken as a whole, offer substantial support for the claim that T-groups have positive outcomes at the individual and perhaps the group level. However, research has not yet clearly established a relationship between attending laboratory training and increased organizational effectiveness or profits (Campbell & Dunnette, 1968; Huse, 1980). Laboratory training, almost from its inception, has been a controversial technique and many criticisms have been directed at it. Some of the most frequent criticisms include the possibility of psychological damage to the participants, possible invasion of privacy, and superficiality of T-group interactions. The blame for these and other deficiencies has been attributed more to trainer incompetence than to the technique itself (Howard, 1972).

Despite the trend to replace laboratory training with more systems-oriented technologies, it is still widely used. The strength of T-groups lies in their ability to modify individual needs, expectancies, skills, and values. However, it is in the transfer of these skills back home that T-groups are weakest (Argyris, 1971).

We like Cooper and Levine's (1978) conclusion: T-groups can be meaningful experiences for certain people under certain circumstances. Since a more satisfying conclusion does not seem possible at this time, there seems to be support neither for those who advocate sensitivity training as the cornerstone of programs for teaching interpersonal skills, nor for those who would prefer to see this strategy eliminated entirely.

Survey feedback

The survey-feedback approach along with laboratory training are the two pioneering OD technologies. Survey feedback was developed at the University of Michigan by Mann (1957, 1961) and his associates. The Institute of Social Research (ISR) at the University of Michigan is constantly updating its survey-feedback instruments and it currently provides survey-feedback services to organizations throughout the country. Over 150,000 individual surveys have been given by the ISR. However, many companies utilize questionnaires developed specifically for them by OD consultants and not those of the ISR.

Description.   Survey feedback is generally a joint effort between the client organization and an OD consultant in developing a questionnaire, using it to collect data about the organization, analyzing the data, interpreting them, and then using the interpretation as the basis for change. It is desirable that members of the client organization be actively involved in developing the attitude-survey questionnaire so that they feel ownership of it. The survey-feedback questionnaire typically contains items on job, company, supervisory and pay satisfaction, leadership, job characteristics such as challenge and autonomy, motivation, decision making, group process, organizational climate, and communication (Bowers & Franklin, 1977).

Three sample items of the type employed in survey-feedback questionnaires were presented in Figure 16–6 (Chapter 16) which you may wish to review. The questionnaire is administered to everyone in the client organization and the responses are then analyzed. If ISR services are utilized, a computer printout of the results is provided for each work group and level of the organization. The results are first presented by the OD consultant to the top management group within the organization.

The top managers are prepared by the OD consultant to conduct data-feedback and discussion meetings with their subordinates. Although the consultant usually attends these meetings, the manager presides. Possible changes to improve current procedures are considered and sometimes implemented immediately. In addition, the group decides how to present the data to the next lower level of the organization. This procedure continues until all members of the organization have an opportunity to participate in the survey-feedback process (Bowers & Franklin, 1977).

The key to successful survey feedback is in providing data relevant to each work group. This encourages work-group members to become involved with the data, and, in turn, should lead them to greater commitment to the change program (Beer, 1976).

Thus, family-group meetings are an essential part of the survey-feedback process. The group meetings put some pressure on the individual members to evaluate their outlook in terms of the group consensus.

In addition, the OD consultant can use the group meeting to help improve the group's problem-solving capabilities. The survey-feedback meeting enables the consultant to obtain useful here-and-now data on the way the group functions (cooperativeness among members, communication, etc.).

Such an analysis and discussion of the way the group handles the feedback phase can itself be a powerful OD technique (Beer, 1976).

Research and critique. The Intercompany Longitudinal Study launched in 1966 was a comprehensive research project conducted by the ISR (Bowers, 1973) to evaluate the effectiveness of the survey-feedback approach. The research was performed in 23 organizations and included almost 15,000 respondents. Repeat measurements were taken yearly. The study compared the effectiveness of laboratory training, a form of process consultation (discussed later), and survey feedback with two types of control groups in which there was no OD. The 16 dependent variables included job satisfaction, organizational climate, and group processes. Bowers concluded that survey feedback was the most effective of the OD technologies. Although the conclusion that survey feedback is the *most* effective of these procedures has been criticized on methodological grounds, there is no question that it is at least a highly effective OD strategy (Passmore, 1976; Huse, 1980).

Grid OD

Blake and Mouton's (1964, 1969, 1978) Grid OD program is the most comprehensive and one of the most widely used of contemporary technologies. Over 200,000 people have attended in-company Grid training sessions. However, very little rigorous evaluative research on Grid OD has been conducted (Huse, 1980). An impetus to the development of Grid OD was the desire to increase the transfer to the back-home situation that plagued laboratory training.

Grid OD is a six-phase program that requires more than three years to implement in an organization. The goal of the Grid OD program is to develop an "ideal strategic corporate model."

The managerial grid. The core of the Grid OD program is Blake and Mouton's Managerial Grid® which rests on a bipolar conceptualization of leadership. The two key dimensions are: (1) concern for production and (2) concern for people. (These are very similar to the dimensions consideration and initiating structure as described in Chapter 15). Each participant completes a Managerial Grid questionnaire which yields a separate score (ranging from 1 to 9) for each dimension. This questionnaire is used as a device for individuals and groups to examine their managerial styles.

FIGURE 17–2
The Managerial Grid®

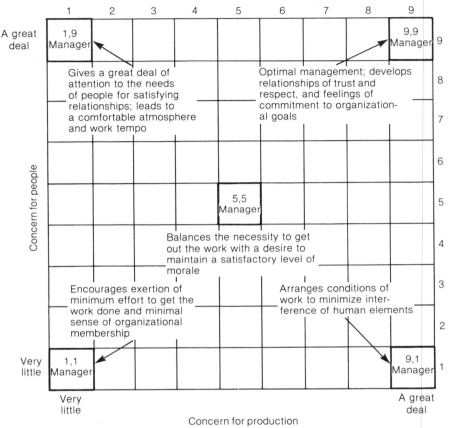

Source: Adapted from R. R. Blake and J. S. Mouton, *The Managerial Grid®* (Houston: Gulf, 1978), p. 10.

The Grid is illustrated in Figure 17–2. It shows the placement of five hypothetical managers. The 1,1 manager behaves in the least desirable fashion. The 9,9 manager, who is maximally concerned both with production and with the people with whom he interacts, is presumed to behave in an optimal manner.

Description.   The six phases of the Grid OD program are based on applied behavioral science and common sense.

Prephase 1: Before an organization begins a Grid OD program, several managers who will later serve as instructors attend a grid seminar. In this week-long experientially-based learning laboratory, managers learn about Grid concepts, assess their own style via the Managerial Grid questionnaire, and learn problem solving, communication, and team-building skills. Some of these managers then attend more advanced Grid courses in which they are taught Phases 2–6 in the program and how to conduct an in-company Phase 1 Grid seminar. Training these managers enables the potential client organization to evaluate the Grid approach and to determine whether or not they think it is a good program to implement throughout their organization. If the company decides to adopt the Grid approach, then Phase 1 begins.

Phase 1: The Grid seminar. A week-long Grid seminar conducted by in-company personnel, is given to all managers in the organization. The training is similar to that described above in Prephase 1. Managers learn Grid theories and strive to become 9,9 managers.

Phase 2: Teamwork development: Work teams in the organization are the focus during this week-long training phase which is usually conducted away from the organization. The goal is to perfect teamwork. The actual work teams (i.e., managers and their subordinates) solve real problems that are hampering their effectiveness within the organization. Each team analyzes and develops its problem-solving, goal-setting, and communication skills. All the managers receive feedback about their own individual and team behavior. This critique enables the manager to understand how others see his strengths and weaknesses.

Phase 3: Intergroup development. Teams that work closely together in the organization learn improved coordination and cooperation. Key members within each team discuss what it would take to create an ideal relationship between the teams. Joint discussions are then held between the key members of each team. Finally, each team works separately to develop a plan to implement the ideal situation which the two groups described.

Phase 4: Developing an ideal strategic corporate model. The organization's top management is assigned the task of designing an ideal strategic corporate model. This model represents what the organization would be like if it were perfect. This process begins with a week-long meeting but it may take as long as a year to perfect the model. As the model is developed, the suggestions of managers at all levels are solicited.

Phase 5: Implementing the ideal strategic model: The model devised in Phase 4 is implemented in a series of steps. First, the organization is reorganized into logical, fairly autonomous subunits. Then, each subunit appoints a planning team whose job it is to determine how its operation can be made more congruent with the ideal model. An additional planning team designs a headquarters to coordinate the subunits. After the planning and assessment procedures are completed, the ideal strategic model is implemented.

Phase 6: Systematic critique: This phase involves a systematic evaluation of the change program. Quantitative measures are taken at the beginning of the program as well as during and after each phase. This critiquing indicates what progress has been made, what obstacles still remain, and what steps need to be taken in the future so that corporate excellence can be attained.

Research and critique.   Despite its widespread use and favorable testimonial evidence, surprisingly little rigorous research has been done with the Grid (Huse, 1980).

The best known study was conducted by Blake, Mouton, Barnes, and Greiner (1964) in a division of a large petroleum corporation employing 800 managers. The changes accompanying the installation of the Grid program were impressive. There was a substantial rise in profits and productivity per worker hour, and a corresponding decrease in costs. There were also substantially more meetings and greater success in organizational problem solving. However, this study was not well controlled. There were no comparison groups and there were several naturally occurring major changes, such as the arrival of a new top manager, just prior to installing the Grid OD program. Therefore, it is impossible to determine if the beneficial changes that occurred were the result of the Grid or extraneous factors. Although it is probable that the Grid OD did have a beneficial effect, the extent of the impact is not clear (Beer, 1976).

Another investigation of the Grid (Blake & Mouton, 1978) involved two organizations that were both owned by a larger corporation. Both of these organizations were engaged in similar businesses and had similar competitive situations. Baseline information on profitability was obtained for both organizations for the years 1961–66. Organization A went through all the phases of the Grid program from 1966 to 1974 while Organization B did not participate in the Grid. The results indicated that the profitability of Organization A was substantially greater over this period than that for Organization B.

Other research on the Grid has produced contradictory results (Huse, 1980). The proportion of organizations that fail to complete all six phases is unknown. Further, considering its widespread application, very little is known about the conditions under which Grid OD is most effective and the conditions under which it is least effective. Despite the viewpoint of Blake and Mouton (1978) that the value of Grid OD has been demonstrated, it appears that much more research is needed.

Process consultation

The most vocal spokesperson for process consultation (P-C) is Schein (1969), although the technology is used by many others. The P-C perspective holds that improvements in the human processes provide the key to organizational development. Thus, the process consultant focuses on communication, member roles and functions in groups, group problem solving and decision making, group norms, leadership and authority, and intergroup cooperation and competition. "P-C is defined as a set of activities on the part of the consultant which help the client to perceive, understand, and act upon process events which occur in the client's environment" (Schein, 1969, p. 9). P-C rests upon a series of seven basic assumptions (Schein, 1969):

1. Managers frequently do not know what is wrong and need help in diagnosing their problems.
2. Managers need to be helped to understand what kind of help consultants can give.
3. Most managers want to improve things but they need help in knowing what to improve and how to do it.
4. Most organizations could be more effective if they could learn to diagnose their strengths and weaknesses.
5. The consultant must work with the members of the organization who know it intimately.
6. The client must be helped to perceive the problems, share actively in the diagnosis, and be completely involved in determining a remedy. The consultant helps provide creative alternative solutions for the client to consider. However, decision making about the solution remains in the client's hands.
7. A P-C must be expert in diagnosing organizational deficiences and establishing helping relationships. Effective P-C requires the transmission of these skills to the client organization.

Description. Process consultants often observe an organization's top-level meetings as a starting point for the intervention. Meetings play an important part in organizational effectiveness because they are where problem solving and decision making frequently occur and as a result they can provide invaluable data about deficiencies within the organization. Depending upon the diagnosis the process consultant selects one (or a combination) of four types of interventions (Schein, 1969):

1. Agenda-setting interventions. The purpose of this type of intervention is to make the group sensitive to how it functions during a meeting. There are several techniques that may be used to accomplish this goal. For example, at the conclusion of a meeting, the group, with the aid of the consultant, may assess how well it functioned. The consultant may have the group complete a survey similar to the one in Figure 17–3 as the basis for constructive discussion. The group may decide to schedule a meeting outside the company to explore and improve its own interpersonal processes. In addition, the group may analyze the procedures it uses for selecting agenda items. During this self-analysis phase, the process consultant frequently provides the group with theory inputs about effective meeting procedures.

2. Feedback of observations on other data. The consultant, at the request of the group, may give feedback on how well it is functioning. Process consultants stress this feedback is to be given *only* when requested by the group and not until the interventionist feels the group is ready for it. Feedback to individuals can also be given while holding to the same prerequisites.

3. Coaching or counseling. Feedback either to individuals or groups invariably leads to coaching or counseling sessions. During these sessions, the

FIGURE 17–3
Sample form for analyzing group effectiveness

Goals

Poor	1	2	3	4	5	6	7	8	9	10	Good

Confused; diverse; conflicting; indifferent; little interest.

Clear to all; shared by all; all care about the goals, feel involved.

Participation

Poor	1	2	3	4	5	6	7	8	9	10	Good

Few dominate; some passive; some not listened to; several talk at once or interrupt.

All get in; all are really listened to.

Leadership

Poor	1	2	3	4	5	6	7	8	9	10	Good

Group needs for leadership not met; group depends too much on single person or on a few persons.

As needs for leadership arise various members meet them ("distributed leadership"); anyone feels free to volunteer as he sees a group need

Decisions

Poor	1	2	3	4	5	6	7	8	9	10	Good

Needed decisions don't get made; decision made by part of group; others uncommitted.

Consensus sought and tested; deviates appreciated and used to improve decision; decisions when made are fully supported.

Trust

Poor	1	2	3	4	5	6	7	8	9	10	Good

Members distrust one another; are polite, careful, closed, guarded; they listen superficially but inwardly reject what others say; are afraid to criticize or to be criticized.

Members trust one another; they reveal to group what they would be reluctant to expose to others; they respect and use the responses they get; they can freely express negative reactions without fearing reprisal.

Source: E. Schein, *Process Consultation: Its Role in Organization Development,* © 1969, Addison-Wesley Publishing Company, Inc., chapter 4, pp. 42–43, Figure 4–3. Reprinted with permission.

consultant helps the group or the individual consider and evaluate alternative courses of action.

4. Structural suggestions. The consultant helps the client organization diagnose its problems and arrive at solutions to structural problems, such as how to improve its communication system. The goal of the process consultant is to improve the client's problem-solving capability. Therefore, the consultant does not solve the problem for the client but teaches the client problem-solving methods.

Research and critique. Kaplan (1979) has summarized the limited amount of research conducted on P-C. He suggests that P-C has some positive effects on the participants as indicated by their self-ratings of greater group effectiveness and greater personal involvement. However, he concludes that there is little, if any, research that demonstrates that P-C leads to increased effectiveness on task activities. Most of the research studies on P-C either did not measure task performance or were inadequately designed. Apparently P-C is a technology implemented by OD practitioners who are generally more concerned with helping their client through a problem than conducting rigorous research on the effectiveness of the technology.

The confrontation meeting

The confrontation meeting (Beckhard, 1967) is a very quick way to mobilize an organization to set action plans. It is probably most useful when an organization is faced with a crisis requiring immediate attention. The confrontation meeting lasts a day and may have as many as 60 participants. It is generally started during the afternoon and completed the next morning. Beckhard states that a confrontation meeting is appropriate where:

a. There is a need for all the managers to examine the organization's functioning with respect to a particular problem.
b. Very limited time is available.
c. Top management needs quick improvement.
d. There is real commitment to resolving the problem.
e. Follow-up can be ensured.

Description. There are six steps involved in a confrontation meeting.

1. Climate setting (one hour). The top manager opens the meeting by explaining its purpose. The need for free and open communication is stressed and attempts are made to set a supportive climate. The consultant then generally gives input on organizational problem solving and communication.

2. Information collecting (one hour). Participants are formed into small (seven- or eight-person) groups. Supervisors and their subordinates are not placed on the same team. Top management meets as a separate group. All the groups are instructed to discuss the following: Think of yourself both as an individual with needs and goals and as a person concerned about the total

organization. What deficiencies exist today? What could make life in this organization better? The results of these discussions are recorded.

3. Information sharing (one hour). Each group's findings are placed, via newsprint, on the walls. The leader compiles a total list which is usually categorized into a few major problem areas.

4. Priority setting and group action planning (one hour). The participants form into their normal work teams to perform these tasks under the direction of their supervisors. First, they identify how the major problems relate to their areas. They set priorities for the problems and determine preliminary solutions to them. Second, they identify the problems they think should be the highest priority for top management. Finally, they decide how they will communicate the results of the confrontation meeting to the lower-level employees who are not present.

5. Immediate follow-up by top management (one to three hours). The top-management team meets after all the other participants leave. They determine what actions should be taken and plan follow-up steps. These plans are communicated to all the other participants.

6. Progress review (two hours). A follow-up meeting with all members of management is held about a month later to review what has transpired since the confrontation meeting.

Beckhard states that the qualities which make the confrontation meeting useful are that it provides rapid diagnosis, release of tension, upward communication, constructive problem solving, involvement and commitment of the entire managerial group, and a shortcut to bureaucratic decision-making barriers.

One potential impediment to successful confrontation meetings is their threatening aspect for some persons. An open climate is essential to the success of the meeting. A confrontation meeting is an attempt to stimulate the open communication that should have been occurring regularly throughout the organization by creating a very special situation where freedom and openness are especially encouraged (Beer, 1976).

Research and critique. Although there are a few case histories of successful interventions (e.g., Beckhard, 1969; Bennis, 1969), the effectiveness of the technology has not been adequately demonstrated.

Job design

The principles of scientific management (Taylor, 1911) emphasized job simplification and task fragmentation as the means for improving efficiency and productivity. However, many studies now indicate that overly simple work often produces such undesirable psychological outcomes as feelings of depersonalization, frustration, and dissatisfaction (Argyris, 1964). These, in turn, can lead to high turnover and absenteeism, low product quality, labor-management problems, and poor mental health. (HEW Special Task

Force, 1973). This implies that what is *logically* efficient in terms of designing jobs may prove to be *psychologically* inefficient.

Herzberg's motivation-hygiene theory (discussed in Chapter 12) initially provided the major theoretical underpinnings for job design efforts. You may recall that this theory states that increased motivation and job satisfaction result from obtaining responsibility, achievement, advancement, and recognition on the job. Herzberg stresses that the only way to provide these things is by changing the job itself, which he terms *job enrichment* (Herzberg, Mausner, & Snyderman, 1959).

Myers (1970) has made a distinction critical to understanding the basic concept of job enrichment. He distinguished between horizontal job loading (or job enlargement) whereby more operations are added to a job, and vertical job loading (or job enrichment) which entails adding more responsibility, planning, and control to a job.

Job-characteristics model. Recent work in the area of job design has been guided more by Hackman and Oldham's (1975) job-characteristics model than by the motivation-hygiene theory. Figure 17–4 provides a summary of the model. It lists five job characteristics, referred to as the *core dimensions* of skill variety, task identity, task significance, autonomy, and feedback,

FIGURE 17–4
The job-characteristics model

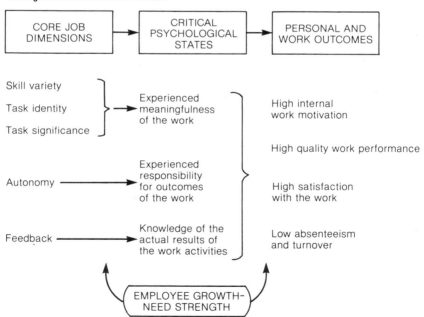

Source: J. Hackman and G. Oldham, "Development of the Job Diagnostic Survey," *Journal of Applied Psychology* 60, p. 161. Copyright 1975 by the American Psychological Association. Reprinted by permission.

which were described under the heading "Components of Job-Satisfaction" in Chapter 13. Please review these pages now. When these core dimensions are present on a job, they are hypothesized to result in some individuals perceiving that: (1) their work is meaningful, (2) they are responsible for the outcomes of their work, and (3) they obtain knowledge of the actual results of their work activities. These perceptions, referred to as critical psychological states, are expected to lead to the personal and work outcomes of high internal work motivation, high quality work performance, high work satisfaction, and low turnover and absenteeism.

The model has a moderating factor referred to as the employee's *growth-need strength*. Individuals high on growth-need strength should be primarily concerned with higher-level needs such as self-fulfillment while individuals low on growth-need strength should be primarily concerned with lower-level needs such as security. The model hypothesizes that individuals who are high on growth-need strength will be more motivated by and react more positively to jobs high on the core dimensions while individuals low on growth-need strength will be less motivated by and react less positively or even negatively to jobs high on these core dimensions.

Description. When job design is performed according to the job-characteristics model, six steps are performed.

1. *Diagnosis.* The Job Diagnostic Survey (JDS) developed by Hackman and Oldham (1975) is administered in order to (*a*) categorize each job as high or low on the core dimensions, (*b*) determine the reactions of individuals to their job and their work setting, and (*c*) ascertain the readiness of individuals to take on jobs that are enriched. If this administration reveals that the jobs can be enriched, the individuals are satisfied with their jobs, and that they are ready to take on enriched jobs, the job-design program proceeds to the second step. Otherwise, remedial programs may need to be implemented or the organization may decide to abandon its job-redesign efforts.

2. *Form natural work units.* As much as possible, individuals are grouped together to form a meaningful work unit. This unit is given continuing responsibility for a body of related work. The objective is to increase the employees' feeling of "ownership" of their job. Forming natural work units should increase the core dimensions of task identity and task significance and result in the perception of increased meaningfulness for the work performed.

3. *Combining tasks.* Jobs that have been fractionated are combined into a larger work module. This is intended to increase both skill variety and task identity.

4. *Establishing client relationships.* As much as possible, employees are put in direct contact with the people who use their product or service. This is designed to increase skill variety, task autonomy, and feedback.

5. *Vertical loading.* The employees are given greater latitude in and responsibility for doing their work. Vertical loading is probably the most important component of a job-redesign program. It should increase all of the core dimensions except feedback.

6. *Opening feedback channels.* Employees are provided with increased feedback on their performance. In contrast with the common practice of providing feedback only during scheduled annual or semiannual performance reviews, job-design programs attempt to implement ongoing, continuous, and immediate feedback.

Research and critique. Research on the job-characteristics model has yielded mixed results. For example, Sims and Szilagyi (1976) found that employees with high-growth needs responded more favorably to jobs that have high levels of skill variety, task identity, autonomy, and feedback. On the other hand Wall, Clegg, and Jackson (1978) concluded that the critical psychological states were not produced by the core job dimensions. Additional research is needed before the value of the job-characteristics model can be determined.

The technology of job design has already been widely attempted and the body of published research is voluminous and generally positive. However, it has been suggested that the literature provides a distorted view: that is, unfavorable results tend to be unpublished (Huse, 1980).

Ford (1969) conducted 18 job-design evaluation studies. Seventeen had positive results and the other mixed results. In addition, Lawler (1969) reviewed 10 job-design studies and found positive results in all the projects. Quality of production increased in all ten studies and quantity increased in four. Increased job satisfaction and motivation have also been shown to result from job-design projects. Many additional studies also supportive of job design have been reported since Lawler's review. Even on those relatively rare occasions when the results have been negative, some evaluators attribute the failure to factors other than the job-design concept. Thus, Frank and Hackman (1975) indicated that an inadequate diagnosis of the situation and a lack of management commitment were responsible for a failure to implement a beneficial job-design program. The authors staunchly defended the technology.

However, job design does have its share of critics. For example, Fein (1974) and Shrank (1974) argue that most Americans, especially those of blue-collar status, do not want enriched jobs. Although that may be an overstatement, there is evidence at least that challenging, enriched jobs are not equally satisfying to all workers (Wanous, 1974).

Moreover, while the evidence as a whole appears to favor job design, most of the studies have lacked methodological rigor (Hulin & Blood, 1968). Finally, the issue of cost-effectiveness has largely been ignored.

THE FUTURE OF OD

OD is a rapidly growing set of strategies, increasingly being selected over more traditional strategies such as management-development seminars. The reasons for the rapid growth of OD include a growing concern for personal and social issues, the knowledge explosion, and rapid product obsolescence (Huse, 1980).

The range of settings in which OD has been applied is also expanding significantly. Recently OD interventions have been performed in the areas of international relations, higher education, health-care delivery, news media, and the military. In addition, numerous large U.S. corporations including General Motors, Sears, Shell, and Texas Instruments have become advocates of OD.

As noted throughout this chapter, one of OD's major shortcomings has been an inclination by earlier advocates to accept it uncritically—almost as a matter of faith. Fortunately, as OD comes of age, its various approaches are increasingly being submitted to rigorous evaluation.

OD is winning over a sizable proportion of the behavioral-science practitioners. According to its supporters, it is alive and well and threatening to have a major influence on many aspects of social design as well as social action (Alderfer, 1977).

SUMMARY

The most frequently cited definition of organization development (OD) is that it "is an effort (1) *planned,* (2) *organization-wide,* and (3) *managed* from the top, to (4) increase *organization effectiveness* and *health* through (5) *planned interventions* in the organization's processes using *behavioral-science* knowledge" (Beckhard, 1969, p. 9). Within the last 15 years, a number of technologies have been developed for intervening in, changing, and developing organizations.

Laboratory training is the forerunner of most contemporary OD technologies and it is still used today. T-groups focus on the here and now and explore the feelings and emotions of the group members. The goals of laboratory training include increased self-awareness and sensitivity to the behavior of others. The strength of T-groups lies in their ability to modify individual expectancies, skills, and values. The lack of transfer of this learning back to the job is the major weakness of this technology.

The survey-feedback approach is a joint effort between the client organization and the consultant in developing a questionnaire, using it to collect data about the organization, analyzing the data, interpreting it, and then using the interpretation as a basis for change. The survey-feedback questionnaire typically contains items on satisfaction with the job and supervisor, organizational climate, and group processes.

Blake and Mouton's Grid OD is a six-phase program that requires at least three years to implement in an organization. The Grid is based on a bipolar conceptualization of leadership. The two dimensions are concern for people, and concern for production. The ideal manager has a 9,9 style, that is, he is high on both of these dimensions. Individuals learn to become 9,9 managers during Grid training. The program also teaches team and intergroup development. An ideal corporate model is designed and implemented within the client organization.

Process consultation is a set of activities performed by the consultant to help the client organization perceive, understand, and act upon process events which occur. Process events include group problem solving and decision making, and intergroup cooperation and competition. Process consultants frequently observe top-level meetings within an organization as the starting point for OD. Interventions include agenda setting, feedback of observations, coaching or counseling, and structural suggestions.

The confrontation meeting is the quickest of the OD technologies to implement. It is generally conducted within a day and is most useful when an organization is faced with a crisis situation. The confrontation meeting is an attempt to stimulate open communication very quickly. The steps in a confrontation meeting are climate setting, information collecting, information sharing, priority setting and group action planning, immediate follow-up by top management, and progress review.

Job design is contrary to the scientific-management approach which emphasized that jobs should be made as simple as possible. However, simple jobs may create depersonalization and dissatisfaction which can lead to low product quality and high turnover and absenteeism. Recent job design efforts have generally been conducted within the framework of the job-characteristics model. The components of this model are the core job dimensions which produce critical psychological states that result in personal and work outcomes. Although support for the model is not strong, job-design efforts have generally produced positive results.

The range of settings in which OD has been applied is expanding significantly and more rigorous research is being employed to evaluate its technologies. The future of OD appears to be extremely promising.

REFERENCES

Alderfer, C. P. Organizational development. *Annual Review of Psychology,* 1977, *28,* 197–223.

Argyris, C. *Integrating the individual and the organization.* New York: Wiley, 1964.

Argyris, C. *Management and organizational development: The path from X_a to X_b.* New York: McGraw-Hill, 1971.

Beckhard, R. The confrontation meeting. *Harvard Business Review,* 1967, *45,* 149–155.

Beckhard, R. *Organization development: Strategies and models.* Reading, Mass.: Addison-Wesley, 1969.

Beer, M. The technology of organization development. In M. D. Dunnette (Ed.), *Handbook of industrial and organizational psychology.* Chicago: Rand McNally, 1976.

Beer, M., & Huse, E. F. A systems approach to organization development. *Journal of Applied Behavioral Science,* 1972, *8,* 79–101.

Bennis, W. F. *Organization development: Its nature, origins, and prospects.* Reading, Mass.: Addison-Wesley, 1969.

Blake, R. R., & Mouton, J. S. *The managerial grid.* Houston: Gulf, 1964.

Blake, R. R., & Mouton, J. S. *Building dynamic organization through grid organization development.* Reading, Mass.: Addison-Wesley, 1969.

Blake, R. R., & Mouton, J. S. *Consultation.* Reading, Mass.: Addison-Wesley, 1976.

Blake, R. R., & Mouton, J. S. *The new managerial grid.* Houston: Gulf, 1978.

Blake, R. R., Mouton, J. S., Barnes, L. B., & Greiner, L. E. Breakthrough in organization development. *Harvard Business Review,* 1964, *42,* 133–155.

Bowers, D. G. OD techniques and their results in 23 organizations: The Michigan ICL study. *Journal of Applied Behavioral Science,* 1973, *9,* 21–43.

Bowers, D. G., & Franklin, J. *Survey-guided development I: Data-based organizational change,* La Jolla, Calif.: University Associates, 1977.

Bowers, D., Frankin, J., & Pecorella, P. Matching problems, precursors, and interventions in OD: A systematic approach. *Journal of Applied Behavioral Science,* 1975, *11,* 391–410.

Buchanan, P. C. Laboratory training and organization development. *Administrative Science Quarterly,* 1969, *14,* 466–480.

Campbell, J. P., & Dunnette, M. D. Effectiveness of T-group experiences in managerial training and development. *Psychological Bulletin,* 1968, *70,* 73–103.

Cooper, C. L., & Levine, N. Implicit values in experiential learning groups: Their functional and dysfunctional consequences. In C. L. Cooper & C. Alderfer (Eds.), *Advances in experiential social processes.* New York: Wiley, 1978.

Fein, M. Job enrichment: A reevaluation. *Sloan Management Review,* 1974, *15,* 69–88.

Ford, R. *Motivation through the work itself.* New York: American Management Association, 1969.

Frank, L. L., & Hackman, J. R. A failure of job enrichment: The case of change that wasn't. *Journal of Applied Behavioral Science,* 1975, *11,* 413–436.

French, W., & Bell, C. *Organization development: Behavioral science interventions for organization improvement* (2nd ed.). Englewood Cliffs, N.J.: Prentice-Hall, 1978.

Hackman, J. R., & Oldham, G. Development of the job diagnostic survey. *Journal of Applied Psychology,* 1975, *6,* 159–170.

Harrison, R. Choosing the depth of organizational intervention. *Journal of Applied Behavioral Science,* 1970, *6,* 181–202.

Herzberg, F., Mausner, B., & Snyderman, B. *The motivation to work.* New York: Wiley, 1959.

HEW Special Task Force. *Work in America.* Cambridge, Mass.: MIT. Press, 1973.

House, R. J. T-group education and leadership effectiveness: A review of empirical literature and a critical evaluation. *Personnel Psychology,* 1967, *20,* 1–32.

Howard, J. *Please touch.* New York: McGraw-Hill, 1972.

Hulin, C., & Blood, M. Job enlargement, individual differences and work responses. *Psychological Bulletin,* 1968, *69,* 41–55.

Huse, E. F. *Organization development and change* (2nd ed.). St. Paul, Minn.: West, 1980.

Kaplan, R. The conspicuous absence of evidence that process consultation enhances task performance. *Journal of Applied Behavioral Science,* 1979, *15,* 346–360.

Lawler, E. E. Job design and employee motivation. *Personnel Psychology,* 1969, *22,* 426–435.

Lundberg, C. Organization development: Current perspectives and future issues. Paper presented to the Southeast Chapter of the American Institute of Decision Sciences, 1974, cited in Huse (1980), see above.

Mann, F. C. Studying and creating change: A means to understanding social organization. In *Research in human relations.* Industrial Relations Research Association Publication No. 17, 1957, 146–167.

Mann, F. C. Studying and creating change. In W. G. Bennis, K. Benne, & R. Chin (Eds.), *The planning of change: Readings in the applied behavioral sciences.* New York: Holt, Rinehart & Winston, 1961.

Myers, M. S. *Every employee a manager.* New York: McGraw-Hill, 1970.

Passmore, W. The Michigan ICL study revisited: An alternative explanation of the results. *Journal of Applied Behavioral Science,* 1976, *12,* 245–251.

Schein, E. H. Process consultation: *Its role in organization development.* Reading, Mass.: Addison-Wesley, 1969.

Schein, E. H., & Bennis, W. G. *Personal and organizational change through group methods: The laboratory approach.* New York: Wiley, 1965.

Sims, H. P., & Szilagyi, A. D. Job characteristic relationships: Individual and structural relationships. *Organizational Behavior and Human Performance,* 1976, *19,* 211–230.

Shrank, R. Work in America: What do workers really want? *Industrial Relations,* 1974, *13,* 124–129.

Tannenbaum, R., Weschler, I. R., & Massarik, F. *Leadership and organization: A behavioral science approach.* New York: McGraw-Hill, 1961.

Taylor, F. W. *The principles of scientific management.* New York: Harper & Bros., 1911.

Wall, T. D., Clegg, C. W., & Jackson, P. R. An evaluation of the job characteristics model. *Journal of Occupational Psychology,* 1978, *51,* 183–196.

Wanous, J. P. Individual differences and reactions to job characteristics. *Journal of Applied Psychology,* 1974, *59,* 616–622.

White, S., & Mitchell, T. Organization development: A review of research content and research design. *Academy of Management Review,* 1976, *1,* 57–73.

chapter 18

Organization Change: Theoretical Models and Case Histories

Although there are still large gaps in our knowledge about organizational psychology, the preceding chapters indicate that relatively recent research efforts are refining our understanding of organizations. However, as we have noted at several earlier points, the practical test of scientific understanding is prediction and control. Thus, organizational theory ultimately must stand the critical test of successful applications in planned organizational-change programs. These applications should include the *transformation* of distressed and troubled organizations into prosperous and healthy ones and the *design* of new organizations that prove to be effective.

This chapter presents two detailed case histories of organization change. They are extremely different. The first case illustrates a dismal failure which occurred when a major university attempted a comprehensive change program. The second case is probably the best researched and one of the most successful of the comprehensive change programs.

We introduce both cases by briefly summarizing organization-change theory.

THEORETICAL MODELS OF ORGANIZATION CHANGE

Until the middle 1960s, interest in organization change was largely theoretical and based on the influential work of Kurt Lewin. Attempts to actually change organizations are thus of recent origin and the pendulum has swung to the other extreme. The balance between theory and practice has now shifted, with practice seemingly leading the way (Alderfer, 1976). This is probably a temporary state of affairs. However, it does explain why two of the four models of organization change presented below were developed over 20 years ago.

Lewin's model

Lewin's (1947) three-stage typology is the pioneering theoretical work in organization change. Although a relatively simple model for organization change, it continues to guide change efforts and is responsible for stimulating the more recent models.

Lewin postulated three stages of organization change:

1. *Unfreezing.* The change process begins by decreasing the strength of previously held attitudes, values, and behaviors. This decrease results from new experiences or information which disconfirms the organizational members' previously held perceptions (of themselves, others, and events).

2. *Moving* (or *changing*). Once existing perceptions are altered, the participants are ready to substitute new attitudes, values, or behaviors for the earlier ones. The psychological mechanisms whereby the members move toward these changed perceptions are identification and internalization.

3. *Refreezing.* Finally, change stabilizes and a new state of equilibrium is established. The organization change is supported by changes in areas such as organization policy and structure, and group norms (Schein, 1961).

This three-stage model can be used to help analyze the effectiveness of the various OD technologies presented in the previous chapter. For example, there is evidence that the strength of T-groups for OD lie in their ability to unfreeze, while their weakness is in refreezing. On the other hand, a properly conducted Grid OD program should have strength at all three stages.

Planned change

The planned-change model (Lippitt, Watson, & Westley, 1958) elaborated Lewin's typology and suggested some practical strategies. Although planned organization change does not necessarily progress in an orderly and logical sequence, the following seven phases are characteristic of most change programs.

Phase 1. Development of a need for change. The client organization becomes aware of its difficulties and wishes to overcome them. This phase is marked by feeling that an external agent (consultant) might help the organization change.

Phase 2. Establishment of a change relationship. The client organization must communicate its need for help in such a way that the potential change agent can understand it and agree to participate in the change process. Lippett, Watson, and Westley stress that this phase is of crucial importance since it is when the parties must intelligently arrive at a decision to work together and define the terms of the helping relationship.

Phase 3. Clarification or diagnosis of the problem. The client organization must provide the change agent with enough information for a comprehensive diagnosis. This often proves to be an especially trying time for management because previously unsuspected ramifications of the original problem are frequently uncovered.

Phase 4. Establishing goals and plans. Organizational management and the change agent must ultimately agree on a course of action after carefully examining alternative goals and procedures for their attainment. Typically some negative feelings are experienced at this stage as management realizes that it will have to relinquish, or at least modify, certain of its long-established and satisfying modes of behavior. Anxieties may arise as the need for new patterns of behavior and/or new management procedures becomes apparent.

Phase 5. Transformation of intentions into change efforts. Because of the departure from previously accustomed patterns of behavior, the client organization may require considerable support and encouragement from the change agent as it attempts to implement new procedures and attain its new goals. Such support and encouragment is possible only in a climate that accepts the desirability of the change.

Phase 6. Generalization and stabilization of change. The diffusion of change throughout the organization and the incorporation of change into the fabric of the organization can be encouraged by management in two ways. First, it must be alert to evidences of appropriate new behavior and reinforce these occurrences. Second, it must institute organizational procedures consistent with the desired change.

Phase 7. Achieving a terminal relationship. The termination of the relationship between the change agent and the organization sometimes proves difficult because of the dependency of the latter upon the skills of the former. It is one of the change agent's responsibilities to wean the organization away from such dependence.

Figure 18–1 summarizes both the Lewin and the Lippitt, Watson, and Westley models of change. The first four stages in the planned-change model closely correspond to Lewin's unfreezing stage: the change effect is equivalent to the moving stage, and the last two stages are very similar to the refreezing stage.

The innermost of the two feedback arrows (I) at the left of the figure indicates that during the generalization and stabilization stage the organization may become aware of some further difficulties generated by the change program itself. These difficulties may lead to further diagnosis and a modification of the change efforts. The other arrow (II) indicates that additional organizational needs may be recognized as the original program nears its conclusion, and may lead to the institution of additional programs. Thus, the planned-change model has a dynamic quality: as organizations become "healthier," they recognize the value of still further improvement.

Action research model

The action-research model is a theoretical description of the steps that should occur in a change program. It is similar to planned change, with the differences between the two being largely that of emphasis. For example, the action-research model places a greater emphasis on periodic evaluation. In

FIGURE 18-1
Lewin's change typology and Lippitt, Watson and Westley's planned change model

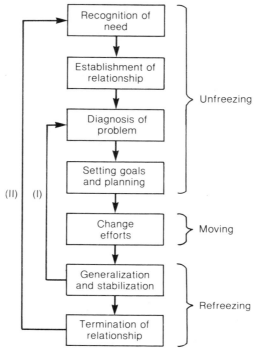

Source: M. Frohman, M. Sashkin, and M. Kavanaugh, *Action Research as an Organization Development Approach* (Binghamton: State University of New York School of Management, 1974).

addition, the action-research model emphasizes selecting a technology after a thorough diagnosis is made, while the planned-change approach may utilize a technology selected prior to the intervention (Huse, 1980).

According to the action-research model, the first step in a change program is the perception of a problem or problems by a key individual within the client organization. A behavioral scientist expert in intervention is then brought in to solve the problem. The interventionist collects data in order to diagnose the situation and determine the impediments which are keeping the organization from achieving its goals. The interventionist then tells the client his diagnosis and the client feeds back its views and information leading to a joint diagnosis of the problem. Then, after considerable interchange, the consultant and the client should decide on the procedures to be used to help the organization solve its problems. This solution phase is implemented and then constantly monitored to maximize its effectiveness. New problems

FIGURE 18–2
The action-research model for OD

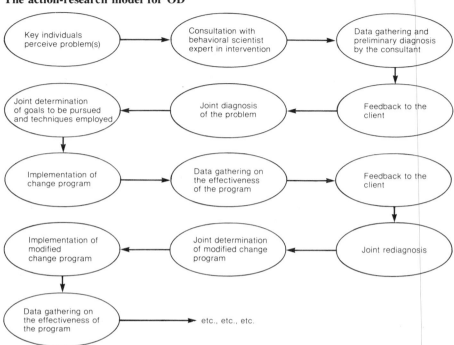

Source: © 1969 by the Regents of the University of California. Adapted from W. French, *Organization Development: Objectives, Assumptions and Strategies, California Management Review,* 12, 23–34, p. 26. Reprinted by permission.

should be diagnosed and solved as they develop. Figure 18–2 depicts the entire action-research model.

Intervention theory and method

A key concept in Argyris' (1970) intervention theory and method is that the client system and the interventionist are separate entities. This means that each party makes its own decisions, and the client organization assumes responsibility for all of its endeavors. While the interventionist does not make the decisions for the client, he/she may help it make its own decisions. Central to Argyris' model are the primary tasks of the interventionist and the implications of these tasks.

Primary tasks of an interventionist. Regardless of the type of problem the client organization is experiencing, there are three tasks on which the interventionist must focus: (1) generating valid and useful information, (2) creating conditions in which clients can make free and informed choices, and (3) helping the clients develop an internal commitment to their choices.

Valid and useful information is regarded as the foundation of an effective intervention. The synthesis of this information (diagnosis phase) should represent the viewpoints of the total client system. The skills of the interventionist are important at this stage because the client organization may be unaware of how to generate valid and useful information about its own problems and functioning. The diagnosis, a joint product of the client system and the interventionist, must include variables that are both significant and changeable so that if the client decides to manipulate them, a more effective state of affairs will follow.

In order to have *free choice,* the clients must have a *cognitive map* of what they wish to accomplish and alternative courses of action. This all depends on the successful completion of the diagnosis phase. Free choice implies that the members of the organization are able to explore freely all the alternatives they consider significant and to select freely those that they consider central to their needs. Free choice places the decision-making authority in the client systems thereby encouraging them to maintain their autonomy and be responsible for their own destiny. The interventionist must often resist pressures to tell the client what to do. Internal commitment is achieved when the course of action once agreed to is internalized by the organization members to the extent that they (*a*) feel that they have ownership of it and (*b*) are responsible for its successful implementation.

Implications of the primary tasks for intervention activity.   These three primary tasks have many implications, two of which are described briefly.

1.   Change is not a primary task. Argyris stresses that the choice about whether or not to change is entirely up to the client organization. He cautions that the interventionist should not a priori consider change good and the status quo bad. The job of the interventionist is to help the organization gather valid data for making a sound decision about whether changes are needed. Argyris warns that change agents may be so taken with the importance of change that they approach situations with an implicit bias against stability.

2.   A criticism frequently leveled against advocates of organization change and development is that the process imposes the interventionist's values on the client organization. Argyris feels that this is avoidable provided both parties focus on the primary tasks. This focus reduces the possibilities that either participant (the client organization or the interventionist) will manipulate the other.

An overview of change models

These four change models are similar in several respects. They are all based on previous behavioral-science theory and the several models of organizational change are complementary. Further they all support the use of the same change technologies (as discussed in Chapter 17).

However, there are some differences. For example, intervention theory and method stresses the point that change is not always necessary. Although this is not a part of the other models, their proponents would probably agree with this position. In addition, intervention theory and method differs from the other models in making the assumption that the client system has the necessary internal resources for a change program, if change is determined to be needed. The action-research model and intervention theory and method place a greater emphasis on both improving the problem-solving skills of the client system and periodically evaluating the change effort than do the other two theoretical approaches (Huse, 1980). In summary, these differences between the four models tend to be those of emphasis rather than reflecting serious disagreements.

AN UNSUCCESSFUL ATTEMPTED CHANGE

The major change attempt at the State University of New York at Buffalo (SUNY-Buffalo) has been reported by Bennis (1972), a prominent OD theorist and practitioner. The following description of the change program captures Bennis' delightful tongue-in-cheek style by quoting him extensively.

The change program

In later 1966, Bennis received a telephone call from an assistant to the president of SUNY-Buffalo. Bennis was informed that an academic paradise with unlimited funding, a new $650 million campus, bold organizational ideas, a visionary president, and exciting new faculty and administration was being created at SUNY-Buffalo. Bennis was asked to take part in this effort to create the "Berkeley of the East" and he accepted.

Shortly before the phone call to Bennis, the state of New York decided to create a top-flight multiversity and had lured their new president from Berkeley to help make the dream materialize. He arrived with a monumental plan to redesign the academic structure. Within two months the faculty senate ratified the following plan:

1. The 90 existing departments were to be restructured into 7 new faculties under the leadership of a provost. (Bennis was to head the social science disciplines).
2. The university was to build 30 small colleges on a new campus. Each college was to house only 400 students with up to 600 commuter students as affiliates. Faculty and students were intended to work together in the intimate atmosphere of these intellectual neighborhoods in an attempt to offset the apathy that characterizes large campuses.
3. Research centers on international, urban, and higher educational issues were to be created to unite faculty and students for work on vital issues.

Bennis was impressed with the new president's plan and was assured that there would be enough money to build a quality faculty on top of the inevitable deadwood already there. Bennis arrived in 1967 and during the next year he recruited 9 new chairmen, 2 deans, and 45 new full-time professors. Buffalo raided Harvard, Yale, and Princeton and each new appointment created more enthusiasm. A flourishing academic community was formed. The change was pervasive. About 75 percent of the academic community was newly appointed.

"For one year, Buffalo was an academic Camelot. The provosts met around the president's conference table to work miracles. Occasionally I got signals that not everyone on campus took us quite as seriously as we took ourselves. One morning I found a Batman cape on my coat rack. The anonymous critic had a point: the atmosphere was a bit heavy with omnipotent fantasy" (p. 114).

Difficulties arise

Rumblings began to occur in paradise. The centers were not doing well. For example, the Center for Higher Education was not attracting new faculty. In addition, rumors were flying about one college which was devoted to independent study and self-evaluation. The rumors said that the class cards in this college were being sold to students who planned to do nothing and then reward themselves with As.

Bennis felt that the many individual accomplishments, the promising new programs, and the appointment of new staff did not add up to a significantly changed university. He feared the gains were not being consolidated and would begin slipping away. These fears were confirmed; "Camelot lasted barely a thousand days" (p. 114).

Four years after the dream was born, the campus mood was dismal. Many of the visionaries had left and the spirit of change was stamped out. The new president "officially disappeared.

"What saddens me is a suspicion that this gross assault would have been successful if we had been more effective. . . . By all appearances, our efforts changed nothing" (p. 120).

Lessons learned

Bennis reports that he can now see with all the unsettling clarity of hindsight, the many mistakes that were made. He offers the following guidelines to those considering change in a university setting.

1. "Plan for change from a solid conceptual base. Have a clear understanding of how to change as well as what to change" (p. 116). Buffalo had a vision of the final result of the change program, but they lacked a clear concept of how the change ought to proceed. They had goals but no well thought-out mechanisms to insure the goals were realized.

2. "Don't settle for rhetorical change" (p. 118). The change at SUNY-Buffalo was accomplished by fiat. The faculty senate announced that they

ratified the new president's plan. However, the senate neither represented faculty sentiment nor understood the plan! There was virtually no commitment to it except as a poetic vision.

3. "Remember that change is most successful when those who are affected are involved in the planning" (p. 120). Bennis feels that nothing makes individuals resist new ideas more than the feeling that those ideas are being imposed on them. The students and faculty at SUNY-Buffalo did not contribute to the planning. Bennis suggests that a clumsier, slower, but more participative approach to changing the university would probably have resulted in more permanent reform.

4. "Build support among like-minded people, whether or not you recruited them" (p. 116). Bennis observes that change-oriented administrators are prone to act as though the organization came into being the moment they arrived. At SUNY the old-guard faculty was neither asked for advice nor invited to social affairs. As a result, the administrators lost the opportunity to gain the loyalty and support of the respected members of the veteran faculty. If they had been made to feel that there was a place for them at the new SUNY-Buffalo, they might have supported the changes with enthusiasm instead of hostility.

5. "Recruit with scrupulous honesty" (p. 114). The new president had a gift as a recruiter. He was able to turn all of the highly visible and terribly real drawbacks at Buffalo into exhilarating challenges. Others, including Bennis, emulated his recruiting approach. The faculty recruiting pitch at Buffalo emphasized the future. Little was made of the past, and the present was deemphasized—Buffalo was to be the university of the future. Although naive, the pitch was effective!

The new faculty had barely enrolled their children in school before reality intruded. A labor dispute, which dragged on for months, delayed construction of the new facilities. After one year, the state legislature began to cut the budget. Many of the new faculty felt they had been conned. They were not told about the ultimate inability of the university's administration to control the legislatively determined budget. "We had promised a new university when our funds could provide only an architect's model" (p. 114).

6. "Appreciate environmental factors" (p. 118). Like other human activities, change proceeds more smoothly in optimal environments. The major environmental problem at SUNY-Buffalo was overcrowding. The new faculty expected to move their academic possessions into futuristic offices. Instead, they moved in on top of the faculty who were already there. Prefab annexes were hastily assembled to accommodate the overflow. The university had to lease an interim campus near the proposed campus. Eleven academic departments moved into this temporary facility. The 15-minute bus trip was a drag to the students and the isolation of the campus was contrary to the spirit of the visionary plan.

SUNY-Buffalo had traditionally been a target for the antiintellectuals in the city. Two years before the major change, powerful groups in the community tried to close down the university. The strength of the opposition was not gauged correctly and, as a result, the administration neglected to protect its new programs from these hostile external forces. One college began an experimental community action program in a building directly across from both a parochial grammar school and a center for retarded children. Whenever a braless coed played her guitar at a window of the center, the residents of the neighborhood reacted. The whole situation got out of hand and this increased the community's normally high level of outrage at the university.

Analysis

The change program at SUNY-Buffalo was unsuccessful despite the fact that it was conducted by gifted and well-meaning people. Some of the key reasons for its failure are clarified by the action-research model. The first step in the action-research model is for a key executive to perceive a problem. This step occurred. The new president perceived a lower-quality university than he desired. The next step in the model is consultation with a behavior scientist expert in intervention.

In this case, the key executive, the new president, was his own change agent. This is somewhat unusual but certainly not unprecedented. Presidents of companies occasionally attempt to conduct massive change programs without consulting with either an internal or external change agent.

From this stage on, the change program and the action-research model depart dramatically. No thorough diagnosis of the problem was made. Rather, the new president appears to have skipped to the solution phase without first determining the nature of the problems. His "master plan" was offered as the solution and imposed upon a largely resistant organization. The organizational members did not interact with reciprocal effects. Goals and procedures established by the president alone were merely rubber stamped by a faculty senate largely unaware of what they had agreed to. Moreover, there was no planned diagnostic procedure to identify the inevitable problems that occur when implementing a change program and there appears to have been no concerted efforts to solve the ones that surfaced.

Other crucial reasons for the failure of the change program can be found by reviewing Argyris' intervention model. Argyris stresses the need for valid information, free and informed choice, and internal commitment. None of these were present. No valid information on which to base the change program appears to have been gathered. Moreover, only a selected few, the new president and those he annointed, had free choice. The majority of the faculty and administration had most of the decisions made for them. Finally, there was very little internal commitment on the part of many to a successful implementation of the plan.

Looking back, it now appears that the attempt to create a Camelot at Buffalo was doomed to fail before the change efforts began. The large number of deficiencies present in this change program was too great to be overcome by the enthusiasm of the new president and his converts.

WELDON COMPANY: A SUCCESS STORY

The Weldon Company was bought by its leading competitor, the Harwood Manufacturing Company in 1962. Both companies made pajamas, using similar manufacturing processes and machinery. Weldon, however, sold its own nationally advertised brand-name items to quality stores, while Harwood sold to large distributors under their own brand names. Through the acquisition of Weldon, Harwood hoped to expand into the leading stores without having to develop a new high-priced line. Harwood had intended to leave the Weldon Company as a separate and independent organization, with the manufacturing and management policies remaining as they were, except for the introduction of minor efficiency changes. However, soon after Harwood assumed control, they discovered unsuspected weaknesses in every area of Weldon's operations.

As a result, the owners of Harwood decided to implement a planned and coordinated change program within the Weldon Company (Marrow, Bowers & Seashore, 1967). The changes, which took place over two years, focused on all areas of the organizational structure, including leadership style, union-management relations, salaries, and communications. Improvements in these areas were introduced by a team of behavioral scientists who acted as change agents. They designed and executed a program based on participative-management principles. Technological advancements were also installed by two groups of engineering consultants. Members of the Survey Research Center of the University of Michigan's Institute for Social Research observed and recorded the events taking place during the changes and the effects that these changes had on employee behavior.

Weldon described

Weldon began operations in the early 1940s and quickly became an industry leader in a seller's market brought on by wartime shortages. By the mid-1950s, the company employed about 3,500 people in five plants. Weldon had two owners, both authoritarian, who personally controlled all managerial practices. One partner supervised production from the Pennsylvania plant and the other partner supervised merchandising from New York. Probably, because of personality clashes, the two partners ran their divisions independently and only conferred on major organizational problems.

The partners' insistence upon personal control and their lack of meetings with each other led to many problems within the organization. Detailed rules were developed to control matters which the partners could not directly supervise, even though these rules involved time loss and work delays. Employees were discouraged from making decisions and suggesting improvements. Poor work relations among the managerial staff and an emphasis on control systems and record-keeping led to high management costs. Communication and organization within Weldon was so poor that two attempts made by the company to expand its markets failed, resulting in large financial losses. The company even resorted to selling its products at prices far below cost to hold its prestige market.

Due to the lack of coordination between the sales and manufacturing departments, impossibly fast deliveries were promised on conflicting dates. This forced changes in production priorities and resulted in partial or rushed deliveries, and unbalanced inventories. Costs soared, resentments deepened, yet the top management failed to recognize its own deficiencies as the real source of the problems. Instead, the partners attempted to alleviate the situation by cutting costs; the staff was greatly reduced, payroll increases were withheld, and obsolete machinery was retained. These attempts seemed to aggravate the already troubled situation.

Soon after the purchase, a thorough study of Weldon's manufacturing facilities was made by a Harwood vice president. He found many shortcomings in the manufacturing process, but believed the basic plant facilities and the Weldon people to be capable of producing a good product. He also found that, although the Weldon plant building was old and unkept, it was more than adequate in size and offered the opportunity for plant rearrangement. The Weldon supervisors and managers were found to be technically skilled, knowledgeable about the manufacturing process, and dedicated to their work. However, they seemed unable to accept responsibility and make decisions.

The Harwood vice president suggested that modern equipment and work methods needed to be introduced to reduce plant costs and to increase employee earnings. He further suggested that these technological changes should be introduced at Weldon before the necessary social changes. He felt this was necessary because Weldon had some staff resources for dealing with technological matters, but practically no resources for dealing with the human aspect of the organization. He believed the technological changes would help provide a background for the social changes since both stressed communication, planning, and responsibility.

Harwood and Weldon compared

The Harwood organization had a long tradition of successfully applying behavioral science principles. It had developed an excellent working relationship with the Survey Research Center of the University of Michigan. Harwood had the center collect information about both Weldon and Harwood before any major changes took place. Additional information was collected during the change program, and after it occurred. It was anticipated that a prechange study of the two companies would offer Weldon some understanding of its situation, and would also offer a standard of comparison for the completed change program.

The study of the two organizations indicated that both were family owned and run by the second generation. Weldon had experienced early and militant labor activity while Harwood had experienced recent, peaceful union activity. The employees of the two firms displayed several similarities: 80 percent of the workers were women, two thirds were married, and most had started, but not finished, high school. The Harwood employees, however, were older and had been employed longer by the company. While the Harwood workers were concerned about not having to work too hard, the Weldon employees were concerned about remaining steadily employed.

An attitude survey indicated that the Harwood company was rated superior in all respects including satisfaction with the company, liking for the job, supervisor support, and supervisor facilitating work. The Survey Research Center classified the managerial approaches of the two companies using the employees'-questionnaire responses. Weldon was found to be on the borderline between an exploitative-authoritative and a benevolent-authorative system. Harwood was found to be on the borderline between a consultative- and participative-group system.

The performance characteristics of the two organizations were also strikingly different. For example, Harwood's return on investment was 17 percent, Weldon's − 15 percent, Harwood's production efficiency was 6 percent, Weldon's − 11 percent, Harwood's monthly turnover was .75 percent, Weldon's 10 percent, and Harwood's monthly absenteeism was 3 percent while Weldon's was 6 percent.

The change program

The comprehensive organization-change program had three main defining features: (1) retaining existing Weldon personnel, (2) modernizing the physical plant and work methods, and (3) introducing a new pattern of organizational life emphasizing participative management. These features were incorporated into a three-phase change effort.

Five different consulting and service organizations were engaged for extended periods of time during the three-phase program. The project involved a joint effort between engineers, accountants, psychologists, and various technical consultants.

Phase 1: Protecting human resources. The employees of Weldon were assured that the plant would continue to operate and that no personnel changes were contemplated. A survey of employee attitudes was taken, and all Weldon managers and supervisors were interviewed. The surveys and interviews focused on morale, interpersonal relations, and motivation. The results were fed back and discussed to help get Weldon past a time of potential disruption.

Phase 2: Technical change program and operator training. The first problem tackled by the team of consulting engineers was employee earnings. Their goals were to retain the piece-rate method and to increase the average performance of the workers. They wanted to reduce the number of daily job changes made by the workers which they felt wasted time and skills and resulted in low earnings and high costs. To accomplish this, they introduced improved production planning and scheduling methods. They also improved the plant layout and work flow, and changed the equipment and methods for many jobs.

After the planning and physical improvements had been made, the engineers offered individual help to all operators whose performance was below standard. The supervisors were simultaneously encouraged to follow proper work methods. The supervisor training was performed both on an individual basis and in staff meetings which emphasized cooperation and communication. This program produced very substantial increases in employee efficiency and earnings.

Turnover was another major problem at Weldon. In 1962, 90 percent of all new employees left within four months of being hired. The major reasons for the high turnover were poor selection and training programs. Therefore, an improved selection program was implemented and a "vestibule" training area was set up. Each new employee was trained for four weeks on regular production materials under regular job conditions and work methods. The selection and training programs caused turnover to decrease to 50 percent within four months. New trainees reached an average level of earnings of 105 percent of standard after four months compared to 87 percent for previous trainees. Training costs were also reduced by more than 50 percent.

Phase 3: OD. A year after the change program began, an evaluation study was conducted. It revealed that productivity was still too low, costs were too high, and morale had improved very little. Improvements in the organization were being blocked by hostilities and suspicions in work relationships.

Therefore, a sensitivity-training program was conducted with the top management as participants. All top managers were required to attend. However, the participants were interviewed before the sessions began and their questions about the program were answered. Three sessions involving different top-level managers were conducted. Due to the positive evaluation of the program by its participants, the sensitivity-training program was expanded to include supervisory personnel at all levels throughout the organization.

In addition, Weldon had a long tradition of serious difficulties on the shop floor between employees and supervisors. To help remedy this deficiency, group problem-solving meetings were initiated. In these meetings, supervisors and operators uncovered joint work problems and developed solutions to them. These group problem-solving meetings were started throughout Weldon after the supervisors had completed the sensitivity-training sessions. The initial reactions to the problem-solving sessions were both hostile and skeptical. However, as the meetings progressed, individual and group communication increased, pride in the work unit appeared, and substantially more positive work relationships and attitudes developed.

The outcome: Weldon, 1964

Weldon improved substantially as judged by several performance measures. Also, it made considerable progress toward employee involvement through participative management.

Performance. The main performance goals set by the new owners were to: (1) attain a good return on invested capital, (2) improve operation-production efficiency, and (3) use manpower-skill resources more economically by reducing absenteeism and turnover. All of these goals were accomplished. The return on invested capital increased from − 15 percent in 1962 to 17 percent in 1964, production efficiency rose from − 11 percent to 14 percent, turnover decreased from 10 percent to 4 percent and absenteeism declined from 6 percent to 3 percent. In addition, Weldon's rate of manufacturing defects was reduced by 39 percent and the rate of customer returns decreased by 57 percent.

Operator performance increased from 89 percent to 114 percent of standard in three years. (See Figure 18–3)

FIGURE 18–3
Mean performance at Weldon January 1962–December 1964

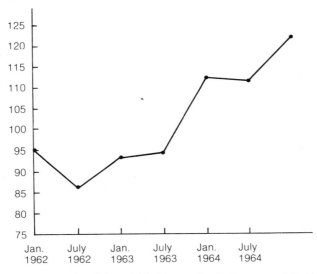

Source: Adapted from A. J. Marrow, D. G. Bowers, and S. E. Seashore, eds., *Management by Participation* (New York: Harper & Row, 1967), p. 154.

An analysis of the operator performance records revealed that the three major reasons for this increase were, in order of importance: (1) remedial training for poorly performing operators, (2) managerial and supervisory training in interpersonal relations, and (3) tighter enforcement of a termination policy for persistently low-performing operators.

Organizational system. The change in Weldon's organizational characteristics is shown in Figure 18–4 which summarizes survey findings. Weldon

FIGURE 18–4
Weldon's progress toward participative management

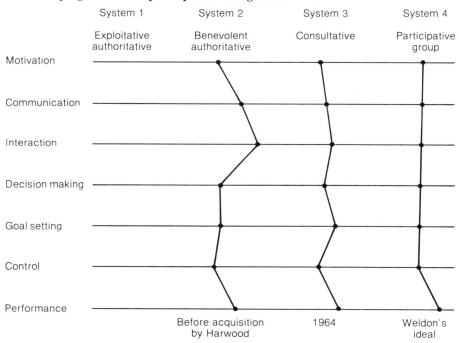

Source: Adapted from A. J. Marrow, D. G. Bowers, and S. E. Seashore, eds., *Management by Participation* (New York: Harper & Row, 1967), p. 219.

changed from an authoritative organization to a consultative one. The results also indicated that the ideal organization according to both Weldon's and Harwood's managers was one based on System 4, participative-group principles. By the end of 1964, Harwood was closer to attaining their ideal than was Weldon.

Analysis

Seashore and Bowers (1970) returned to Weldon in 1969 to determine if the organization-change program had produced durable results or if the benefits had just faded away. They administered questionnaires during a one-day visit and collected additional data from Weldon's files.

Seashore and Bowers report that they were prepared for the worst since Weldon had spent very little on consultants since 1964. However, they found Weldon to be healthy and thriving. A slight improvement in employee attitudes was found. Moreover, the organization had become more participative and the business indicators were still excellent. Return on capital was very high and substantial gains in efficiency and volume had occurred.

The success of the organization-change program at Weldon was very dramatic and the beneficial results were still visible five years after the change agents had left. As a matter of fact, Weldon in 1969 was a healthier and more prosperous organization than it was in 1964. (Likert uses the Weldon case as support for his theoretical positions which were presented in Chapter 16.)

What are the reasons for the success at Weldon?

One likely reason is that the change at Weldon was a multidisciplinary project. Engineers, accountants, and technical consultants, as well as OD psychologists, all participated in the program. Each change agent installed a program in his/her own area of expertise. The diverse interventions included setting up a selection program, training the low-performing operators, sensitivity training for the managers, group problem-solving sessions for the workers and supervisors, installing new equipment, and redesigning the work set-up. While each consultant may have been an expert in just his/her one area, effective planning produced a smoothly coordinated overall effort. The program at Weldon is a classic example of the benefits of a system-wide multidisciplinary approach to organization change.

Weldon's success story can also be viewed from the theoretical perspectives introduced earlier in this chapter. Consider Lippitt, Watson, and Westley's planned-change model. All seven phases occurred at Weldon and they occurred in the sequence advocated by the model. First, the recognition of need was implicit when Weldon sold out to Harwood. Then, a relationship was established with several consulting organizations who performed thorough diagnoses of the state of affairs at Weldon. Goals were set, plans made, and the change efforts were conducted. The change occurred throughout Weldon and the relationship with the consultants was terminated in 1964.

Another potential reason for the success at Weldon can be found in Argyris' model of the three primary tasks of the interventionist: generating valid information, free and informed choice, and internal commitment. The new owners of Weldon stressed generating valid information. They had one of the vice presidents from Harwood, several consulting organizations, and the Survey Research Center of the University of Michigan collect data before any changes were planned. However, the changes were planned by the owners of Harwood and not by Weldon employees. The new owners retained the free and informed choice for themselves. Therefore, it is reasonable to expect, and there is also evidence to indicate, that there was little or no internal commitment from the employees at Weldon to the change program planned by their new owners.

The initial changes at Weldon were largely technical and they did not produce very substantial results. Then, sensitivity-training labs were conducted and group problem-solving sessions were implemented throughout the organization. It was at this point in time that the inputs of the workers, supervisors, and managers at Weldon were obtained and changes were made based on these inputs. It was after these efforts, and as a result of them, that Weldon changed from an authoritative organization to a consultative one.

It is reasonable to assume that after their own inputs had been utilized the employees of Weldon began to be committed to the program's success. Not surprisingly, at this time, production and profits began to rise, and absenteeism and turnover declined. There is no experimental proof that the beneficial changes occurred partly because the Weldon employees obtained free and informed choice and developed internal commitment to the change program, but the circumstantial evidence in support of this contention is very solid.

SUMMARY

The theories and research findings of organizational psychologists ultimately *must* stand the test of successful application in planned organization-change programs. Unfortunately, the area of organization change is in its infancy. There are only a few theoretical models and most of them were developed over 20 years ago. However, the number of case histories on organization change is increasing rapidly.

Four theoretical models of organization change were presented. Lewin's model is the pioneering theoretical work and it is a three-stage typology. The first stage is unfreezing. During this stage, the strength of previously held attitudes and beliefs decrease. This prepares the organization for the moving or change stage in which new attitudes, values, and behaviors are developed. The final stage is refreezing in which the change stabilizes and a new state of equilibrium is established.

The planned-change model is composed of seven phases. They are: development of a need for change, establishment of a change relationship, clarification or diagnosis of the problem, establishing goals and plans, transformation of intentions into change efforts, generalization and stabilization of change, and achieving a terminal relationship. Although planned organization change does not necessarily progress in this orderly and logical sequence, the preceeding phases are characteristic of most change programs.

The action-research model views change as a cyclical process which should include the following characteristics: (1) a joint effort between the client system and the interventionist, (2) a strong emphasis on a diagnostic data collection phase prior to deciding on objectives and goals, (3) periodic data collection to evaluate the effectiveness of the change program leading to (4) modifications of the change program.

According to intervention theory and method, regardless of the type of problem the client organization is experiencing, there are three tasks on which the interventionist should focus: (1) generating valid and useful information, (2) creating conditions in which clients can make free and informed choices, and (3) helping the clients develop an internal commitment to their choices.

These four theoretical models tend to be complimentary in their viewpoint rather than competitive, although there are some differences in emphasis.

Two case histories of organization change were presented. The first was the unsuccessful attempt to make SUNY-Buffalo the Berkeley of the East. A new president of that university tried to impose his master plan for reorganization on the university community. After an initial flurry of success, the plan failed dismally. Possible reasons for the failure were discussed. One analysis of the failure was based on Argyris' three primary tasks. Unfortunately, the change program at SUNY-Buffalo was not based on valid information. Moreover, most of the university community did not have free and informed choice and, therefore, very little internal commitment to the change program developed. Looking back with the wisdom of hindsight, some suggestions for future change efforts at universities were made. These included the need to: plan for change from a solid conceptual base, involve the individuals who are affected in the planning, recruit with scrupulous honesty, and appreciate environmental factors.

The second case was the successful organization-change program at the Weldon pajama company. This program was a multidisciplinary, system-wide effort conducted over a two-year period. At the time of its purchase, Weldon was financially distressed, had severe morale problems, and was authoritative in management style. The change program had three main phases: (1) protecting human resources, (2) the installation of technical improvements, and (3) transforming the human organization to a more participative style through OD. The outcomes of the change program were dramatic. All three of the goals set by the new owners were attained: (1) obtaining a good return on invested capital, (2) improving operator-production efficiency, and (3) using manpower-skill resources more efficiently. A follow-up study conducted five years after the change agents had left indicated that the beneficial effects had not only endured but that the organization was even more prosperous and participative in style. Possible reasons for the success of the change program at Weldon include its multidisciplinary approach using engineers, accountants, and psychologists, its strict adherence to the seven stages of the planned-change model, and its achievement of the three primary tasks: generating valid information, obtaining free and informed choice, and striving for internal commitment.

REFERENCES

Alderfer, C. P.   Change processes in organizations. In M. D. Dunnette (Ed.), *Handbook of industrial and organizational psychology*. Chicago: Rand McNally, 1976.

Argyris, C. *Intervention theory and method,* Reading, Mass.: Addison-Wesley, 1970.

Bennis, W. The sociology of institutions or who sank the yellow submarine. *Psychology Today,* 1972, *6* (6), 112–120.

Frohman, M., Sashkin, M., & Kavanaugh, M. *Action Research as an organization development approach.* Binghamton: State University of New York School of Management, 1974.

Huse, E. F. *Organization development and change* (2nd ed.). St. Paul: West, 1980.

Lewin, K. Group decision and social change. In E. E. Maccoby, T. Newcomb, & E. Hartley (Eds.), *Readings in social psychology.* New York: Holt, Rinehart & Winston, 1947, 330–344.

Lippitt, R., Watson, J., & Westley, B. *The dynamics of planned change.* New York: Harcourt, Brace & World, 1958.

Marrow, A. J., Bowers, D. G., & Seashore, S. E. (Eds.), *Management by participation.* New York: Harper & Row, 1967.

Schein, E. H. Management development as a process of influence. *Industrial Management Review,* 1961, *2,* 59–77.

Seashore, S. E., & Bowers, D. G. Durability of organizational change. *American Psychologist,* 1970, *25,* 227–233.

postscript

The Weldon case is rather a nice upbeat ending for our introduction to *Personnel and Organizational Psychology*. A troubled organization was changed through improved selection, training, work procedures, managerial style, and other elements of OD. Productivity, participation in decision making, employee satisfaction, and profits were all improved. Although not all efforts of I/O psychologists are as comprehensive or as successful, the I/O psychologist as scientist learns from the failures as well as the successes.

We join with other authors who have observed that you never finish a book; you merely decide to end it. You have come with us on a journey which we end here knowing that there are some topics of special interest, such as consumer behavior, that we have not touched at all, and others that we have addressed only superficially. Nevertheless, we have attempted to convey much of the flavor of our field—at this time. We invite instructors and students who have used the book to send us comments in care of the publisher, Richard D. Irwin, Inc.

I/O psychology has thus far made important contributions to its parent discipline and to society generally by helping to develop scientific bases and effective practical strategies for helping human beings lead more productive and satisfying lives. While we are proud of these accomplishments, we are humbled by the tremendous gaps in our knowledge, and challenged by the opportunities to learn more about people and their jobs.

The "quality of life" is rapidly becoming an overworked and trite phrase, perhaps because it is so relevant to fundamental human needs throughout the world. For most of us the quality of our lives and the quality of our working lives are inseparable. We have yet a long way to go before work-life quality becomes even marginally acceptable for a major proportion of the world's population and a substantial proportion of our own nation's population. Employment in a safe and healthy environment, in settings encouraging persons to make the most effective use of their present abilities and to develop new ones, and in work that is intellectually and emotionally satisfying is more than a worthy goal. It is an imperative for civilization which must be constructively approached by all fields, ranging from the humanities to the hard sciences.

We look forward confidently to I/O psychology's future contributions as part of this broad human effort.

appendix

Taylor-Russell Tables[1] for Group Prediction[2]

Proportion of Employees Considered Satisfactory = 0.05

	Selection Ratio										
r	0.05	0.10	0.20	0.30	0.40	0.50	0.60	0.70	0.80	0.90	0.95
0.00	0.05	0.05	0.05	0.05	0.05	0.05	0.05	0.05	0.05	0.05	0.05
0.05	0.06	0.06	0.06	0.06	0.06	0.05	0.05	0.05	0.05	0.05	0.05
0.10	0.07	0.07	0.07	0.06	0.06	0.06	0.06	0.05	0.05	0.05	0.05
0.15	0.09	0.08	0.07	0.07	0.07	0.06	0.06	0.06	0.05	0.05	0.05
0.20	0.11	0.09	0.08	0.08	0.07	0.07	0.06	0.06	0.06	0.05	0.05
0.25	0.12	0.11	0.09	0.08	0.08	0.07	0.07	0.06	0.06	0.05	0.05
0.30	0.14	0.12	0.10	0.09	0.08	0.07	0.07	0.06	0.06	0.05	0.05
0.35	0.17	0.14	0.11	0.10	0.09	0.08	0.07	0.06	0.06	0.05	0.05
0.40	0.19	0.16	0.12	0.10	0.09	0.08	0.07	0.07	0.06	0.05	0.05
0.45	0.22	0.17	0.13	0.11	0.10	0.08	0.08	0.07	0.06	0.06	0.05
0.50	0.24	0.19	0.15	0.12	0.10	0.09	0.08	0.07	0.06	0.06	0.05
0.55	0.28	0.22	0.16	0.13	0.11	0.09	0.08	0.07	0.06	0.06	0.05
0.60	0.31	0.24	0.17	0.13	0.11	0.09	0.08	0.07	0.06	0.06	0.05
0.65	0.35	0.26	0.18	0.14	0.11	0.10	0.08	0.07	0.06	0.06	0.05
0.70	0.39	0.29	0.20	0.15	0.12	0.10	0.08	0.07	0.06	0.06	0.05
0.75	0.44	0.32	0.21	0.15	0.12	0.10	0.08	0.07	0.06	0.06	0.05
0.80	0.50	0.35	0.22	0.16	0.12	0.10	0.08	0.07	0.06	0.06	0.05
0.85	0.56	0.39	0.23	0.16	0.12	0.10	0.08	0.07	0.06	0.06	0.05
0.90	0.64	0.43	0.24	0.17	0.13	0.10	0.08	0.07	0.06	0.06	0.05
0.95	0.73	0.47	0.25	0.17	0.13	0.10	0.08	0.07	0.06	0.06	0.05
1.00	1.00	0.50	0.25	0.17	0.13	0.10	0.08	0.07	0.06	0.06	0.05

[1] H. C. Taylor and J. T. Russell, "The Relationship of Validity Coefficients to the Practical Effectiveness of Tests in Selection," *Journal of Applied Psychology*, 1939:23, 565–578.

[2] Entries are the proportions of employees who will be satisfactory among those selected under specified conditions.

Proportion of Employees Considered Satisfactory = 0.10

	Selection Ratio										
r	0.05	0.10	0.20	0.30	0.40	0.50	0.60	0.70	0.80	0.90	0.95
0.00	0.10	0.10	0.10	0.10	0.10	0.10	0.10	0.10	0.10	0.10	0.10
0.05	0.12	0.12	0.11	0.11	0.11	0.11	0.11	0.10	0.10	0.10	0.10
0.10	0.14	0.13	0.13	0.12	0.12	0.11	0.11	0.11	0.11	0.10	0.10
0.15	0.16	0.15	0.14	0.13	0.13	0.12	0.12	0.11	0.11	0.10	0.10
0.20	0.19	0.17	0.15	0.14	0.14	0.13	0.12	0.12	0.11	0.11	0.10
0.25	0.22	0.19	0.17	0.16	0.14	0.13	0.13	0.12	0.11	0.11	0.10
0.30	0.25	0.22	0.19	0.17	0.15	0.14	0.13	0.12	0.12	0.11	0.10
0.35	0.28	0.24	0.20	0.18	0.16	0.15	0.14	0.13	0.12	0.11	0.10
0.40	0.31	0.27	0.22	0.19	0.17	0.16	0.14	0.13	0.12	0.11	0.10
0.45	0.35	0.29	0.24	0.20	0.18	0.16	0.15	0.13	0.12	0.11	0.10
0.50	0.39	0.32	0.26	0.22	0.19	0.17	0.15	0.13	0.12	0.11	0.11
0.55	0.43	0.36	0.28	0.23	0.20	0.17	0.15	0.14	0.12	0.11	0.11
0.60	0.48	0.39	0.30	0.25	0.21	0.18	0.16	0.14	0.12	0.11	0.11
0.65	0.53	0.43	0.32	0.26	0.22	0.18	0.16	0.14	0.12	0.11	0.11
0.70	0.58	0.47	0.35	0.27	0.22	0.19	0.16	0.14	0.12	0.11	0.11
0.75	0.64	0.51	0.37	0.29	0.23	0.19	0.16	0.14	0.12	0.11	0.11
0.80	0.71	0.56	0.40	0.30	0.24	0.20	0.17	0.14	0.12	0.11	0.11
0.85	0.78	0.62	0.43	0.31	0.25	0.20	0.17	0.14	0.12	0.11	0.11
0.90	0.86	0.69	0.46	0.33	0.25	0.20	0.17	0.14	0.12	0.11	0.11
0.95	0.95	0.78	0.49	0.33	0.25	0.20	0.17	0.14	0.12	0.11	0.11
1.00	1.00	1.00	0.50	0.33	0.25	0.20	0.17	0.14	0.13	0.11	0.11

Proportion of Employees Considered Satisfactory $= 0.20$

						Selection Ratio					
r	0.05	0.10	0.20	0.30	0.40	0.50	0.60	0.70	0.80	0.90	0.95
0.00	0.20	0.20	0.20	0.20	0.20	0.20	0.20	0.20	0.20	0.20	0.20
0.05	0.23	0.23	0.22	0.22	0.21	0.21	0.21	0.21	0.20	0.20	0.20
0.10	0.26	0.25	0.24	0.23	0.23	0.22	0.22	0.21	0.21	0.21	0.20
0.15	0.30	0.28	0.26	0.25	0.24	0.23	0.23	0.22	0.21	0.21	0.20
0.20	0.33	0.31	0.28	0.27	0.26	0.25	0.24	0.23	0.22	0.21	0.21
0.25	0.37	0.34	0.31	0.29	0.27	0.26	0.24	0.23	0.22	0.21	0.21
0.30	0.41	0.37	0.33	0.30	0.28	0.27	0.25	0.24	0.23	0.21	0.21
0.35	0.45	0.41	0.36	0.32	0.30	0.28	0.26	0.24	0.23	0.22	0.21
0.40	0.49	0.44	0.38	0.34	0.31	0.29	0.27	0.25	0.23	0.22	0.21
0.45	0.54	0.48	0.41	0.36	0.33	0.30	0.28	0.26	0.24	0.22	0.21
0.50	0.59	0.52	0.44	0.38	0.35	0.31	0.29	0.26	0.24	0.22	0.21
0.55	0.63	0.56	0.47	0.41	0.36	0.32	0.29	0.27	0.24	0.22	0.21
0.60	0.68	0.60	0.50	0.43	0.38	0.34	0.30	0.27	0.24	0.22	0.21
0.65	0.73	0.64	0.53	0.45	0.39	0.35	0.31	0.27	0.25	0.22	0.21
0.70	0.79	0.69	0.56	0.48	0.41	0.36	0.31	0.28	0.25	0.22	0.21
0.75	0.84	0.74	0.60	0.50	0.43	0.37	0.32	0.28	0.25	0.22	0.21
0.80	0.89	0.79	0.64	0.53	0.45	0.38	0.33	0.28	0.25	0.22	0.21
0.85	0.94	0.85	0.69	0.56	0.47	0.39	0.33	0.28	0.25	0.22	0.21
0.90	0.98	0.91	0.75	0.60	0.48	0.40	0.33	0.29	0.25	0.22	0.21
0.95	1.00	0.97	0.82	0.64	0.50	0.40	0.33	0.29	0.25	0.22	0.21
1.00	1.00	1.00	1.00	0.67	0.50	0.40	0.33	0.29	0.25	0.22	0.21

Proportion of Employees Considered Satisfactory = 0.30

					Selection Ratio						
r	0.05	0.10	0.20	0.30	0.40	0.50	0.60	0.70	0.80	0.90	0.95
0.00	0.30	0.30	0.30	0.30	0.30	0.30	0.30	0.30	0.30	0.30	0.30
0.05	0.34	0.33	0.33	0.32	0.32	0.31	0.31	0.31	0.31	0.30	0.30
0.10	0.38	0.36	0.35	0.34	0.33	0.33	0.32	0.32	0.31	0.31	0.30
0.15	0.42	0.40	0.38	0.36	0.35	0.34	0.33	0.33	0.32	0.31	0.31
0.20	0.46	0.43	0.40	0.38	0.37	0.36	0.34	0.33	0.32	0.31	0.31
0.25	0.50	0.47	0.43	0.41	0.39	0.37	0.36	0.34	0.33	0.32	0.31
0.30	0.54	0.50	0.46	0.43	0.40	0.38	0.37	0.35	0.33	0.32	0.31
0.35	0.58	0.54	0.49	0.45	0.42	0.40	0.38	0.36	0.34	0.32	0.31
0.40	0.63	0.58	0.51	0.47	0.44	0.41	0.39	0.37	0.34	0.32	0.31
0.45	0.67	0.61	0.55	0.50	0.46	0.43	0.40	0.37	0.35	0.32	0.31
0.50	0.72	0.65	0.58	0.52	0.48	0.44	0.41	0.38	0.35	0.33	0.31
0.55	0.76	0.69	0.61	0.55	0.50	0.46	0.42	0.39	0.36	0.33	0.31
0.60	0.81	0.74	0.64	0.58	0.52	0.47	0.43	0.40	0.36	0.33	0.31
0.65	0.85	0.78	0.68	0.60	0.54	0.49	0.44	0.40	0.37	0.33	0.32
0.70	0.89	0.82	0.72	0.63	0.57	0.51	0.46	0.41	0.37	0.33	0.32
0.75	0.93	0.86	0.76	0.67	0.59	0.52	0.47	0.42	0.37	0.33	0.32
0.80	0.96	0.90	0.80	0.70	0.62	0.54	0.48	0.42	0.37	0.33	0.32
0.85	0.99	0.94	0.85	0.74	0.65	0.56	0.49	0.43	0.37	0.33	0.32
0.90	1.00	0.98	0.90	0.79	0.68	0.58	0.49	0.43	0.37	0.33	0.32
0.95	1.00	1.00	0.96	0.85	0.72	0.60	0.50	0.43	0.37	0.33	0.32
1.00	1.00	1.00	1.00	1.00	0.75	0.60	0.50	0.43	0.38	0.33	0.32

Proportion of Employees Considered Satisfactory = 0.40

r	Selection Ratio										
	0.05	0.10	0.20	0.30	0.40	0.50	0.60	0.70	0.80	0.90	0.95
0.00	0.40	0.40	0.40	0.40	0.40	0.40	0.40	0.40	0.40	0.40	0.40
0.05	0.44	0.43	0.43	0.42	0.42	0.42	0.41	0.41	0.41	0.40	0.40
0.10	0.48	0.47	0.46	0.45	0.44	0.43	0.42	0.42	0.41	0.41	0.40
0.15	0.52	0.50	0.48	0.47	0.46	0.45	0.44	0.43	0.42	0.41	0.41
0.20	0.57	0.54	0.51	0.49	0.48	0.46	0.45	0.44	0.43	0.41	0.41
0.25	0.61	0.58	0.54	0.51	0.49	0.48	0.46	0.45	0.43	0.42	0.41
0.30	0.65	0.61	0.57	0.54	0.51	0.49	0.47	0.46	0.44	0.42	0.41
0.35	0.69	0.65	0.60	0.56	0.53	0.51	0.49	0.47	0.45	0.42	0.41
0.40	0.73	0.69	0.63	0.59	0.56	0.53	0.50	0.48	0.45	0.43	0.41
0.45	0.77	0.72	0.66	0.61	0.58	0.54	0.51	0.49	0.46	0.43	0.42
0.50	0.81	0.76	0.69	0.64	0.60	0.56	0.53	0.49	0.46	0.43	0.42
0.55	0.85	0.79	0.72	0.67	0.62	0.58	0.54	0.50	0.47	0.44	0.42
0.60	0.89	0.83	0.75	0.69	0.64	0.60	0.55	0.51	0.48	0.44	0.42
0.65	0.92	0.87	0.79	0.72	0.67	0.62	0.57	0.52	0.48	0.44	0.42
0.70	0.95	0.90	0.82	0.76	0.69	0.64	0.58	0.53	0.49	0.44	0.42
0.75	0.97	0.93	0.86	0.79	0.72	0.66	0.60	0.54	0.49	0.44	0.42
0.80	0.99	0.96	0.89	0.82	0.75	0.68	0.61	0.55	0.49	0.44	0.42
0.85	1.00	0.98	0.93	0.86	0.79	0.71	0.63	0.56	0.50	0.44	0.42
0.90	1.00	1.00	0.97	0.91	0.82	0.74	0.65	0.57	0.50	0.44	0.42
0.95	1.00	1.00	0.99	0.96	0.87	0.77	0.66	0.57	0.50	0.44	0.42
1.00	1.00	1.00	1.00	1.00	1.00	0.80	0.67	0.57	0.50	0.44	0.42

Proportion of Employees Considered Satisfactory = 0.50

	Selection Ratio										
r	0.05	0.10	0.20	0.30	0.40	0.50	0.60	0.70	0.80	0.90	0.95
0.00	0.50	0.50	0.50	0.50	0.50	0.50	0.50	0.50	0.50	0.50	0.50
0.05	0.54	0.54	0.53	0.52	0.52	0.52	0.51	0.51	0.51	0.50	0.50
0.10	0.58	0.57	0.56	0.55	0.54	0.53	0.53	0.52	0.51	0.51	0.50
0.15	0.63	0.61	0.58	0.57	0.56	0.55	0.54	0.53	0.52	0.51	0.51
0.20	0.67	0.64	0.61	0.59	0.58	0.56	0.55	0.54	0.53	0.52	0.51
0.25	0.70	0.67	0.64	0.62	0.60	0.58	0.56	0.55	0.54	0.52	0.51
0.30	0.74	0.71	0.67	0.64	0.62	0.60	0.58	0.56	0.54	0.52	0.51
0.35	0.78	0.74	0.70	0.66	0.64	0.61	0.59	0.57	0.55	0.53	0.51
0.40	0.82	0.78	0.73	0.69	0.66	0.63	0.61	0.58	0.56	0.53	0.52
0.45	0.85	0.81	0.75	0.71	0.68	0.65	0.62	0.59	0.56	0.53	0.52
0.50	0.88	0.84	0.78	0.74	0.70	0.67	0.63	0.60	0.57	0.54	0.52
0.55	0.91	0.87	0.81	0.76	0.72	0.69	0.65	0.61	0.58	0.54	0.52
0.60	0.94	0.90	0.84	0.79	0.75	0.70	0.66	0.62	0.59	0.54	0.52
0.65	0.96	0.92	0.87	0.82	0.77	0.73	0.68	0.64	0.59	0.55	0.52
0.70	0.98	0.95	0.90	0.85	0.80	0.75	0.70	0.65	0.60	0.55	0.53
0.75	0.99	0.97	0.92	0.87	0.82	0.77	0.72	0.66	0.61	0.55	0.53
0.80	1.00	0.99	0.95	0.90	0.85	0.80	0.73	0.67	0.61	0.55	0.53
0.85	1.00	0.99	0.97	0.94	0.88	0.82	0.76	0.69	0.62	0.55	0.53
0.90	1.00	1.00	0.99	0.97	0.92	0.86	0.78	0.70	0.62	0.56	0.53
0.95	1.00	1.00	1.00	0.99	0.96	0.90	0.81	0.71	0.63	0.56	0.53
1.00	1.00	1.00	1.00	1.00	1.00	1.00	0.83	0.71	0.63	0.56	0.53

Proportion of Employees Considered Satisfactory = 0.60

	Selection Ratio										
r	0.05	0.10	0.20	0.30	0.40	0.50	0.60	0.70	0.80	0.90	0.95
0.00	0.60	0.60	0.60	0.60	0.60	0.60	0.60	0.60	0.60	0.60	0.60
0.05	0.64	0.63	0.63	0.62	0.62	0.62	0.61	0.61	0.61	0.60	0.60
0.10	0.68	0.67	0.65	0.64	0.64	0.63	0.63	0.62	0.61	0.61	0.60
0.15	0.71	0.70	0.68	0.67	0.66	0.65	0.64	0.63	0.62	0.61	0.61
0.20	0.75	0.73	0.71	0.69	0.67	0.66	0.65	0.64	0.63	0.62	0.61
0.25	0.78	0.76	0.73	0.71	0.69	0.68	0.66	0.65	0.63	0.62	0.61
0.30	0.82	0.79	0.76	0.73	0.71	0.69	0.68	0.66	0.64	0.62	0.61
0.35	0.85	0.82	0.78	0.75	0.73	0.71	0.69	0.67	0.65	0.63	0.62
0.40	0.88	0.85	0.81	0.78	0.75	0.73	0.70	0.68	0.66	0.63	0.62
0.45	0.90	0.87	0.83	0.80	0.77	0.74	0.72	0.69	0.66	0.64	0.62
0.50	0.93	0.90	0.86	0.82	0.79	0.76	0.73	0.70	0.67	0.64	0.62
0.55	0.95	0.92	0.88	0.84	0.81	0.78	0.75	0.71	0.68	0.64	0.62
0.60	0.96	0.94	0.90	0.87	0.83	0.80	0.76	0.73	0.69	0.65	0.63
0.65	0.98	0.96	0.92	0.89	0.85	0.82	0.78	0.74	0.70	0.65	0.63
0.70	0.99	0.97	0.94	0.91	0.87	0.84	0.80	0.75	0.71	0.66	0.63
0.75	0.99	0.99	0.96	0.93	0.90	0.86	0.81	0.77	0.71	0.66	0.63
0.80	1.00	0.99	0.98	0.95	0.92	0.88	0.83	0.78	0.72	0.66	0.63
0.85	1.00	1.00	0.99	0.97	0.95	0.91	0.86	0.80	0.73	0.66	0.63
0.90	1.00	1.00	1.00	0.99	0.97	0.94	0.88	0.82	0.74	0.67	0.63
0.95	1.00	1.00	1.00	1.00	0.99	0.97	0.92	0.84	0.75	0.67	0.63
1.00	1.00	1.00	1.00	1.00	1.00	1.00	1.00	0.86	0.75	0.67	0.63

Proportion of Employees Considered Satisfactory = 0.70

	Selection Ratio										
r	0.05	0.10	0.20	0.30	0.40	0.50	0.60	0.70	0.80	0.90	0.95
0.00	0.70	0.70	0.70	0.70	0.70	0.70	0.70	0.70	0.70	0.70	0.70
0.05	0.73	0.73	0.72	0.72	0.72	0.71	0.71	0.71	0.71	0.70	0.70
0.10	0.77	0.76	0.75	0.74	0.73	0.73	0.72	0.72	0.71	0.71	0.70
0.15	0.80	0.79	0.77	0.76	0.75	0.74	0.73	0.73	0.72	0.71	0.71
0.20	0.83	0.81	0.79	0.78	0.77	0.76	0.75	0.74	0.73	0.71	0.71
0.25	0.86	0.84	0.81	0.80	0.78	0.77	0.76	0.75	0.73	0.72	0.71
0.30	0.88	0.86	0.84	0.82	0.80	0.78	0.77	0.75	0.74	0.72	0.71
0.35	0.91	0.89	0.86	0.83	0.82	0.80	0.78	0.76	0.75	0.73	0.71
0.40	0.93	0.91	0.88	0.85	0.83	0.81	0.79	0.77	0.75	0.73	0.72
0.45	0.94	0.93	0.90	0.87	0.85	0.83	0.81	0.78	0.76	0.73	0.72
0.50	0.96	0.94	0.91	0.89	0.87	0.84	0.82	0.80	0.77	0.74	0.72
0.55	0.97	0.96	0.93	0.91	0.88	0.86	0.83	0.81	0.78	0.74	0.72
0.60	0.98	0.97	0.95	0.92	0.90	0.87	0.85	0.82	0.79	0.75	0.73
0.65	0.99	0.98	0.96	0.94	0.92	0.89	0.86	0.83	0.80	0.75	0.73
0.70	1.00	0.99	0.97	0.96	0.93	0.91	0.88	0.84	0.80	0.76	0.73
0.75	1.00	1.00	0.98	0.97	0.95	0.92	0.89	0.86	0.81	0.76	0.73
0.80	1.00	1.00	0.99	0.98	0.97	0.94	0.91	0.87	0.82	0.77	0.73
0.85	1.00	1.00	1.00	0.99	0.98	0.96	0.93	0.89	0.84	0.77	0.74
0.90	1.00	1.00	1.00	1.00	0.99	0.98	0.95	0.91	0.85	0.78	0.74
0.95	1.00	1.00	1.00	1.00	1.00	0.99	0.98	0.94	0.86	0.78	0.74
1.00	1.00	1.00	1.00	1.00	1.00	1.00	1.00	1.00	0.88	0.78	0.74

Proportion of Employees Considered Satisfactory = 0.80

	Selection Ratio										
r	0.05	0.10	0.20	0.30	0.40	0.50	0.60	0.70	0.80	0.90	0.95
0.00	0.80	0.80	0.80	0.80	0.80	0.80	0.80	0.80	0.80	0.80	0.80
0.05	0.83	0.82	0.82	0.82	0.81	0.81	0.81	0.81	0.81	0.80	0.80
0.10	0.85	0.85	0.84	0.83	0.83	0.82	0.82	0.81	0.81	0.81	0.80
0.15	0.88	0.87	0.86	0.85	0.84	0.83	0.83	0.82	0.82	0.81	0.81
0.20	0.90	0.89	0.87	0.86	0.85	0.84	0.84	0.83	0.82	0.81	0.81
0.25	0.92	0.91	0.89	0.88	0.87	0.86	0.85	0.84	0.83	0.82	0.81
0.30	0.94	0.92	0.90	0.89	0.88	0.87	0.86	0.84	0.83	0.82	0.81
0.35	0.95	0.94	0.92	0.90	0.89	0.89	0.87	0.85	0.84	0.82	0.81
0.40	0.96	0.95	0.93	0.92	0.90	0.89	0.88	0.86	0.85	0.83	0.82
0.45	0.97	0.96	0.95	0.93	0.92	0.90	0.89	0.87	0.85	0.83	0.82
0.50	0.98	0.97	0.96	0.94	0.93	0.91	0.90	0.88	0.86	0.84	0.82
0.55	0.99	0.98	0.97	0.95	0.94	0.92	0.91	0.89	0.87	0.84	0.82
0.60	0.99	0.99	0.98	0.96	0.95	0.94	0.92	0.90	0.87	0.84	0.83
0.65	1.00	0.99	0.98	0.97	0.96	0.95	0.93	0.91	0.88	0.85	0.83
0.70	1.00	1.00	0.99	0.98	0.97	0.96	0.94	0.92	0.89	0.85	0.83
0.75	1.00	1.00	1.00	0.99	0.98	0.97	0.95	0.93	0.90	0.86	0.83
0.80	1.00	1.00	1.00	1.00	0.99	0.98	0.96	0.94	0.91	0.87	0.84
0.85	1.00	1.00	1.00	1.00	1.00	0.99	0.98	0.96	0.92	0.87	0.84
0.90	1.00	1.00	1.00	1.00	1.00	1.00	0.99	0.97	0.94	0.88	0.84
0.95	1.00	1.00	1.00	1.00	1.00	1.00	1.00	0.99	0.96	0.89	0.84
1.00	1.00	1.00	1.00	1.00	1.00	1.00	1.00	1.00	1.00	0.89	0.84

Proportion of Employees Considered Satisfactory $= 0.90$

					Selection Ratio						
r	0.05	0.10	0.20	0.30	0.40	0.50	0.60	0.70	0.80	0.90	0.95
0.00	0.90	0.90	0.90	0.90	0.90	0.90	0.90	0.90	0.90	0.90	0.90
0.05	0.92	0.91	0.91	0.91	0.91	0.91	0.91	0.90	0.90	0.90	0.90
0.10	0.93	0.93	0.92	0.92	0.92	0.91	0.91	0.91	0.91	0.90	0.90
0.15	0.95	0.94	0.93	0.93	0.92	0.92	0.92	0.91	0.91	0.91	0.90
0.20	0.96	0.95	0.94	0.94	0.93	0.93	0.92	0.92	0.91	0.91	0.90
0.25	0.97	0.96	0.95	0.95	0.94	0.93	0.93	0.92	0.92	0.91	0.91
0.30	0.98	0.97	0.96	0.95	0.95	0.94	0.94	0.93	0.92	0.91	0.91
0.35	0.98	0.98	0.97	0.96	0.95	0.95	0.94	0.93	0.93	0.92	0.91
0.40	0.99	0.98	0.98	0.97	0.96	0.95	0.95	0.94	0.93	0.92	0.91
0.45	0.99	0.99	0.98	0.98	0.97	0.96	0.95	0.94	0.93	0.92	0.91
0.50	1.00	0.99	0.99	0.98	0.97	0.97	0.96	0.95	0.94	0.92	0.92
0.55	1.00	1.00	0.99	0.99	0.98	0.97	0.97	0.96	0.94	0.93	0.92
0.60	1.00	1.00	0.99	0.99	0.99	0.98	0.97	0.96	0.95	0.93	0.92
0.65	1.00	1.00	1.00	0.99	0.99	0.98	0.98	0.97	0.96	0.94	0.92
0.70	1.00	1.00	1.00	1.00	0.99	0.99	0.98	0.97	0.96	0.94	0.93
0.75	1.00	1.00	1.00	1.00	1.00	0.99	0.99	0.98	0.97	0.95	0.93
0.80	1.00	1.00	1.00	1.00	1.00	1.00	0.99	0.99	0.97	0.95	0.93
0.85	1.00	1.00	1.00	1.00	1.00	1.00	1.00	0.99	0.98	0.96	0.94
0.90	1.00	1.00	1.00	1.00	1.00	1.00	1.00	1.00	0.99	0.97	0.94
0.95	1.00	1.00	1.00	1.00	1.00	1.00	1.00	1.00	1.00	0.98	0.94
1.00	1.00	1.00	1.00	1.00	1.00	1.00	1.00	1.00	1.00	1.00	0.95

name index

subject index

439

*This book has been set VIP in 10 and 9 point
Times Roman, leaded 2 points. Section numbers
are 27 point Times Roman. Section titles and
chapter numbers and titles are 20 point Times
Roman. The size of the type page is 28 by 47
picas.*

DATE DUE
